Choosing Methods in Mental Health Research

Choosing Methods in Mental Health Research develops a new framework for mental health research. It is concerned with how to choose the most appropriate mental health research method, not only to address a specific question, but also to maximise the potential impact on shaping mental health care.

Mike Slade and Stefan Priebe focus attention on the types of audience that the researcher is seeking to influence, the types of evidence each audience accepts as valid, and the relative strengths and limitations of each type of methodology. A range of research methodologies are described and critically appraised, and the use of evidence by different groups is discussed. This produces some important findings about the interplay between research production and consumption, and highlights directions for future mental health research theory and practice.

The findings presented here will be relevant to mental health service users and professionals who use research evidence to inform decision making. It will also prove an invaluable resource for students and researchers in the field of mental health.

Mike Slade is Clinical Senior Lecturer in the Health Services Research Department at the Institute of Psychiatry and a Consultant Clinical Psychologist in Rehabilitation, South London and Maudsley NHS Trust.

Stefan Priebe is Professor of Social and Community Psychiatry at Barts and the London School of Medicine, Queen Mary, University of London. He has published widely on concepts, therapeutic processes and outcomes in mental health care.

Contributors: Thomas Becker, Peter Beresford, Pat Bracken, Terry Brugha, Tom Burns, Lorenzo Burti, Joan Busfield, Simon Gilbody, Sunjai Gupta OBE, Lars Hansson, Dave Harper, Karen Henwood, Frank Holloway, Rachel Jenkins, Heinrich Kunze, John S. Lyons, Rosemarie McCabe, Howard Meltzer, Sophie Petit-Zeman, Vanessa Pinfold, Stefan Priebe, Bernd Puschner, Mike Slade, Phil Thomas, Graham Thornicroft, Andre Tylee, Paul Walters, Simon Wessely, Barbara A. Wilson, Whitney P. Witt

Choosing Methods in Mental Health Research

Mental health research from theory to practice

Edited by Mike Slade and
Stefan Priebe

Routledge
Taylor & Francis Group

LONDON AND NEW YORK

First published 2006 by Routledge
27 Church Road, Hove, East Sussex BN3 2FA

Simultaneously published in the USA and Canada
by Taylor & Francis Inc
270 Madison Avenue, New York, NY 10016

*Routledge is an imprint of the Taylor & Francis Group,
an informa business*

Typeset in Times by
RefineCatch Limited, Bungay, Suffolk
Printed and bound in Great Britain by
TJ International Ltd, Padstow, Cornwall
Cover design by Sandra Heath

British Library Cataloguing in Publication Data
A catalogue record for this book is available from the British Library

Library of Congress Cataloging in Publication Data
Choosing methods in mental health research : mental health research
  from theory to practice / edited by Mike Slade & Stefan Priebe.
    p. cm.
  Includes bibliographical references and index.
  ISBN-13: 978-1-58391-844-9 (hbk.)
  ISBN-10: 1-58391-844-2 (hbk.)
  1. Mental illness—Research.   2. Mental illness—Research—
Methodology.   I. Slade, Mike.   II. Priebe, Stefan, 1953–   .
  [DNLM: 1. Health Services Research.   2. Mental Health Services.
3. Research Design.   WM 30 C548 2006]
RA790.C456 2006
362.2072—dc22   2006010647

ISBN10: 1-58391-844-2

ISBN13: 978-1-58391-844-9

Contents

Contributors

Prof. Thomas Becker, Department of Psychiatry II, University of Ulm, Bezirkskrankenhaus Günzburg, Ludwig-Heilmeyer-Strasse 2, D-89312 Günzburg, Germany

Prof. Peter Beresford, OSP, Tempo House, 15 Falcon Road, London SW11 2PJ, UK

Dr Pat Bracken, Department of Psychiatry, Bantry General Hospital, Bantry, Co. Cork, Ireland

Prof. Terry Brugha, Department of Health Sciences, University of Leicester, Brandon Mental Health Unit, Leicester General Hospital, Gwendolen Road, Leicester LE5 4PW, UK

Prof. Tom Burns, University of Oxford, Department of Psychiatry, Warneford Hospital, Oxford OX3 7JX, UK

Prof. Lorenzo Burti, Section of Psychiatry and Clinical Psychology, Policlinico G.B. Rossi, Piazzale L.A. Scuro 10, 37134 Verona, Italy

Prof. Joan Busfield, Department of Sociology, University of Essex, Colchester CO4 3SQ, UK

Dr Simon Gilbody, Department of Health Sciences, Alcuin College, University of York, York YO10 5DD, UK

Dr Sunjai Gupta OBE, Department of Health, UK

Prof. Lars Hansson, Department of Health Sciences, Lund University, PO Box 157, SE-22100 Lund, Sweden

Dr Dave Harper, School of Psychology, University of East London, Romford Road, London E15 4LZ, UK

Dr Karen Henwood, School of Medicine, Health Policy and Practice, University of East Anglia, Norwich NR4 7TJ, UK

Dr Frank Holloway, Croydon Integrated Adult Mental Health Service, Bethlem Royal Hospital, Monks Orchard Road, Beckenham, Kent BR3 3BX, UK

Prof. Rachel Jenkins, Health Services Research Department, Institute of Psychiatry, De Crespigny Park, London SE5 8AF, UK

Prof. Dr Heinrich Kunze, Klinik für Psychiatrie u. Psychotherapie, Zentrum für Soziale Psychiatrie Kurhessen, Landgraf-Philipp-Str. 9, D-34308 Bad Emstal, Germany

Prof. John S. Lyons, Mental Health Services and Policy Program, Northwestern University, 710 N. Lake Shore Drive, Abbott 1205, Chicago, IL 60611, USA

Dr Rosemarie McCabe, Unit for Social and Community Psychiatry, Department of Psychiatry, Queen Mary, University of London, Newham Centre for Mental Health, Glen Road, London E13 8SP, UK

Howard Meltzer, Health and Care Division, Office for National Statistics, 1 Drummond Gate, Pimlico, London SW1V 2QQ, UK

Dr Sophie Petit-Zeman, Association of Medical Research Charities, 61 Gray's Inn Road, London WC1X 8TL, UK

Dr Vanessa Pinfold, Rethink Severe Mental Illness, 28 Castle Street, Kingston-Upon-Thames, Surrey KT1 1SS, UK

Dr Bernd Puschner, Department of Psychiatry II, University of Ulm, Bezirkskrankenhaus Günzburg, Ludwig-Heilmeyer-Strasse 2, D-89312 Günzburg, Germany

Dr Phil Thomas, Centre for Citizenship and Community Mental Health, School of Health Studies, University of Bradford, 25 Trinity Road, Bradford BD7 0BB, UK

Prof. Graham Thornicroft, Health Services Research Department (P029), Institute of Psychiatry, King's College London, De Crespigny Park, London SE5 8AF, UK

Prof. Andre Tylee, Health Services Research Department (P028), Institute of Psychiatry, King's College London, De Crespigny Park, London SE5 8AF, UK

Dr Paul Walters, Health Services Research Department (P028), Institute of Psychiatry, King's College London, De Crespigny Park, London SE5 8AF, UK

Prof. Simon Wessely, Academic Department of Psychological Medicine, Guy's, King's and St Thomas's School of Medicine and Institute of Psychiatry, 103 Denmark Hill, London SE5 8AF, UK

Prof. Barbara A. Wilson, MRC Cognition and Brain Science Unit, Box 58, Addenbrooke's Hospital, Hills Road, Cambridge CB2 2QQ, UK

Dr Whitney P. Witt, Northwestern University, 676 North Saint Clair Street, Suite 200, Chicago, IL 60611, USA

Foreword

This book fulfils an undoubted need, with clear descriptions of different research methods written by informed enthusiasts for each method, followed by examples of how actual practice is affected in various clinical settings and different countries by particular research projects. A final section is dedicated to linking the production of research to the consumers of the various findings.

The model for research proposed by the authors in Chapter 1 (Figure 1.1) and amended by them at the end of the book (Figure 21.1) is one concerned only with health services research. They are on strong ground when they argue that when one is trying to change mental health policies, or to persuade mental health professionals to change their ways, the revised model is the more effective one. There is little point in devoting effort to research that is not seen or heeded by the people who need to take action on the results.

However, it should not be thought that the only point of health services research is influencing policy – evaluating treatment methods, better understanding of individual cases (Wilson, Chapter 2) and better understanding of process (McCabe, Chapter 3) are other important purposes. Many important studies in the rest of the mental illness field benefit greatly from a hypothesis-testing design, as described in Chapter 1.

The section of this interesting book in which authors give examples of research that has had major impact on mental health policies in their country set me thinking about the research that has had most impact in my professional lifetime, over the past 40 years. Oddly enough, the first study (Wing & Brown 1970) is mentioned only once (by Puschner et al in Chapter 14) and the second (Stein & Test 1980) again only once (by Burns in Chapter 10) – probably because most authors have considered recent research.

Wing and Brown's 'three hospitals study', published as *Institutionalism and Schizophrenia* (1970), not only documented by ingenious measures the changes that were typical of institutionalisation, but conclusively demonstrated that the conditions in which patients were kept in mental hospitals, and the length of time they stayed there, had profound effects on the clinical syndromes of schizophrenia. The clear relationship between an impoverished environment and the negative symptoms of schizophrenia was described here. It is true that by this time psychiatrists in the UK were engaged in rehabilitation activities and attempting the earlier discharge of their patients – but after this book, there was no turning back. The book perhaps had a comparable effect to Basaglia's best-seller in Italy that gave *direct evidence* of the inhuman conditions of inmates of Italian mental hospitals at that time, and convinced the authors of the need for a concrete change (Burti, Chapter 15).

The second study was the demonstration by Stein and Test (1980) that a brief admission followed by community care is preferable to long stays in a mental hospital – both clinically and economically – for acute episodes of schizophrenia. This set of papers was followed by studies in other countries, and was taken up by public health doctors working within health authorities. Unfortunately, many of them believed that admission to hospital was no longer necessary, whereas not only were all the patients admitted briefly, but there were many exclusions from the study. The impetus that this work in the USA had on the development of community mental health services worldwide is difficult to overestimate.

Henwood (Chapter 5) correctly states that grounded theory emerged in the 1960s, but the account that follows mysteriously jumps the next 30 years, until the general discovery of the technique by psychologists. However, in this void is to be found the whole work of George Brown and Tirril Harris on depression and life events. They have consistently used grounded theory to illuminate our understanding of not only depression, but also other episodes of illnesses both psychological and physical.

As the authors of several chapters explain, mental health policies are devised by Ministers, who are in turn influenced by both their professional advisers in the government and media coverage of sensational cases. In the UK, such media coverage has produced such questionable concepts as dangerous and severe personality disorders (DSPD), whereby incarceration in a secure unit can take place before any offence has been committed, and the knee-jerk statement by the Secretary of State for Health that 'community care had failed', simply because one brutal murder had received wide publicity.

As Holloway argues in his excellent chapter (13), the diversion of resources to pay for the various nostrums suggested by central government often have the effect of depriving standard mental health teams of their staff, and their patients of a satisfactory service.

In the minds of many health service researchers, there is a notion that 'placebo effects' are confined to pharmacological treatments. Thus, Lyons (Chapter 17), giving possible reasons for the low salience of the Collaborative Depression Study in the USA, states that 'about one-third of patients in the placebo condition showed a reliable clinical response' (p. 211). He comments, 'This either means that the sample was quite suggestive or the placebo had an active treatment component imbedded.' Not only do many episodes of depression resolve with time, but if an active interest is taken in the patient and he or she is given an expectation of improvement, there will be an even greater recovery rate. It is better to term such improvements a 'case management effect', and to acknowledge that such non-specific effects are found in all treatments, both psychological and physical.

There is a pleasing lack of consensus about some ways of organising community services: the 'care programme approach' is highly valued by Burns (Chapter 10), but criticised by Gilbody (Chapter 7) and Holloway (Chapter 13). It is pleasing because in the organisation of services we deal with differing shades of grey, rather than with black and white. In a service treatment, we must ask what the comparator is, as well as how enthusiastically are the different treatments being carried out by the staff.

The book achieves high marks for describing a wide range of methodologies clearly and helpfully. The descriptions of services in different countries reminds us of the extent to which service developments are not entirely dependent on the findings of health services research, but rather depend on the amount of resource a country spends on its mental health services, on the various pressures put on politicians, but most of all on the values of people in each country.

David Goldberg

Preface

This book outlines how to choose the most helpful and appropriate mental health research method, not only to address a given research question, but also to maximise the potential impact of the research on shaping mental health care.

The impetus for the book arose from a previous book, which demonstrated the inadequacy of any single research methodology for investigating the plethora of mental health service research questions, and the need to develop a multimethod approach (Priebe & Slade, 2002). Building on this, we contend that there is an interplay of political, social and scientific forces which influence what type of evidence is generated and what type is taken notice of and used. The aim of this book is to make this interplay explicit, so that it is amenable to debate and can be considered in commissioning, designing and using research. International experts argue for 'their' research methodology, and representative research consumers highlight what types of evidence have relevance for them. The result is a rich description of the relationships between evidence production and consumption, which is intended to open a critical space for thinking and new options to plan and utilise research.

We hope that *policy makers* and *funding bodies* will find this book relevant to their need to sift different types of evidence, mediate between often conflicting claims from the research literature, and commission new research.

For research producers such as *clinical academics* and other *researchers*, the book will help to meet the imperative of generating *influential* research. This may require the use of different methods to produce new types of evidence.

Research consumers, such as *mental health service users* and their *carers*, along with clinicians, including *general practitioners*, *psychiatrists*, *psychologists* and *nurses*, may benefit from the explicit discussion of the assumptions of each methodology. This may cause re-evaluation of the importance of their favoured form of evidence, and new interest in alternative approaches.

Finally, *students* will develop improved critical appraisal skills by learning more about the merits of specific methodologies for particular uses, and will be able to make more informed choices when developing and carrying out their own research studies.

As clinical academics who both produce and consume research, we express two hopes. First, that the goal of moving 'science' closer to society will be seen as a virtue, rather than a vice. We advocate strengthening scientific rigour and not abandoning it, but argue that the impact of research will be enhanced when the potential of different methodologies is considered in a wider context. Good practice guidelines have been established for qualitative methodologies (Murphy et al, 1998), systematic reviews (Moher et al, 1999), and randomised, controlled trials (Altman et al, 2001), as well as the use and reporting of non-randomised trials (Britton et al, 1998; Des Jarlais et al, 2004). Every mental health services researcher should be familiar with these quality assurance standards. However, if the status of evidence is moving from a revealed and generalisable 'truths' to 'explanations' that help to advance mental health care in the real world, the challenge is now to maximise the strength of explanations as produced by research.

Our second hope is that our colleagues will focus on the forward-looking optimism embedded in this book, rather than any implicit criticism of past practice. Many publications have informed our thinking, both from within mental health (e.g. Bolton & Hill, 1996; Long & Dixon, 1996; Ellwood, 1988) and outside it (Baron & Kenny, 1986; Pawson & Tilley, 1997). Individual people, including (in addition to the chapter contributors) Alison Faulkner, Gyles Glover, Elizabeth Kuipers, Diana Rose, Mirella Ruggeri, Heinz-Peter Schmiedebach, Jim van Os and Til Wykes, have also shaped our understanding of the complex network of scientific, social and political forces we have tried to encompass. Our sincere thanks to all.

Mike Slade
Stefan Priebe
October 2005

Part I

Research methods

Chapter 1

Who is research for?

Mike Slade and Stefan Priebe

Introduction

This book has the aim of positioning methods of mental health service research in a wider context, by considering the potential and actual impact of evidence from different methods on a range of target audiences. There is clearly a need to use a variety of methodologies: to address the different types of research questions, to explore and answer the same question in a number of ways, to ensure that proportionate effort and resources are applied, and so forth. However, different research methods produce different types of evidence, and each type of evidence may have distinct levels of credibility with each audience of research consumers.

Research has a purpose in society, although this may often be forgotten in the everyday work in research. The purpose is to produce evidence that will help to improve mental health care and, hence, the lives of many people with mental health problems. The relationship between research production and research consumption is likely to be complex, and will be analysed in this book. This will be done from different angles, with the aim of providing a comprehensive picture.

The impact of research may be mediated through the evidence that the research provides. Yet, there are different concepts of evidence. For example, postmodern epistemology (among others) would challenge the assertion that evidence exists as an absolute concept, irrespective of the context, type of question, and the person or group using the evidence. Rather, evidence may be better seen as meaning 'explanation', with each type of evidence varying in its social force on the basis of what it is used for and who is using it. In other words, the impact of research does not depend only on the inherent qualities of research, but also on the willingness and ability of audiences to take notice of and accept different types of evidence, and on factors influencing the relationship between research production and its impact in the real world. Considering this relationship may help in research planning and commissioning.

Traditional model of research

The traditional model of health service research is shown in Figure 1.1.

This model places the initial stages of research and the selection of methods in a kind of vacuum, and changes currently occurring in society raise challenges for this model. Recent events in the UK illustrate these changes. An article in the *Lancet* in February 1998 suggested a link between the measles, mumps and rubella (MMR) vaccine and autism (Wakefield et al, 1998). What happened next starkly demonstrates some of the societal changes – in relation to knowledge, trust, risk and choice – which are taking place.

- *The hierarchy of evidence employed by the public differs from that employed in evidence-based medicine (Faulkner & Thomas, 2002)*. The *Lancet* study involved 12 children (Wakefield et al, 1998). Within an evidence-based medicine approach, a case series has limited value in establishing a causal relationship, and is the wrong scientific method for confirming a causal relationship between relatively common events. As a method, it ranks very low on the hierarchy of evidence used in evidence-based medicine (Geddes & Harrison, 1997). For the public, by contrast, it is plausible that the small numbers increased the salience. Certainly, most members of the public were unfamiliar with the Finnish study of 1.8 million children (Peltola et al, 1998) or the Danish study of 537,000 children (Madsen et al, 2002), which, along with all other scientifically robust studies, refuted any connection between the vaccine and autism.
- *The expert may be less trusted by society*. Numerous clinical academics and researchers gave press and media briefings to inform concerned parents about the safety of the vaccine. Despite these reassurances, take-up rates fell from 91% in 1998 to 79% in 2003. Latest published figures (the year to March 2004) show the uptake rate stabilising at 80%. The subsequent uncovering of an undisclosed financial interest by the first author of the original study (reported online by the *Lancet* on 23 February 2004) increased this process of public disenfranchisement from scientific expertise. This indicates that medical doctors may be less trusted by the public, although research on the subject still shows a high level of trust in them.
- *There is an increased preoccupation with risk (Beck, 1986)*. A central theme in the debate was the concept of 'risk'. For the scientists, risk was

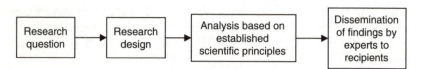

Figure 1.1 Traditional model of scientific enquiry.

used in the sense of potential danger. By this definition, risk is unavoid-able, and the goal is to balance different types of risk (i.e. the risk of developing autism following the vaccination and the risk of developing any of the conditions being vaccinated against). For concerned parents, risk was being used in the sense of actual danger. By this definition, any risk is unacceptable, and the goal is to avoid risk. The societal preoccu-pation with risk in the UK since the late 1990s, and the difference in meaning between scientific and non-scientific audiences, came into focus when experts proved unwilling to state categorically that the vaccine did not cause autism.

- *There has been a rise of consumerism, choice and empowerment (Muir Gray, 1999)*. Individuals are encouraged to choose what sort of health care to access and use. This has led to the development of the 'informed patient', who is given the best available information and then supported by the clinician in deciding what health-care interventions (if any) to opt for. The MMR debate illustrates how the assumption that giving parents information would lead them to make the 'right' (i.e. scientifically indi-cated) decision about vaccinations proved false. As noted, the vacci-nation rate fell to well below the 95% rate recommended by the World Health Organisation for 'herd immunity'. Consequently, there were 467 confirmed cases of mumps in April to June 2003 in England, compared with 84 for the same period in 2002. Similarly, measles incidence rose for the same period from 52 in 2002 to 145 in 2003. The public health implications of moving from decision making by experts to decision making by individuals are both profound and unexplored.

These changes are consistent with postmodernist concepts, and have implica-tions for mental health service research.

The position of mental health care

Psychiatry has a chequered past. Modern psychiatry was established as a medical profession with the rise of the Enlightenment approximately two centuries ago, and since then has been characterised by specific tensions that have not been shared – or at least not to the same extent – by other medical specialties. One specific issue has been the long struggle of psychiatrists to be part of conventional medicine, having the same prestige, status, income and power as other medical doctors. Another issue has been the balance between therapeutic aspiration and social control, psychiatry being the only medical specialty that treats a significant proportion of patients against their will. Other aspects make psychiatry unique within medicine. Psychiatry has been misused as an instrument of state control and political oppression. These cases may have been rare, but may nevertheless have tainted the reputa-tion of psychiatry. Historical examples include the 'sluggishly progressing schizophrenia' diagnosis given to Soviet political dissidents, and – less publicised – the recent role of psychiatry in China in relation to the Falun Gong sect (Stone, 2002). More widely, the very concept of mental illness has been challenged (Szasz, 1961), in a way not found in other branches of medicine (Bracken & Thomas, 2001).

Psychiatry survived the antipsychiatry assault in the 1960s. Perhaps it is now sufficiently developed as a discipline to embrace rather than withstand the concerns of 'post-psychiatry' (Bracken & Thomas, 2001). One important element of this response concerns research – the lifeblood of any respectable scientific profession. Here, too, traditional practice has been criticised. A gap exists between professional and service user priorities for research (Thornicroft et al, 2002), and there is a call for user-led mental health service research (Faulkner & Thomas, 2002). We therefore turn now to the role of mental health service research in the modern world.

Mental health service research

The era of the trusted expert, who uses the best available research evidence to inform advice to ideally passive patients, might have passed. Individuals can now much more readily access and use a range of information – some 'scientific', some not – to inform their health behaviours. Even when scientific evidence is present in the information 'market place', the MMR debate highlights that the media and the public may interpret research evidence in different ways from that planned by researchers.

One possible response from the scientific establishment to this analysis of social changes is to do nothing. This risks scientific evidence becoming increasingly marginalised and subjected to spin in important health-related debates.

A second possible response, which is becomingly increasingly common, is to embark on a public education approach. The aim is to explain more clearly the strengths and limitations of research evidence to non-scientifically trained members of the population. The success of this approach has not been formally evaluated, but is based on the assumption that society, having 'moved' in the ways outlined earlier, can be persuaded to move back. On the basis of the available anecdotal evidence (e.g. from the MMR debate), we are unconvinced that this assumption is correct.

A third option is that well-worn phrase, a 'paradigm shift' (Kuhn, 1962), and this is what we argue for. Specifically, we suggest that research planning and research production should not take place in isolation without considering research consumption. Rather, the intended target audience for a research study should inform the design of the study – including the choice of method – and the dissemination and presentation of the findings. To put this from the perspective of research commissioners, the likely impact of a study can be used as a relevant criterion for evaluating the quality of a research proposal.

'Applied' research which is more likely to affect the target audience should be prioritised over 'applied' research which is less likely to have an impact. We need to develop methods for differentiating between the two.

The book explores the implications of this suggestion.

Goals of the book

Previous books on research methods in mental health have focused on the link between research question and research design (e.g. Prince et al, 2003; Parry & Watts, 2004). This book, by contrast, investigates the link between research design, the intended target audience and the potential impact. We seek to focus attention more explicitly on the type of audience which the researcher is seeking to influence, the types of evidence which each audience accepts as valid and relevant, and the relative strengths and limitations of different scientific methods for providing different types of evidence.

The book has the following four goals:

1   to present the perspectives of a wide range of academic disciplines on mental health service research
2   to provide a learning resource for students and more experienced mental health service researchers to broaden their conceptual and technical knowledge
3   to develop a sophisticated understanding of the relative merits of different research designs
4   to inform the selection of the best research method, with due consideration paid to the intended audience for the research.

Structure of the book

The book has three parts. Part I reviews a wide range of methods. Each chapter provides a brief outline of the methodology, providing pointers to more detailed texts for the interested reader. The link with other methods is then explored, by elaborating their embedded assumptions. The types of evidence which is produced by the methodology are then discussed, leading to consideration of what research questions the approach is most applicable to. The existing contribution of the methodology to mental health research is then reviewed, illustrated by a case study. Finally, future potential for the approach is considered. Each chapter follows the same structure, so that the reader can compare potentials and limitations, strengths and weaknesses of the different methods. The order of chapters progresses from investigation of individuals to research at a population level. The methodologies chosen for inclusion are not exhaustive – omissions include non-randomised designs, anthropological designs and consensus techniques. The included methodologies were selected to illustrate the range of research in mental health. Part I is intended to provide a set of connections within and between methods, so that the reader can judge the current and potential level of importance attributed to the approach.

Part II investigates the use of research to change behaviour or practice. Contributors to this section are representative of, or expert in influencing, different target audiences. Each chapter begins by describing the types of evidence that have high salience for the specific audience, illustrating with a case study. Non-scientific evidence that is influential for the target group is then identified. It is said that history repeats itself, possibly because nobody listens. Each chapter therefore concludes with a case study of research which has not had the intended impact, with the aim of informing future research design. Influencing policy is a particularly important issue, and so separate chapters are devoted to experiences in the UK, Germany, Italy, Sweden and the USA.

Part III moves from description to intervention. We seek to synthesise the observations made about research production in Part I and research consumption in Part II. Consistent with its philosophical underpinnings, we do not seek in this book to make universally valid recommendations – the book is structured to open up questions, rather than prescribe action. The concept of evidence is considered in Part III from sociological, mental health service user, and postmodern perspectives. We end by outlining an emergent conceptual framework for mental health service research.

Using the book

Some guidance for the reader who wishes to dip in may be helpful.

For the postgraduate (or ambitious undergraduate) needing to select a research method for a thesis, Part I provides a rich description of the relative merits and issues with a wide range of methods. Similarly, critical appraisal skills will be enhanced by learning more about *when* (rather than just *how*) to use the different methodologies.

For the clinical reader looking for a summary of the ideas (in order, perhaps, to state authoritatively at a clinical team meeting, 'The evidence clearly shows . . .'), Part III summarises the key emergent themes.

For research commissioners, the central message of this book is that the type of research to commission is a function not just of the research question but also of the target audience. The chapters in Part II may help clarify thinking about the intended target audience. Researchers need assistance to do things differently. Part III may help commissioners to guide the research community toward developing high-impact (and not just high-quality) proposals.

And, finally, for mental health service researchers, such as ourselves, Parts I and II may provide a different perspective on scientific 'quality', by considering impact as well as scientific rigour. It will be a challenge to change practice, and Part III is intended to give practical pointers for action.

Chapter 2

Single-case experimental designs

Barbara A. Wilson

Historical origins and development of single experimental designs

The science of psychology began with studies of individuals. In 1860, Fechner published one of the first studies in sensory perception. He established the just noticeable difference (or the minimum distance) between two objects before an individual can determine whether one or two pinpricks have been given (described in Boring, 1950). Fechner was also one of the first to apply statistical methods to psychological problems (Hersen & Barlow, 1976). Wundt, Ebbinghaus and others followed suit in working with individual subjects, and from such work came important findings with wide generality (ibid.). In neurology, Broca (1861) published his famous case of 'Tan', so called because this was the only 'word' the patient could say. 'Tan' had a lesion in a particular part of the brain, now known as Broca's area, that results in expressive aphasia. Most patients with lesions in this area have problems with expressive language, so, again, the study of an individual led to findings that go far beyond the individual. Coming closer to our own time, another famous neurological patient, H.M., described by Scoville and Milner (1957), had bilateral hippocampal lesions that resulted in dense amnesia. The finding that such lesions result in severe memory problems is robust, and any patient with hippocampal damage is almost certainly going to have significant memory problems.

If the study of individuals was once so important in psychology, physiology and neurology, why was it, in the last century, that those who chose to study single cases rather than groups were considered to be revolutionary or eccentric? Hersen and Barlow (1976) suggest there were two main reasons. First, the growth of statistics, particularly from Fisher's work, changed attitudes. Fisher, whose first interest was agricultural research, developed sophisticated statistical methods to allow him to generalise from the sample studied to a wider population. These statistics became so influential that the whole style of psychological research changed, and Fisher's concern with averages and intersubject variability caused 'the intensive study of the single organism, so popular in the early history of psychology, to fall out of favor' (Hersen & Barlow, 1976, p. 8).

The second reason why single-case studies lost credibility is that proponents of the case study method, favoured by psychiatrists and others, had little awareness of basic scientific principles and so were unable to evaluate the success or failure of their treatments adequately. When group comparisons were made of collections of case studies, the results were at best confusing. Typically, as in most group studies, and some patients improve, and some do not, and averaging out the results leads to an overall effect of no difference. The basic question facing all clinicians is, 'Is this patient changing and, if so, is the change because of my intervention or would it have happened anyway?' We cannot answer this question with group comparisons. Group studies answer questions about groups such as, 'How many people improve under this particular treatment regime?' but they cannot tell us about an individual's response to treatment. After decades of being in the wilderness, in the mid-twentieth century, single-case designs started to become respectable again due both to a more sophisticated approach to basic research design and to the awareness that we can apply research principles to individuals.

Brief description of methodology

The basic assumptions in single-case experimental designs are that we are studying change in an individual – we are concerned with intrasubject variability rather than intersubject variability. Instead of measuring 50 people on one occasion, we can measure one person on 50 (or whatever) occasions, and each subject is his or her own control. Instead of a control group with which to compare the experimental group, we establish a baseline with which to compare change after the introduction of treatment.

The main design used in clinical practice is the ABAB or reversal design (and variations on this theme), where the first A is the first baseline, the first B is the introduction of treatment, the second A is the second baseline after the removal of treatment and the second B is the reintroduction of treatment. This allows for comparison of treatment after a baseline and then what happens when the treatment is removed and when it is reinstated. Variations include the ABA design, where the treatment is not reintroduced; the ABAC design, where B is one kind of treatment and C is a second kind of treatment; the ABACACD design, where the second treatment C is combined with a third treatment D (Alderman & Ward, 1991); and so forth. Although these are useful designs, they are not always appropriate in clinical practice, as it may be impossible, unethical or impractical to revert to baseline conditions. For example, if you have taught someone to use a telephone, you cannot unteach this; if you have taught a self-injuring child to stop head banging, it would be unethical to revert to baseline; if you have taught a head-injured person to stop shouting in therapy sessions, the therapist might be very annoyed if you go back to baseline to establish a principle. Figure 2.1A and B, however, shows how an ABA design was used to establish the efficacy of a paging system for people with memory problems after brain injury. It can be seen that the two patients showed different responses once the pager was removed, that is, when we reverted to baseline conditions. Clinically, this was useful, as it told us that the first client did not need the pager long term – he learned to carry out his necessary everyday activities after a few weeks with the pager, whereas the second needed the pager on a long-term basis as he was as bad in the second A phase as he had been in the first.

Multiple-baseline designs are also widely used single-case experimental designs. The underlying principle here is the staggering of the introduction of treatment. In a multiple baseline across behaviours (or across problems) design, one takes baselines on several behaviours or problems and then starts

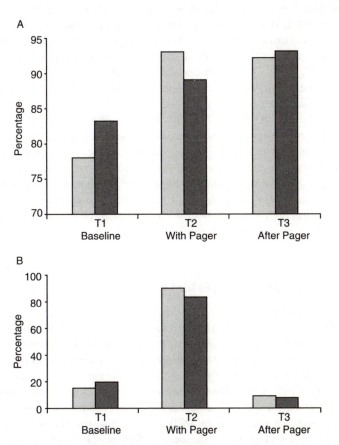

Figure 2.1 Percentage of targets achieved in the baseline, treatment and post-treatment stages for two people (A and B) with memory impairments.

treating one problem at a time while measuring the others. At a certain point, one would start treating a second problem and then a third and so on. The rationale behind this is that improvement should occur only after the introduction of treatment. If natural recovery or some non-specific factor is responsible for the change, there should not be a direct link with the introduction of treatment. A similar procedure follows the other multiple-baseline designs, so in a multiple baseline across settings, one staggers the introduction of treatment across settings. If a patient is planning to learn to use a memory aid, one could obtain a baseline of how frequently this is used before training in physiotherapy, speech therapy, occupational therapy, clinical psychology and on the ward. The next step is to teach use of the aid in one setting only while monitoring the other settings, and then teach use of the aid in the second setting and so forth. Again, if the teaching is successful, one should get an improvement only after the teaching is introduced. The third main multiple baseline is a multiple baseline across subjects design. Although, strictly speaking, this is a small group rather than a single-case design, one can still address intrasubject variability. The principle of staggering the introduction of treatment is the same. Examples of these designs can be seen in Wilson (1987, 1999). The main problem of multiple-baseline designs is that there may be a carry-over from one problem or setting to another, so if someone has learned to use an aid in speech therapy, the aid may be automatically used in the other therapy sessions.

There are other designs one can employ, such as mixed designs. These include alternating-treatment designs, whereby one can compare several different treatments in one session, and embedded designs, which are a mixture of reversal and multiple-baseline designs – see Singh et al (1981) and Wong and Liberman (1981) for examples. Finally, one can compare two or more treatments directly just as one would in a group study, but, instead of having two groups, one compares two procedures on a number of occasions. An example of this is provided in Table 2.1 (from Wilson, 1987).

Assumptions and theoretical framework

The main assumptions of single-case experimental designs are described above. Perhaps the most important assumptions are, first, that one can determine whether change is due to a specific treatment or intervention, or whether it is due to some other cause, such as natural recovery or extra attention; second, that baselines rather than control groups are used to determine the difference between two or more conditions; and third, that group studies are the method of choice for answering questions about groups, while single-case designs are the method of choice for answering questions about individuals. The main theoretical framework behind these designs comes from behavioural analysis and learning theory. Given the necessity for measuring and evaluating change with the introduction of behavioural

Table 2.1 A comparison of two strategies to enhance verbal recall for a man with severe amnesia

Session	PQRST		Rote rehearsal	
	Immediate	*Delayed*	*Immediate*	*Delayed*
1	75	50	25	0
2	75	50	100	25
3	100	50	75	25
4	75	75	75	50
5	25	0	50	25
6	100	50	25	0
7	75	50	75	0
8	75	50	75	0
X	77.7	47.1	62.5	15.6

treatments and behaviour modification, single-case experimental designs became an invaluable tool.

The theoretical influences underlying behavioural treatments are also diverse, drawing on a number of fields, such as experimental psychology, learning theory, information processing, psycholinguistics and so forth. Nevertheless, several features or characteristics are common to all these influences. Behavioural psychology is an applied science in which it is imperative to carry out treatments so that unambiguous and meaningful information can be obtained. This information will be used to evaluate the efficacy of treatment. In addition, treatment targets should be specified at the beginning of treatment, and not at the end, as one would find with interpretative psychotherapy. The targets should be specific, and not too general or broad; for example, one would not set as a goal 'improve concentration' or 'increase motivation', as these are almost impossible to measure. Thus, measurement is crucial in a behavioural approach, as we must avoid subjective or intuitive impressions.

A comparison of single-case and group studies

There is no one right or wrong way to carry out research. It depends on the question to be answered. As stated earlier, group designs are to be preferred if the research question is about groups, and single-case experimental designs are to be preferred if the question is about individuals. Group studies use many subjects. It is recognised that each subject is unique, so we have to make allowances for individual differences. Randomisation is used to share out these differences between groups. We try to ensure that there is about an equal amount of individual variation between our groups. Control groups are often used as part of the randomisation. Alternatively, we may randomly allocate each participant to treatment first, or waiting list first, as was done in the

NeuroPage study evaluating the use of a pager, as mentioned previously (Wilson et al, 2001). Another option is randomly to allocate each participant to one of two conditions and then switch conditions, as was done in the Baddeley and Wilson (1994) study of errorless learning. Half the subjects had a trial-and-error (errorful) condition first, and half had an errorless condition first.

Single-case studies, on the other hand, do not have to concern themselves with this variation across individuals, as each subject is his or her own control. Thus, baselines are used to establish control. We determine the pattern of behaviour in the baseline period and compare this to the pattern of behaviour seen after the introduction of treatment.

Statistical analysis is an important element in group studies, allowing us to determine whether any differences seen are due to individual variation or to the variable being tested. Although statistics may be used in single-case experimental designs, these are not always necessary. In Figure 2.1B, for example, it is clear that the differences between baseline and treatment, and treatment and after treatment were marked. Nevertheless, the pattern of results is not always clear-cut, and non-parametric statistics can be employed to determine whether there is a significant difference between conditions or a significant difference between the rate of change during the baseline and the treatment phases. Kazdin (in Hersen & Barlow, 1976), Edgington (1982) and Morley and Adams (1991) all discuss statistics in single-case experimental designs. The difference between statistics in the two types of design is that group designs employ intergroup and intragroup comparisons, whereas single-case designs employ intersubject and intrasubject comparisons.

The number of measures taken from each participant in the study also differs between group and single-case experimental designs. In group studies, we typically take one or two measures from each individual. Because there are many individuals and because any one response may not be representative, it is both impractical to take many measures from each person and necessary to have a large number of responses so that atypical responses are masked. In single-case designs, however, we take many measures, as we need to be sure that the response pattern is typical or representative of a person's behaviour under different circumstances.

In group studies, data analysis is usually carried out at the end of the experiment, partly to avoid experimenter bias and partly because one wants to have all the data collected before applying the statistical procedures. Thus, data are monitored simultaneously. In single-case experimental designs, however, we usually plot the data continually throughout the experiment. Indeed, it is necessary to note each measurement as it occurs. Thus, data are monitored consecutively. This means that we can adjust the variables during a single-case design; for example, if we feel it is beneficial to allow extra time or carry out the treatment at a different time of the day when the patient is less fatigued, we can do this in single-case, but not in group, designs.

Table 2.2 A comparison of differences between small N and large N studies (based on Robinson & Foster, 1979)

	Small N	Large N
Number of subjects	1–5	Many
Measures	Many	Few
Monitoring data	Throughout experiment	After all data collected
Time sequence	Consecutive	Simultaneous
Adjustment of variables during experiment	Yes	No
Determining significance	Visual examination: intrasubject/intersubject comparisons	Statistics: intergroup and intragroup comparisons

A summary of these differences can be seen in Table 2.2.

In some circumstances, it is imperative to employ a group design. For example, if we want to know how many people benefited from a particular regime or whether limb activation training is better than scanning training for most stroke patients with unilateral neglect, we need a group study to answer this question. There are, however, limitations to group studies when working with individual patients.

Limitations of group studies

Results from group studies apply to groups of people, and not necessarily to individuals. The individual patient we are seeing may be unlike the patients or control subjects in the group study. Often patients with very pure deficits are selected for group studies, but in rehabilitation most patients have a variety of problems. Not only may our patient be different, but also the group study results are averaged among all the participants so individual responses (even within the group study) may be very unlike the average. If we are averaging scores of 5, 10, 15 and 20 – that is, a mean of 12.5 – then two of the individuals in the group of four are a long way from the mean.

Another limitation is that results from group studies may confuse clinical and statistical significance. A statistically significant result does not mean that *every* person within the group did better, and some may have even deteriorated as a result of the treatment or intervention. Nor does it mean that the statistically significant results mean anything in clinical practice. One can show, for example, that biofeedback has a significant effect on control of a muscle, yet the patient who shows this effect may still be unable to use the muscle functionally. Furthermore, it is easy to confuse the *numbers* who change with the *amount* of change. If there is a 75% improvement after a particular treatment, does this mean 75% of the participants improved or the average improvement across the group was 75%?

Certain theoretical questions can be answered only by single-case designs. Take, for example, the question of short-term and long-term memory deficits. If we looked at groups of people to determine whether these two aspects of memory are dissociated, we would be unable to answer the question. The rare person with a digit span of one or two (a characteristic of a person with a short-term memory deficit) would be masked by the group averages. Instead, we have to find individuals who demonstrate poor short-term and normal long-term memory and other individuals who show the reverse pattern. Once we have established this double dissociation, we can be sure that there really are two qualitatively different memory systems.

Of great interest to neuropsychologists are patients with rare syndromes, such as Balint's syndrome, or visual object agnosia. Even if one wanted to evaluate a treatment that would apply to groups of people with these syndromes, it would be just about impossible to do it, for one would be unable to find groups of such patients. So, if we are working with people with unusual syndromes, we have to employ single-case or small-group studies.

A similar case can be made if we are interested in following people over a long period of time. See, for example, Luria's, *the Man with a Shattered World* (1981). The practicalities of this method preclude group studies. One can only do such detailed investigations by the single-case approach.

Finally, group studies are of very limited use when we want to evaluate an individual's response to treatment. As noted earlier, our patient may be unlike the ones in the group study. Furthermore, during treatment, we are interested in the *pattern* of change. This is not measured in group studies. Nor do these studies allow us to see what happens if we adjust the procedure, as by giving extra time. We cannot tailor the treatment to the individual if we simply follow the procedure laid down in the group studies. I once taught a Korsakoff patient to programme a message into an electronic aid. We started by using verbal instructions, but he became bored. I quickly switched to written instructions, so that he could work at his own pace. I still assessed his successes and his mistakes, and was able to determine how long it took him to learn the task. If I had not adjusted during the treatment session, he would have left the room.

What kind of evidence do single-case experimental designs produce?

The main question in psychological treatment concerns change. 'Is this person changing and, if so, is it a result of the intervention or would it have happened anyway?' Single-case designs are one of the main ways we can establish the answer to this question. If the treatment employed results in a significant change after a stable baseline, or if the rate of change is significantly greater after the introduction of treatment, we have evidence that the treatment was successful. Our confidence in this evidence is enhanced if removal of treatment leads to a return to baseline levels (ABA design), and further enhanced if reintroduction of treatment leads, once more, to improvement (ABAB design). As stated above, ABAB or reversal designs are not always appropriate, and sometimes multiple-baseline or mixed designs should be employed. Again, if introduction of treatment is staggered across problems, settings or subjects, and improvement occurs only *after* the introduction rather than in a random manner, this is evidence that the treatment itself is the cause of change, and not some non-specific factor. In the case of mixed designs, one is looking for improvement that is associated with one kind of treatment only, and not associated with the other kinds of treatment. There are, of course, situations where the evidence is unclear. This can occur when patients do *not* return to baseline in an ABA(B) design. It may be that the treatment was successful and the patients learned to cope during the treatment stage (as happened in Figure 2A) or because the improvement was not due to treatment and just happened to coincide with the introduction of treatment. In situations like this, one can look at the difference between the baseline and treatment phases. If there is a big improvement, one can be more confident that the treatment was responsible than if there is a small improvement. Even more importantly, one can repeat the design over a number of individuals. Wilson et al (1997), for example, evaluated NeuroPage with 15 people. Each had an ABA design. In every case, there was a significant improvement between baseline and treatment. For the group as a whole, the average success in the baseline (first A) phase was 36% and in the treatment phase over 85%. Thus, a series of single-case studies was also a group study of 15 people.

What types of questions can single-case experimental designs answer?

As noted above, questions about groups can best be answered with group studies, but questions about individuals need to be answered with single-case studies. Single-case experimental designs are best able to answer questions about individuals' responses to treatment or how individuals respond after the introduction of a change of regime. We have already discussed the reasons why large group studies are of limited value when one is working with patients or clients. In treatment or rehabilitation, we usually need to take repeated measures. We may want to change the treatment during the course of therapy to see, for example, whether or not responses alter at different times of the day or when a particular person is present. These variations cannot take place in group studies, as such studies do not concern themselves with the pattern of change, but only with one or two responses at set points in time. Kazdin (1982) says that the two central characteristics of single-case studies are that, first, they require '*continuous assessment* of behaviour over time; measures are administered on multiple occasions within separate phases; continuous assessment is used as a basis for drawing inferences about intervention effects; and patterns of performance can be detected by obtaining several data points under different conditions. Second, *intervention effects are replicated within the same subject* over time' (pp. 291–292). So these designs are for questions that require continuous assessment and replication.

What are the key strengths of single-case designs?

One of the main strengths of these designs is that they allow us to determine whether or not our treatment is effective with each individual patient or client that we see. They are powerful tools with which to determine the effect of treatment, the course of treatment (whether change is sudden or gradual), whether time of day or the presence or absence of particular individuals has an effect, and whether or not treatment effects are maintained. They are also the ideal tool for studying rare or unusual cases, and, as Gianutsos and Gianutsos (1987) point out, 'Single case experimental designs rarely conflict with the goals and ethics of clinical practice' (p. 468). No one need be denied treatment, as it is usually the timing of treatment that is varied, not the withholding of treatment. These designs are more compatible with the therapeutic process, as measurement is carried out over a period of time during the therapy sessions. Group studies are more appropriate for one-off interventions, such as surgery or a course of pharmacological interventions. For rehabilitation or psychotherapy, where the process is re-educational and longer lasting, we need a different approach to evaluation.

What are the key limitations of single-case experimental designs and what risks arise from inappropriate use?

The most commonly perceived criticism of these designs is that one cannot generalise from the results. This is not entirely true, however, and will be addressed later. In fact, the main limitation is that they do not always work in the way one expects. In reversal or ABAB designs, for example, it is sometimes impossible to revert to baseline conditions, or it is unethical to do so, or it is not practical to do so. These points have been addressed above. In the multiple baselines, there may be carry-over or interference effects from one problem or setting to another. For example, if one is able to reduce severe head banging in a learning-disabled child, other self-injurious behaviours, such as eye gouging or tongue biting, may also improve *before* one has implemented treatment for these behaviours. Another problem that can arise with any one of the designs is that one cannot obtain a stable baseline. If the patient is improving and the baseline is changing at a steady rate, one may just want to accept that change is happening without treatment because of natural recovery, general stimulation or some other reason, and this may be a good thing. If the baseline is simply too erratic, it might be worth beginning treatment and looking to see whether the baseline pattern changes. It is in circumstances like this that one may need statistical analysis to determine whether or not there are real changes.

The main risks of inappropriate use of these designs is that one might perceive change where there is no real change. For example, if behaviour is steadily increasing during the baseline period and continues to increase after the introduction of treatment, this might look like improvement in behaviour after several weeks, when in fact the *rate* of change is no different in the two phases.

Case study of a single-case experimental design in rehabilitation

Clare et al (1999) describe how V.J., a man with Alzheimer's disease (AD), was retaught the names of the people at his social club. A multiple baseline across behaviours was used to plan and evaluate treatment efficacy (each name was considered to be a different behaviour). V.J. was 62 years old and had been diagnosed with AD 6 years earlier. He lived with his sister and attended a social club every week. He had forgotten the names of most of the people there, and, as this caused him some embarrassment, he chose to focus on relearning these names. These became the therapeutic goals. Prior to the initial baseline, 14 photographs were obtained of club members. Six baselines were then taken in which V.J. was shown the photographs, one at a time, and asked to name each one. V.J. almost always correctly named three photographs, but these were still included in each session, as some success was considered to be good for his morale. Results, however, are based on the 11 names selected for training. Following the six baseline sessions, the remaining 11 names were taught, one at a time during twice-weekly sessions at V.J.'s home. At the end of each session, all names were presented for assessment. The order of training was determined by random allocation. The training consisted of the following steps. First, V.J. was shown the photograph and told the name, such as 'This is Gloria'. Second, V.J. was encouraged to think of a way he might remember the name, such as 'Gloria with the gleaming smile'. Third, a vanishing cues procedure was employed (Glisky et al, 1986), in which the name was written down with an increasing number of letters omitted for V.J. to complete: *GLORI_; GLOR_ _; GLO_ _ _;* etc. Fourth, consolidation was attempted through an expanding rehearsal procedure (Landauer & Bjork, 1978); for example, V.J. was tested on the name after 30 seconds, and then after 1, 2, 5 and 10 minutes. A correction procedure was applied if required. If he had forgotten the name, he was asked to look at the back of the photograph, where the correct name was written, and the previous interval was repeated. If he was still incorrect, testing occurred after a shorter interval. The criterion for success was correct recall after a 10-minute interval. After this, all names were presented for the test trial. The overriding principle was one of errorless learning (Baddeley & Wilson, 1994). V.J. was prevented, as far as possible, from making mistakes during learning. He was asked not to guess if he was unsure of the name but to check on the back of the photograph. In the test trials, a correct response was one where he did not have to check.

After 21 treatment sessions when V.J. was able to recall reliably all names, the generalisation phase was implemented. This consisted of training at the social club, where V.J. was asked to match the photograph to the person and then name the person. Again, he was encouraged not to guess. Eight general-isation sessions were conducted and once more a test trial was conducted. In the post-intervention phase, V.J.'s ability to name the photographs was assessed on nine occasions. He was then followed up for 3, 6 and 9 months. The results can be seen in Figures 2.2 and 2.3. Figure 2.2 looks at the learning of individual names from baseline to the end of the post-intervention phase, and Figure 2.3 shows the average learning in each of the treatment phases.

Not only was this a very successful treatment procedure, but it was also one that improved V.J.'s self-esteem (he commented, 'I thought I would never be able to learn anything new again and now look at me'). The treatment effects lasted for 9 months (V.J. was practising each day during this period). The photographs were then removed, so the only practice occurred during the weekly visits to the club. Even then, although retention of the names

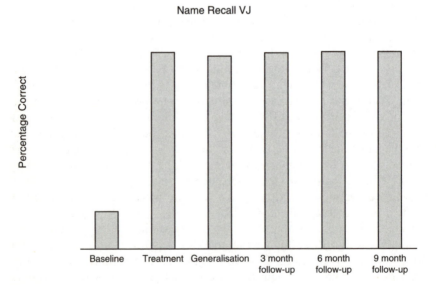

Figure 2.2 Learning of 11 names by a man with Alzheimer's disease.

No																														

Baseline and Intervention | Post-intervention

Key:

(i) the columns represent successive trials

(ii) the stepped heavy line separates baseline trials from intervention-phase trials, and indicates for each name when the intervention was introduced

(iii) the vertical heavy line separates intervention from post-intervention baseline trials

(iv) a ✓ represents a correct response

(v) a ✗ represents a failure to give the correct name

(vi) for reasons of space, generalisations and follow-up trials are not included

Figure 2..3 Summary of name learning from baseline to follow-up.

declined, it was still significantly above baseline levels (Clare et al, 2001). Finally, the success occurred and was maintained even though the AD was progressing. Potentially, this is a very important clinical finding. If we can teach useful everyday information to people with AD and they can retain this information with progression of the disease, we might be able to enable them to remain outside care for a longer period and reduce the stress on families and carers.

Overview of single-case experimental designs in the mental health services

There is little doubt that these designs are both accepted and influential in neuropsychology and neuropsychological rehabilitation. Theoretically, they have played a part from the early days of neuropsychology in such patients as Broca's 'Tan'. Clinically, these designs appeared later on the scene and were, for the most part, derived from learning theory, behaviour therapy and behaviour modification. Behavioural treatments have proved useful in adult and child mental health; in learning disability; in medical conditions such as epilepsy, cardiac rehabilitation and diabetes; and in addictive behaviours. In all cases, such treatments are committed to the empirical evaluation of treatments and interventions, and single-case experimental designs enable us to uphold that commitment for every patient we see. Without measurement, we are in danger of giving subjective or intuitive opinions about change or the efficacy of treatment. These designs allow us to individualise treatment to the characteristics of the individual in front of us. Although most clinical and neuropsychologists, and some psychiatrists, are convinced of their value, members of the medical profession often remain sceptical and consider large-group studies, particularly double-blind, randomised, control trials (RCTs) to be the only designs worth considering. This is despite the fact that we cannot do double-blind studies in psychological treatments. Andrews (1991) said, 'The RCT is a tool to be used, not a god to be worshipped. They are fine for pharmaceutical studies but are very limited for the long term, re-educative treatment that many of us are engaged in' (p. 5).

Perhaps our main task for the future is to convince the medical profession and the purchasers of health care that evidence from single-case designs is as worthy as any other experimental designs. It was pointed out earlier that there is a common perception that one cannot generalise from the results of single-case studies, yet this is not necessarily true. First, the language deficits first identified in Broca's Tan have been generalised to other patients with lesions in this area. The finding from Scoville and Milner's H.M. that bilateral lesions in the hippocampus lead to severe memory deficits holds up universally. Furthermore, as mentioned earlier, we often cannot generalise from group studies, as the group results are averaged and therefore are not always representative of the individuals within the group.

Finally, Gianutsos and Gianutsos (1987) argue that the only safe way to generalise is from single-case experimental designs. One simply replicates the procedure with more patients (direct replication) and then one can systematically vary patient characteristics or treatment characteristics to delineate the crucial variables. Several studies have shown that errorless learning is superior to trial-and-error learning in people with organic memory deficits (Wilson et al, 1994; Squires et al, 1997; Clare et al, 1999, etc). All these were single-case studies with results that have held up across individuals. The same is true of the NeuroPage studies. From the initial 15 people in the pilot study (Wilson et al, 1997), each of whom was studied by an ABA design, two further single-case studies showed the efficacy of the pager (Evans et al, 1998; Wilson et al, 2000); finally, after establishment of the likelihood of success and generalisation, an RCT was adopted (Wilson et al, 2001).

Seminal textbooks

The main textbook is Hersen and Barlow (1976), *Single Case Experimental Designs: Strategies for Studying Behavior Change*. This is the major resource book for single-case experimental designs. It includes a chapter by Kazdin on statistical analysis. A later edition appeared in 1992. Kazdin (1982), *Single-Case Research Designs: Methods for Clinical and Applied Settings*, is also a very useful book. Krishef (1991), *Fundamental Approaches to Single Subject Design and Analysis*, is the third of the main textbooks in this area. A recent book on statistics is Todman and Dugard (2001), *Single Case and Small-N Experimental Designs: A Practical Guide to Randomization Tests*.

Chapter 3

Conversation analysis

Rosemarie McCabe

Historical origins and development of conversation analysis (CA)

Conversation analysis (CA) encompasses a theoretical approach and method to analyse naturally occurring conversation, or talk-in-interaction. It emerged in the late 1960s in California, pioneered by sociologists Harvey Sacks, Emmanuel Schegloff and Gail Jefferson. Its emergence was influenced by both Erving Goffman's observations of people in interaction and Harold Garfinkel's ethnomethodology, that is, the study of how ordinary people reason in practice and accomplish the activities of everyday life. This set of approaches arose from dissatisfaction with the widespread application of quantitative techniques and arbitrary use of a priori categories in American sociological research at the time (Levinson, 1983). CA represented a fusion of Goffman's and Garfinkel's approaches in devising an empirical method to analyse how people produce order, that is, coordinate and accomplish activities, *in* actual interaction. It crystallised an interest in observable, empirical and reliable study of the social world (Vehviläinen, 1999). This was facilitated by audio-recording technology, which could provide a record of an interactional event to be replayed for analytic purposes. For Sacks, the most important virtue of this kind of record was that it could be played back and so was available for others to check whether they agreed with the analyst's interpretation of the record. This marked an innovative turning point in social scientific research in proposing a method that could 'handle the details of actual events' (Sacks, 1984, p. 26).

Although the earliest CA work was on talk in institutional settings (telephone calls to a suicide-prevention centre and group-therapy sessions), since then two main strands of work have emerged, sometimes referred to as 'pure' and 'applied' CA (cf. Ten Have, 1999). So-called pure CA analyses commonplace conversations (e.g. a family at the dinner table, telephone calls between friends), whereas 'applied' CA analyses conversations that take place in an institutional setting. The distinction is best summarised by Heritage (2004):

There are . . . at least two kinds of conversation analytic research going on today, and, though they overlap in various ways, they are distinct in focus. The first examines the institution *of* interaction as an entity in its own right; the second studies the management of social institutions *in* interaction.

(p. 223)

Contemporary CA encompasses both 'pure' and 'applied' studies, both approaches contributing to the amassing of empirical findings on how commonplace and institutional conversations are organised. Although its roots lie in the field of sociology, CA has penetrated other disciplines such as linguistics, social psychology and medicine. As Hutchby and Wooffitt (2003) note, CA continues to evolve as an interdisciplinary field of study, starting with questions that emerge in specific disciplines but turn out to have wider relevance.

Brief description of methodology

CA is a specific research technique that analyses naturally occurring talk in interaction. It is a qualitative method that analyses what people do rather than what they say they do. It focuses on how participants in an interaction negotiate meaning on a turn-by-turn basis, and this distinguishes it from approaches which interpret talk with reference to what a person might be thinking.

The starting point of CA is the audio(visual) recording of naturalistic interaction. Typically, conversation analysts work with large datasets. For example, Heritage and Stivers (1999) analysed 335 recordings of doctor–patient interaction from 19 practices, while Heath (1986) analysed more than 1000 consultations in his study on body movement and speech in medical interaction. From the recording, a written transcript of the interaction is produced through close, repeated listenings to it. Transcripts are produced using standardised transcription conventions developed by Gail Jefferson. Both *what* people say (the words as spoken) and *how* they say the words are transcribed. The latter include features such as pauses, overlapping speech, volume, pace and stress intonation. Non-verbal aspects of communication, such as eye gaze, gesture and postural orientation, may also be transcribed. As Ten Have (1999) has noted, the transcription system used in CA has been designed to highlight the sequential features of talk, that is, the relative positioning of any given utterance after the preceding and before the next one. CA transcription is a labour-intensive activity, with 1 hour of talk taking approximately 30 hours to transcribe at the Jeffersonian level of notation (Antaki, personal communication, 3 June 2004).

Producing transcripts at this level of detail is part of the analytic process (Atkinson & Heritage, 1984). Precisely because the analyst must attend to details of the interaction that an ordinary listener would not notice, the act of transcribing prompts 'noticings' that otherwise would not take place (cf. Ten Have, 1999). The transcript is used in conjunction with the recording during analysis. The aim of analysis to identify systematic, recurrent patterns in how talk is organised along with the interactional consequences of these patterns.

Systematic, recurrent patterns in talk are identified through an analysis of the sequential pattern of talk. The primary units of analysis are sequences and turns within sequences (Heritage, 1984) The analyst repeatedly asks why this now? A set of key conversational structures identified in early CA research provide some tools for systematic analysis. An example, the adjacency pair, may serve to illustrate how these basic structures are used to analyse talk. In its minimal form, an adjacency pair is a two-part utterance, with the two utterances adjacently positioned and uttered by two different speakers (Schegloff & Sacks, 1973). Examples are question-answer, greeting-greeting and offer-acceptance/refusal sequences. Adjacency pairs are closely ordered and composed of a first-pair part and a second-pair part, which fit together. If a question (the first-pair part) is asked in conversation, a pertinent response (second-pair part) is made relevant. If a response is not provided, this is an accountable issue, which the speaker of the question makes sense of in terms of the recipient having some trouble in responding. The reason for the trouble would then be further analysed in the context of the specific interaction. Other tools of analysis (cf. Ten Have, 1999) include examining how sequences of talk are organised with respect to:

- turn-taking, i.e. how participants manage speaker transition
- repair, i.e. sources of trouble, through mishearing or misunderstanding
- turn design, i.e. the way in which utterances are constructed or formulated (as a meaningful choice, given the range of alternatives) for that recipient at that point in the interaction.

Having examined these structures and identified a phenomenon of interest, the analyst collects all instances of the phenomenon and constantly compares their structure with respect to turn-taking, repair, turn design, etc. Close attention is paid to deviant cases, which are used to test emerging hypotheses. Peräkylä (1997) describes how Schegloff's analysis of a single deviant case in a corpus of 500 telephone call openings led him to abandon his initial hypothesis in favour of a revised interpretation which accommodated all of the cases, that is, the 499 regular cases and one deviant case.

Assumptions and theoretical framework

CA grew out of a particular form of social enquiry, ethnomethodology, in the field of sociology. Ethnomethodology is the study of participants' own (ethnic) methods of constructing and maintaining social order (Levinson, 1983). Social order is assumed to be produced by participants *in situ*, and CA is concerned with the organisation of social action as identified in inter-actional practices. Hence, conversation analysts focus on naturalistic, non-experimental data. The CA endeavour is less concerned with 'language use' than with the explanation of social action as configured in interaction. According to Sacks (1984):

> It is not any particular conversation that we are interested in. Our aim is to get into a position to transform . . . our view of 'what happened', from a matter of a particular interaction done by particular people, to a matter of interactions as products of a machinery. We are trying to find the machinery. In order to do so, we have to get access to its products. At this point, it is conversation that provides us such access.
>
> (pp. 26–27)

Within this framework, there is little role for premature theorising and an ideal of unmotivated looking (Sacks, 1984). Theorising should take place on the basis of the analytic categories that participants themselves are oriented to and that the analyst has shown to be used in interaction.

The central assumptions of CA are as follows:

1   talk is sequentially organised and highly systematic
2   conversational practices are, to a large extent, recurrent
3   talk is contextually oriented.

The first assumption was a somewhat radical one, given its emergence against the Chomskian view of talk as largely disordered and unsystematic (Drew & Heritage, 1992). Paradoxically, CA's focus on talk in its naturally occurring social context led to the discovery that talk has a tightly organised structure with discernible patterns. CA has shown that participants deploy specific interactional resources in a systematic way to produce the orderly patterns found in talk (Ten Have, 1990). Moreover, these patterns are stable or recur-rent across different forms of talk. However, talk is also negotiated on a turn-by-turn basis by the participants in the talk. Hence, the importance of the notion of context in CA. According to Heritage (2004):

> In constructing their talk, participants normally address themselves to preceding talk and, most commonly, the immediately preceding talk. . . . In this simple and direct sense, their talk is *context-shaped*. . . . In doing some current action, participants normally project (empirically) and require (normatively) that some 'next action' . . . should be done by a subsequent participant. . . . They thus *create* (or *maintain* or *renew*) a context for the next person's talk. . . . By producing their next actions,

participants show an understanding of prior action. . . . These understandings are (tacitly) confirmed or can become the objects of repair.

(p. 224)

At first glance, the second and third assumptions may appear somewhat
contradictory but can be explained by a key tenet of CA, namely, that the
structure of conversation is both 'context-free' and 'context-sensitive' (Sacks
et al, 1974, p. 699). This idea is elaborated by Hutchby and Wooffitt (2003):

> The resources are context free in the sense that the techniques any set of
> conversationalists may use to get some interactional work done are not
> tied to the local circumstances of that specific occasion. Rather, we find
> that conversational patterns are enormously recursive: the same kinds of
> techniques are used by different participants in different circumstances.
> Yet at the same time, the use of those resources is context sensitive in the
> sense that, on that specific occasion, *these* participants in particular are
> designing their talk in the light of what has happened before in *this*
> conversation, and possibly also in their relationship as a whole, among
> other contextual specifics.

(p. 35)

Although the same kinds of techniques are used accomplish different activities, they are used to construct utterances which are designed for that particular conversation, that particular recipient at that particular moment in the
conversation, that is, in response to the preceding utterance and projecting
the next utterance. Thus, analysts anchor their analysis of how understanding
is specifically negotiated in that context within the broader framework of
conversational organisation. For example, a recent study by Drew (2003)
compared the same conversational practice, that is, formulations or statements that propose the upshot of the previous talk, in four different settings:
news interviews, psychotherapy, radio call-in programmes and workplace
negotiations. Drew (2003) showed that while a formulation is a generic
conversational practice, the forms through which it is realised in different
contexts is not. A formulation is designed somewhat distinctively according
to the specific contingencies and activities in that setting, demonstrating the
interface between context-free (or general) and context-sensitive (particular)
conversational structures.

What does CA highlight as the assumptions of other methodologies?

The theoretical assumptions underlying CA and what they highlight as
the assumptions of other methodologies reflect different underlying epistemologies and paradigms (see Schegloff, 1993; Hutchby & Wooffitt, 2003,

pp. 115–119). Perhaps the main contrast between CA and *quantitative* methodologies relates to what is assumed to be relevant to the phenomenon being investigated. Quantitative methods define a priori categories with which to code the data that is collected. CA, on the other hand, has an ideal of unmotivated looking, and the analysis itself must demonstrate that the categories which the analyst identifies are those that the participants themselves are oriented to. Hence, CA can be characterised as a form of inductive analysis (Silverman, 1997), as it examines a range of cases or instances, identifies patterns and then generalises from particular instances to a theory.

CA's focus on naturally occurring interaction was motivated by Sacks's dissatisfaction with other methods of collecting data about behaviour (Heritage, 1984). They included interviewing, which treats people's verbal accounts as an adequate substitute for observing actual behaviour. Peräkylä (2004) notes that

> in the context of quantitative research, there is an underlying, background assumption about a separation between the 'raw' observations and the issues that these observations stand for or represent. Responses to questionnaires, for example, can be more or less valid representations of underlying social phenomena, such as the respondents' attitudes or values. . . . Conversation analysis is in stark contrast to this kind of approach: the core of its very aim is to investigate talk-in-interaction, not as a 'screen on which are projected other processes', but as a phenomenon in its own right (Schegloff, 1992a: xviii).
>
> (p. 289)

Thus, CA findings do not represent underlying social phenomena but describe social interaction as *the* phenomenon in its own right. Sacks's worries about treating verbal accounts as an adequate substitute for observing behaviour were well founded. It is now well established in social scientific research that asking people what they do is not reliable. Our accounts of our actions are characterised by various perceptual, attitudinal and memory biases. A strength of CA in this respect is that it looks for 'recurrent and systematic patterns, which do not arise from or depend upon participants' idiosyncratic styles, particular personalities or other individual or psychological dispositions' (Drew et al, 2001, p. 60).

CA studies of interviews, especially structured surveys and semistructured interviews, have shown that they are not straightforward methods of eliciting information (e.g. Suchman & Jordan, 1990; Lavin & Maynard, 2001; Antaki et al, 2002). In their aim to be objective and neutral, they end up being somewhat contrived in their conversational format (cf. Suchman & Jordan, 1990). The requirement to ask all, or at least some, questions in a standardised way to all respondents deviates from how we conduct 'normal' conversation. The resultant conversational exchange lacks many of the resources we normally use to ensure mutual understanding, such as clarification questions and designing questions for a particular recipient at that particular point in an exchange. More importantly, the inability to use these resources influences how the information offered by the respondent is recorded by the interviewer and then treated as raw data. As Ten Have (2004) remarks, 'interview expressions are collaborative "constructions", rather than purely individual expressions of the "mind" ' (p. 76).

Equally problematic are observational methods that rely on field notes (although ethnographic observational methods suffer fewer limitations) or precoded inventories, using intuition to invent examples of interactional conduct and experiments involving the intervention in and manipulation of behaviour (Heritage, 1984).

Some of the aforementioned methods are characterised by 'idealisation' about how interaction works and loss of the specific details of what actually happened (Heritage, 1984).

An important contrast with other *qualitative* methods (e.g. some forms of discourse analysis and social constructionism) is that CA does not emphasise the open-endedness of meaning (Peräkylä, 2004). As Peräkylä (2004) notes, this is because the meaning of an utterance, if it is interpreted in isolation, is open to endless and varying interpretation. However, if an utterance is considered in the interactive context in which it occurs, after the previous utterance and before the next utterance, it can be interpreted in line with how it is understood by the co-participant(s).

Other methods used to analyse health-care communication, which code and count professional communicative behaviours, such as 'information giving', 'positive talk' and 'negative talk', have considerable shortcomings (e.g. Stewart, 1984; Roter et al, 1987). These, mostly content-analytic methods, identify types of behaviour but do not analyse crucial information about how these behaviours are communicated and their interactional import. These approaches have been criticised by Peräkylä (1997) and described by Pendleton (1983) as 'like the listing of ingredients in a cake without the analysis to put the ingredients together'. For example, information giving can be done in different ways: it can be presented in an affectively congruent or incongruent way; it might be accepted or rejected by the patient; and it might be accepted or rejected to varying degrees. These subtleties become apparent only when the detailed interactional management of an exchange is analysed. CA attends to these details of microlevel communication in analysing sequences of talk and their interactional consequences (see also Haakana's comments on and attempt to code and quantify laughter (2001, pp. 9–10)).

What types of evidence does CA produce?

Evidence is concerned with how we substantiate propositions. In research, this raises questions about the reliability and validity of research findings. As

Silverman (1997) argues, attempts to bypass the issue of reliability by appealing to differing ontological positions (in some qualitative research) are unconvincing. CA prescribes a set of techniques to ensure that both reliability and validity are addressed in a rigorous fashion (cf. Silverman, 1997; Peräkylä, 2004).

The reliability of CA findings is addressed through the selection of recordings, the technical quality of the recordings and the adequacy of transcripts (Peräkylä, 2004). As Sacks (1984) emphasised, recorded interactions can be replayed. From the recording, a highly detailed written transcript is produced. A transcript makes what was said and how it was said available for consideration both by the analyst and by others. Thus, the transcript provides people other than the analyst with 'independent access' to the raw data (Ten Have, 1999) and the opportunity to disagree with the analyst's observations.

Validity is addressed in the transparence of analytic claims, and validation through 'next turn' and deviant case analysis (Peräkylä, 2004). Although CA findings are descriptive, the analytic claims are transparent and have what Peräkylä (2004; after Kirk & Miller, 1986) calls *apparent validity*. On reading the findings of a rigorous CA study, one is convinced that they hold true. As noted elsewhere, the analyst's interpretations are validated through ensuring that they are consistent with those of the participants themselves, as demonstrated in each participant's next turn in the interaction. Deviant case analysis

> involves examining cases where the general pattern is departed from and examining whether, and in what ways, the participants orient to such departures. Used in this way, deviant case analysis is an important resource for determining whether the basic pattern simply embodies an empirical regularity that happens to occur, or whether it involves something that is oriented to as a normative interactional procedure.
>
> (Heritage, 1997, p. 399)

If the participants themselves are responding 'deviantly' to the case because it departs from the expected course of events, this provides additional support for the analyst's observations (Peräkylä, 2004). Hence, deviant cases are not treated as outliers or discrepancies, and great care is taken to incorporate them into the analysis. This technique is a safeguard against selective analysis, which focuses only on cases that support an emerging observation.

Although there are no prescriptions for sample size, as noted previously, large corpora of data tend to be collected. The point, however, is not to collect enough cases to make statistical generalisations. Statistical generalisation assumes random sampling, which is rarely the case in CA research. Nevertheless, CA researchers are rigorous in their attempts to ensure that the patterns they identify are systematic and recurrent in the context they are studying. As the number of CA studies has increased, many findings have been shown to be generalisable from one context to another, particularly findings from 'ordinary' conversation. Peräkylä (2004) notes that when the focus is on conversational practices in specific institutional settings, the generalisability of findings will remain unknown at least until large-scale comparative studies are conducted. The scarcity of multicentre CA studies is no doubt due to the practical problems of transcribing and analysing the number of data gathered in such studies. One notable exception, Silverman's work (1997) on HIV counselling, included a comparative component analysing multiple settings in Britain, along with centres in the USA and Trinidad. Even across these apparently diverse settings, Silverman has described as fascinating the 'degree of invariance that we are discovering in the local management of delicacy' (p. 33).

What types of question can CA answer?

As CA is a method to analyse the organisation of talk-in-interaction, and talk is central to all forms of social organisation, it can be applied to a very wide range of subject areas. With respect to health care, much of it is delivered in interactions, whether they are face-to-face, on the telephone or, increasingly, via the Internet. Hence, the applicability of CA as a research method is wide. CA is well suited to any research question which asks how people do things in practice in naturally occurring rather than experimental contexts. Its sociological roots inform studies of how social institutions (e.g. medicine) are 'talked into being' (Heritage, 1984, p. 290). By taking the 'baseline' of ordinary conversation, it can identify how this varies in 'institutional' conversation (Silverman, 1997, p. 29) and examine how different conversational practices implicate particular roles, identities and relationships.

Its main application in health care has been to analyse professional–patient communication (e.g. Heath, 1986, 1992; Peräkylä, 1993, 1997, 1998, 2002; Silverman, 1997; Heritage et al, 2001; Ruusuvuori, 2001; Maynard, 2003; Stivers et al, 2003). This can involve a relatively specific analytic focus (e.g. how psychiatrists elicit information from patients whose mental state is at issue) or a more general focus (e.g. the importance of coordinating gaze and body movement in displays of engagement in doctor–patient interaction). Indeed, as mentioned previously, specific issues frequently turn out to have a wider relevance than the context in which they were originally studied. For example, the ways in which the behaviour of prospective involuntary patients is constructed as 'delicate' (Bergmann, 1992) has parallels with talk about a delicate issue, that is, the possibility of death, in HIV counselling (Silverman, 1997). Similarly, Maynard (2003) has analysed the delivery of bad news in everyday talk and in clinical settings. CA can also address more applied questions vis-à-vis people's competencies and deficits; for example, can an alleged communicative deficit be shown to be present in actual interaction (see below).

What are the key strengths of CA?

Perhaps the key strength of CA is that 'from close looking at the world we can find things that we could not, by imagination, assert were there. We would not know that they were "typical".... Indeed, we might not have noticed that they happen' (Sacks, 1984, p. 25).

CA involves collecting the best available records of human conduct in social scientific research. Moreover, as a method to analyse social interaction, CA is the most detailed and sensitive method available. It analyses microlevel aspects of communication, including the non-verbal features of gaze, gesture and postural orientation. Not only does it analyse what is said, when and how but it also attends to how these elements co-occur to make utterances understood in one way rather than another. As noted previously, meaning is not endlessly open-ended because utterances are interpreted in the context in which they occur. Interpretation derives only from the givens in the data and does not appeal to external factors, such as participants' sex, social identity, motives and power, unless they are made relevant by the participants themselves in the interaction. Hence, CA identifies categories participants themselves use rather than those generated by analysts. Heritage (1984) summarises why this is possible:

> Conversational interaction is structured by an organization of action which is implemented on a turn-by-turn basis. By means of this organization, a context of publicly displayed and continuously updated inter-subjective understandings is systematically sustained. It is through this 'turn-by-turn' character of talk that the participants display their understandings of 'the state of the talk' for one another ... because these understandings are publicly produced, they are available as a resource for social scientific analysis.
>
> (p. 259)

This contrasts with coding systems that specify a priori a particular meaning or function of the phenomenon being studied. Haakana (2002) notes the shortcomings of many of the coding systems which have been used to assess medical interaction (e.g. Roter, 1989). For example, laughter is included in the category 'positive talk', but laughter does not always mark humorous or unproblematic talk. Sometimes, it indicates that a delicate issue is under discussion and can be a sign of interactional discomfort (Haakana, 2002; McCabe et al, 2002).

What are the key limitations of CA, and what risks arise from inappropriate use?

The main challenge in CA research is quantifying highly detailed descriptive findings. Conversation analysts do quantify their findings (e.g. Peräkylä, 2002), but this is a secondary rather than a preliminary activity (Hutchby & Wooffitt, 2003). In the context of health-care research, an interest in quantification derives from linking findings about the procedures that people use to produce understanding in interaction and the outcomes of these interactions. A question at the heart of health-care communication is how to categorise and quantify descriptive findings from analyses of microlevel communicative processes so that they can be tested for their impact on concurrent and future behaviours and outcomes. This entails a substantive methodological problem, that is, translating, in a valid way, rich descriptive findings into a form that can be quantified and then integrated into statistical analyses to predict outcome from interactional processes.

Some proponents of CA are concerned that quantitative interactional analysis may be premature (e.g. Schegloff, 1993; Hutchby & Wooffitt, 2003). This concern is warranted given the tension between preserving the unique character of each individual case and identifying regularities across cases. Hutchby and Wooffitt (2003) state:

> Conversation analysts use collections in order to reveal systematic patterns in talk-in-interaction across differing contexts and involving various participants. But that aim is underpinned by a recognition that while there may be regularities across cases, each case is ultimately unique.
>
> (p. 116)

Schegloff (1993) cautions against quantification being used as a substitute for comprehensive analysis and suggests that detailed single-case analyses followed by collections of cases must form the basis of any quantitative analysis.

Haakana (2002), who quantified laughter in medical interaction, found that his quantification proved to be too simplistic to deal with the complexity of interactional sequences when doctors and patients laughed together. One of the parameters he coded in these sequences was whether and to what extent the laughter was inviting, that is, called for reciprocation:

> The coding of the sequences for instance with the parameter inviting–non-inviting is very difficult. The question of when laughter is or is not inviting is highly complex: it seems to depend on several issues, e.g., the type of activity, the way the activity is constructed, the placement of the laughter in the whole consultation, and also perhaps on the quality (strength, pitch, etc.) of the laughter itself . . . the findings presented here can be used to build better coding systems for quantitative interactional

work on laughter but it is important to remember that each sequence of interaction has a dynamic of its own.

(Haakana, 2002, p. 227)

Notwithstanding the foregoing complexities, some researchers have successfully operationalised and quantified communicative practices. However, the handful of such studies reflects the complexities involved. In one notable example, Stivers et al (2003) investigated parental expectations for antibiotics, parent communicative behaviours and doctors' perceptions of parental expectations for antibiotics. They applied CA to identify communicative behaviours associated with the prescribing of antibiotics in the consultation itself, identified their frequency and merged this data with the survey data on parents' expectations and doctors' perceptions of parents' expectations. They found that parents' use of 'candidate diagnoses' during the consultation increased the likelihood that doctors would perceive parents as expecting antibiotics, a feature which is associated with increased rates of prescribing.

From the viewpoint of a conventional quantitative researcher, CA might appear to be too concerned with detail and context. However, CA has been criticised for analysing conversational encounters outside a more extensive investigation of the setting in which they occur (e.g. Lynch, 1985), particularly in the case of specialised (e.g. institutional) settings. The concern here is that conversation analysts study instances of 'shop talk' in isolation from their context without in-depth knowledge of the participants, and their tasks and competencies along with the work being done by them (Lynch, 1985).

Case study of CA use in mental health service research

We recently conducted a study of 32 audio-visually recorded outpatient consultations between psychiatrists and people with a diagnosis of schizophrenia or schizoaffective disorder (McCabe et al, 2002; McCabe & Priebe, 2003a, 2003b). Informal carers, typically the patient's partner or parent, were present in about one-third of the consultations. The consultations lasted approximately 15 minutes and were analysed by CA.

A typical consultation involved the psychiatrist asking patients how they had been since the last visit, asking carers for their account of how things had been, reviewing medication and side effects, and discussing social aspects of care such as daily activities and living arrangements. The psychiatrist tended to ask patients whether they were (still) experiencing symptoms, such as hearing voices or having unusual thoughts, and, if so, how often and to what degree. This kind of talk was not especially problematic.

The patients, on the other hand, attempted to talk about the content of their psychotic symptoms, along with the emotional consequences (such as fear or embarrassment), and why others disagreed with their claims and beliefs. This kind of patient-initiated talk was not easily introduced into the consultation. Patients used certain conversational strategies in an attempt to make these concerns a legitimate topic for discussion. For example, they repeated statements or questions about their symptoms, asked direct questions and introduced this talk in the preclosing phase of the consultation. When patients did succeed in topicalising their concerns about these symptoms, it was a source of tangible interactional tension. Psychiatrists displayed reluctance and discomfort in talking about these aspects of psychotic symptoms. They hesitated and avoided answering these questions.

The presence of carers also seemed to influence patients' ability to express their concerns. When a carer was present, the doctor also smiled or laughed in response to patients' assessments of and questions about their symptoms. In telling about troubles, it is usually the teller who laughs and the recipient who produces a serious response (Jefferson, 1984). In medical interactions, laughter tends to be used more by patients than by doctors, often for delicate interactional tasks (Haakana, 2001, 2002). In our study, the doctors' use of laughter seemed to be problematic as a response to serious talk (questions) from the patient and may have indicated embarrassment when faced with such delicate questions from patients about the causes of their distress.

This study was presented at national and international conferences and then published in the *British Medical Journal* (http://bmj.com/cgi/content/-full/325/7373/1148) and the *Journal of Primary Care and Mental Health*. It stimulated debate about an issue at the heart of psychiatric practice in relation to psychosis, that is, whether or not clinicians should actively engage with the content of people's psychotic symptoms (http://bmj.bmj-journals.com/cgi/eletters/325/7373/1148). This study showed that, in practice, psychiatrists avoided engaging with the content of the symptoms, focusing instead on their frequency and severity. However, this avoidance led to the issue's resurfacing later in the consultation, often in a more confrontational manner.

What caused the greatest interactional tension were questions from patients highlighting others' disbelief in their claims (Figure 3.1). In any interaction, successful communication rests on participants' creating mutual understanding and resolving sources of misunderstanding. These findings show the practical problem of coming to a shared understanding or agreement about psychotic phenomena and the challenge of responding therapeutically to questions about the 'reality' of patients' anomalous experiences. For psychiatrists, this might present a paradoxical task. On the one hand, their role is to diagnose these symptoms as based on 'unreal', that is, pathological, perceptions and thought contents. On the other hand, patients are trying to seek a shared understanding of their 'unreal' experiences, which the psychiatrist cannot confirm as real for them. The psychiatrists' diagnostic role may conflict with their therapeutic role, creating a therapeutic dilemma in the care of these patients.

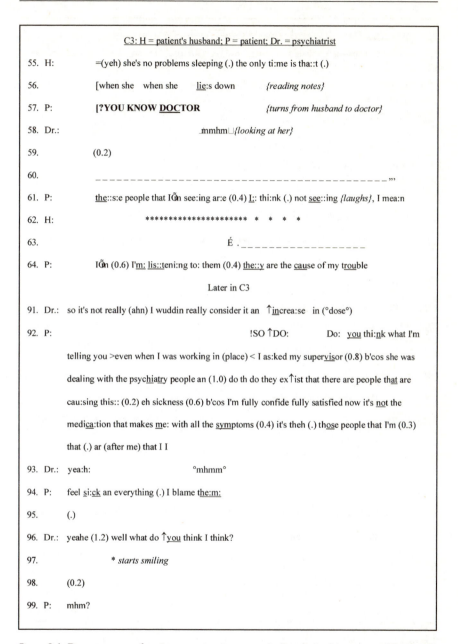

C3: H = patient's husband; P = patient; Dr. = psychiatrist

55. H: =(yeh) she's no problems sleeping (.) the only ti:me is tha::t (.)

56.   [when she   when she   lie:s down   {reading notes}

57. P: [?YOU KNOW DOCTOR   {turns from husband to doctor}

58. Dr.:   mmhm⌐{looking at her}

59.   (0.2)

60.   _ ,,,

61. P: the::s:e people that I'ᵐ see:ing ar:e (0.4) I:: thi:nk (.) not see::ing {laughs}, I mea:n

62. H: *********************   *   *   *   *

63.   É . _ _ _ _ _ _ _ _ _ _ _ _ _ _ _ _ _ _

64. P: I'ᵐ (0.6) I'm: lis::teni:ng to: them (0.4) the::y are the cause of my trouble

                          Later in C3

91. Dr.: so it's not really (ahn) I wuddin really consider it an   ↑increa:se in (°dose°)

92. P: !SO ↑DO: Do: you thi:nk what I'm

          telling you >even when I was working in (place) < I as:ked my supervisor (0.8) b'cos she was

          dealing with the psychiatry people an (1.0) do th do they ex↑ist that there are people that are

          cau:sing this:: (0.2) eh sickness (0.6) b'cos I'm fully confide fully satisfied now it's not the

          medica:tion that makes me: with all the symptoms (0.4) it's theh (.) those people that I'm (0.3)

          that (.) ar (after me) that I I

93. Dr.: yea:h: °mhmm°

94. P: feel si:ck an everything (.) I blame the:m:

95.   (.)

96. Dr.: yeahe (1.2) well what do ↑you think I think?

97.   * starts smiling

98.   (0.2)

99. P: mhm?

Figure 3.1 Data extracts of patients attempting to topicalise their claims.   (*Continued*)

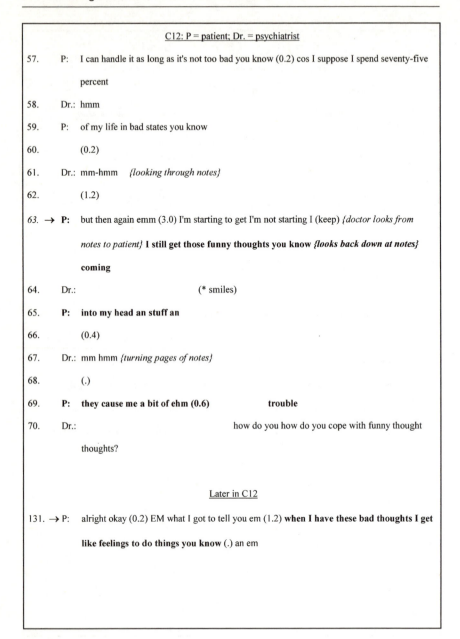

57. P: I can handle it as long as it's not too bad you know (0.2) cos I suppose I spend seventy-five

percent

58. Dr.: hmm

59. P: of my life in bad states you know

60. (0.2)

61. Dr.: mm-hmm *{looking through notes}*

62. (1.2)

63. → **P:** but then again emm (3.0) I'm starting to get I'm not starting I (keep) *{doctor looks from*

notes to patient} **I still get those funny thoughts you know** *{looks back down at notes}*

coming

64. Dr.:   (* smiles)

65. **P:** **into my head an stuff an**

66. (0.4)

67. Dr.: mm hmm *{turning pages of notes}*

68. (.)

69. **P:** **they cause me a bit of ehm (0.6)**   **trouble**

70. Dr.:   how do you how do you cope with funny thought

thoughts?

Later in C12

131. → P: alright okay (0.2) EM what I got to tell you em (1.2) **when I have these bad thoughts I get**

like feelings to do things you know (.) an em

Figure 3.1 Continued

		C9: P = patient; Dr. = psychiatrist; H = patient's husband

103.   H: her sister you know she the same (0.8) they took her scanning for her head (.) why the? I don't know

104.   (.)

105.   Dr: yeh

106.   (1.0)

107. → P: **do you think it's mental ment ment (_ _ _ illness) because I'm getting disability allowance an I don't I don't find myself mentally ill ment (0.6) I think it's <u>fear</u> (1.0) some kind of <u>fear</u> I have**

108.   (0.4)

109.   Dr: ↑oh↓<u>kay</u>

110.   (2.9)

111.   P: and it probably <u>will</u> come out

112.   (1.2)

113.   Dr: well (0.2) I think think that ehh (0.4) weh eh at the moment you are quite disabled aren't you? (.) in (0.2) uh many respects (I mean)?

114.   (0.6)

115.   P: I don't know Dr. (name_ _ _ _ _ _ _) I'm so confused I don't know what's wrong with me (.) I mean (_ _ _ _ _ _ I don't think _ _ _ _ _ _ _ I don't)

116.   (0.8)

117.   Dr.: I mean I must say for (0.2) for once (.) that eh (0.2) you know (1.0) eh (0.8) over time it's a lot easier to talk to you than it was in the past

118.   (0.2)

119.   P: mm-hmm=

120.   Dr: =you know (0.2) because eh when I first saw you eh you ehm (0.4) you know were you know able to: hh

121.   (0.4)

122.   P: **I think it's im<u>pul</u>sive isn't it? (0.6) what do you think?**

123.   (0.8)

124.   P: I'm too <u>impuls</u>ive (0.2) or too (fright to wait) I don't know

125.   (0.8)

126.   Dr: °mmhmm°

132. → P: **Do you think it's a <u>rea</u>:l pro(b)lem that?**

133.   (0.3)

134.   Dr. I thought it was <u>done</u> (.) didhin't okay (I mean) I:: I might be wrong *{looking at Husband}*

135.   (.)

136.   H: whahds thah wha(h)ds that <u>actually</u> <u>for</u>?

137.   (0.8)

138.   Dr: it's just eh that in <u>some</u> cases (.) what happen

139.   H: see if there's anything blocking or something isn't it

140.   Dr: that there might be some other reason for this illness

141.   (1.2)

142. → P: \<I mean\> <u>unbalanced</u>

143.   Dr.   (but) I wuddint rea::lly (0.3) worry about it

144.   (.)

145.   H: no ↑thaht's al↓right (I was   )

146. → P: ih(t)s unbal↑anced Dr.? (0.2) (name)

147.   Dr.   °pardon°?

148.   (.)

149. → P: °(I mean)° iht's un<u>balanced</u>?

150.   (1.2)

151. → P: of <u>mi::nd</u>?

152.   (.)

153.   H: un<u>balanced</u> she mean=

154. → P: =do you thi<u>nk</u> my mi:nd is un<u>balanced</u>?

155.   (1.0)

Figure 3.1 Continued

This study has been influential in two ways. Firstly, it has drawn attention to the challenge of communicating effectively with people when they are psychotic. Through a detailed analysis of actual consultations, it showed

1 how psychiatrists avoid taking up patients' attempts to talk about the content of their symptoms and the emotional distress it causes them
2 how after repeated attempts to raise this issue, patients use increasingly direct conversational strategies (mainly questions) to secure some response from psychiatrists
3 how these questions are met with discomfort by psychiatrists and may present a therapeutic dilemma for them.

Secondly, this study has highlighted the potential of the CA method to analyse communication in health service research. In a commentary on the study, Skelton (2002) wrote that the study 'raises fascinating issues about conversation analysis as a methodology and about the way that doctors and patients with psychotic illness communicate', and that 'conversation analysis . . . offers the reader a way of thinking about the obvious and rediscovering it as profound' (p. 1151).

Overview of the impact CA has had on mental health services

Few studies have applied CA to the study of mental health or mental health services. Bergmann (1992) analysed psychiatric admission interviews in West Germany. Briefly, he identified ways in which psychiatrists elicited information from patients about their activities leading to admission. Psychiatrists used indirect descriptive practices such as mitigating elements (e.g. 'not so completely dressed', 'kind of irritated a little bit', acting 'a little bit' peculiarly) and euphemisms (e.g. an early description, 'you withdrew very much', is later reformulated as 'you had yourself barricaded') in eliciting information. Bergmann (1992) identified two possible ways that patients respond to psychiatrists' discreet 'fishing' for information. They could respond either in a 'neutral' and 'friendly' way, thus implicitly accepting the suggestion of wrong doing in the psychiatrist's utterance, or in a negative protest and turn against the psychiatrist, thus leading to the judgement that the patient is exhibiting strange and aggressive behaviour.

Bergmann's take on this data is sociological. It led him to observe that psychiatry is an institution that has to manage the contradictory demands of practising medicine, that is, dealing in a neutral, disengaged way with illness, and practising morality, that is, dealing with people whose behaviour is treated as morally improper. In the light of theoretical writings about how morality and values come into psychiatric assessment and diagnosis (cf. Fulford, 1989), it is interesting to see how the contradictory structure of medicine and morality 'materializes itself at the level of turn-by-turn inter-action in the various manifestations of psychiatric discretion' (Bergmann, 1992, p. 158).

A recent development in CA research has been the application of CA to interactions involving people with a psychiatric disorder to investigate how their symptoms are manifested in real social interaction. In practice, it is in the interaction between the clinician and patient that the signs and symptoms of mental illness are manifested, identified and treated. Moreover, studying interaction directly has distinct advantages in identifying how a particular skill, as operationalised and tested in experimental situations, can be general-ised to everyday reasoning and interaction. The particular strength of CA in analysing the talk of people whose diagnosis implicates problems in com-municating is that it can identify in what way their talk is orderly and in what way it is disorderly (cf. Hutchby & Wooffitt, 2003; Schegloff, 2003). Dickerson et al (2005) used CA to investigate whether children with autism display problems in achieving joint focus of attention in social interaction. They found that, contrary to theories of autism and associated diagnostic systems, autistic children successfully manage joint attention through the use of gaze and pointing, which previous research claimed was deficient among autistic children.

We have conducted studies with a similar focus on how the symptoms of schizophrenia are manifested in social interaction (McCabe et al, 2004; McCabe, in press). It has been proposed that schizophrenia is a disorder of theory of mind (Frith, 1992). This theory predicts that people with schizo-phrenia will have problems representing their own and others' states of minds, that is, thoughts, beliefs, intentions, etc. However, in a study of naturalistic social interaction, we have shown that people with schizophrenia accurately represent and report mental states of others and design their contributions to conversations on the basis of what they think their communicative partners know and intend (McCabe et al, 2004).

In a similar vein, Palmer (2000) has applied CA to schizophrenic patient talk about delusions. He observed that it was not the falsity of belief that provided the basis for identifying talk as delusional. Instead, it was how patients deemed delusional used evidence to support their claim. He con-trasted the conversational practices that characterise delusional talk with the practices that characterise non-delusional accounts of paranormal activity. In the latter, people who are not delusional are concerned with the grounds on which their stories might be doubted and attempt to undercut those grounds. By contrast, in delusional accounts, there is a lack of concern that one's story is open to doubt.

We have also used CA to analyse talk with delusional content (McCabe, in press). We found that patients

1   failed to provide convincing evidence to warrant their claims
2   recognised that others did not agree with their claims
3   were confused by their failure to convince others of their claims
4   maintained their claims despite repeated exposure to competing formulations from others.

Contrary to Spitzer's (1990) suggestion that schizophrenic patients are not concerned with 'intersubjective feedback' or reasoning about anything pertaining to these claims, we found that they were concerned with others' beliefs and attempted to reason about and provide evidence for their claims. Moreover, they displayed discomfort in the face of others' disagreement. It is their resistance to revision of their beliefs that appears to be the striking feature of delusions. Hence, there is mounting evidence from interactional analysis that it is not the falsity of a belief that makes it delusional but the way in which a person provides evidence for the belief in question and the tenacity with which they hold the belief.

Thinking about mental health more broadly, there is a burgeoning field of CA research on primary care (e.g. Heath, 1986, 1992; Ruusuvuori, 2001; Haakana, 2002; Maynard, 2003; Heritage & Maynard, in press), which is increasingly managing patients with mental health problems, and on therapeutic discourse more generally (e.g. Peräkylä, 1995; Silverman, 1997; Vehviläinen, 1999). For example, in the context of AIDS counselling, Peräkylä (1993) has examined a particular type of questioning, hypothetical questioning (e.g. 'Say you got so ill that you couldn't kind of make decisions for yourself'), in which the counsellor's description of a hypothetical future situation is followed by an enquiry about the patient's fears or ways of coping in this situation. This is a questioning technique that encourages clients to discuss matters they might otherwise choose not to discuss. Peräkylä's analysis is relevant to counsellors and therapists in describing where to place such questions and how to design them so as to increase the chances of getting patients to talk about threatening futures (Pomerantz, 1993). Moreover, in his analysis of AIDS counselling, Peräkylä's (1995) analysis of 'circular questioning', that is, questions that elicit the client's view of his or her significant others, has been used to teach this method in family therapy training in Finland (personal communication, 2 June 2004).

The evidence that CA produces is strong and, as noted previously, has apparent validity. For example, in the aforementioned case study, while there was debate about whether or not psychiatrists should talk to patients about the content of their psychotic symptoms, the finding that psychiatrists were reluctant to do so was not disputed. However, it is early days for CA research in the field of mental health and, indeed, health care more generally. As with other qualitative methods, there is increasing receptivity in the psychiatric field, which CA is only starting to penetrate. Currently, CA is not a widely known method and its chief proponents are researchers. Hence, it has yet to influence decision making by policy makers, practitioners or service users. However, given that users of psychiatric services consider the quality of the therapeutic relationship to be the most important factor in psychiatric care (Johannson & Eklund, 2003), we may see increasing calls from service users for studies investigating professional–patient communication in mental health care.

How should CA be used in future mental health research?

CA is gaining increasing attention in health-care research for its potential to shed new light on professional–patient communication (e.g. Peräkylä, 1997; Drew et al, 2001), and this potential should be exploited in future mental health research. While it is likely that many of the findings from medical interaction in general (e.g. rejecting advice in a service encounter (Jefferson & Lee, 1992)) will be found to be relevant to mental health care, CA will also identify issues specific to the treatment of mental illness (c.f. McCabe et al, 2002), attention to which will advance the field and the quality of care provided.

CA could make a significant contribution to the training and supervision of mental health professionals in communication skills. Silverman (1997) argues strongly for the contribution that theoretically guided analysis of actual consultations can make to practice in that field:

> The implication is that effective training begins from a close analysis of the skills of counsellors and their clients revealed in careful research rather than from normative standards of good practice. As our workshops with counsellors show, professionals respond to research which seeks to document the fine detail of their practice, while acknowledging the structural constraints to which they must respond. Put another way, this means that we should aim to identify the interactional skills of the participants rather than their failings. Although the researcher cannot tell practitioners how they should behave, understanding the intended and unintended consequences of actions can provide the basis for a fruitful dialogue.
>
> (p. 223)

Basing skills training on what people do and the constraints within which they work in their routine practice could considerably enhance training, which currently relies on idealised or, at best, 'tidied-up' scenarios of clinical practice. However, as CA reveals the richness and complexity of communication, there is a tension between imparting, on the one hand, general rules of thumb, insensitive to the context, and, on the other hand, useful guidelines that lead to enhanced communication skills. While this needs to be acknowledged, CA could be used to sensitise clinicians to both what they are doing when they do X rather than Y (e.g. inhibiting or facilitating further pursuit of a topic), and what their patients are doing when they do X rather than Y (e.g. agreeing or disagreeing with advice).

As noted previously, CA lends itself to the study of any area of actual practice. Hence, it could be applied to various stages in the development and evaluation of complex interventions in mental health services (cf. Medical Research Council, 2000). Currently, most interventions are designed on the basis of assumptions about practice rather than empirical findings. CA could analyse existing clinical practice and identify specific areas that cause inter-actional trouble along with more or less problematic ways of responding to this trouble. This analysis could develop recommendations for improving that area of practice. The Medical Research Council document (2000) highlights the problem that many researchers face in defining precisely what the active ingredients of an intervention are and how they relate to each other. It argues that future research designs will have to take this into account. Although randomised, controlled trials (RCTs) are generally accepted as the reference standard in research, simple RCTs produce only descriptions of outcomes, rather than explanations of why interventions work or not (e.g. Pawson & Tilley, 1997). Methods that link process and outcome are required to address this lack of explanatory power.

Methodological challenges notwithstanding, CA is promising in its po-tential to contribute to this endeavour (e.g. Stivers et al, 2003). In another exemplary study, Boyd (1998) examined the negotiation of treatment decisions between doctors and medical insurance representatives and the outcome of these negotiations, that is, a decision regarding the financial coverage of an operation. She found that the way in which the first topic of the discussion was initiated, that is, either collegial (a general, non-bureaucratic question inviting the doctor to identify the most relevant features of a case) or bureaucratic (focusing on some documentary of clerical aspect of the case as a problem) predicted the outcome. Collegial formats were significantly more likely than bureaucratic formats to lead to a decision that the surgery be approved.

In summary, CA can access a range of phenomena that occur in inter-action. It can address a wide range of issues from general ones, such as what professionals and patients do when they meet or how is technology deployed in service encounters, to specific issues, such as how illness is diagnosed in talk-in-interaction, what interactional competencies and deficits people with different illnesses display in social interaction, how the practice of a psy-chiatrist is different from that of a psychiatric nurse or social worker, or how can the human–computer interface be designed in a way that is sensitive to actual rather than assumed use.

Seminal textbooks and electronic resources for CA

Atkinson, J.M., Heritage, J. (1984) *Structures of Social Action*. Cambridge: Cambridge University Press.

Drew, P., Heritage, J. (1992) *Talk at Work: Interaction in Institutional Settings*. Cambridge: Cambridge University Press.

Garfinkel, H. (1967) *Studies in Ethnomethodology*. Cambridge: Polity Press.

Heritage, J. (1984) *Garfinkel and Ethnomethodology*. Cambridge: Polity Press.

Hutchby, I., Wooffitt, R. (2003) *Conversation Analysis*. Cambridge: Polity Press.

Peräkylä, A. (2004) Reliability and validity in research based on naturally occurring social interaction. In D. Silverman (ed.), *Qualitative Research: Theory, Method and Practice*. London: Sage.

Sacks, H. (1996) *Lectures on Conversation*. Cambridge, MA: Blackwell.

Sacks, H., Schegloff, E.A., Jefferson, G. (1974) A simplest systematics for the organization of turn-taking for conversation. *Language*, 50, 696–735.

Silverman, D. (1998) *Harvey Sacks and Conversation Analysis*. Cambridge: Polity Press.

Silverman, D. (2004) *Qualitative Research: Theory, Method and Practice*. London: Sage.

Ten Have, P. (1999) *Doing Conversation Analysis: A Practical Guide*. London: Sage.

www2.fmg.uva.nl/emca/. Information and resources on ethnomethodology and conversation analysis.

www.sscnet.ucla.edu/soc/faculty/schegloff/. Emanuel Schegloff's web pages with a very useful publications archive.

www.sscnet.ucla.edu/soc/faculty/heritage/. John Heritage's web pages with many of his publications available to download.

www-staff.lboro.ac.uk/~sscal/index.htm. Charles Antaki's introductory tutorial on conversation analysis.

www.leaonline.com/loi/rlsi. A key journal, *Research on Language and Social Interaction*.

Chapter 4

Discourse analysis

Dave Harper

A brief history of discourse analysis (DA)

Discourse analysis (DA), a qualitative research method, is an umbrella term for a number of different approaches to the study of language. Potter and Wetherell (1987) note that the term 'discourse' can mean 'all forms of spoken interaction, formal and informal, and written texts of all kinds' (p. 7). Some have argued that there is a danger that this is overly restrictive and have used DA to study 'texts' which are neither written or spoken (Parker & Bolton Discourse Network, 1999).

In this chapter, I will be focusing on forms of DA which have become popular in psychology, especially British social psychology. They became popular because of a growing disenchantment with a strictly experimental, quantitative and decontextualised research tradition that seemed to reify cognitive structures, such as 'attitudes', which were seen to lie within individuals. Humanistic qualitative research methods have been generally seen as the alternative to this tradition, but DA also emerged in response to a disenchantment with these approaches, and many critics felt that a way out of this 'crisis' (cf. Parker, 1989) was to develop methods which focused on language and context.

Powers and Knapp (1990) define DA as 'an examination of language use – the assumptions that structure ways of talking and thinking about the topic of interest and the social functions that the discourse serves' (p. 40). There are a number of types of DA, some being very similar to conversation analysis (CA) (Chapter 3 in this volume). At times, it seems there are as many types of DA as there are discourse analysts. Potter and Wetherell (1987) concur: 'Perhaps the only thing all commentators are agreed on in this area is that terminological confusions abound' (p. 6). This, they argue, has occurred because of simultaneous developments around the topic of discourse in a number of disciplines, rendering the term 'discourse analysis' a generic one. For reasons of space and accessibility, the two main approaches I will describe here are discursive psychology (DP), which is influenced by work broadly in the fields of semiology, CA and ethnomethodology (e.g. Potter &

Wetherell, 1987); and Foucauldian DA (FDA), which is influenced by feminism, Marxism, critical psychology, psychoanalysis and the writings of post-structuralists[1] like Michel Foucault and Jacques Derrida (e.g. Burman & Parker, 1993; Parker, 2003).

Key ideas in DA

The principles of DA from a discursive psychology approach have developed over time. In early DP writings, talk is seen as varied or contradictory, since people construct what they say in order to perform certain (not necessarily intentional) functions (Potter & Wetherell, 1987; Edwards & Potter, 1992). Within talk, it is possible to elucidate different 'interpretative repertoires' or systematic ways of talking about a topic. Thus, in contrast to a traditional psychological view, language is not seen as descriptive of the world, but rather as *constitutive*, and is viewed not as a path to finding out about something else (e.g. about 'cognitions') but as something worthy of study in itself. Wetherell and Potter (1988) comment that 'the fact that discourse is oriented, consciously or not, to particular functions, which in turn throw up a mass of linguistic variation, tells us that discourse is being used *constructively*' (p. 171). Traditionally, mainstream researchers have attempted to suppress such variability through the use of concepts such as reliability. Discourse analysts, on the other hand, embrace such variability on the assumption that it is a consequence of the way texts are organised to perform certain actions. More recently, the principles of DP have been delineated as a focus on the action orientation, the constructed-ness and the situated-ness of talk (Hepburn & Potter, 2003; Potter, 2003). One strand in DP work has been a focus on how facts get constructed in talk. Thus, Edwards and Potter (1992) have described a number of ways in which speakers use rhetorical devices that have the effect of making what they are saying appear factual – often when there is some disagreement about the facts and when the speaker has a stake in the outcome. Discursive psychologists are particularly interested in what might be termed the microlevel of interaction; in discursive *practices*.

Foucauldian discourse analysts, on the other hand, are more interested in the macrolevel of interaction; in discursive *resources*. They focus on how ways of talking about a topic are located in particular historical and institutional contexts or, in Rose's (1990) words, how language makes 'new sectors of reality thinkable and practicable' (pp. 105–106). As a result, they use the term 'discourse' rather than 'interpretative repertoires', following Foucault's use of this term, which sees ways of talking as more than just words but as

---

1 Post-structuralists are those theorists who rejected 'structuralism's search for explanatory structures underlying social phenomena' (Burr, 2003, p. 204).

embedded in sets of power relations, supported by institutions (e.g. legal, medical, etc.) and existing at a particular historical moment. Foucauldian discourse analysts often produce historical analyses of how certain discourses have developed. These discourses mean that certain things become real through language. In other words, they construct particular objects – for example, 'attitudes' – and particular 'subject positions' – ways in which objects or people take up or are placed in particular positions – for example, as doctor or patient (Davies & Harré, 1990; Harré & Van Langenhove, 1999; Harré & Moghaddam, 2003). Foucauldian discourse analysts may analyse the ways in which individual speakers draw upon discourses in their talk and explore the effects of this (e.g. in terms of which positions are then made available to them). They also use 'deconstruction' – a concept introduced by Derrida – which refers to the elucidation of taken-for-granted meanings in texts, such as the oppositional assumptions implied in texts. Thus, for example, for the notion of 'health' to make any sense, we need to draw on a notion of 'illness'.

It is worth noting that some are concerned with the construction of two distinct DA 'camps'. Wetherell (1998), for example, has argued for a more integrative approach, noting that both orientations address equally important research questions.

DA is a reactive, recursive and interactive endeavour. Two primary concerns can be said to shape the analytic attitude: a search for patterns in the data (shared features of accounts or differences between them); and consideration of the functions, effects and consequences of accounts. DA is a process of reading from a position of curiosity, formulating questions about what one is reading, and then crafting a coherent written analysis.

In much social constructionist and post-positivist work, method is problematised because of a desire to avoid an overly prescriptive, 'cookbook' approach (Hollway, 1989). However, there are now a number of guides to doing DA (see the list at the end of the chapter), and some work in which the actual process of analytic choices is described (Harper, 2003). In Box 4.1, I have adapted Billig's (1997) stages to outline some of the key steps in an analysis.

Assumptions and theoretical framework

DA is broadly based on a social constructionist epistemological[2] framework. There is no one definition of social constructionist theory since it is, in reality, more of a framework, and workers within this tradition constitute a broad church. Gergen (1985) has argued, however, that there are four assumptions

---

2 'Epistemology' refers to the study of the nature of knowledge and the methods for obtaining it, whereas the related term, 'ontology', refers to the attempt to discover the fundamental categories of what exists (Burr, 2003).

Box 4.1 Steps in doing discourse analysis (DA) (adapted from Billig, 1997, and Potter, 1998)

1   Decide on a topic and then read both background material about the topic you wish to study and DA material on this and related topics.
2   Decide on the type of data you wish to study. Discourse analysts have studied a wide range of texts, broadly defined. Access to certain sensitive material (e.g. recordings of psychotherapy sessions) will need to be negotiated carefully with all participants and will need proper consideration by relevant research and ethics committees.
3   Collect data. If they are printed materials, go to step 9.
4   Listen to/view recordings.
5   Transcribe the recordings. The length of this process depends on the detail you require for your analysis (some CA transcriptions may take up to 30 times as long as the original recording to transcribe), the quality of the recording (e.g. extraneous noise in background) and the content of the recording (e.g. one or two people talking versus a group discussion, in which people may interrupt each other and it may be difficult to tell voices apart).
6   Check the transcriptions against the tapes.
7   Read the transcriptions/data.
8   Keep reading them; start looking for interesting features and developing 'intuitive hunches'.
9   Start indexing for themes and discursive features (see Harper, 2003, for more detail on analytic decision making).
10 Read, read and read, especially to check out 'intuitive hunches' against the data; always try to look for counter-examples. Potter (2003) suggests that analysis may involve examining variation in the texts, small details (such as hesitation), the rhetorical organisation of discourse (i.e. its argumentative context), how speakers make their actions accountable (i.e. how they are made to seem sensible, rational, etc), how they manage their stake and interest, and how the current analysis builds on previous research. Identify key discursive features by, for example, delineating binary oppositions; recurrent terms, phrases and metaphors; and subject positions in the texts (Terre Blanche & Durrheim, 2002a). What social practices are warranted by speakers' accounts?
11 Start writing preliminary analyses, testing your 'hunches' against the details of the data; always be critical. Think about the discursive features, their effects and contexts (Terre Blanche & Durrheim, 2002a).

12 Keep drafting and redrafting analyses, comparing different extracts, looking in detail at extracts and being aware of counter-examples.
13 Keep writing, reading, thinking and analysing until you produce a version with which you are not totally dissatisfied.
14 Be prepared to return to step 1.

implicit in most social constructionist work: a radical doubt in the taken-for-granted world; the viewing of knowledge as historically, socially and culturally specific; the belief that knowledge is not fundamentally dependent on empirical validity but is rather sustained by social processes; and that descriptions and explanations of phenomena can never be neutral but constitute social action which serves to sustain certain patterns to the exclusion of others. Social constructionist assumptions can be difficult to understand, and readers are referred to Burr (2003) for an accessible introduction. Here I will try to touch on some key issues.

First, social constructionists are epistemologically anti-essentialist in that they do not search for innate discoverable psychological essences such as 'personality', 'cognitions' or even 'emotions' (this is different from the ontological claim that they do not exist at all). Second, they adopt a questioning approach to realism. It is assumed that we cannot directly perceive a naively objective reality 'out there'. This should not be interpreted to mean that social constructionists deny that reality exists – rather, that what we know as 'reality' is socially constructed and, indeed, that there are often different competing versions of reality, which may be a source of dispute between speakers. Thus, in considering the notion of depression, a social constructionist would not deny that people talk about feeling deeply unhappy and distressed, but they would be curious about the terms we use in noticing, talking about and seeking help for it in ways which are culturally and historically located. Historians tell us that sufferers from melancholia in the Middle Ages recognised it and talked about it in different ways and sought different kinds of help and from different people than we do today.

A third difference is that social constructionists assume that knowledge is bound by time and culture; therefore, grand theories which attempt to explain phenomena in an ahistorical and culture-free manner are ultimately flawed. Thus, theories should be explicit about their local and provisional status. Fourth, language is not a peripheral matter, but is central to the way we view the world. Fifth, language is seen as a form of social action and is constitutive rather than merely descriptive. Social constructionist discourse analysts do not see particular accounts given by speakers as arising from their intentions; rather, the analyst might talk about how 'certain discourses operate in a particular text, or that the text draws on, or is informed by, these discourses' (Terre et al, 2002a, p. 156).

It is important to emphasise however that approaches to DA are not homogeneous and there are wide differences of view on central issues such as reality, and the ideological functions and effects of accounts (Parker, 1998; Nightingale & Cromby, 1999). As a result, some discourse analysts argue for epistemological relativism – a rigorous doubting of the basis of all claims (Edwards et al, 1995) – while others adopt critical realism, which 'is the view that, although we cannot be directly aware of the material objects in the world, nevertheless our perceptions do give us some kind of knowledge of them' (Burr, 2003, p. 204).

Many discourse analysts also draw on ideas from critical psychology (Fox & Prilleltensky, 1997; Hepburn, 2003), a field which is both critical of 'society or at least some basic elements of its institutions, organisations or practices', and critical of psychology itself, asking questions 'about its assumptions, its practices and its broader influences' (Hepburn, 2003, p. 1).

How are the assumptions of other methodologies viewed from a DA viewpoint?

DA and social constructionism developed as a critical response to naively realist approaches in psychology. Willig (2001) says of discursive psychology that 'it does not make claims about the nature of the world, the existence of underlying causal laws or mechanisms, or entities which give rise to psychological phenomena' (p. 103). Foucauldian discourse analysts similarly 'do not seek to understand the "true nature" of psychological phenomena' (Willig, 2001, p. 120). However, because they are concerned with the social, psychological and material effects of discourse, they do seek to understand the social and historical conditions which support certain discourses at particular times.

In contrast to more realist approaches such as content analysis – which is a hybrid quantitative/qualitative method – there is no assumption that the frequency with which a feature appears is an indicator of its importance: some low-frequency features in talk may be extremely important. Moreover, discourse analysts aim to go beyond a simple description of talk summarised into themes related to broader factors. Indeed, DA represents a radical break from the tendency to read for gist or summary (Potter, 1998). Foucauldian discourse analysts would also be very interested in the 'why now?' question: why these particular discursive resources are being drawn on at this point in history.

As I have already noted, DA is constructionist rather than essentialist in orientation, and thus discourse is not seen as a route to investigating inferred mental constructs. Such an approach is very different from the traditional ways in which language is studied in mental health as, for example, a potential sign of pathology (e.g. Oxman et al., 1982). Rather than inferring mental constructs from, say, responses to paper and pencil questionnaires, discourse analysts study how language produces effects by examining talk itself. This standpoint is extremely useful when studying phenomena such as psychiatric categories. As Wetherell (1994) has noted, the discursive examination of such categories thus moves from using them as an explanatory resource (e.g. 'she is doing that because she is depressed') to regarding them as a topic to be explored (e.g. 'what effects does the notion of "depression" have in this context?').

This is not to fetishise language. Discourse analysts do not argue that it should be the only thing studied, since it is equally important how concepts such as psychiatric diagnoses become enshrined in certain kinds of institutional spaces and practices (e.g. admission to hospital or the prescription of neuroleptic medication) that are anything but simply linguistic. However, language provides one way into an analysis of this realm.

Those new to qualitative approaches sometimes assume that they are theoretically homogeneous because they are non-numeric, but this is not the case (Potter, 1998). Qualitative methods draw on some very different epistemological traditions (see Willig, 2001, for more detail on this). We can examine the way different research methods might tackle the issue of subjective experience. Phenomenological approaches (of which there are also many varieties), for example, tend to focus on careful and rich descriptions of subjective experience, often from an 'insider's perspective' (Smith, 1996). Language is thus seen as a route to understanding the essential qualities of that experience. Because of its social constructionist epistemology, discourse analysts would view it differently. Discursive psychologists would see a description of subjective experience as, primarily, a particular kind of *account*, a rhetorical move, drawing on particular discursive resources and action-oriented. A Foucauldian discourse analyst would see experience as a thing constructed by drawing on particular discursive resources, which then set up a variety of positions for the speaker and others rather than a description of, say, an internal state. Some other qualitative approaches are *constructivist* rather than social constructionist in that they generally acknowledge that individuals construct their own views of the world, but do not view (as discourse analysts do) those individual constructions as occurring in a social world where different constructions have different social power.

What types of evidence does DA produce?

Roy-Chowdhury (2003) makes a powerful case for seeing the kinds of insights provided by DA as 'evidence' in the context of the currently dominant discourse of evidence-based practice. Different kinds of DA can provide different kinds of evidence.

History of psychiatric categories

DA can be used to trace the history of psychiatric categories, detailing the discursive effects instanced by their creation (Hepworth, 1999). It can also focus on the use of those categories, examining the positions that are available in such discourses for diagnoser and diagnosed (Hallam, 1994; Harper, 1994a; Malson, 1997; Hepworth, 1999; Blackman, 2001).

Delineating discursive resources and the positions afforded through their use

DA can also be used both to identify the kinds of discursive resources drawn on in arenas such as psychiatric diagnosis and therapy, and describe how a multiplicity of discursive positions are set up through speakers drawing on them. Examples of contexts range from feminist psychotherapy, family therapy sessions, the diagnosis of delusion and writing case notes to analysing doctors' accounts of their interactions with pharmaceutical representatives (Foreman & Dallos, 1992; Burman, 1995; Harper, 1995, 1996, 2003; Lewis, 1995; Swann & Ussher, 1995; Frosh et al, 1996; Swartz, 1996; Gillett, 1997; Malson, 1997; Stancombe & White, 1997; Terre Blanche, 1997; Stoppard, 1998; Aitken & Burman, 1999; Hepworth, 1999; Georgaca, 2000, 2004; Blackman, 2001; Caudle, 2002; Boyle, 2002, 2003; Messari & Hallam, 2003; Reavey & Warner, 2003; Roy-Chowdhury, 2003).

A focus on the interaction as evidenced in the practice of diagnosis and psychotherapy

A focus on discursive practice can help us appreciate the interactional nature of many of the conversations which occur in the clinical context, showing how participants' accounts are action-oriented. Again, studies here range over a wide variety of contexts from psychotherapy sessions to child protection telephone calls and multidisciplinary team meetings (Barrett, 1988; Marks, 1993; Soyland, 1994, 1995; Edwards, 1995; Morris & Chenail, 1995; Peräkylä, 1995; Kogan & Gale, 1997; Madill & Barkham, 1997; Griffiths, 2001; Madill et al, 2001; Harper 1994b; Hepburn & Potter, 2003; Rapley, 2004).

What types of question can DA answer?

In common with most qualitative research, DA does not begin with clearly structured hypotheses. Most DA researchers usually have some broad and relatively open-ended questions or areas of interest. The breadth is permissive in that there is a reluctance to close down areas of interest a priori, and often research questions develop over a period of time as a result of the interaction between the analyst and the texts being studied.

Depending on the form of analysis one uses, there may be different research questions. Thus, discursive psychologists seek to produce 'an understanding of the processes by which things are "talked into being" through the use of interpretative repertoires and discursive devices' (Willig, 2001, p. 103). Thus, a typical project might ask, 'how do participants use language to manage stake in social interactions?' (Willig, 2001, p. 121). There is a concern with *how* people use language in interaction and what they are trying to *do* (again, not necessarily intentionally) through their talk. Foucauldian discourse analysts, on the other hand, aim to 'map the discursive worlds people inhabit and to trace possible ways-of-being afforded by them. Some discourse analysts also ask questions about the historical origin of discourses and their relationship with institutions and social structures' (Willig, 2001, p. 120). A typical project here might ask, 'what characterises the discursive worlds people inhabit and what are their implications for possible ways-of-being?' (Willig, 2001, p. 121). Thus, there is a concern with *what* discursive resources people draw on, *how* those resources came to be culturally available and *what effects* they have in terms of the kinds of objects, subjects and positions which those resources make available – that is, 'what this means for us as human subjects (for our sense of self, for our subjectivity, for our experiences)' (Willig, 2001, p. 120).

What are the key strengths of DA?

One of the key strengths of DA is that, in common with many other qualitative methods, validity is not sacrificed in the service of repeatability and reliability, as with much quantitative research (Sherrard, 1997). Readers of good-quality discourse analyses often comment on their internal coherence (they tell a good clear story); they have face validity (it resonates with readers), and also offer new theoretical insights and generate fruitful further questions.

Social constructionist work is useful because it does not attempt to set a fixed meaning on concepts a priori, nor does it attempt to compare concepts with a notion of an unproblematically, independently existing reality. As a result, it becomes a useful theoretical resource from which to analyse the ways in which a concept emerges historically and the different ways in which it functions in different domains in culture (e.g. Parker et al, 1995; Hepworth, 1999). For example, the study of psychotherapy can move from asking whether or not a particular psychological theory is true or false to examining how it is used in a particular psychotherapy session (Roy-Chowdhury, 2003). DA is most useful to clinicians when they share its epistemological assumptions, and so it has been embraced by many narrative and systemic therapists influenced by social constructionism and post-structuralism (e.g. Foreman & Dallos, 1992; Frosh et al, 1996; Kogan & Gale, 1997; Stancombe & White, 1997; Roy-Chowdhury, 2003).

Because discourse analysts do not transform their data into numerical form (e.g. by reducing it to group means or averages) or into inferred mental constructs (e.g. 'personality', 'beliefs' or 'attitudes'), and because the data are reported so that readers can judge the interpretations for themselves, it is, like other qualitative approaches, in a sense more truly empirical than many quantitative approaches (Harré, 2004). Potter (1998) argues that DA provides a 'rigorous way of directly studying human practices' (p. 139), and thus it is able to examine the difference between what we, as clinicians, do and what we think we do (Potter, 1998; Roy-Chowdhury, 2003).

Finally, given their emphasis on the constructed nature of language, discourse analysts see the researcher as an active author of interpretations, and thus no analysis is presented as the only 'true' reading – rather, it is presented as one possible reading of many. As a result, analysts need to practise reflexivity – that is, reflect on their own position in their research. Discourse analysts may seek to make themselves accountable, but not through the 'agonising confessional work' (Parker, 1999a, p. 31) seen in some other qualitative approaches or through a simple listing of the social locations they occupy in order to render them unproblematic (Bola et al, 1998). Rather, discourse analysts may seek to identify those aspects of their social identity which might influence the study (e.g. Coyle & Rafalin, 2000) and trace their influence on the subsequent analysis.

What are the key limitations of DA?

One of the key limitations of discursive research arises from the continuing dominance of more traditional, especially naively realist, quantitative approaches. This leads to a situation where research questions may be framed (e.g. by research-funding bodies) and studies judged (e.g. by journal reviewers and editors) according to the assumptions of the dominant paradigm. Methods such as DA that ask those questions in different ways or that ask different kinds of questions run the risk of being devalued. Those socialised in hypothetico-deductive approaches often frame questions in terms of comparison or change over time, or in relation to inferred constructs – these kinds of questions are more appropriately addressed by other methods (Barker et al, 2002). Potter notes that for those beginning to use qualitative methods 'the failure to properly conceptualise a research question that fits with the research method is a major source of confusion' (1988, p. 122).

Discourse analysts note that there are a number of difficulties with the method (e.g. Burman & Parker, 1993; Coyle, 2000), a few of which are worth noting here. The first is that, because of its questioning of taken-for-granted notions and analysis of speakers' positions, some approaches to DA can be seen as implying personal criticism of those speakers (Marks, 1993). One way of avoiding this is for analysts to be scrupulous in ensuring that they do not imply that individual speakers intentionally use discourse in particular ways. Another difficulty is what has been termed 'ontological gerrymandering' (Gill, 1995), which is the criticism that critical realist discourse analysts follow a relativist and constructionist style of analysis but then implicitly claim their account is true and refuse to see some things as equally constructed. One response to this is to argue, not that one's analysis is more real, but, rather, that it is *better* than others (Harper, 1999).

A much more pernicious difficulty is the danger of 'trawling a set of transcripts for quotes to illustrate preconceived ideas' (Potter, 1998, p. 127); this can be avoided through attention to detail and a much slower pace of analysis – Antaki et al (2003) note some other features of poor analysis.

Quantitative researchers used to large sample sizes which aim to be representative of the population at large may criticise discourse analysts because of their relatively small samples. A standard response to this in qualitative research is to state that one's analysis applies only to the sample studied. As Eric Emerson (personal communication) has argued, this might seem odd, since researchers often seek to extrapolate their findings beyond their samples. It can be argued that some level of generalisability may be possible so long as the grounds for this are clearly stated. This might include the consistency of features with those reported by other researchers (e.g. DA studies on other topics or research from different standpoints on the same topic). The report may have very strong face validity. Under these conditions, some generalisability may be possible (see Mason, 1996, for a description of the different theoretical bases of generalisability in qualitative research). Of course, one would not then claim that the sample was representative.

Similarly, it may be possible to engage in 'theoretical sampling', whereby participants are sought who might tell a different story or draw on different discursive resources because of their particular social position. The question then becomes, 'how is it that this person in this position draws on these resources?' rather than 'how representative is this person's account?'. Discursive psychologists may be more interested in establishing the operation of some normative organisation in the materials being analysed, which may be more robust than the statistically significant but small effects seen in traditional quantitative analysis of small data sets (Potter, personal communication).

A final limitation of DA is that it is not a simple technique which can be mechanistically learned and applied. Analysis is an active endeavour, and those using DA need to become familiar with a wide range of literature. The relatively unstructured nature of the analytic process means that it requires time and confidence on the part of the researcher and a willingness to understand and use concepts that are often not traditionally taught in the original disciplines of mental health researchers.

Of course, many of the limitations of, and difficulties with, qualitative research noted by its critics are also present in quantitative research but are simply more visible (since they are openly acknowledged) in the former.

An example of DA in practice: paranoia and the social construction of risk

The example I will describe here is from my own research. I had begun using DA in 1990 in some research on the social construction of paranoia (i.e. persecutory delusions) in interviews with clinical psychologists and psychiatrists (Harper, 1994b). In the early 1990s, I embarked on a new study that developed ideas from this earlier project on the same topic; it comprised three parts. The first section included a use of both DP and FDA in three domains: texts on the history of paranoia, how mental health professionals constructed paranoia in the academic literature, and the way it was represented in popular culture. The analysis showed how paranoia was constructed through delineating some of the assumptions implicit in the notion of paranoid delusions as revealed in these texts and the array of subject positions afforded by these accounts.

The second section included a DA of the transcripts of 21 semistructured interviews conducted by me: nine with users of mental health services that had been identified by mental health professionals as having experienced paranoid delusions, and 12 with professionals who worked with them, including psychiatrists, community psychiatric nurses and general practitioners.

Briefly, the analysis of the interview material explored three topics: the cluster of emotions, actions and beliefs felt to be associated with paranoia; how accounts of the plausibility of 'beliefs' was discursively constructed; and a 'map' of the discursive resources drawn on in talk about psychiatric medication (a topic in which I had not previously been interested but which seemed a rich area for investigation). The third section of the study considered both aspects of reflexivity and some of the tensions and dilemmas in going beyond an analysis of discourse to outline implications for intervention.

Limitations of space mean that I can give only a flavour of the study here – there is a more descriptive account of the structure and process of analysis in Harper (2003), and the study itself can be read on the World Wide Web.[3] Rather than give examples of general findings, it is probably most helpful to give an example of the analysis of one of the interview extracts.

Box 4.2 shows an extract from my interview with Dr Smith, a consultant

---

3 <www.criticalmethods.org/thesis0.htm> (accessed 15 February 2004).

Box 4.2 Interview extract[4]

431   Dave: Right, right (.) and with both Mike and Geoff, they, they
432   were both sectioned at, at various times. What, what, what was it
433   that led you to, to, to consider the section/

439   Dr Smith: <Dave: Right> (.) With erm (.)
440   Mr Stewart the reason was erm (.) er sort of risk to others, risk,
441   quite substantial risk that he might act er (.) because of his belief
442   er there was substantial risk er because he was keeping er er a
443   sharp axe erm and he was keeping it really, sharpening it. There
444   was, there was considerable worry on our part that er he might
       act er
445   on that basis.

---

psychiatrist, concerning Mr Stewart, a patient of his.[5] It is possible to present two readings of this extract, drawing on both DP and FDA approaches to analysis. For the discursive psychologist, the analysis would begin with an acknowledgement that the interactional sequence is part of an interview, which is a particular kind of conversation. For instance, here, the interviewee is called upon by my question to produce a justification of his decision to place Mr Stewart in hospital under a section of the UK Mental Health Act. The extract contains a number of rhetorical devices (Edwards & Potter, 1992) that can have the effect of making an account more persuasive and appear more factual. Thus, when Dr Smith says the reason is 'risk' (line 440), this has a certain weight because he is speaking from a position of being a psychiatrist – this is an example of category entitlement (that is, that people in particular categories are expected to know about certain things – in this case, a psychiatrist might be expected to know about diagnosis and risk). However, the speaker adds both a qualifier here ('sort of risk', line 440) – which might

---

4 As the line numbers indicate, six lines of the transcript referring to another interviewee (Mike Sullivan) are omitted here in order to reduce the space needed for the analysis. The transcription conventions used are a much simplified version of that in Potter and Wetherell (1987). Noticeable pauses are indicated by a full stop in brackets: (.). The timing of pause lengths was not considered to contribute to this analysis and so are omitted. A slash (/) indicates an interruption by the other speaker. Short interruptions are placed in angled brackets: <Dave: Right>. Extracts are punctuated to facilitate reading. Interviewees gave their consent for interviews to be tape-recorded, transcribed and published in journal articles and they are identified with a pseudonym.
5 Both these names are pseudonyms.

function to inoculate against a potential challenge to this judgement (that is, that Mr Stewart does not pose a risk) – and also an element of quantification (the risk is 'substantial' (line 442), and there is 'considerable worry' (line 444)), one effect of which is to bolster the judgement. The notion that the speaker's worry about Mr Stewart is shared with others ('considerable worry on our part', line 444) adds an element of corroboration to his account. This further strengthens the force of the emerging narrative of risk and danger, as does the repetition of key words ('risk' is mentioned four times, 'sharp' or 'sharpening', is mentioned twice). Thus, although only a few lines are presented here, we see a strong account of Mr Stewart's risk being developed, which is also structured to inoculate against potential criticism (from me as the interviewer).

It is important to state here that the discourse analyst is not concerned with whether or not it was right that Mr Stewart was considered a risk, but rather, with *how* accounts of his risk are produced and what some of the *effects* might be of these kinds of accounts. For Foucauldian discourse analysts, there might be less concern with the immediate interactional context. Instead, they might be interested in what subjects and objects are constructed in the accounts. One striking aspect is the kind of subject position which is constructed for Mr Stewart here: he is presented as a mysterious Other, unpredictable and possibly capable of anything. In order to illustrate this, imagine other descriptions which could have been given here, such as a humanistic psychological account that might have included an account of Mr Stewart's hopes, feelings and wishes. However, in the account presented in the extract, Mr Stewart's subjectivity is composed of an array of signs and symptoms (e.g. beliefs, actions, risk). Risk is one of the objects constructed here, and this has both a particular historical trajectory in UK mental health policy (Rose, 1996) and a range of effects, some of which can be seen at work here. Thus, we can see that danger (of Mr Stewart using the axe to harm someone) can be implied by a range of factors or actions that are not necessarily dangerous in themselves (Mr Stewart's sharpening the axe). Decisions are based on the likelihood of potential actions in the future rather than actual actions in the past. They are also based on a range of other objects – inferred constructs such as Mr Stewart's beliefs. It is implied that certain beliefs (considered elsewhere in the transcript by Dr Smith to be delusional) may lead to certain (undefined but worrying) actions. Such accounts have important social and political consequences too. Thus, the focus for health professionals, such as Dr Smith, shifts from a discourse of care to one of public safety (Rose, 1996). Moreover, the ethical and political dimensions of risk and its management (e.g. compulsory psychiatric treatment in a hospital) are obscured by the construction of risk assessment as primarily a technical endeavour.

Now to move onto dissemination and the influence of the research. Rather than start at the level of my analysis and see what might be 'applied', I found it helpful to focus on different groups of potential consumers of research:

academic researchers in psychiatry and allied fields such as nursing, social work and clinical psychology; practitioners in those fields; the wider group of practitioners involved in providing psychotherapy and counselling; users of mental health services and their relatives and friends; and citizens and mental health activists (Harper, 1999). It was important to ask what might be of interest or of use to them and what might be the most influential medium of communication for each group.

Some elements of this study have been published in academic books and journals (e.g. Harper, 1996, 1999, 2003, 2004), including journals with a high practitioner readership (e.g. Harper, 1995). However, since journals in general tend to be read mainly by academics and by only a small proportion of practitioners, I have deliberately sought to publish in a wider variety of outlets, including publications more likely to be seen by practising clinical psychologists (e.g. Harper, 1998); publications read by service users, their friends and relatives (e.g. Harper, 2002); and the World Wide Web.

It is difficult to tell what influence this study has had for a number of reasons. Firstly, there is a need to develop a critical mass of this kind of research before it begins to make an impact in the mainstream. It is also difficult to disentangle the effects of research from other policy and political interventions that are consistent with the study's 'findings' – thus, for example, my analysis of the construction of risk has been helpful in responding to UK government proposals to reform the Mental Health Act (Harper, in press). Interventions do not flow in a straightforward way from research; rather, the use of these ideas is a matter of practical engagement through one's standpoint – to note of all the possible interventions one could make, which ones seem to be the 'better' or most 'useful' (Misra, 1993) in the light of the study, and which are most consistent with its conclusions and thus can be informed by them.

Thus, one could argue that even if forms of DA and deconstruction are not used explicitly they may still *inform* interventions. I would also argue that dissemination needs to reach beyond those who read mental health publications, and so I use the knowledge gained through these projects in engaging with sympathetic journalists for background material for articles about mental health policy, including the recent UK proposals to reform the Mental Health Act (Leason, 2002) and the media's perjorative use of mental health terminology (e.g. Radcliffe, 2003).

What impact has DA had on mental health research and services?

From a social constructionist perspective, it is important to question taken-for-granted notions such as impact and applicability. Although the notion of applicability has strong rhetorical power (especially in terms of legitimating professional groups), it seems to happen less in practice than might be supposed (Harper et al, 2003). From his DA study, Potter (1982) argued that the work of psychology practitioners is not directly influenced by research for the simple reason that theory and practice are often institutionally separated – for example, through researchers and practitioners attending different kinds of conferences or publishing in different outlets. Indeed, some medical sociologists have argued that theory often seems to follow developments in treatment as a post hoc justification (Gabbay, 1982), while Potter comments that 'it is not hard to conceive of theories being used as a gloss on application which has been undertaken for quite different reasons' (1982, p. 46).

Willig (1999a) takes up these points and develops them further, specifically in relation to DA. One of her criticisms is that DA studies are often disseminated through academic texts, meaning that these ideas often reach only a minority of those one might wish to influence. She argues that it is possible to find DA research that is of use in developing guides to reforms of current practices, and she lists the following different strategies of or types of intervention: exposing how dominant discourses operate, providing a space for alternative constructions, therapeutic interventions, education/consciousness raising, campaigning and lobbying.[6]

Judging the impact that DA has had is a difficult task, as qualitative methods in general have only started to make an impact in mental health research in recent years. There have been special issues on qualitative research in *Clinical Psychology Forum* (1998) and the *Journal of Mental Health* (1995), which have included DA studies, but it has taken time for it to be recognised as a valid approach, in contrast to more realist qualitative methods. Indeed, in many reviews (e.g. Buston et al, 1998), social constructionist (as opposed to phenomenological or more realist) methods such as DA are absent, reflecting a tendency to downplay epistemological differences. Some commentators have noted how radical qualitative methods may be transformed so as not to threaten the status quo (Boyle, 1998).

However, there are clear signs that DA is beginning to be more accepted – mental health research methods books have begun to include it as a valid approach (e.g. Potter, 1998; McLeod, 2001; Barker et al., 2002; Marks & Yardley, 2004), and articles using it have now been published in the *British Medical Journal* (Elwyn & Gwyn, 1999); the *Australian and New Zealand Journal of Psychiatry* (Allen & Nairn, 1997), the *Journal of Family Therapy* (e.g. Foreman & Dallos, 1992), the *British Journal of Medical Psychology* (e.g. Stowell-Smith & McKeown, 1999) and the *British Journal of Clinical Psychology* (Messari & Hallam, 2003).

The impact of DA on mental health services is even more difficult to judge.

---

6 Shakespeare (1998), drawing on the experience of a variety of liberation movements, has argued that the adoption of a social constructionist standpoint can be a useful political strategy for marginalised groups and so be a form of intervention in itself.

One interesting feature of many DA studies is that they are conducted by mental health practitioners that seek to understand their own and others' practice by placing it in both an interactional and a wider social context. In particular, DA has proved most useful in exploring issues which are contested in some way – for example, the role of 'culture' (Roy-Chowdhury, 2003) or 'change' in systemic psychotherapy sessions (Frosh et al, 1996; Stancombe & White, 1997), or the social context of psychiatric diagnoses such as eating disorders (e.g. Hepworth, 1999), ME (Horton-Salway, 2001) or sexual abuse (Reavey & Warner, 2003). Potter (1998) has noted, however, that the impetus for DA studies in clinical settings comes not only from practitioners and researchers that have found social constructionist ideas useful (e.g. the contributors to McNamee & Gergen, 1992 and Parker, 1999b) but also from academic researchers that have extended theoretical developments in discourse studies to these settings. He argues that the different aims of these groups could lead to tensions, particularly about the stance taken on therapy. However, this need not necessarily be a problem, provided those involved in the studies are clear about their aims.

Aside from research, some have suggested that DA may be useful in the training and supervision of mental health professionals and therapists (Marks, 1992, 1993). McKenzie and Monk (1997) describe how they invite trainee therapists to practise identifying discourses and positions adopted by themselves and their clients in therapy. Such an approach can enhance trainees' curiosity about the conflicting demands made upon them; the different positions they can adopt, be forced into and place others in; and the personal and social effects of different discourses and positions. This kind of approach can also be helpful in broadening the context explored in psychotherapy supervision (Heenan, 1998).

Judging the credibility of the evidence produced by DA has been a source of much debate. For qualitative research methods, especially those not based on a naively realist paradigm, the traditional evaluative criteria of reliability and validity are inappropriate.[7] It has taken some time to develop more appropriate criteria, although there are several versions now available (e.g. Henwood & Pidgeon, 1992, 1994; Stiles, 1993; Turpin et al, 1997; Elliott et al, 1999). However, many of these criteria are also inappropriate for DA because of its social constructionist epistemology (Elliott et al, 2000; Reicher, 2000). As a result, some have formulated general criteria which need to be interpreted in the light of each method's underlying epistemology (Yardley, 2000; Gough et al, 2003; Spencer et al, 2003); in addition, DA-specific criteria have been developed (Potter & Wetherell, 1987; Potter, 1996, 1998; Antaki et al,

---

7 Limitation of space prohibits a detailed discussion of this, and the reader is referred to the wide literature on the evaluation of qualitative and discursive research cited here.

2003; Burman, 2004). Good practice for DA researchers should include explaining which criteria are appropriate for judging the credibility of their study (Coyle, 2000).

To those unfamiliar with it, DA can seem inaccessible and inapplicable, and this, combined with the tendency in health service research to frame research questions in line with the dominant modernist paradigm, may account for its limited take-up by research consumers and impact on decision makers so far. As I have noted, DA research in mental health is still in its early days – the first textbooks on DA and social psychology appeared just over 15 years ago, and it will take time for mental health consumers and commissioners to judge which questions DA can address and which it cannot. Moreover, some within the DA community have now begun to produce publications aimed at bringing it to a wider audience (Willig, 1999b). Indeed, DA has become popular among those sympathetic to social constructionism; for example, critical mental health professionals and psychotherapists (e.g. narrative and systemic).

How should DA be used in future mental health research?

DA could be used much more than it currently is in mental health research. However, for this to occur, it will be important for commissioners and publishing gatekeepers of research to be open to their questions being reframed if they are based on modernist and realist assumptions. DA can offer genuinely exciting, innovative and thought-provoking ways of approaching topics. It is particularly useful for exploring contested topics or situations, and few issues in mental health are uncontested.

There are a number of considerations to bear in mind as DA becomes accepted as a method in mental health research. Firstly, it is important to avoid the temptation to think that some approaches to DA are necessarily superior to others – instead, the most important issue is the extent to which a method appropriately addresses a research question. It is also important to reflect on the kinds of material studied with DA. For example, Potter (2003) has cautioned against what he sees as the inappropriate and overuse of interview methods in DA studies. It is certainly true that interviews create particular kinds of interaction (Gilbert, 1980), and they should not be seen as a proxy for more 'naturally occurring' kinds of conversations. However, interviews may be an important source of data for some of the questions in which discourse researchers are interested (e.g. what kinds of justifications do mental health professionals give for their decisions?), but they should not be inappropriately used when more 'naturalistic' data might be better. This may pose particular challenges for professional training courses that see the interview as the data-collection method of choice for all qualitative research. There is a danger of overemphasising talk at the expense of more mundane activities, and discourse analyses are likely to be enhanced by those informed by an ethnographic sensitivity to context (Potter, 1998).

Although discursive methods are becoming more popular among mental health researchers, it is, unfortunately, still not unusual to hear of inappropriate demands made by journal reviewers and editors on the one hand, or supervisors or examiners on the other. For example, some training courses for mental health professionals, where trainees submit doctoral-level theses after 1–2 years of empirical research, require them to conduct up to 20 interviews in order to meet reliability and validity criteria more suited to quantitative work. Such a demand inevitably means that the researcher will produce only a very superficial analysis in the allotted time. Similarly, some hold an excessively narrow interpretation of the definition of a 'clinically relevant' research question, one that is often informed by the dominant modernist research paradigm. Another problem is that some courses promote 'mixed methods' approaches emphasising the importance of using both quantitative and qualitative research methods. While this can work where the methods share epistemological assumptions, it is extremely difficult, if not impossible, if they do not.[8] Those in such situations need to cite the extant literature to demonstrate both how inappropriate the demands are and other ways of addressing what may be legitimate underlying concerns. It is important to write with one's target audience (busy clinician, examiner, etc.) in mind so that one is able to anticipate and address any concerns they might have with what may be an unfamiliar approach.

Those beginning to use DA should try to attend relevant workshops and conferences, read widely and seek support from both peers and others experienced in using the methodology. Discursive mental health researchers need to keep abreast of current developments and debates in discourse work. There is often a time lag between the development of particular research methods and their use in mental health settings; as a result, there is a danger that particular approaches to DA become reified and frozen in aspic, whereas the field is characterised by vigorous debate about issues such as embodiment, subjectivity, identity and reality (see Parker, 1998; Nightingale & Cromby, 1999).

Finally, given the increasing focus on user-led research (Faulkner & Thomas, 2002), there is a need to ask where the meeting points might be between the aims of service users and critical DA researchers with an interest in questioning dominant conceptualisations of mental health. Those who have used DA for the first time often comment that it offers a very different and exciting way of viewing issues in mental health. In time, research in this

8 There are, however, examples of researchers using quantitative methods from a more critical perspective (e.g. Terre Blanche & Durrheim, 2002a, b).

area may open up new possibilities, not only for researchers, but also for practitioners and users of services.

Acknowledgements

I am very grateful to Anne Cooke, Pippa Dell, Genie Georgaca, Ian Parker, Jonathan Potter, Sim Roy-Chowdhury, Martin Terre Blanche and Vanessa Cowle for helpful comments on an earlier version of this chapter.

What are the seminal textbooks and electronic resources for DA?

Electronic resources

Centre for Narrative Research: <http://www.uel.ac.uk/cnr/index.htm> (accessed 15 March 2006).
Critical Methods Collective: <http://www.criticalmethods.org/> (accessed 15 March 2006).
Critical Psychology International: <http://www.criticalpsychology.com/> (accessed 15 March 2006).
Discourse Analysis Online: <http://extra.shu.ac.uk/daol/> (accessed 15 March 2006).
Ken Gergen's home page: <http://www.swarthmore.edu/SocSci/kgergen1/web/page.phtml?st=home&id=home> (accessed 15 March 2006).
Loughborough Discourse and Rhetoric Group (DARG): <http://www.lboro.ac.uk/departments/ss/centres/dargindex.htm> (accessed 15 March 2006).
Loughborough DARG's Conversation Analysis tutorial: <http://www-staff.lboro.ac.uk/~ssca1/sitemenu.htm> (accessed 15 March 2006).
Manchester Discourse Unit: <http://www.psychology.mmu.ac.uk/research/research_discourse.htm>
Discourse Unit.com (includes downloadable copies of out-of-print books by Erica Burman, Ian Parker etc): <http://www.discourseunit.com/> (accessed 15 March 2006).
Jonathan Potter's homepage (including papers, resources for transcription etc): <http://homepage.ntlworld.com/jonathan.potter1/potterhomepage.htm> (accessed 15 March 2006).
The Virtual Faculty (lots of resources including free access articles): <http://www.massey.ac.nz/~alock/virtual/welcome.htm> (accessed 15 March 2006).

Seminal textbooks (* Good introductory reading)

*Banister, P., Burman, E., Parker, I. et al (1994) *Qualitative Methods in Psychology: A Research Guide*. Buckingham: Open University Press.
*Burr, V. (2003) *Social Constructionism* (2nd edn). London: Routledge.
*Coyle, A. (2000) Discourse analysis. In G.M. Breakwell, S. Hammond, C. Fife-Shaw (eds), *Research Methods in Psychology* (2nd edn). London: Sage.

*Hepburn, A., Potter, J. (2003) Discourse analytic practice. In C. Seale, D. Silverman, J. Gubrium et al (eds), *Qualitative Research Practice*. London: Sage.

*Hollway, W. (1989) *Subjectivity and Method in Psychology: Gender, Meaning and Science*. London: Sage.

Parker, I. (2002) *Critical Discursive Psychology*. London: Palgrave-Macmillan.

*Potter, J. (2003) Discourse analysis. In M. Hardy, A. Bryman (eds), *Handbook of Data Analysis*. London: Sage.

*Potter, J., Wetherell, M. (1987) *Discourse and Social Psychology: Beyond Attitudes and Behaviour*. London: Sage.

*Potter, J.A. (1998) Qualitative and discourse analysis. In A.S. Bellack, M. Hersen (eds), *Comprehensive Clinical Psychology* (vol. 3). Oxford: Pergamon.

*Terre Blanche, M., Durrheim, K. (2002) Social constructionist methods. In M. Terre Blanche, K. Durrheim (eds), *Research in Practice: Applied Methods for the Social Sciences*. Cape Town: University of Cape Town Press.

Wetherell, M., Taylor, S., Yates, S.J. (2001) *Discourse Theory and Practice: A Reader*. London: Sage.

Wetherell, M., Taylor, S., Yates, S.J. (2001) *Discourse as Data: A Guide for Analysis*. London: Sage.

*Willig, C. (2001) *Introducing Qualitative Research in Psychology*. Buckingham: Open University Press.

*Wood, L.A., Kroger, R.O. (2000) *Doing DA: Methods for Studying Action in Talk and Text*. London: Sage.

Chapter 5

Grounded theory

Karen Henwood

Historical origins and development of the method

The idea that understanding, explaining and theorising should be well grounded in the processes and products of empirical enquiry is well established within social, psychological, health and clinical research. The term 'grounded theory' was first introduced by two collaborating sociologists, Barney Glaser and Anselm Strauss, within sociology in the 1960s to signify a general methodological approach to primarily (though not exclusively) qualitative data gathering and analysis, along with an associated set of formalised methods for putting those principles into practice.

First published in *The Discovery of Grounded Theory* (1967), Glaser and Strauss' methodological proposals were put forward at that time as part of an argument against the degree of influence that was being exerted by a logic of scientific enquiry that privileged the gathering and analysis of quantitative data and the testing of hypotheses derived from a few grand sociological theories. Glaser and Strauss succeeded in presenting a quite different 'logic of enquiry' (Charmaz, 1995) or 'methodological outlook' (Dey, 2004) that stressed the importance of developing ideas and theory generation through the creative and systematic investigation of a range of rich and meaningful sources of 'real world' data (Henwood & Pidgeon, 1992). They extended an invitation to researchers in sociology and across social science disciplines more widely to become more engaged with substantive domains of enquiry, and envisaged the data that researchers would examine as part of their enquiries as a mix of socially experienced realities, symbolic constructions and communicated meanings. They aimed to foster the production of far more widely intelligible, relevant and applicable conceptualisations and theories. This characteristic of grounded theory is especially valuable today, as it enhances the accessibility of the research to a diverse range of categories of research users.

Grounded theory methodology, like any other, has had to move with the times, and it is important to be aware that there are controversies surrounding the way it is being taken up and used; for example, the question of whether it enforces an unhelpful shift to 'technical essentialism' (e.g. Barbour, 2003). Some have argued forcefully in favour of reinforcing a single 'true' account of grounded theory, and there is a risk of revisionist accounts eroding what is distinctive about any research methodology. However, the view taken in this chapter is that inflexible approaches that cannot take account of important developments in thinking and practice are likely to become fossilised and restricted in their range of use.

Grounded theory's epistemological positioning is a key arena of controversy. The dominant reading of *The Discovery of Grounded Theory* is that it rests upon a positivist empiricist philosophy in that it espouses an inductivist view of the process of 'discovering' theory from data. However, this account glosses over a significant tension in the grounded theory approach, and one that has been discussed more generally as the 'dilemma of qualitative method' (Hammersley, 1989). This tension arises from a simultaneous commitment, on the one hand, to science and realism by the claim to reflect the data objectively, and on the other hand, to a form of constructionism that recognises the multiple meanings and subjectivities involved in any research encounter, and that certainly feature prominently whenever researchers are concerned with opening up new insights and generating theory.

In fact, philosophically speaking, theory cannot simply emerge from data, because interpretation and analysis in qualitative research methodology are always conducted within some conceptual framework that is, at least in part, brought to the task by the analyst, and this raises the thorny question of 'what grounds grounded theory?' (Henwood & Pidgeon, 1992, 2003). This issue is recognised in many of the classic and most influential writings on grounded theory, which suggest that researchers must be able to retain their disciplinary knowledges and utilise their 'theoretical sensitivities' (Glaser, 1978; Charmaz, 1990, 1995, 2000; see also Bulmer, 1979; Hammersley, 1989). It would be a false hope to start out on a grounded theory study, thinking that it is possible to escape the inevitable complexities involved in qualitative research around the interplay between data and theory.

Description of methodology

Figure 5.1 depicts the flow of work in grounded theory studies that makes a significant contribution to the logical character or methodological outlook of the research. In addition, the methodology of grounded theory is affected by the sets of disciplinary assumptions, knowledges, resources, framings and sensitivities brought by the analyst to the project. For some grounded theory studies, and especially those taken forward through teamwork (as is commonly the case in social and health service research settings), the methodological outlook of the project may be further influenced by an explicit commitment to interdisciplinary, transdisciplinary or, cross-professional working.

Unremarkably, the flow of work is broadly linear, reflecting the need for all

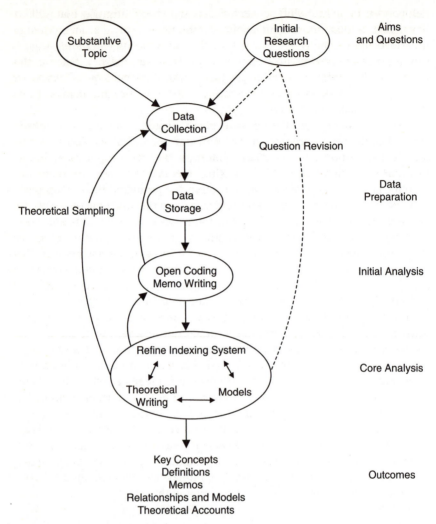

Figure 5.1 The flow of work in grounded theory studies.

Reprinted with permission of Sage Publications from M. Hardy and A. Bryman (eds), *Handbook of Data Analysis* (2004).

planned projects (and especially student projects and applications for research funding) to have at least a nominal start and end point, and for the activities between these points to involve anticipating any foreseeable difficulties (Pidgeon & Henwood, 2004). But it is also characteristically flexible and iterative, as the analyst is simultaneously involved in data gathering and analysis. This simultaneous involvement of the analyst in data gathering and analysis underpins at a practical level the 'flip-flop' (see e.g. Bulmer, 1979;

Henwood & Pidgeon, 1992) between data and conceptualisation that is often articulated within more philosophical discussions of the methodology already mentioned above.

A particular emphasis is given to the intertwining of data gathering and analysis in classical accounts of grounded theory methodology, because it clearly distinguishes the approach from the principles and practices of hypo-thetico-deductive method (Glaser & Strauss, 1967). Clearly, if data are being gathered to test specifically prior hypotheses, it would be anathema to change the data to fit the hypotheses, since this would undermine the verificationist or falsificationist logic of that mode of enquiry. However, in grounded theory, the logic of enquiry is quite different. The researcher seeks to work creatively, systematically and dialogically with rich, relevant and possibly wide-ranging sources of data, so as to generate understandings and explanations of the phenomena under investigation that are most plausible, credible and non-reductive in the circumstances. The importance of *theoretical sampling*, or using data analysis to guide further data gathering to develop emerging con-cepts and theoretical accounts, is also stressed from a practical point of view, as a means of helping researchers to guard against becoming overwhelmed by increasingly large volumes of unwieldy and initially ill-structured data as a study progresses (Charmaz, 1995).

As shown in Figure 5.1, the researcher moves from an initial topic or set of research questions to data gathering, through initial treatment of materials, using operations such as *coding* and *memo writing*, onto a set of theoretical categories, interpretations, models and written accounts of theory. Early on, 'open coding' – the development of tentative labels to encapsulate the mean-ings in the material obtained that are relevant to the topic under investigation – is a major focus of activity, supported, as necessary, by the accumulation of research memoranda written to reflect upon issues such as the coding process, the development of the analysis, or the quality of the data. In fact, such memoranda can usefully be written on anything associated with the aspects of the enquiry that would typically be written about by qualitative researchers in their fieldwork logs or research diaries. The flow of work underscored by such operations is accompanied by a gradual development of the level of analysis away from the local descriptions inherent in the initially ill-structured data toward more ordered, analytic (theoretical) concepts and categories.

As Figure 5.1 also illustrates, the researcher will move from later back to earlier operations as the analysis proceeds. Initial ways of categorising the coded data may be reorganised after emergent theoretical analysis, or the reali-sation by the analyst that the initial codes and terms did not fit the data in the ways that had been originally assumed. New rounds of data collection may be prompted to check out the emerging ideas or to extend the richness and scope of the emerging analysis until *theoretical saturation* has been reached; that is, when the decision has been reached by the researcher that further sampling and analysis are unlikely to result in the generation of further insights.

Many aspects of the grounded theory method can be likened to the process of stepping further into a maze of complexity (Pidgeon et al, 1991). Hence, suitable ways out of the maze have to be found for the researcher to reach a sufficient level of integration or closure to produce research findings and draw conclusions from the study. The *method of constant comparison* is one of grounded theorists' core strategies for doing this. It occurs initially at the level of data (as by comparing the various instances or exemplars that have been coded and then categorised similarly), and then by exploring similarities and differences between separate categories, and also, perhaps, more holistically by using selected categories to make comparisons between sampled cases. This process of making constant comparisons helps to establish analytic claims about the conceptual meaning of categories and the possible relationships between categories, and to lead to more holistic accounts and models.

Kathy Charmaz (1995) provides an elegant example from her study of people living with chronic illness of how constant comparison helped to focus the coding and develop the categorising of her data. Her initial category, 'living one day at a time', did not fully cover people's experiences of constantly struggling for survival, so she recoded and subcategorised these instances as 'existing from day to day'. Likewise, with my own study of mother–adult daughter relationships, more detailed comparison of data instances that had been initially coded together under the heading 'relational closeness' gave rise to a separate but linked category, 'over-closeness', depicting the emotional intensity and ambivalence of the women's relationship, feelings of painful gratitude and debt, hypersensitivity to criticism, and desire to flee from the relationship (Henwood, 1993). The use of a further core grounded theory strategy, writing a theoretical memorandum (in this case based directly on the key instances of comparative work in the data), was then used as a stimulus for further conceptual development, and to serve as a major resource for writing the paper that followed, reporting the main study findings. *Theoretical memoranda* are ways of articulating points of synergy between the data and key areas, aspects, and controversies within existing theory. Along with constant comparison, they can be a major means of moving between substantive and more abstract modes of theorising.

Not uncommonly, grounded theory studies involve drawing up *visual and spatial representations* depicting relationships and concepts that have become the main focus of the analysis, and drawing attention to the overall purpose and features of theoretical accounts and models. Today, computer-assisted data analysis packages (such as NVivo and ATLAS.ti) help with data handling, coding, categorising, and reclassifying and visual modelling. These packages can cut down on much of the drudgery associated with the practical side of the methodological work involved in grounded theory studies. However, they are in themselves highly labour- and time-intensive, especially at early stages of setting up coding schemes and when coding data. Moreover, they do not replace the creative interpretive and analytic work that is done, as ever, by the individual researcher or collaborative team.

The above commentary has highlighted some of the core methodological strategies and tactics that are most commonly utilised in grounded theory studies (see, also, Appendix 5.1 for a summary list, and Turner, 1981; Strauss & Corbin, 1990; Pidgeon & Henwood, 1996, 2004, for more detailed and systematic treatments). The broad assumptions and theoretical frameworks of grounded theory studies within which these strategies and tactics are situated are considered in the next section.

Assumptions, theoretical frameworks, research questions

Thus far, grounded theory methodology has been characterised by its logic of enquiry; how this translates into a set of principles and practices for collecting, analysing and interpreting data; and by the way it takes an iterative approach to the processes of qualitative enquiry. This way of presenting grounded theory methodology reflects a number of the key assumptions that underpin the appeal and popularity of the approach. One such assumption is that it can be stimulating, enlightening or liberating for the researcher's theoretical imagination to explore creatively the complexities, intricacies and inconsistencies of problems and data sources in the 'real world'. Another, closely related assumption is that these forms of engagement are made possible by the systematic set of procedures and practices offered by the approach. However, as flagged up earlier in the introduction to this chapter, it would be misleading to suggest that these assumptions and supportive practices make the grounded theory approach theory-free, either at the outset of any particular investigation or in its relation to a broader spectrum of accumulated theoretical knowledge.

Grounded theory is most closely associated, in historical terms, with the American pragmatist and symbolic interactionist theoretical traditions that emerged in the late nineteenth and early twentieth centuries. This was a time when behaviourism held sway in psychology, and when there was also a strong predilection in sociology for applying the natural science model of research to investigations of the social world. Behaviourism reduces the study of human activity to the observation or objective analysis of behaviour; it also assumes that neither the mind of the researcher nor the subjective experiences of those being researched should have any place in scientific attempts to understand, explain and predict what people do. However, it is now widely appreciated, both within and beyond psychology, just how little can be understood about social activity in the absence of showing any interest in questions about human subjectivity and intentionality, and about the contextual framing of the goals and tasks of social interaction (Harré & Moghaddam, 2001; Harré & Secord, 1972). Likewise, within sociology, it rapidly became apparent that holding too exclusive or strong a commitment to scientific measurement, control and prediction can risk reifying the properties of human action and social interaction (Blumer, 1954, 1969).

Symbolic interactionism provided a coherent alternative to research premised on these pre-existing intellectual traditions, and established and foregrounded a number of guiding enquiry principles. These included:

1   seeking to understand the meaningfulness of everyday life to the people living through it
2   showing sensitivity to the interpretation and situatedness of social interactions and routines
3   appreciating the role of symbolism and communication in enabling people to make sense of their lives and social organisation.

Grounded theory provided sociologists, and later other social, health and clinical researchers, with a systematic and yet creative methodology for broaching the kinds of research questions that are raised against this set of background concerns.

In their recent book chapter on grounded theory for research in health and clinical psychology, Chamberlain et al (2004) propose specific links between grounded theory and phenomenology. Linking grounded theory and phenomenology in this way usefully reflects the current situation in health and clinical psychology, and some other health-care studies, where grounded theory studies are, indeed, often used to investigate people's lived experiences and conscious thoughts about the phenomena that exist as part of their 'lifeworlds'. It is important to note, however, that grounded theory studies have always been part of a much broader qualitative and interpretive enquiry tradition (e.g. Denzin & Lincoln, 2000; Seale, 2004) spanning ideas from diverse theoretical and research approaches. This broader tradition includes hermeneutics, social constructionism and, latterly, postmodernism, in addition to phenomenology and symbolic interactionism with their more long-standing associations with grounded theory. This means that, potentially, a much wider range of forms of theorising are available to inform the design and execution of grounded theory studies, and to foster methodological integrity throughout the grounded theory research process.

The following list is indicative of the kinds of research questions asked by researchers who have undertaken grounded theory studies. Most of the questions are taken from actual studies, but some are hypothetical.[1] The list also

---

1   Where the questions are from actual studies, they give a clear gloss of the study concerned, rather than representing quotations from published work. The published studies are Glaser & Strauss, 1964; Houston & Venkatesh, 1996; Baszanger, 1997; Turner & Pidgeon, 1997; Kendall, 1999.

embraces studies that are focused on developing theory at a more abstract or formal level (e.g. the question about socio-technical systems) and ones that have more localised, substantive concerns (e.g. the one about bereavement services and support).

- How aware are patients who are near to death in different kinds of settings (hospitals, hospices) that they are dying? How do professional workers orient to their dying patients, and how do their orientations affect the experiences of the dying?
- How does having a child with attention-deficit disorder affect the routines of family life? What are the consequences of any changes for family functioning?
- What are the procedures and practices for handling illegal drugs in organisations?
- How do disasters develop in socio-technical systems? Do events and people's responses to them follow orderly sequences, and might such sequences make accidents predictable?
- How do people with facial disfigurements manage their reputations and identities in face-threatening interactions?
- How do general practitioners in different organisations approach the task of diagnosing illness? And how are the distinctive styles, strategies and practices developed?
- Do bereavement support groups provide valued services to group members? Are these services able, for example, to support efforts by group members to create coherent narratives linking their past, present and future selves?
- What are the cultural beliefs, practices and values of communities of recent immigrants to the USA, and how do they affect their consumption of health care?

As the grounded theory research process is iterative, and research questions can be refined as part of the research process, these research questions may or may not be in the form in which they started at the beginning of each study. Research questions in grounded theory can be more open-ended than in other types of study. Contrary to some accounts of the grounded theory method, making explicit links at the outset to a theoretical framework is not anathema to grounded theory studies. This is because the higher level of conceptualisation it brings can be beneficial in terms of clarifying the focus on the research problem – especially for novice researchers (e.g. Strauss & Corbin, 1990; Miles & Huberman, 1994; Cutliffe, 2000). However, it can also result in too little openness, and this can leave the question insufficiently intriguing from the point of view of a qualitative investigation concerned with the interpretation of participants' understandings and with social meanings *in situ*. For a useful commentary on getting a balance that includes the openness of research questions in qualitative studies generally, see Mason (2002). Pidgeon and Henwood (2004) also provide some comment on the parting of ways that took place between Glaser and Strauss on this issue of how open or closed to make the initial formulation of one's research question in grounded theories.

Methodological differences, different methodologies

When grounded theory first emerged on the scene in UK psychology in the early 1990s (Henwood & Pidgeon, 1992), the main focus of methodological discussion was upon its difference from quantitative research, and especially the challenge it posed to methodological orthodoxy in the form of hypo-thetico-deductive and verificationist method.[2] Historically, psychology had privileged the use of experiments, measurement and statistical methods, but, in so doing, psychological researchers had been denied the opportunities that could be offered to them by a wide variety of naturalistic, real-world and qualitative enquiry methods (Lincoln & Guba, 1985; Robson, 1993; Henwood & Nicolson, 1995). At that time, grounded theory offered much needed resources to psychologists wishing to develop their methodological skills in a number of areas: handling and analysis of large volumes of ill-structured qualitative data, conceptual development and theory generation, and interpretive thematic analysis of the meanings of qualitative data. These remain the same today but now have to be viewed in relation to a far greater range of qualitative methodologies.

There has been a rapid expansion in psychologists' familiarity with and proficiency in using qualitative approaches and methods (e.g. Camic et al, 2003). The range of available approaches and methods covered in the latest social, health and clinical psychology services research texts (e.g. Rice & Ezzy, 1999; Willig, 2001; Marks & Yardley, 2004) include content and thematic analysis, grounded theory, case studies, ethnographic/fieldwork methods, individual interviews and focus groups, participatory and action research, and specialist methods for the analysis of talk and text (such as discourse analysis, narrative analysis and semiotics). At the same time, the assumptions of different qualitative methods have become better recognised, and schemas have been put in place to aid decision making about the kinds of research problems for which different qualitative methods are best used.

2 As part of these arguments, it was pointed out that scientific method involves far more than theory testing, and that, therefore, there were gaps in psychology's scientific credentials. To support its claims to be scientific, psychology also needed to cultivate skills in theory gener-ation. Accordingly, grounded theory was desirable for psychologists on two counts: first, it was a methodology for theory generation and, second, as a qualitative methodology, it fitted within both interpretivist and scientific traditions.

Marks and Yardley's schema describes grounded theory methodology as best suited to the 'interpretive analysis of subjective meanings' and, specifically, to the 'content and structure of meanings that result from that process' (Chamberlain et al, 2004). In a useful development, they link case studies with grounded theory, since they provide further methodological resources for the holistic analysis of such processes in specific settings (such as health-care settings). Both offer 'deep engagement with the meanings of the data' while minimising the risk of researchers 'offering a purely descriptive account'. By contrast, discourse and narrative analysis (Yardley & Murray, 2004) ask different kinds of questions of a similar range of kinds of data – documents, interviews, naturally occurring interactions – although discourse analysis places a much greater emphasis on detailed recordings to facilitate more fine-grained analysis of talk and text. Whereas grounded theorists derive meaning with reference to their analysis of reality, discourse analysts regard meanings as being actively constructed through the use and functions of language and talk. Narrative analysis has a particular focus on the temporal structure of stories and the way this can enable people to make sense of their social world, life experiences and, otherwise, potentially disorderly life events.

Different methodological assumptions underpin the kinds of questions asked by researchers when using one or other of these comparable methodologies. Bryman (2001) points out that the associations between epistemological assumptions and research approaches should not be drawn too tightly, as this would constrain rather than inform creative methodological practice. Nevertheless, researchers do need to bear these differences in mind if they are to appreciate the kinds of research questions, types of evidence, and claims made in different studies. A three-way epistemological framework distinguishing contextualist, constructionist and realist approaches has been developed to help in this regard (Henwood & Pidgeon, 1994).

- 'Contextualism' (or 'constructionist contextualism'[3]) involves researchers in discerning, through analysis and interpretation, the meanings in the data, so that they can offer an explanatory account of key categories bearing a meaningful relationship to participants' subjective experiences and interpretations and/or interactional, communicative and symbolic practices and processes.[4]
- 'Constructionism' (or 'radical constructionism') involves the researcher in a form of interpretive practice that 'deconstructs' common-sense meanings by highlighting the assumptions upon which they are built, and

3 In parentheses are Madill et al's (2000) revisions of the schema headings used in Henwood and Pidgeon (1994), and also discussed in Parker (1994).
4 The precise set of foci will reflect the particular concerns of the study.

by questioning the grounds for the analysis or the account that has been offered of those meanings.

• 'Realism', the taken-for-granted norm within many areas of psychology, is not concerned with exploring the indeterminacy, complexity and context specificity of subjective and social meanings. Hence, it is not an interpretive practice in the sense of the other two positions. Rather, objective methods are used to determine units of data and what they contain, and it is assumed that these categories will reveal the important properties of people's experiences and social realities.

This schema is a reminder of the fact that researchers who opt to gather and analyse qualitative data face a choice: they can embrace the researcher's role in the interpretive analysis of meaning, or use standardised methods of enquiry that are designed to be researcher free (so as to rule out subjective bias). This point is especially relevant to grounded theory, since it epitomises the dilemma of qualitative method (as described in the opening section). Hence, it can be informed by different epistemological positions, even though this may not always be apparent to a researcher opting to use the core methodology (Ritchie and Lewis, 2003). Grounded theory studies could risk being poorly executed if researchers are unreflective about the consequences of their epistemological choice for the ways in which they approach the research process and the claims that are made for the findings.

It is particularly important for researchers to be aware of the differences between the practices and aims of coding and analysing data in grounded theory and those of objective coding methods such as content analysis (Henwood, 1996; Joffe & Yardley, 2004). Content analysis involves arriving at definitive criteria prior to data coding and analysis of the precise categories that will be used, and what they will and will not contain (although, in some cases, these may be drawn up through an open-ended inspection of a subset of the data). Subsequently, the frequencies with which data units are coded into the categories will be tabulated or analysed statistically. It is assumed that this kind of process will make the quality of the analysis easier to judge, as any 'inferences should be made by systematically and objectively identifying characteristics of the text' (Joffe & Yardley, 2004, p. 57). This is different from grounded theory, since, here, the researcher seeks to develop a meaningful understanding of the data by generating and refining codes and categories (or themes) in the course of data analysis, and uses various strategies to shift that understanding to a more abstract or conceptual level. While it would be possible to use the categories generated by a grounded theory study as the prior coding scheme for a content analysis study, knowledge is typically built up in different ways in qualitative enquiry traditions (see section below on types of evidence, credibility and impact).

Developing this contrast between grounded theory and content analysis has been important to highlight the characteristic features of an *interpretive, qualitative approach to thematic coding and analysis.* Such an approach does not assume that meanings inhere within the data or that boundaries between data segments that have been coded similarly are fixed (as is assumed in objective coding methods, such as content analysis). Rather, it is assumed that codes or themes that have been identified in the data contain meanings that can be analysed at multiple levels. In interpretive approaches to qualitative thematic analysis, there is an important distinction to be made between manifest meanings (observable meanings in the data) and latent meanings (which have to be inferred by the researcher). As latent meanings require reference to other parts of the data to discern their meanings, their analysis involves a process of 'contextualisation', a key element of interpretive practice. Analysis of latent meanings is, therefore, a different approach from content analysis, as the latter involves fixing meaning by applying a standardised coding frame to the data.

It is possible to conduct a thematic qualitative analysis without fully adopting the grounded theory logic of moving from analysis and interpretation to theoretical explanation. Rice and Ezzy (1999), therefore, reserve the term 'thematic analysis' for studies that use techniques for data analysis that are broadly similar to grounded theory but that do not use theoretical sampling. Joffe and Yardley (2004) view thematic analysis as more similar to content analysis than grounded theory, but as paying more attention than do objective coding methods to the analysis of latent meanings.

Illustrative case studies

Karp and Tanarugsachock's (2000) study of mental illness, caregiving and emotion management is featured as the main case study to illustrate the principles and practices of grounded theory in use, and to highlight the relevance of more social-psychologically framed approaches to grounded theory for research in mental health. Subsequently, Bolger's (1999) grounded theory study of emotional pain is briefly introduced as an example of a phenomenologically informed study that looks in more detail at the structure and content of participants' experiences in psychotherapy.

Karp and Tanarugsachock explicitly describe their study as following the logic of producing grounded theory, in that their aim is to provide an explanatory account of caregivers' changing perceptions of their obligations and responsibilities over time, along with the corresponding emotional shifts at different turning points in their 'joint caring careers'.[5]

The study has a number of real-world characteristics in that the topic is of

---

5 That is, the moments in their life history that they share with the family members who are suffering from severe mental health problems.

social and personal relevance to the people involved, and to mental health service providers. The approach to data gathering also involved the principal investigator in periods of ethnographic observation over a number of years, initially of a self-help group for people suffering from depression and manic depression. Subsequently, and for the purpose of the cited study, the observations were of a support group for family and friends. The main data were 2–3-hour interviews with those family members who agreed to volunteer and other participants recruited by other means. Although, as described in the published article, the approach to sampling is not informed in distinctive ways by grounded theory (theoretical sampling techniques were not used), the approach to data analysis and presentation of findings is far more so.

Karp and Tanarugsachock (2000) present a well-developed and lengthy data analysis section in the published account of their study. This is thoroughly (although not, of course, exhaustively) descriptive of key aspects of the data, as well as allowing for examination of the authors' core analytic claims that there is a 'mutually transformative relationship between situational interpretations of obligation norms and emergent emotions', and that 'beliefs about the propriety of emotions at any moment in time may be rooted in a prior history of affect' (p. 8).

From the account that is given of the study methodology, and from the products of the data analysis, the processes of data analysis have involved a range of grounded theory techniques. However, these were not followed slavishly; rather, they were tailored to the specific circumstances and analysis tasks of the study. 'All materials[6] were closely read, and any materials related to the emotions accompanying duty, obligation and responsibility collated in a single data book.' Codes were established by 'making voluminous marginal notations in the emotions data book', longer memos were written 'on emerging themes', and an 'index was constructed to identify the pages in the notebook where materials related to each constructed code could be found' (all quotations, p. 10).

The authors give a particularly clear account of the processes by which they focused their research aims and refined their specific research questions. It started with a 'larger researcher agenda to comprehend the experience of caring for family members suffering from one of three major mental illnesses'. The study 'did not begin with any explicit hypotheses to be tested' but, rather, 'began with broad sensitising questions about the variety of meanings that respondents attach to their role . . . and the way in which they spoke about their obligations and responsibilities toward the ill family member in their lives'. As the coding and analysis developed, it became clear how 'central and problematic [study participants] considered the issue of

---

6 That is, transcribed interviews and fieldwork notes.

managing the emotions between themselves and their sick spouse, parent, child or sibling' (all quotations, p. 9). From here, the central research question developed.

The wider theoretical concerns of the study are with the emotion work involved when mental illness poses an implicit threat to the concrete routines and symbolic order of daily life. The authors show how they used these concerns to develop the focus and rationale of their study and their analysis, and to interpret their findings. Hence, a high level of methodological consistency is shown throughout.

The goal of Bolger's (1999) study is to 'enhance the understanding of the phenomenon of emotional pain, and to illuminate the process of working through pain' (p. 343). The guiding methodological principle is to explore emotional pain from the subjective view of people who were working through painful experiences in their lives. The seven adult children of alcoholics who took part in the repeat one-to-one interviews (four at 6-month intervals) had been receiving group psychotherapy for over a year. The researcher attended the group to foster collaborative relationships with the group members and, in this way, secure permission from seven group members to interview them after completion of their group therapy sessions, and to supplement the interview data with selected data from the group psychotherapy sessions.

Grounded theory was chosen, as it 'values individual experience and the client's reflexivity (Rennie, 1992)' and is known to be effective in psychotherapy research (Rennie et al, 1988). The analysis procedures involved working with 'meaning units', shortening them into summary 'property statements', placing these into appropriate descriptive categories to 'preserve as much variation in the data as possible', and intensively exploring the linkages between categories and reorganising the data (all quotations, p. 346). These processes continued until a hierarchical model emerged with one category 'the broken self' standing in relation to higher-order categories ('covered' and 'transformed' selves).

The results section provides a detailed and highly organised description of the structure and content of people's painful experience, and their shameful feelings about themselves, especially those of brokenness. Awareness of the latter featured centrally within the proposed process model of working through pain. Discussion of the model is in terms of the support it offers to diverse areas of psychotherapy research, and the surprising elements of the findings, as, 'although pain had forced a positive change in some, for others it had been wholly destructive' (p. 358). This surprise narrative constitutes the major justification for the study findings, as a number of potential threats to their validity are raised. The key issue of how to justify the collaborative aspects of the design in the light of such criticisms is not addressed in the published paper.

Types of evidence, credibility and impact of the methodology

What constitutes appropriate research evidence for these kinds of studies? When are they judged to be credible?

As a first requirement of any grounded theory study, the author should be able to demonstrate that their analytic account is the product of a creative and rigorous analysis process with a rich and detailed data set that has been chosen for its relevance to the problem at hand. By describing the application of the kinds of data analysis procedures and practices previously described to a specific set of data, the author should be able to make transparent how the analysis has involved extensive efforts to work with the data. Assuming that the data have been generated with an appropriate sampling strategy for a grounded theory study, this will in itself provide a strong logical character for the researcher's claims and interpretations. Both of these features of the study represent a key resource for demonstrating the analytic integrity and interpretive validity of the claims and interpretations that are made for the data. It is customary in grounded theory studies to use carefully chosen data extracts to exemplify or typify the kinds of claims that are being made for the analysis, either in part or as a whole. Ideally (although consistent with the need to protect respondents' identities), sufficient details about the source of the extract will be given so that they are clearly contextualised, and so that readers can make sense of the extract and judge for themselves how well it supports the claims being made by the analyst. The account that is given of the research will also demonstrate goodness of fit between any theoretical resources that have been used to support the researcher's interpretive practices and, in particular, the kinds of interpretive claims that are being made for the data.

Where grounded theory studies seek to have an impact beyond the local domain of enquiry, they frequently do so by creating or strengthening links with existing theories and frameworks of interpretation. Grounded theory researchers and practitioners work on different kinds of research problems and substantive research areas, and in a range of similar – but not identical – settings. Accordingly, one of the main ways in which their single-domain studies can be made more intelligible and usable by others is by reflecting upon the wider implications of their findings for theory and research. This issue is important even if a study has been undertaken with the immediate aim of informing practice, as is often the case within service research projects. This latter issue has become a matter of much recent attention in debates about how to identify and enhance ways of synthesising the findings from disparate research efforts. The need for grounded theory researchers to engage in what is sometimes known as qualitative forms of meta-analysis is pertinent to the strengths and weaknesses of grounded theory.

Strengths and weaknesses of the approach

As the strengths of the approach have been articulated throughout this chapter, the potential weaknesses of the approach are addressed in this section.

Given the large measure of inductive thinking that can inform grounded theory studies, the theoretical resources drawn upon by researchers are often not embraced explicitly as part of the adopted methodological approach. This does not mean that it is any less important for grounded theory studies to be overt about their guiding enquiry principles (of the kind noted above), however. Strategies for developing and maintaining clear thinking about theoretical influences on research methodology are highly valued in all varieties of research, and grounded theory studies are no exception in this respect. One possible strategy for maximising the methodological integrity of any study is to utilise a common set of principles, drawn from pertinent traditions of enquiry, as sources of guidance and consistency of approach when making key research decisions. Often, the issue of theoretically informed decision making about methodology is not very well addressed in either philosophical or practical writings about grounded theory. Nonetheless, key moments when guidance and consistency are likely to be necessary include formulating research questions, selection of categories for comparison, finding ways to link concepts together, and interpreting the significance of findings for research and theory.

Use in future research

One of the major future challenges lies in utilising grounded theory methodology for multidisciplinary and cross-professional working. Grounded theory, as with qualitative research generally, involves intellectual connoisseurship (Turner, 1987), so ways may need to be found to mesh this feature of grounded theory work with the creative effort that is also required to build research collaborations.

Grounded theory remains a significant influence on qualitative, applied policy and evaluation research. Recently, however, framework (Madill et al, 2000) and template (King, 1998) models have begun to be widely publicised, to simplify and hasten the coding and analysis process. Therefore, it is possible that the nature of the commitment researchers have to more demanding aspects of the methodology will alter. The changing context for funding qualitative studies is prompting some re-evaluation and formalisation of ways of judging the credibility of such work, although it is unclear how much influence the new quality-control checklists will have on research practice.

Questions about how to integrate, mix or combine different methodologies, and the circumstances when it is appropriate to do this, have become a major focus of interest among researchers seeking to develop methodological innovation and improve skills. Findings from these investigations may create new opportunities for adapting and using the methodology.

Further useful resources

- contrasting book chapters by Strauss and Corbin (1994) and Charmaz (2000) in the first and second editions of Denzin and Lincoln's *Handbook of Qualitative Research*
- recent chapters by Henwood and Pidgeon in Camic et al's *Qualitative Research in Psychology* (2003) and in Hardy and Bryman's *Handbook of Data Analysis* (2004)
- Strauss and Corbin's *Grounded Theory in Practice* (1997)
- studies using grounded theory to investigate topics of relevance to social, health and clinical research in journals such as *Social Science and Medicine, Qualitative Health Research*, and *Health*. Many articles in *Qualitative Health Research* also discuss methodological issues in the context of service and practice research.

Appendix 5.1

List of core grounded theory strategies

1   developing open-coding schemes to capture the detail, variation and complexity of observations and other material obtained
2   sampling data and cases on theoretical grounds, and, as analysis progresses, extending the emergent theory ('theoretical sampling')
3   constantly comparing data instances, cases and categories for conceptual similarities and differences (the method of 'constant comparison')
4   writing theoretical memoranda to explore emerging concepts and links to existing theory
5   continuing to make comparisons and with theoretical sampling until the point at which no new or further relevant insights are being reached ('saturation')
6   engaging in more focused coding of selected core categories
7   tactics to force analysis from descriptive to more theoretical levels (such as writing definitions of core categories and building conceptual models).

Chapter 6

Randomised, controlled trials

Simon Wessely

Introduction

> At the end of the day it is the faith of those NHS doctors mostly closely involved with the work of the Cancer Centre . . . which provides us with the most meaningful statistic of all. That when both patients and their doctors can testify to the intrinsic work of something they are unlikely to be proved wrong.
>
> Anon, 1990

My introductory quotation from this chapter comes from a medical magazine, and is written by a doctor. The subject matter, the *Lancet* outcome study of patients treated at the Bristol Cancer Centre, is probably now only of historic interest. But the quotation emphasises why this chapter is necessary. It is pithy, eloquent, inspiring and usually wrong.

Doctors almost invariably believe that what they are doing is right for the patient, or they would not be doing it. Mental health professionals, who are perhaps more reflective than some doctors, usually believe they are right as well. Most health-care professionals are well-meaning people who believe they do their best and that what they do is reasonably successful. They could not work otherwise. And usually they are right, because most illnesses, especially the ones we see in psychiatry, usually do improve. If not, they at least wax and wane, to give the illusion of improvement – as in depression or asthma. Patients come to see us when they are at their worst, and, providing we do not mess things up, they are likely to improve anyway – this is called 'regression to the mean' or the 'physician's friend'. From the patients' perspective, providing they meet a doctor or therapist who is nice, courteous and respectful, things are not normally too bad. Most patients report good outcomes because they may have got better anyway, and because they like their doctor or therapist. Finally, all treatments seem to work better in acute single illnesses, as opposed to chronic, complex conditions occurring in patients with other multiple risk factors and disadvantages, so it is not surprising that we prefer to give our best treatments to those who seem most likely to benefit. These issues are elaborated later.

We need randomised, controlled trials (RCTs) – because it is the methodology that can most reliably overcome these hurdles.

Historical origins and development of the RCT method

There is some dispute about when RCTs first entered medicine and psychiatry, because people have been confused about what exactly an RCT is. The history of RCTs is actually two separate stories. The first is the history of attempts to avoid observer bias – the history of placebos, and of blinding (Kaptchuk, 1998).

The second story is the history of attempts to avoid selection bias (Chalmers, 2001). According to Iain Chalmers, the first exposition of random allocation came from the Flemish physician Jean Baptiste van Helmont, writing in 1662, in which he advocated casting lots to decide which patients would receive bloodletting and which would not, and that the outcome measure would be the number of funerals in each group. However, there is no evidence that any contemporary physician accepted the challenge. Instead, many consider that the experiment performed by naval surgeon James Lind, in which he demonstrated the ability of citrus fruits to prevent scurvy, was the first practical controlled trial in medicine.

In 1816, army surgeon Alexander Hamilton apparently used alternate allocation in a further attempt to ascertain the effectiveness or otherwise of bloodletting, although later historians have cast doubt on whether or not he ever did the experiments as reported.

One of the earliest accounts of the principles of randomisation comes from the work of Thomas Balfour at the Royal Military Asylum in Chelsea in 1854. It is quoted by Chalmers (2001), and worth reproducing, since it conveys the essence of why randomisation remains the best method of deciding whether a treatment works. Balfour was unimpressed by the claims made of the ability of a homeopathic medicine to prevent scarlet fever in the orphan boys in his care.

> There were 151 boys of whom I had tolerably satisfactory evidence that they had not had scarlatina: I divided them into two sections, taking them alternately from the list, to prevent the imputation of selection. To the first section (76) I gave belladonna: to the second (75) I gave none: the result was that two in each section were attacked by the disease. The numbers are too small to justify deductions as to the prophylactic power of belladonna, but the observation is good, because it shows how apt we are to be misled by imperfect observation. Had I given the remedy to all of the boys, I should probably have attributed to it the cessation of the epidemic.

As Chalmers comments, everything is there. The need for sound eligibility criteria (boys who had not yet had scarlet fever), the randomisation (in this case by alternation), the problem of type 2 errors (Balfour considered that his numbers were too small, and there remained a chance that belladonna did prevent scarlet fever, albeit very weakly), and the tangible risk of drawing an incorrect inference from uncontrolled data (the epidemic would appear to have been either over, or less virulent than previously thought, leading physicians to believe falsely that the relative absence of scarlet fever in the orphanage was due to belladonna).

Another milestone in the evolution of randomisation can be partly claimed by psychiatry, since it concerns the work of William Fletcher, who demonstrated the role of polished rice in the aetiology of beriberi, and how this could be overcome by using uncured rice. He did so by randomly allocating (again by alternation) patients who were inmates of the 'lunatic asylum' in Kuala Lumpur.

By the 1930s, there were numerous examples of clinical trials in which selection was determined by the toss of a coin, or alternative numbers. Why, then, is it traditional to describe the first true RCT as being the 1948 Medical Research Council (MRC) trial of streptomycin for tuberculosis? The answer is because of the role of the statistician, Austin Bradford Hill. The innovation he introduced in the 1948 trial was to tackle allocation concealment by introducing sealed envelopes. He did so specifically to prevent any possibility of investigators influencing the selection of treatments. It is for that reason that the 1948 study is justly celebrated as being the first of the modern generation of true RCTs. The purist might point out that the MRC whooping cough trial actually preceded the tuberculosis trial, but it was the latter that was reported first, and has justly received the plaudits (Doll, 1998).

It is unclear who carried out the first true RCT in psychiatry. David Healy (1997) gives the following four candidates:

1   a placebo-controlled, randomly allocated trial of chlorpromazine for treating schizophrenia carried out in 1954 in Birmingham, UK, by the husband and wife team of Joel and Charmain Elkes

2   again in 1954, a trial performed by Linford Rees, who randomly allocated 100 anxious patients to either placebo or chlorpromazine

3   a trial undertaken at the Maudsley Hospital in London by David Davies and Michael Shepherd to study the use of reserpine for treating depression. This trial began in 1953, but reports of it did not appear until 1955. (Ironically, most modern psychiatrists who have heard of reserpine associate it with producing, rather than alleviating, depression!)

4   finally, during the same time period, Morgens Schou and Eric Stromgren's randomised trial to determine the effectiveness of lithium as a treatment for mania.

Since trials take place over many years, it may be invidious to try to label any one trial as the first in psychiatry. However, perhaps the first 'modern' large-scale trial, whose influence continues to this day, is the 1965 MRC clinical trial of the treatment of depressive illness (Medical Research Council, 1965). The trial, which was conducted in three geographically dispersed regions within the UK, involved some 55 psychiatrists, recruited 269 patients with depression, randomised them to one of four treatment groups (two classes of antidepressant drug, electroconvulsive therapy (ECT) and a place-bo), and followed them for almost 6 months. The list of personnel associated with the trial now reads like a *Who's Who* of British psychiatry and statistics, including Bob Cawley, Archie Cochrane and Austin Bradford Hill. It, more than any other, signalled a new era in the assessment of psychiatric treatments.

Brief description of methodology

One of the principal changes in medical practice and culture during the last 100 years has been the increasing realisation that it is not enough for a doctor to say that his or her treatment works, nor is it enough for a patient to say likewise. These forms of anecdotal evidence, even if expanded into a series of anecdotes (dignified by the title of case series), are inadequate for the task.

There are many reasons why this is so across medicine, but especially so in psychiatry. Clearly, if one takes a disease such as bacterial meningitis, which was 100% fatal, and then introduce penicillin, after which it becomes almost 100% curable, assuming treatment is given in a timely fashion, a series of case reports is sufficient to establish benefit, and no one would even dream of doing a RCT. Likewise, the treatment of cardiac arrest would come under the same heading. However, this situation has never yet applied to psychiatry, and, I suspect, never will. Why not?

First of all, many disorders in psychiatry improve spontaneously. Thus, any treatment that the patient may have received is likely to be credited for this improvement by both patient and doctor. This accounts for much of the success of alternative therapies throughout history. We should not forget that generations of physicians would, in all honesty, have reported bleeding to be an effective treatment, and would have been supported in this claim by those patients lucky enough to survive the intervention. Thus, in any disorder which is not universally fatal, anecdotal opinion alone will invariably support any treatment claim.

Second, this process of spontaneous recovery is accentuated by what is called 'regression to the mean'. The symptoms of many disorders, such as depression, wax and wane. People tend to go to the doctor when their symptoms are worse. Inevitably, symptoms improve over time, as this is the natural history of the condition. However, the physician will falsely conclude that his or her intervention was responsible for this improvement, unaware of the fact that he or she is usually seeing the patient at their worst. For this reason, regression to the mean is also called 'the physician's friend'.

Third, we have 'non-specific' effects of treatment, which may also include the placebo effect. The simple act of taking an interest in some one, listening to them, paying attention and giving them the expectation that you will do something, anything, is itself a powerful intervention. For that reason, many charismatic doctors have, over the years, claimed great success for their particular treatment, whatever it may be, when the real intervention was provided by their character.

The fourth factor is selection bias. If one offers a treatment to 100 people, not all of them accept. Often in psychiatry, only a small proportion actually do. But this proportion is not random, and will almost invariably contain an overrepresentation of those with a good prognosis anyway. It may include those with more stable backgrounds, less severe illness, less comorbidity (such as drugs or alcohol), a greater chance of a job to return to, a more supportive home environment, and so on. All of these will be associated with both the decision to accept treatment, and also a better prognosis anyway. Thus, if someone gets better on treatment A, it may be that treatment A actually works, or it may be that those who accepted treatment A have a better outcome anyway. All of these factors that are associated with both the decision to accept treatment and the outcome of the treatment are alternative explanations for why the treatment seems to work. The technical term is *confounders*.

Assumptions and theoretical framework

So if anecdote and number of people successfully treated alone is no guide, how can we decide whether a specific treatment works or not? The answer is simple – randomisation (Kleijnen et al, 1997; Wessely, 2001). Randomisation deals with all these confounders by ensuring that they are distributed randomly (and hence without bias) between those who do and those who do not receive the treatment. That way we can be sure that those who receive the treatment are not going to do better, or worse, because of some factor unrelated to treatment. If patients have been randomly allocated to treatment or no treatment, then all of these factors should be equally distributed between the two groups, and any differences between the groups will be due either to the play of chance (and for that reason trials have to be reasonably large to eliminate that possibility) or to the fact that the treatment actually works. This is the unique property of randomisation.

Therefore, randomisation deals with selection bias. Other aspects of the controlled clinical trial deal with other biases – hence placebos, blindness, rating scales and so on are all employed to reduce observer bias, but randomisation is the only way of overcoming selection bias. Its purpose is to ensure that like is being compared with like, and that hidden biases favouring one arm of the trial or the other have not crept in.

The beauty of randomisation is that it deals with not only the confounders that you thought of, but those that you did not (Sibbald & Roland, 1998). You might be aware that responses to a particular intervention are better in females than males. Gender would then be a confounder, since if you had one arm of the trial that had more females than males, that treatment would falsely appear to be superior. However, knowing that, you could ensure by matching that the two arms have equal numbers of males and females, and thus eliminate the confounder. But what if you did not know that, and it only came out later? What about confounders that you have never heard of, but the referees of your paper have? And what about confounders that are simply unknown at the present time? Much is mysterious in psychiatry, and we can say with confidence that there is much we do not know about why some people respond better to any given treatment than others.

Here is the elegance of randomisation. You do not need to worry about unknown confounders, either now, when you submit your paper, or in the future, since so long as randomisation has been performed properly, all those confounders will have been taken care off, including those you have never heard of.

What do RCTs highlight as the assumptions of other methodologies?

One way of determining what RCTs reveal is to consider what happens if you do not randomise. The answer is simple. You are more likely to come up with the wrong answer. A series of studies has established beyond all doubt that when you do not randomise, all sorts of biases creep in (Sacks et al, 1982, 1987; Chalmers et al, 1983; Antman et al, 1992; Schultz et al, 1994; Schultz et al, 1995; Kleijnen et al, 1997; Kunz & Oxman, 1998). And what these biases do is to overstate systematically the effectiveness of the new treatment. Study after study that compares the results of evaluations of new treatments that do not include randomisation find that these designs are far more likely to report that the new treatment works. Now it could be that for some perverse reason doctors tend to perform RCTs on weaker, less effective treatments, reserving the inferior research designs for the more powerful treatments. However, one can show the same even within RCTs – the better the design of the trial, and the greater the protection from bias, the less the chance of showing that the new treatment works. Hence the importance given to what is called 'allocation concealment': preventing the investigator from being able to influence the choice of treatment. We know that the greater the chance of the investigator being able to guess the next treatment, the more likely is the trial to be positive. Investigators have been known to do virtually anything to compromise randomisation – holding 'opaque' envelopes to the light being merely one common trick – because of instances in which they are convinced that they already know what is best for the patient (Schultz &

Grimes, 2002). But what this actually shows is the unique power of the adequately concealed RCT to deliver unbiased information.

What types of evidence do RCTs produce?

It is not for nothing that RCTs come at the top of the hierarchy of knowledge, a position first accorded them nearly 30 years ago (Byar, 1978), because of their unique ability to deal with bias. And because bias, in all its shapes and sizes, is the single biggest threat to all other forms of assessment, RCTs are indeed the king or queen of assessment techniques.

Randomisation does not mean that you always get the 'right' answer. There are numerous examples of positive RCTs of treatments that later trials find ineffective. St John's wort as a treatment for depression is one instance (Shelton, 2001). The use of magnesium in the treatment of heart attacks is a very famous non-psychiatric example. And one could argue that every positive trial of homeopathy provides another. There are numerous reasons why even properly randomised trials can still give incorrect answers, although, almost invariably, it comes down to sample size and the play of chance. However, what randomisation does is protect against bias. You might be unlucky in a small trial and still get more treatment successes in the active group than the placebo group. But, provided that randomisation was successful, this will be due not to bias, but to chance, and the risk of this diminishes as the sample size increases. Bias, on the other hand, is not affected by sample size. A large biased study is even more dangerous that a small biased study, because people are more likely to be taken in by the number of noughts in the P value. All that shows is that these results did not occur by chance alone – it does not protect you from bias. In general, one can say that large treatment effects in small trials are inherently less believable and more likely to be due to some violation of the principles of the RCT than small treatment effects in large trials. Moderate (but worthwhile) effects on major outcomes are generally more plausible than large effects (Collins et al, 1996).

What types of question can the RCT methodology answer?

Again, this is very simple. The RCT addresses the question of does treatment A do more good than harm (or vice versa) than treatment B in condition C. It does not tell us why a treatment might work, although the use of placebo conditions can often shed much light on processes, and is widely used in psychological experiments. However, that is an additional benefit from some RCTs, not a prime reason for their existence. It does not tell us that treatment A will work on patient B, just that, on balance, treatment A is more likely to do good than harm in a series of patient Bs. It does not tell us that treatment A works on condition D, if that was not the focus of the original trial. Nor does it tell us whether it works on patient E, if patient E systematically differs from the patients in the original trial. But what it uniquely tells us is whether or not the benefits of treatment outweigh the risks and, if so, by how much. All treatments have side effects – there is no effective intervention without side effects. There are reports even of side effects to homeopathy! What the RCT does is assess what is the balance between risk and benefit.

What are the key strengths of RCTs?

Bias is the enemy of all attempts to determine whether our treatment, as opposed to our charm, luck or the natural history of illness, really does work. RCTs are concerned with the removal of bias. Confounding occurs when it appears that a treatment works, but this is because of some other factor, shared by those receiving the treatment, that is the real determinant of outcome. I have already detailed the issues around bias and confounding that bedevil other forms of assessment. The key strength of randomisation is that, if performed properly, it removes confounding. That is the only unique feature of randomisation. Other aspects of the RCT, such as accurate measurement, removal of observer bias (blinding) and so on, can indeed be claimed by other forms of assessment (sometimes), but the control of confounding cannot.

What are the key limitations of RCTs, and what risks arise from inappropriate use?

There have been a number of well-reasoned criticisms of the use of RCTs to evaluate mental health treatments. It has, for example, been argued that psychiatric treatments are simply too variable and/or too complex to permit generalisations from the particular. An alternative case that has been made is that psychiatric patients are themselves too complex to permit extrapolation from one patient to the wider community. And, of course, there is the continuing claim that the results from most psychiatric trials have little relevance for the day-to-day treatment of the mentally ill; that is, the results are not generalisable.

Psychiatry is not 'cookbook' medicine. So, does the same diversity that makes psychiatry or psychology both fascinating and challenging mean that the RCT is both inappropriate and inadequate to assess our success or failure in treatment? For example, taking one voice from many, Silberschatz articulates the principal arguments against RCTs in psychiatry from the perspective of a psychotherapist (Persons & Silberschatz, 1998). For him, the important questions are what is bothering the patient? What do they hope to achieve? Why have they not achieved that? And so on. The argument continues that manualisation, deemed essential in psychological treatment trials to enable another clinician to be able to repeat the intervention later, and to ensure that the therapy is replicable, removes the heart of psychological treatment – empathy, therapeutic alliance and so on. What is lost, it is claimed, is the essential individual nature of psychological treatments. People are different, problems are different, and, therefore, the argument goes, so should treatments be different.

How can we counter such arguments against trying to evaluate psychiatric treatments scientifically by RCTs? Of course, it is true that people are different, but this applies across medicine. A hundred or so years of writing on the 'art of medicine', the recent growth of 'narrative-based medicine', and the seemingly endless critiques of the limitations, or at least the perceived limited scope, and, indeed, limited success of narrowly oriented biomedicine, show that across the entire medical profession, no one should seriously dispute the importance of understanding the individual.

But if that was all there was, if every patient was indeed unique and every problem without precedent, medicine in general and psychiatry in particular would come to a full stop. If there were no communalities between our patients, and no identifiable general patterns in particular groups of patients, there would be no purpose in medical education, or any purpose in clinical experience and training. It is these shared factors that permit clinicians to draw on what they have learnt from both their training and their experience to assess and understand the specific patient now requiring their attention. After all, an intelligent clinician does not treat every person as a completely unique entity; rather, we classify patterns and information to be able to apply hard-won knowledge about similar people encountered in the past, to the person at hand.

And it is the existence of patterns of disease that make clinical trials viable. The observation of some phenomenon in a patient population of interest, be it a certain cancer, a particular behaviour, a biochemical abnormality or an emotional reaction, means that there is something that might form the basis for a clinical trial. The systematically acquired information that results can be used to help future patients, without forgetting that what is truly unique about a patient (and so cannot be studied in a clinical trial) still has to be taken into account in caring for the patient, and for this, the treating clinician will often need large amounts of intuition, experience and empathy.

The next argument is that psychiatric disorders are too complex. True, psychiatric disorders are frequently not straightforward, and psychiatric patients often display challenging and complex behaviours that might at first sight appear incompatible with the tightly controlled demands of most clinical trials. Broad categories such as depression or schizophrenia hide several subgroups, whose boundaries are imperfectly delineated. Many psychiatric patients have more than one diagnosis – the problem of *comorbidity*. What use is it studying those rare patients in whom depression does not coexist with other disorders, such as anxiety or substance abuse, when, in 'real life', these so often go together? And is it really possible to recruit members of 'difficult' patient populations and to maintain them in a trial according to the often, stringent requirements of the trial protocol?

Complications of diagnosis and patient complexity can both be difficult challenges for psychiatric trialists, but neither provides *fundamental* objections to the use of RCTs in psychiatry. Comorbidity may, for example, affect generalisation, if the index trial was performed on an unusually 'pure' subgroup of patients, but the validity of the data is unaffected. And trials can be (and have been) conducted, and conducted to a high standard, in populations and situations that might seem insuperable to the faint hearted. Schizophrenia and substance abuse, for example, does not seem an auspicious subject for an RCT, since patients with both problems ('dual diagnosis' in the jargon) are sometime seen as 'unascertainable, unconsentable, untreatable and untrackable'. But a research group in Manchester in the UK performed just such a trial to good effect (Barrowclough, 2001). Again, it might be predicted that it is impossible to carry out randomised trials in violent forensic patients, yet there is a seminal trial in which 321 mentally disordered offenders were randomly assigned to either release or outpatient compulsory treatment (Swartz, 2001).

It has also been argued that interventions in mental health are simply too complex to be reduced to the simplicities of a clinical trial. Certainly, in mental health, we seem to have a vested interest in making things more complex than is necessary. Diagnostic issues in psychiatry, for example, can become something of a fetish, and taken to extremes can undermine the inherent simplicity of the clinical trial; few clinicians really care, for example, about the subdivisions of somatoform disorders or whether someone has dysthymia or double depression. And psychiatrists use far too many rating scales to measure far too many things in their trials, increasing the chances of false-positive findings (as the Oxford, UK, group of trialists note, 'Many trials would be of much greater scientific value if they collected 10 times less data on 10 times more patients'). An analysis of trials on the Cochrane Schizophrenia Data Base found that over 640 different rating scales had been employed (Thornley & Adams, 1998; Gilbody et al, 2002a). The use of a large number of outcome measures is driven by the fear of missing something that might be 'clinically significant' even if that 'something' was not the primary reason for carrying out the study. But any advantages of such an approach are usually outweighed by the disadvantages, in particular those of multiple testing, and loss of simplicity both in analysis and in understanding of results.

The next criticism concerns the generalisability of RCTs. Critics point out that many clinical trials take place in 'pure' populations, for example, those free from all forms of comorbidity, with participants keen to attend followups, happy to take medication and so on, with the consequence that the results are not considered relevant to the vast majority of the population who *do* suffer from comorbidity, and who are, in general, reluctant to do any of the things mentioned. Likewise, prognostic features of patients in clinical trials may vary, even within trials, and it is certainly true that one cannot assume that because a treatment has been successful in a well-conducted clinical trial, the results will apply to all patients with the same diagnosis (Rothwell, 1995).

This is indeed a powerful argument for more pragmatic trials in psychiatry. I accept that the main criticism that can be sustained against the RCT in psychiatry as currently undertaken is the issue of generalisability (McKee et al, 1999). But note the rider, 'as currently undertaken'. The fault lies not with the principles of the randomised clinical trial, but simply with the way such trials are often conducted at present. The answer is not for psychiatry to turn its back on the RCT, but to push for larger, simpler trials, and to lobby against the increasing bureaucratisation of the clinical trial that stands in the way of achieving these objectives.

Case study; the example of debriefing

There are numerous examples of instances in which the evidence produced by RCTs has proved the RCT superior to other forms of assessment. If we had not done clinical trials, we would still be giving insulin coma in schizophrenia. In my time, I remember when I was a real doctor, the standard treatment for septicaemic shock, was high-dose steroids. We now know, because of RCTs, that more people die when you give them steroids than when you do not. Likewise, at the time I qualified, the treatment of cerebral malaria was high-dose steroids, except that trials showed that, too, killed more people than it cured. When I was a senior house officer in cardiology, working on coronary care, we used to give a drug called lignocaine, a local anaesthetic agent, to people whose electrocardiograms showed plenty of ventricular ectopics. It 'worked' because it did indeed suppress ventricular ectopics, and this was thought to be a good thing. Except it was not. Again, the trials showed that more people died from being given lignocaine than from not receiving it. How could that have been shown except by a clinical trial with random allocation of treatment? If one of my patients, to whom I had just given lignocaine, died, I could always reassure myself with the thought, 'this is a coronary care unit – people here have had heart attacks, and lots do die'. It is only in a randomised trial that you can actually spot the fact that your treatment may be doing more harm than good.

Let me now cite a classic example from the mental health literature and, more specifically, the debriefing controversy. Most people will be familiar with the concept of single-session psychological debriefing. This is a fairly structured procedure in which a mental health professional carries out an intervention with people, either individually or in groups, very shortly after they have been exposed to some form of adversity. The procedure involves some element of telling the story of the event, asking how people felt emotionally during the event and now, and teaching about likely further emotional reactions over time. Its purpose, enthusiastically proclaimed by its advocates, is to prevent later psychiatric disorder such as post-traumatic stress disorder (PTSD).

In our contemporary culture, the arrival of what the media inevitably call 'trained counsellors' has become as much a part of the theatre of disaster as that of the emergency services. It has become part of the social recognition of disaster, and our collective desire that 'something must be done' (Gist, 2002). And it seems to be very sensible. What harm could possibly come to talking to someone who has been exposed to a trauma? 'Better out than in' is now very much the fashion. Who could possibly think this is not a good idea? Very few, judging by the number of indications for stress debriefing – in a quick literature search, I recently found over 56 different scenarios in which stress debriefing is used or advocated.

Does it work? Even to ask the question is to invite ridicule from some quarters. Early attempts by several investigators in the field to mount an RCT were blocked because some ethical committees felt that it was unethical to deny debriefing to disaster victims. The aficionados of debriefing, and there are many, meanwhile claim that there is no need for such trials, since the evidence already exists. 'The experiences of over 700 CISM teams in more than 40,000 debriefings cannot be ignored, especially so when the majority of reports are extremely positive' ... 'numerous studies have already shown positive results ... [proving] the clinical effectiveness beyond reasonable doubt' (Mitchell & Everly, 2003).

Unfortunately, the opposite is true. The RCTs of debriefing are overwhelmingly negative. In the Cochrane meta-analysis, the Peto odds ratio for short-term psychological distress is firmly anchored around unity. What is more, the two studies with the highest-quality scores and the longest follow-up show a significant increase in the risk of PTSD in those receiving debriefing. (Wessely et al, 2000), confirmed by a very different *Lancet* meta-analysis (Emmerik et al, 2002).

Armed with this information, we can now come up with many possible reasons for the ineffectiveness and possible harm of debriefing. Psychologists might argue that it exposes people to the risk of retraumatisation, without providing any subsequent therapy. Certainly, trials that involve several sessions, and of cognitive behavioural therapy rather than debriefing, do provide more encouragement. Sociologists wonder about the professionalisation of distress, and that debriefing impedes the normal ways in which we deal with adversity – talking to our friends, family, doctor, vicar and so on. However, the point is that only randomisation could have given this information, and overcome the problems of regression to the mean, high satisfaction (as opposed to efficacy – very different things) and multiple confounding. Without these trials, it would have proven impossible to question the wisdom of debriefing. We would have continued debriefing happily enough, safe in the knowledge that regression to the mean will ensure that most get better anyway, and that those that do not – well, they were indeed exposed to something nasty so perhaps they were going to get PTSD whatever we did.

How should RCTs be used in future mental health research?

The short answer is, more often. The longer answer is, more often, with more patients, and fewer measures. We must make psychiatric trials 'bigger' (larger numbers of patients), 'simpler' (fewer outcome measures, for example) and more 'lifelike' (in psychiatry, perhaps more so than any other discipline, the case for more pragmatic trials that reflect real clinical practice is compelling). But the problem of size, or power, remains the biggest challenge. When one has conditions of major public health importance, which includes most psychiatric disorders, even modest treatment effects may have a major impact on populations. Yet, almost invariably, mental health trials are so small that they can detect only major treatment effects, which are often inherently implausible.

Take depression, for example. We know that both the tricyclics and the selective serotonin reuptake inhibitors (SSRIs) are effective in management. But which is better? And what do we mean by 'better' anyway? We can agree that should one class of drugs be, say, 50%, better (however defined) than the other, this class would immediately become the treatment of choice, and the results would represent a dramatic breakthrough in treatment. Even a 25% improvement in outcome from one class of antidepressants over the other would be of considerable importance, and, indeed, still be close to being a 'dramatic breakthrough'. But since depression is a very common problem worldwide (the World Bank analysis predicts that it will be the second most common cause of disability across the world by 2020), even a 10% improvement produced by one class of drugs over the other would be a very worthwhile benefit.

There have been over 100 trials comparing tricyclics and SSRIs, so, presumably, we should by now know the answer to this question. But we do not, and the reason is simple – the trials were too small. Hotopf and colleagues analysed 121 trials that compared tricyclics 'head to head' with SSRIs (Hotopf, 1997). Many of the trials were sufficiently large to show that SSRIs were about 50% better in improving outcome than tricyclics; of course, none did, and such a quantum leap in efficacy was always improbable. Fewer than a dozen could have detected a 20% difference. And if the differences were 10%, perhaps the most realistic possibility, not a single trial could have come anywhere near detecting what would still be an important improvement in the management of depressed patients.

We need more trials, bigger trials, and better trials.

I began with a quotation, and end with one. It is from Richard Horton, the editor of the *Lancet*, in what is often a critical look at modern trials. He is talking about all of medicine, but his rhetoric applies just as much to psychiatry as elsewhere.

> All health-care professionals directly or peripherally involved in clinical trials need to recommit themselves to explaining, proselytising, promoting, understanding, encouraging, studying, protecting, strengthening, and reflecting on the clinical trial process.
>
> (Horton, 2001)

What seminal textbooks and electronic resources exist for RCTs?

CONSORT Statement: www.consort-statement.org. The only way to report a clinical trial.

Pocock, S. (1985) *Clinical Trials: A Practical Approach*. Chichester: Wiley. A classic text.

Everitt, B., Wessely, S. (2004) *The Randomised Controlled Trial in Psychiatry*. Oxford: Oxford University Press. Not a classic text, but the only text specifically aimed at psychiatry.

MHRA EU CTD pages. http://medicines.mhra.gov.uk/ourwork/licensingmeds/types/clintrialdir.htm.

Resource Centre for Randomised Trials (RCRT). www.rcrt.ox.ac.uk. An outstanding resource centre covering most aspects of designing and undertaking RCTs.

UK Clinical Trial Managers' Network. www.tmn.ac.uk.

Chapter 7

Systematic reviews and meta-analysis

Simon Gilbody

Historical origins of systematic reviews

Systematic reviews now form the cornerstone of evidence-based decision making. They have risen in prominence over the past 10 years, largely through efforts such as those of the Cochrane Collaboration and investment in research synthesis and dissemination by the UK Department of Health in establishing the NHS Centre for Reviews and Dissemination. Systemic reviews and meta-analyses, however, are nothing new, and this method of synthesising research evidence has its roots in mental health and social science (Smith & Glass, 1977).

Gene Glass coined the term 'meta-analysis' (Glass, 1976) for the mathematical technique that he developed to investigate the effectiveness of psychotherapy. His ground-breaking meta-analyses in the 1970s established that most psychotherapies do have an effect and led Lester Luborsky to comment (quoting the Dodo from *Alice in Wonderland*) that 'everyone has won and all must have prizes' (Luborsky et al, 1975).

The origin of systematic reviews within mental health seems to have been lost from the historical narrative, and the rationale and need for more systematic summaries of research evidence are commonly attributed to Cynthia Mulrow (1987) and Andy Oxman (Oxman & Guyatt, 1988). In the late 1980s, they bemoaned the lack of rigour and potential for bias in the preparation of overviews or review articles. From this emerged a growing consensus that review articles must be prepared with the same level of rigour as primary research, if their results are to be trusted.

The most notable early success in applying systematic review methods was in establishing beyond doubt that streptokinase is a life-saving treatment for myocardial infarction. Retrospective overviews of randomised data demonstrated that if meta-analysis had been applied at an earlier stage, hundreds of thousands of lives might have been saved (Antman et al, 1992).

The establishment of the international Cochrane Collaboration – named after British epidemiologist Archie Cochrane – has facilitated the conduct and dissemination of systematic review in all areas of health care, including mental health. The Cochrane library holds more than 6000 completed reviews, and there are collaborative research groups active in all the major areas of mental health services research.

Brief description of systematic reviews

Consumers of research evidence include practitioners, service users, policy makers and decision makers at every level. They often want answers to questions such as what works? What helps? What harms? What caused something? What are the longer-term consequences of a disorder or course of treatment? What is the most efficient way in which to allocate scarce health-care resources?

In answering such questions, people ought to search out the best or least-biased answer, obtained from the highest-quality research evidence. The research must use the correct research method for the question being asked – either quantitative or qualitative.

When faced with such questions, we have two options: either find the research evidence and consider its quality and relevance for ourselves, or have someone else do that for us. Finding and appraising all the research evidence is a daunting task. There are vast numbers of scientific papers published each year, and these are incompletely and inconsistently held by libraries and indexed within bibliographic databases such as MEDLINE (Adams et al, 1994). Most people, understandably, prefer to get others to do this for them. For this reason, review articles have always been very popular as sources of authoritative and accessible information for people with questions. Often, these are produced by content experts – that is, those who have actively researched a topic.

The main concerns with traditional review articles are that they are open to bias and lack transparency (Mulrow, 1987). For example, individual pieces of primary research might use different methods, and some might be more rigorous or believable than others. How, in this case, should we believe the results of one piece of evidence over another? How should the quality and relevance of research be considered, and contradictions between research evidence reconciled? Similarly, authors of reviews can, either consciously or unconsciously, be selective in the research that they include in a review. The point of systematic reviews is to acknowledge these sources of bias and to ensure that all sources of bias are made explicit and, where possible, minimised.

The way in which systematic reviews seek to avoid and minimise bias is through working to an explicit and transparent method. It is through the use of a method and the publication of a 'method section' that the review becomes just like any other piece of primary scientific research. A typical systematic review includes:

1   a research review question or hypothesis
2   explicit inclusion and exclusion criteria
3   a comprehensive system of locating studies
4   an explicit framework to assess study quality
5   a method for synthesising results (either quantitative or qualitative).

Meta-analysis refers to a specific quantitative method of synthesising results, and this method is not always sensible or appropriate to use. For this reason, the term 'systematic review' will be used throughout this chapter to describe the overall approach in summarising literature in an explicit and replicable manner. The terms 'systematic review' and 'meta-analysis' should not be used interchangeably, although this is often done in the literature.

Assumptions and theoretical framework

A common misconception is that systematic reviews and meta-analyses are useful only for summarising randomised, controlled trials, and that they have an inherent biomedical bias, since the randomised trial is most commonly used in the evaluation of drug treatments. Nothing could be further from the truth.

The main theoretical assumption is that reviewing the literature is a potentially biased procedure. Biases creep in at every level, from both the person reviewing the literature, and from the literature being reviewed. Steps are taken to minimise all sources of bias. Examples include the use of an explicit protocol, which is drawn up in advance of the literature review and subject to extensive peer review, without foreknowledge of what the results of the review might be. Similarly, biases in the location of studies are minimised through extensive literature searches, and biases in extracting information from studies are minimised by using two independent researchers.

Systematic reviews show no inherent theoretical framework that allies them with any specific theoretical orientation – either qualitative or quantitative. However, a theoretical orientation is introduced through being explicit about what sort of research evidence should be included in order to answer a specific question or hypothesis. This theoretical framework is also made explicit by specifying how the quality or rigour of this research should be judged. This orientation has historically tended to be an empirical one, and the theoretical framework has been that of quantitative epidemiology, for questions relating to what works and for whom. There is no reason why other orientations cannot be applied, so long as the notion of what constitutes evidence and how the quality of that evidence should be judged is made explicit (Mays et al, 2001).

What do systematic reviews highlight as the assumptions of other methodologies?

Systematic reviews seek to draw together individual pieces of primary research in order to provide an overview that is more generalisable than the results of individual primary research – that is, the whole is greater than the sum of the parts. For data drawn from individual clinical trials, this approach is especially appealing since individual studies, especially in mental health, are frequently underpowered. Similarly, trials can be conducted upon such highly selected groups that their results are difficult to apply in routine clinical settings (Gilbody et al, 2002a). Therefore, systematic reviews increase statistical power and enhance generalisability. However, a tension can exist between generalisability and specificity. For example, a systematic review can produce results about what level of benefit might be the expected for an *average* individual within a population, but might be uninformative for a *specific* individual with an idiosyncratic combination of personal, social and psychological factors that determine outcome and potential to benefit. Results of systematic reviews might therefore be informative for macrolevel policy making, but less informative for microlevel clinical decision making.

Qualitative studies, single-case studies and small-scale clinical trials work on the assumption that it is important to understand the *how* and *why* aspects of, for example, effectiveness and risk. The inherent appeal of systematic reviews as they have come to be used in the evaluation of average effectiveness is their utility in macrolevel decision making. As will be seen, this is largely an artefact of how systematic reviews have come to be used, rather than an assumption that is inherent in systematic reviews themselves. Systematic reviews are largely 'assumption free', other than that they seek to make explicit and minimise the biases that exist in primary research. The assumptions that are imposed upon the systematic review are largely those of the reviewer – and include notions of what constitutes good-quality research and what sources of bias are important. Theoretically, systematic reviews can be used to summarise all forms of primary research – qualitative, quantitative or otherwise. A major misconception about reviews is that they can be used only to synthesise quantitative epidemiological data, and that they ignore the contribution of a qualitative dimension or the individual patient perspective (Petticrew, 2001).

What types of evidence do systematic reviews produce?

Systematic reviews synthesise primary research literature in order to highlight consistencies and differences between individual studies. Sometimes, this synthesis can be quantitative, whereby primary studies have been deemed sufficiently similar in terms of setting, population, intervention/exposure and outcome to justify some form of pooling to get an overall estimate of, for example, effectiveness or association. The most common mathematical tool used for quantitative synthesis is the technique of meta-analysis (Sutton et al, 1999).

Sometimes, however, this synthesis is more narrative. In this case, where a quantitative synthesis cannot be justified, important areas of consistency and disagreement between individual component studies are described and explained.

In both quantitative and narrative synthesis, it is important to explore plausible sources of difference between studies – termed 'heterogeneity'. Sources of heterogeneity often give important insights into how interventions or aetiological factors work in different populations and in different settings (Thompson, 1995).

What types of question can systematic reviews answer?

Systematic reviews are most commonly used to provide answers to questions of efficacy and effectiveness of interventions. However, this dominance of reviews of effectiveness reflects the fact that some of the major research activities and developments have been in this area, and that consumers of research (including funders) have sought this evidence. For example, the Cochrane Collaboration sets out in its guiding principles that their reviews address questions of effectiveness, and holds the randomised, controlled trial to be the least-biased method of answering this type of question (Mulrow & Oxman, 1999). However, the dominance of reviews of effectiveness should not be taken to mean that this method cannot and should not be applied elsewhere, and for other types of questions.

The principle of systematic review can (by and large) be applied to the synthesis of any type of research literature answering any type of question (NHS Centre for Reviews and Dissemination, 2001b). This is true, so long as the guiding principles of setting an explicit question, deciding inclusion/ exclusion criteria, searching in a comprehensive manner, and examining the quality of all potentially relevant research are adhered to.

Hence, systematic reviews can answer the following questions:

- What are effects of exposure to a putative aetiological agent?
- What is the best diagnostic method for a certain condition/problem?
- What is the longer-term consequence or outcome of a certain disorder or problem?
- What are the costs and consequences of a certain intervention?

Systematic review methods have less readily been applied to the understanding *how* and *why* questions, which have been more readily addressed by qualitative research methods. There is no reason why this should be the case, and there is an emerging consensus about how reviews of qualitative research can be prepared (Popay et al, 1998). Perhaps one reason that reviews of quantitative evidence predominate is the fact that there is now a strong consensus on what constitutes rigour and quality within clinical epidemiology (Sackett et al, 1991) and health economics (Drummond & Jefferson, 1996). This consensus is emerging but is less developed within the sphere of qualitative research (Popay et al, 1998; Dixon-Woods & Fitzpatrick, 2001).

What are the key strengths of systematic reviews?

The key strengths of the systematic reviews are fivefold:

1   A systematic review starts with an explicit research question/hypothesis that can be answered, accepted or rejected, just as with any other type of research. The focus and limits of the review are therefore made explicit. This is generally not the case with a non-systematic narrative expert review.
2   Systematic reviews have advanced the science of searching for literature, and have harnessed potentially powerful electronic bibliographical databases such as MEDLINE. We know which databases need to be searched, how to search them and the biases that emerge from reliance on bibliographical databases of published research (publication bias) (Gilbody et al, 2000).
3   Systematic reviews make explicit what are the types of evidence in terms of research design, population, setting and outcomes that are needed to answer the question that is set. These are set a priori, within a protocol for research, which can be subjected to peer review.
4   Systematic reviews seek to sort good-quality evidence from biased and misleading evidence by introducing and making explicit the idea of *quality appraisal* of potentially relevant research.
5   Systematic reviews provide an explicit method that can be replicated or even questioned from the perspective of the critical reader. These are all in contrast to the traditional review article, where it was impossible to know where the results came from and whether they should be trusted.

What are the key limitations and what risks arise from inappropriate use?

Perhaps the key limitation of the systematic review relates to the 'garbage in – garbage out' theory of health services research. In many instances, an area of interest or importance has been underresearched, or the research that does exist is of such poor quality that no conclusions can or should be drawn from the evidence (Gilbody et al, 2002a). This is not a failing of systematic reviews, but is a genuine reflection of the state of research knowledge in a specific area (Petticrew, 2003).

Risks emerge when those applying systematic review methods ignore these limits and go beyond the data within a review. Trying to make a silk purse from a sow's ear is the major abuse of systematic review methods and should always be checked for, as in all areas of research.

One common abuse of systematic review is also the misuse of statistical techniques, such as meta-analysis, through pooling individual studies that are clearly heterogeneous in search of some overall 'grand mean'. This, termed 'mixing apples and oranges', led a prominent epidemiologist to accuse those who conduct meta-analysis of being 'statistical alchemists' (Feinstein, 1995) that attempt to forge evidence-based gold from epidemiologically base metals.

Another potential problem with systematic reviews is that of 'publication bias'. Often the published research literature is not a representative sample of the totality of research, since favourable studies may have been published in preference to negative or equivocal studies. This publication bias is especially problematic in certain areas, such as the evaluation of new drugs or psycho-therapies, where those publishing research have a pecuniary interest in the results of their research (such as pharmaceutical companies or strong sup-porters or originators of a certain psychological therapy or approach). For-tunately, this source of bias can be checked for, and steps can be taken to minimise its effects, as for example, by contacting authors in search of unpublished or negative research. One of the key advantages of the system-atic approach is that this, as with other sources of bias, is made explicit and steps are taken to minimise its effects (Gilbody et al, 2000).

Case study of one systematic review in mental health services research

Depression is the most common mental health problem, and the majority of those with depression are managed in primary care settings. Unfortunately, a substantial proportion of those with depression are either missed or the quality of the care that they receive is poor (Katon et al, 1997). Quality-improvement strategies targeted within a primary care setting therefore have the potential to have the greatest impact on depression and the burden of suffering within the population. A number of strategies have been advocated to improve the recognition and management of depression, including the routine use of paper-and-pencil, case-finding questionnaires (such as the General Health Questionnaire) (Wright, 1994) and the development and dis-semination of guidelines and educational strategies for general practitioners (Paykel & Priest, 1992). Screening questionnaires are, on the face of it, a low-cost intervention with little potential for harm. Likewise, the education of practitioners and the dissemination of guidelines on best practice by such august bodies as the Royal College of General Practitioners and the Royal College of Psychiatrists could surely only be seen as a good thing. Policy-making and treatment recommendations should be guided by the best-quality evidence (Black, 2001), and it was decided to subject both these issues to systematic review. The approaches taken to these two problems highlight the variations on the methods involved in systematic reviews, depending upon the question being asked.

The routine administration of questionnaires and their feedback to practitioners is a fairly straightforward intervention that can be readily subjected to randomisation. In this case, one patient receives a screening questionnaire and has the results of this questionnaire fed back to the general practitioner of prior consultation, while another receives a questionnaire but has the results withheld from the practitioner. In this example, it was likely both that there would be a randomised evidence base to draw upon and that outcomes of interest – such as recognition rates of depression and the management and outcome of depression over time – would be available. A systematic review of this topic was therefore conducted (Gilbody et al, 2001). The methods and results of this review are shown in Box 7.1, and illustrate the key stages in the conduct of a systematic review.

It is clear from this review that studies were sufficiently similar in terms of setting, intervention and outcome to justify the application of meta-analytic pooling, giving an overall summary statistic – expressed as an odds ratio, with attendant confidence intervals. The results of this review were that the administration of questionnaires had little impact on the management of depression.

The evaluation of guidelines and educational strategies has a long history within health services research (Grimshaw & Russell, 1993), and the synthesis of robust research evidence is relatively well developed, largely through the efforts of groups such as the Cochrane Effective Practice and Organisation of Care (EPOC) group (Bero et al, 1998). Educational strategies and guidelines are often implemented at a national level, and educational strategies in particular are often delivered to groups of clinicians, where randomisation is difficult (though certainly not impossible) to achieve. In order to conduct a systematic review in this area, it was decided in advance that, although randomised trials would constitute the most believable form of evidence, it was important to consider other potentially rigorous but non-randomised sources of evidence. The study designs included in this review were therefore both randomised and non-randomised, controlled trials, interrupted time series analyses, and controlled before-and-after studies (Grimshaw et al, 2001). Additionally, it was anticipated that studies would be too heterogeneous, in terms of their interventions, populations, settings and outcomes, to justify meta-analytic pooling. A narrative synthesis was therefore planned. The methodology and results of this review are detailed in Box 7.2 (Gilbody et al, 2003).

Box 7.1 The routine administration of screening questionnaires for depression (Gilbody, 2001)

Objectives: To examine the effect of routinely administered psychiatric questionnaires on the recognition, management and outcome of psychiatric disorders in non-psychiatric settings.

Data sources: EMBASE, MEDLINE, PsycLIT, Cinahl, Cochrane Controlled Trials Register and hand searches of key journals.

Methods: A systematic review of randomised, controlled trials of the administration and routine feedback of psychiatric screening and outcome questionnaires to clinicians in non-psychiatric settings. Narrative overview of key design features and end points, together with a random effects quantitative synthesis of comparable studies.

Main outcome measures: Recognition of psychiatric disorders following feedback of questionnaire results; interventions for psychiatric disorders; outcome of psychiatric disorders.

Results: Nine randomised studies were identified that examined the use of common psychiatric instruments in primary care and general hospital settings. Studies compared the effect of the administration of these instruments followed by the feedback of their results to clinicians, to administration with no feedback. Meta-analytic pooling was possible for four of these studies (N=2457 patients), which measured the effect of feedback on the recognition of depressive disorders. Routine administration and feedback of scores for all patients (irrespective of score) did not increase the overall rate of recognition of mental disorders, such as anxiety and depression in (relative risk of detection of depression by clinician following feedback – 0.95, 95% CI = 0.83–1.09). There is some suggestion from two studies that routine administration followed by selective feedback for only high scorers did increase the rate of recognition of depression (relative risk of detection of depression following feedback = 2.64, 95% CI = 1.62–4.31). However, this increased recognition did not translate into an increased rate of intervention. Overall, studies of routine administration of psychiatric measures did not show an effect on eventual patient outcome.

Conclusions: Routine outcome measurement is a costly exercise, and there is no evidence to suggest that it is of benefit in improving psychosocial outcomes of patients with psychiatric disorder managed in non-psychiatric settings.

Box 7.2 Guidelines, and educational and organisational interventions to improve the quality of primary care for depression (Gilbody et al, 2003)

Objective: To evaluate systematically the effectiveness of organisational and educational interventions to improve the recognition and management of depression in primary care settings.

Data sources: Electronic medical and psychological databases from inception to March 2003 (MEDLINE, PsycLIT, EMBASE, CINAHL, Cochrane Controlled Trials Register, NHS Economic Evaluations Database, Cochrane Depression Anxiety and Neurosis Group Register, Cochrane Effective Professional and Organisational Change Group Specialist Register). Correspondence with authors and searches of reference lists.

Study selection: We selected 36 studies including 29 randomised, controlled trials (RCTs) and non-randomised controlled clinical trials (CCTs), five controlled before-and-after (CBA) studies, and two interrupted time series (ITS) studies. Outcomes relating to recognition, management and outcome of depression were sought.

Data extraction: Methodological details and outcomes were extracted and checked by two reviewers. Summary risk ratios were, where possible, calculated from original data, and attempts were made to correct for unit of analysis error.

Data synthesis: A narrative synthesis was conducted. Twenty-one positive studies were found. Strategies effective in improving patient outcome were generally complex interventions that incorporated clinician education, an enhanced role of the nurse (nurse case management) and a greater degree of integration between primary and secondary care (consultation liaison). Telephone medication counselling delivered by practice nurses or trained counsellors was also effective. Simple guideline implementation and educational strategies were generally ineffective.

Conclusion: There is substantial potential to improve the recognition and management of depression in primary care. Commonly used guidelines and educational strategies are likely to be ineffective. The implementation of the findings from this research will require substantial investment in primary care services and a major shift in the organisation and delivery of care.

The results of this review were that simplistic and passive guideline dissemination strategies (such as the Royal Colleges sending written guidance to each of their members) were largely ineffective. Similarly, GP educational strategies had no demonstrable effect on the actual management of depression for their patients. However, organisational enhancements, such as nurse case managers, and telephone follow-up of patients, did improve management and outcome.

Both of these reviews were published in paper form within high-impact journals – the traditional conduit for the dissemination of research evidence – and have subsequently been widely cited. However, a more direct approach was taken to ensure that this research had a greater probability of reaching its key target audiences. Both reviews were rewritten in a less technical language and published in the UK as an Effective Health Care Bulletin by the University of York (Gilbody et al, 2002b). This bulletin was mailed to GP practices, health-care trusts, primary care trusts and key academics in the UK (65,000 copies were produced), and was made available to download for free from the Internet (www.york.ac.uk/crd). Since evidence is dynamic rather than static, the production of an Effective Health-Care Bulletin allowed the update of these reviews, in order to ensure that the most recent and relevant research was incorporated. It is anticipated that both these reviews will eventually be published on the electronic Cochrane Library and will be periodically updated as further evidence emerges.

Overview of the impact that that systematic reviews have had on mental health services

When judging the impact of systematic reviews on mental health services, it is useful to consider both their role in routine clinical decision making for the individual patient, and their impact on macrolevel decision making, as in the formulation of mental health policy.

The degree to which systematic reviews are used in everyday clinical decision making is difficult to assess. It is clear that the rational use of research evidence now forms a key component of professional training programmes for all mainstream mental health care professions in the UK. Within this is an appreciation of the role of systematic reviews. The areas where systematic reviews have had most impact is probably in deciding what works for whom. Several innovations have sought to increase the accessibility of systematic reviews, such that they can be more readily incorporated into routine decision making. One example is the production of brief evidence summaries for individual conditions and their treatments, such as those published in *Clinical Evidence* (Godlee et al, 1999). Here, summaries of treatment options for common mental health problems, such as depression and schizophrenia, are presented, together with a 'bottom line' on the evidence, drawn from systematic reviews. Other innovations have been the development of readily accessible Internet summaries of systematic reviews, such as the Database of

Abstracts of Reviews of Effectiveness (DARE), produced by the University of York (www.york.ac.uk/crd), and the Mental Health Library, produced by the National Health Service (NHS) National electronic Library for Health (NeLH) (www.nelmh.org). Despite these innovations, and a raised awareness of the importance and potential contribution of systematic reviews, the degree to which they are incorporated into everyday decision making remains unknown.

Within the context of macrolevel decision making, systematic reviews increasingly form the basis of policies, treatment recommendations and clinical guidelines. Where policy making occurs in the absence of an explicit consideration of the evidence base, reviews are often subsequently commissioned or conducted by researchers to question the wisdom of mental health policies.

Clinical guidelines are increasingly used in order to improve the quality and outcome of care. It is now well established that clinical guidelines are likely to have little influence on care unless they are supported by a clear and rational examination of the evidence (Grimshaw & Russell, 1993). Within the UK, early guidelines for the management of depression in primary care were largely 'evidence-free' initiatives, produced and disseminated by royal colleges (e.g. Paykel & Priest, 1992). However, in the USA, national guidelines were based upon explicit evidence summaries and systematic reviews from an early stage (e.g. Agency for Health Care Policy Research, 1993). Within the UK, guidelines produced by the National Institute for Clinical Effectiveness (NICE) (www.nice.org.uk) are now explicitly based upon systematic reviews of the research evidence. Evidence-based NICE guidelines have been produced on the management of schizophrenia, depression, bipolar illness and the use of electroconvulsive therapy (ECT). Interestingly, the review of ECT included systematic reviews of effectiveness (does it work and for whom?), alongside systematic reviews of patient experience of the treatment based upon qualitative research literature (Rose et al, 2003). It is still too early to judge the degree to which these guidelines will influence practice. Systematic reviews have also been used to examine the most effective ways in which depression treatment guidelines can be implemented in routine practice (Gilbody et al, 2002b) – see above.

Policy making often precedes a rigorous consideration of the evidence, and systematic reviews represent a powerful critique of misguided policies or a means of supporting those that are sensible. Two examples drawn from UK mental health policy serve to illustrate this point, the Care Programme Approach (CPA) and the National Service Framework (NSF).

The CPA was a high-profile UK health policy introduced in the 1990s as a means of organising and delivering community care for people with severe mental health problems, such as schizophrenia. This generated much debate and some resentment among clinicians and users of care alike, and there was concern that this represented a profligate and bureaucratic exercise, with little evidence to support its value (Tyrer, 1998). A series of important systematic reviews (Marshall et al, 2001; Marshall & Lockwood, 2001) conducted under the auspices of the Cochrane Collaboration produced robust evidence to show that the CPA, as originally conceived, was likely to be ineffective in improving patient outcomes. An effective approach, based upon an Assertive Community Treatment programme, was likely to require substantial investment prior to implementation. It is likely that these reviews, although uncomfortable for policy makers at the time, have influenced the subsequent implementation of mental health policy.

The NSF was a bold piece of national health policy, which laid out seven core principles to guide the development of mental health services (Secretary of State for Health, 1999). These principles were laid out in advance of an explicit appraisal of the evidence to support their value, or methods to support their implementation. Subsequent work was commissioned by the UK Department of Health to examine what evidence was available from systematic reviews, in terms of clinical and cost-effectiveness (NHS Centre for Reviews and Dissemination, 2001a).

How should systematic reviews be used in future mental health services research?

There is growing acknowledgement that systematic reviews provide the highest-quality summaries of research evidence. One key purpose of systematic reviews should be to highlight the shortcomings of the research evidence and to demonstrate the need for further high-quality research. For example, the UK Medical Research Council now requires that applicants for research funds have conducted a systematic review of the existing research literature in advance of funding new primary research. Similarly, technology appraisals conducted on behalf of the National Institute of Clinical Excellence and the UK Health Technology Assessment programme are now used to help refine and shape the primary research agenda in a specific field.

Two key developments are likely to become more accepted and widespread in the near future, and these relate to enhancing the relevance and contextualising the results of systematic reviews. Systematic reviews often produce results but also raise questions about the relevance and rigour of primary research evidence. For example, several of the studies highlighted in the review of guidelines and organisational interventions for depression in primary care have limited follow-up periods, or have been conducted in the insurance-based US health-care system. Therefore, what are the longer-term outcomes or transferability of these options in the socialised model of care in the UK? One strategy than can be used in this instance is that of *decision modelling*, whereby longer-term outcomes and cost-effectiveness can be examined by combining the results of rigorous systematic reviews with longer-term observational data and resource use data from a specific health-care system (Petitti, 2000).

The relevance of systematic reviews can also be enhanced by combining the results of both qualitative and quantitative research (Dixon-Woods & Fitzpatrick, 2001). For example, the negative results of the review of screening for depression (Gilbody et al, 2001) may need to be understood by considering or undertaking qualitative research into how clinicians use questionnaires in the process of routine clinical decision making. The practical implications of routine screening can also be understood from qualitative research conducted alongside randomised trials. In this case, routinely administered question-naires are not the resource-free strategy that supporters would claim, and when used in the GP waiting room, they frequently caused 'bottlenecks' and required that a research assistant be employed to administer and score them (Rost et al, 2000).

The methods that have evolved in the synthesis of epidemiological and economic data are now relatively well established and accepted. Future research activity is likely to focus on the definitions and development of commonly accepted quality criteria for qualitative and organisational research, and a consensus about how qualitative and quantitative research can be integrated and synthesised.

What are the seminal textbooks and electronic resources for systematic reviews?

For an interesting introduction to the historical development of the science of research synthesis, a book by Hunt (1997) is both readable and accessible.

For those wishing to understand the rationale behind research synthesis, an edited book by Ian Chalmers and Doug Altman (1995) is both accessible and brief.

More advanced textbooks and resources on the conduct of systematic reviews and meta-analysis include that by Egger et al (2000), which represents an up-to-date collection of papers by leading authors in the conduct of all types of review, and the seminal textbook by Cooper and Hedges (1994), which gives a more technical overview of the mathematics of meta-analysis. In addition, an authoritative and freely available summary of the methods used in systematic reviews has been produced by the NHS Health Technology Assessment Programme (Sutton et al, 1999).

For those who wish to undertake a systematic review, two freely available resources are of note. The first is the *Cochrane Handbook* (Mulrow & Oxman, 2002), which provides a step-by-step introduction for those designing a Cochrane review. The second is the update of report no. 4 from the NHS Centre for Reviews and Dissemination (2001b), which is less focused on reviews of randomised, controlled trials than the *Cochrane Handbook*. For example, it gives clear instructions on formulating review questions; literature searching; and the synthesis of epidemiological, economic and qualitative data.

Chapter 8

Surveys

Rachel Jenkins, Howard Meltzer, Terry Brugha and Sunjai Gupta OBE

Historical origins and development of surveys

Surveys began in order to answer specific questions which could not be answered by routine service use data such as hospital admission data, outpatient attendance data, local case register data, GP consultation data or mortality data. There is a long history of studies that describe and characterise the psychiatric morbidity seen in the community by standardised assessments.

In the first generation of surveys (e.g. Stromgren, 1938; Roth & Luton, 1942; Sjogren, 1948), trained psychiatrists interviewed informants and reached a diagnosis by using their skills in the ordinary way. There was no formal attempt to standardise case definition. These surveys produced values for morbid risk, which were very similar for the major psychoses but which varied considerably for the neuroses.

The second generation of surveys made real attempts at standardisation in the 1950s (Srole et al, 1962; Leighton et al, 1963). Self-report schedules provide a standard coverage of possible symptoms. However, they used summed symptom scores as position indicators on a continuum from health to abnormality, and subjects were divided into groups according to their degree of impairment. These divisions were regarded merely as statistical conveniences. These studies used brief checklists of symptoms (e.g. Langner, 1962), but concerns were increasingly expressed about the validity of these measures and the lack of diagnostic information they supplied.

The authors of the third generation of community surveys felt strongly that classification was a crucial part of the study of psychiatric disorder, and that reliable and comparable measures could be established if the classifying rules were made explicit and precise. This permits the identification of cases comparable with those seen and treated by psychiatric clinicians.

Thus, the US-UK study (Cooper et al, 1972) saw a dramatic change in the development of standardised psychiatric assessments. The assessments were developed from the way in which clinical judgements were used in characterising psychiatric disorder in the more severely ill patients treated in specialist settings (Wing et al, 1974). As the interviews were administered by specialists, the opportunities for mounting large-scale surveys were severely limited. There have been a number of community surveys carried out in the UK, but these have been limited in geographical and diagnostic coverage and have made use of differing definitions, populations and methodologies (Taylor & Chave, 1964; Hare & Shaw, 1965; Brown et al, 1977; Brown & Harris, 1978; Cochrane et al, 1980; Bebbington et al, 1981; Surtees et al, 1983). They have also been carried out at different times over the last few decades, so it is difficult and probably invalid to extrapolate the findings of these small-scale surveys to the countries as a whole or even to combine the results of those that have been carried out.

Some surveys with a national coverage have used shorter questionnaires to elicit psychiatric symptoms; for example, the General Health Questionnaire (GHQ) (Cox et al, 1987; Buck et al, 1994). Although the GHQ has good sensitivity and specificity for neurotic disorder, there are concerns about its validity in some groups (Stansfeld & Marmot, 1992; Lewis & Araya, 1995), and it provides little information to characterise psychiatric disorder or for diagnoses. These studies did not link data on psychiatric disorder to use of health or social services.

The most recent generation of large-scale surveys in the Western world include those based on the GHQ, and those using more detailed assessments of mental state, such as the Columbia Impairment Scale (CIS), the Composite International Diagnostic Interview (CIDI) and the Diagnostic Interview Schedule (DIS). Those relying exclusively on the GHQ include the UK annual health surveys for England, repeated annually between 1992 and 1999; the Health and Lifestyle Survey 1984; and its follow-up in 1991–2, the British Household Panel Survey 1991–2. Surveys using more detailed assessment instruments include the Edmonton Survey of Psychiatric Disorders in Canada in 1983–6, which used the diagnostic interview schedule and the GHQ 30; the Epidemiological Catchment Area programme (Eaton & Kessler, 1985; Robins & Regier, 1991); the National Comorbidity Survey (1990–2) in the USA, which used the CIDI (Kessler, 1994); the British National Survey Programme (1993–present), which uses the Clinical Interview Schedule–Revised; the Australian National Mental Health Survey 1997, which used the CIDI; the Netherlands Mental Health Survey and Incidence Study (NEMESIS), which used the CIDI and the GHQ 12; and, most recently, the World Mental Health Survey in 26 countries, which used the CIDI.

Brief description of methodology

The methodology of surveys comprises objective setting, sampling design and strategy, choice of assessment tools, piloting and implementation.

Objectives

This involves a choice of age groups, or settings and of specific questions to be answered. Age groups include children, adolescents, adults and the elderly. Possible settings include private households; the homeless; and institutions such as prisons, hospitals, orphanages, schools and workplaces. Potential research objectives are as follows:

1   to estimate the prevalence of psychiatric morbidity – individual symptoms, specific disorders, and the above threshold disorders combined
2   to investigate associations between psychiatric disorders and substance use and abuse
3   to identify the nature and extent of social disabilities associated with mental illness, social disability here referring to limitations in function and restriction in activities within the various domains of housing, occupation, social relationships, finance, family, etc.
4   to describe the use of primary and secondary health services, private facilities. social services and voluntary services by people with psychiatric morbidity, and to relate these to ICD-10 psychiatric disorders, symptoms and associated disability
5   to investigate the association between psychiatric morbidity and recent life events, the experience of social support and socio-economic circumstances, in a cross-sectional survey
6   to investigate the links to other potential risk factors such as measures of deprivation, living conditions, employment and housing
7   to investigate the links to physical illness and physiological measures
8   to gather health economic data, often concerning the costs of interventions, and the costs for people and their families.

The sampling design

The specific sampling design depends on the objectives of the study, the age group and setting concerned, and the contextual structures available to help in drawing up a sample frame. For example, in the British household surveys 1993 and 2000, the small users' Postcode Address File (PAF) was chosen as the sampling frame because it gives accurate, up-to-date representation of private households, which can be used to produce nationally representative prevalence rates. For the 1993 survey, postal sectors in the PAF were stratified by regional health authority and by the proportion in manual socio-economic groups as defined by the OPCS Classification of Occupations. Ninety delivery points within 200 postal sectors were selected, yielding a sample of 18,000 delivery points. This sample was designed to yield 10,000 subjects. In a pilot household survey in Kenya, the national census of the preceding year was used to identify all houses, allocate house numbering, and draw a random sample. In the British institutional survey, the sampling design was based on lists of hospitals and residential homes obtained from government departments, and a list of alternative forms of residential care hostels, group homes, etc., obtained from health and local authorities. The institutions were selected randomly, stratified by institutional size. In the British prison survey, all prisons were surveyed, and prisoners were selected randomly with specific sampling fractions for male remand, female remand, male sentenced and female sentenced prisoners.

Choice of assessment instruments

The decisions behind the choice of instruments will depend on the objectives of the survey, the age group and the setting, as well as on the resources available and the experience of the interviewers, which can be used.

It is widely acknowledged that assessments of medical conditions, including psychiatric disorders, must be standardised in community surveys. Standardisation is the process of incorporating clinical assessment concepts into rules, and its purpose is to reduce between-observer variations and to allow comparability within and between studies. It is also important to contrast the needs of clinicians for whom accuracy in the individual case is paramount with those of a researcher for whom reducing systematic bias or error also has a high priority. Reducing systematic bias is one of the most important advantages of standardisation.

The decisions behind the choice of instruments will depend on the objectives of the survey, the age group and the setting, as well as on the resources available and the experience of the interviewers. Current survey instruments include the CIDI, the CIS-R and the SCAN.

Choice of interviewers

Depending on resources available, interviewers may be mental health professionals, general health professionals, lay interviewers, and medical students. In the British surveys among adults, an initial interview was carried out by ONS interviewers using computer-assisted interviewing (CAI), and, for selected subsamples, psychiatrists were employed to assess psychosis and personality disorder.

Deployment of interviewers

Whoever the interviewers are, they need training in the structure and administration of the interview, the rules for its application and the implementation of the design to ensure the correct interviewees are selected, as this will otherwise be a source of bias. The interviewers will need to be given a realistic list and timetable of their interviews, such as two interviews per day over a period of 3 months.

Run pilot study

A pilot study is essential to test whether the interviewers can handle the interview, whether respondents find the interview acceptable, the likely response rate and the length of the interview.

Data analysis

After implementation of the main study, data will need to be entered into a database, separated from information which could identify specific individuals, and analysed with a specific programme, such as SPSS or STATA.

Dissemination of results

Results need to be disseminated in a variety of ways, by articles, talks and reports to specified audiences in government, health and social care management, the research community, etc.

Assumptions and theoretical framework

The central methodological assumptions in community psychiatric surveys concern the threshold for recognising disorder and the reliability of case finding. Relatively small shifts in threshold lead to appreciable changes in prevalence, as cases in the community tend to cluster around the threshold. It cannot be assumed that because we have instruments that provide reasonable, consistent results for populations, they will necessarily identify individual cases in a consistent way. There is likely to be disagreement both when two people use the same instrument and when one person uses different instruments or a substantially modified version of an instrument.

What does survey methodology highlight as the assumptions of other methodologies?

Survey methodology highlights the assumptions made about the generalisability of the findings of other methodologies. For example, individual case studies are not generalisable beyond the case itself, and small-scale surveys are not generalisable to national populations. In surveys, it is possible to be clear about what the biases are, such as that produced by the relative non-response rates of different age groups, so that the data can be weighted to take account of the population age structures. Routinely collected administration data, such as hospital admission data, are collected by numerous individuals whose training in data collection is variable, so it is difficult to be sure of the quality.

Surveys highlight the difference between clinical and research diagnoses. Clinical diagnoses are reached by a clinician after a clinical interview consisting of a set of questions, normally following a broad pattern but nonetheless specifically varied by the clinician, and influenced by his training and experience and by cues from the patient, whereas research diagnoses are derived from diagnostic algorithms applied to a systematic set of questions asked in the same way of all respondents.

Hospital admission and discharge data are not based on standardised diagnoses, individuals are not linked to episodes, and the number of admissions does not correspond with the number of patients. Admission statistics provide no data on individuals with less severe conditions who are not admitted to hospital, and, increasingly, even the severely ill are treated outside hospital.

Local case registers have been set up in a few parts of the world. For example, seven areas of the UK have had such registers, and the Aarhus register in Denmark is famous. These overcome the problem common in national statistics of providing data only on admissions and episodes, rather than on individuals. However, there is no standardisation in the collection of diagnostic information, and only those contacting the specialist psychiatric services are included. In Denmark, there is one psychiatrist per 2,000 population, whereas in the UK there is one psychiatrist per 25–50,000 population, so it can be seen that case registers in Denmark are likely to reflect more closely population morbidity than case registers in the UK. The main source of information from primary care in Britain is the Morbidity Survey in General Practice (1992) (McCormick et al, 1995). This survey was last carried out in 1991–2 in several hundred volunteer general practices; it has produced information on primary care consultations and episodes of illness as diagnosed by the GP. Even if this sample were representative of all primary care practices, and it is not, there is considerable diagnostic variation within general practice (Jenkins et al, 1988). Studies that have used standardised assessments of psychiatric morbidity within primary care have necessarily been small and located in unrepresentative practices. Consultation with a GP is influenced by many factors in addition to the presence of psychiatric disorder (Goldberg & Huxley, 1992) and information is difficult to generalise to a household sample in the community.

What types of evidence do surveys produce?

Surveys can produce hard, numerical and reproducible data and softer, more qualitative and narrative data.

Surveys vary in their mode of administration (which may be by post, telephone, the Internet, personal interview, self-completion or a mixture of these); in the type of information gathered, whether qualitative or quantitative, factual or attitudinal; and in the setting and the specific population in which the survey is carried out (general population; prisons; the homeless; schools; or clinical populations in primary care, outpatients, inpatients or long-term residential care, or subgroups, such as people caring for someone with a chronic illness, or children looked after by the state).

Surveys can produce information about detailed symptomatology as well as about specific disorders, and they can examine symptoms and disorders in dimensional ways as well as categorical ways. Surveys are helpful for needs assessment. They work well if one wants to look at strengths of specific associations. They solve problems of sampling, measurement, reliability, etc. They can indicate, for a public health purpose, what groups at a population level need treatment. Accurate classification is difficult even in clinical settings and even in the physical health arena.

What types of questions can surveys answer?

The types of questions which surveys can answer are those on the prevalence of psychiatric morbidity, whether individual symptoms, specific disorders or the above threshold disorders combined; the associations between psychiatric disorders and substance use and abuse; the nature and extent of social disabilities associated with mental illness; the use of health and social services; the association between psychiatric morbidity and recent life events, the experience of social support and socio-economic circumstances; the links to other potential risk factors, such as measures of deprivation, living conditions, employment and housing; the links to physical illness and physiological measures; and the cost-effectiveness of interventions, and the costs for people and their families. Surveys can compare findings between populations or within populations, compare health trends over time, estimate the likely impact of potentially preventable health problems, and describe the impact of health problems.

What are the key strengths of surveys?

One of the key strengths of surveys is that they are representative of the population sample frame covered, in terms of age, sex, social class and region. Thus, a national sample is representative of the country. A district sample is representative of that district. Another key strength is the capacity to link prevalence estimates with other variables, such as housing, employment, risk factors, protective factors and the consequences of illness, which can all be assessed within the same interview.

National surveys are normally commissioned by the government, and this gives the government ownership of the data, making government officials much more likely to make use of it for health planning, than if they feel the research comes directly from academics, whom governments often perceive as having vested interests in the results. National surveys can be used to provide local estimates that can be used for local planning.

In surveys, each respondent is asked about everything, so there is a coherent set of data on all the included variables, and everyone should have been posed each question in the same way.

Thus, the key strengths of surveys are that they can be tailor-made to the purpose, can be made nationally representative, can give authoritative answers to policy questions, and can test hypotheses derived from smaller-scale research.

What are the key limitations of surveys and what risks arise from inappropriate use?

A particular limitation of surveys is that it is difficult to get accurate answers to questions about use of clinical services and treatment, because people often do not know exactly which type of professional they have been treated by, or the exact type of treatment which they have received. A second problem is the differences in prevalence estimates obtained by lay interviewers and clinicians. If the respondent does not understand an attitudinal question, a lay interviewer is not allowed to explain it, but must simply repeat the question; otherwise, bias will be introduced. Clinicians do provide clarifications, and these may introduce bias.

A third problem is that of the quality of accurate and meaningful translation into other languages, a particular risk with ethnic minority groups. Europe is a political structure with 20 or more primary languages, and there is not enough investment in translation. Surveys need to be tailored to the local culture and need to cope with the different varieties of somatic expression of distress.

A fourth limitation is posed by the response rates achieved in surveys. Young men in particular tend to be underrepresented. Their involvement has declined across all countries where surveys have been conducted in recent years.

Fifth, some surveys use very small sample sizes, which cannot give very precise estimates among subgroups. Sixth, some survey designs do not incorporate the Kish grid method of selecting one person at random from each household, resulting in a tendency to overselect heads of households, leading to significant bias. Significant time and money are required for feasibility, pilot testing and reliability in order to enhance the quality of the final survey data. Different instruments have been used for surveys of children, adults and the elderly, and are not all validated to the specific age ranges on which they are used. There is a need to look at the transition between adulthood and childhood, research which is currently impeded by the use of such different instruments for the different age groups. Some questions are particularly sensitive to being asked by lay interviewers, such as questions relating to childhood sexual abuse, post-traumatic stress disorder (PTSD) and suicidal ideation.

When one calculates the magnitude of the effect of taking antidepressants on the overall national prevalence of depression, the British survey of 10,000 was still too small to detect the effect on national prevalence rates. One needs a very cheap screening method to be able to magnify sample size greatly to achieve such high numbers.

People who have had no involvement in planning and implementing the survey often find it difficult to understand how the data have been weighted; moreover, they use the survey for purposes for which it was not designed. It is important not to use instruments inappropriately. For example, the GHQ should not be used to make diagnoses.

National surveys may not be relevant to local populations without specific modelling, and they can be expensive. Cross-sectional surveys give associations but cannot supply causal links. There are frequently requests to use local data from within a national survey to give information relevant to a specific local population. However, in general, this cannot be ethically done without running the risk of revealing identifiable data.

Use of psychiatric surveys by the Department of Health: a case study

In the early part of the twentieth century, infectious illnesses were the main cause of death, often early in life. However, in later decades, cardiovascular disease accounted for the largest proportion of deaths, and cancer also grew steadily in importance as a cause of death over the course of the century.

Accompanying these shifts in the pattern of *death* was a corresponding change in the pattern of *disease*, as the predominant disease pattern in most developed countries became one of the chronic or long-term illness.

These trends continued right up into the last years of the twentieth century and are still continuing. For example, Figure 8.1 shows the proportions of the population in Great Britain who reported having a long-standing illness of different kinds in 1994 and 1998 in the General Household Survey. Although not many people reported having a mental illness in 1984, this proportion increased by nearly a half between 1994 and 1998. These data on mental illness are based on a simple set of questions asking people whether or not they had a long-standing illness and, if so, what this was due to. A way of approaching the issue is to carry out a dedicated survey on psychiatric morbidity using trained interviewers. This was done in 1993 and then repeated in 2000 with substantially the same methodology.

These surveys showed a number of interesting things. Firstly, the prevalence of neurotic mental illness was much higher than appeared at first glance from the General Household Survey illustrated in Figure 8.2. Secondly, a

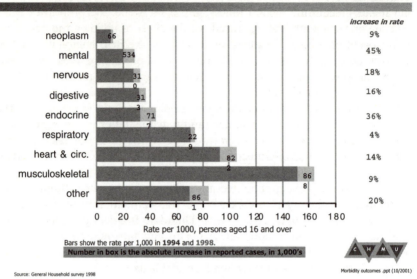

Increase of long-standing conditions between 1994 and 1998
Great Britain

increase in rate

Condition		increase in rate
neoplasm	66	9%
mental	534	45%
nervous	31 / 0	18%
digestive	31 / 3	16%
endocrine	71 / 7	36%
respiratory	22 / 9	4%
heart & circ.	82 / 2	14%
musculoskeletal	86 / 8	9%
other	86 / 1	20%

0   20   40   60   80   100   120   140   160   180
Rate per 1000, persons aged 16 and over

Bars show the rate per 1,000 in **1994** and **1998**.
Number in box is the absolute increase in reported cases, in 1,000's

Source: General Household survey 1998

Morbidity outcomes .ppt (10/2001)

Figure 8.1 Change in long-standing illness by cause.

Source: General Household survey 1998.

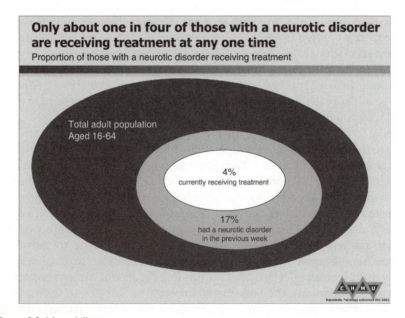

Only about one in four of those with a neurotic disorder are receiving treatment at any one time
Proportion of those with a neurotic disorder receiving treatment

Total adult population
Aged 16-64

4%
currently receiving treatment

17%
had a neurotic disorder
in the previous week

Figure 8.2 Mental illness.

Source: National Psychiatric Morbidity Survey 2000.

very high proportion of those who were thought to have a neurosis were not receiving any form of medical care or treatment. Lastly, although the overall prevalence of neurotic mental illness stayed the same, the proportion who *were* under treatment had increased substantially, even over the relatively short period of 7 years. However, even in the year 2000, only about one in four of those with a neurosis were actually receiving treatment for it.

So, although the prevalence of neurosis may have stayed roughly the same, a higher proportion of sufferers who had in the past remained outside the health-care system have found their way into it. Thus, the filters or barriers that prevent access for those with a common mental illness may have become more permeable over time. This is not to say that they are necessarily equally permeable to all groups. For example, the Fourth National Survey of Ethnic Minorities has shown that people of Afro-Caribbean origin had higher rates of depression than white people, but were far less likely than the latter to receive treatment for it (Gupta, 1999). Similarly, local studies have shown that, among those who exceeded the threshold for a possible psychiatric disorder as assessed by a screening questionnaire, south Asian patients were less likely to be diagnosed as having a psychiatric disorder. Similarly, in some areas, case recognition by GPs is higher among white than among black or south Asian people (Gupta, 1999).

Surveys can thus be used to establish population-level prevalence rates of mental illness and to define trends not only in these but in the proportions of those in need who are receiving treatment and care, and inequities and inequalities in this between different subgroups of the population. All of this has important policy and service implications for the Department of Health and the NHS, to establish strategies to enhance access to treatment in general, and for underserved populations.

Overview of the impact surveys have had on mental health services

Information from mental health surveys is generally relevant to planning mental health services, but, in practice, insufficient consideration is taken of them. The 1993 survey highlighted the poor correlation between mental health needs and the services that were provided, the high level of unmet needs and the need for primary care to be involved in delivery of care. Following a number of primary care pilot projects in the early 1990s, the national service framework included primary care of mental disorder as a key component. Similarly, the children's survey has produced a predictive scale for childhood disorder, which will be helpful for teachers to use as a screening tool, and the prison mental health survey (1998) continues to have a considerable policy impact on the escalating provision of mental health services in prisons.

Clinical information and interviews are not underutilised, but survey data often are, because of insufficient investment in the data analysis. Use of survey data is also restricted by the view that surveys have a limited shelf-life.

How should surveys be used in future mental health research?

Future mental health research should include surveys based on larger samples, in order to look for less common disorders that may have a prevalence rate of less than 1%, and in order to give greater precision to our current prevalence estimates. Future surveys should also build in longitudinal components to examine the course of disorders and the resolution of symptoms, to obtain more power for the effect of predictive factors for certain subgroups of disorders. Large samples allow multilevel modelling. It will also be helpful to insert batteries of mental health questions into more general physical health and social surveys, thus giving access to larger samples, and also to link mental health variables with a wider range of physical and social variables, including the possibility of biological samples. More qualitative information may be helpful to include in future mental health surveys, as in the children's mental health survey (Meltzer et al, 2000).

What are the seminal textbooks and electronic resources for surveys?

Goldberg, D.P. (1972) *The detection of psychiatric illness by questionnaire GHQ* (Maudsley Monograph 21). London: Oxford University Press.

Gupta, S. (1999) The fourth national survey of ethnic minorities. In D. Bhugra, V. Bahl (eds), *Ethnicity: An Agenda for Mental Health*. London: Gaskell.

Institute of Medicine (2001) *Neurological, Psychiatric and Developmental Disorders: Meeting the Challenge in the Developing World*. Washington, DC: National Academy Press (www.iom.edu).

Jenkins, R., Meltzer, D. 2003 A decade of national surveys of psychiatric epidemiology in Great Britain; 1990–2000. *International Review of Psychiatry*, 15, nos 1 and 2.

Lewis, G., Pelosi, A., Araya, R. (1992) Measuring psychiatric disorder in the community: a standardized assessment for use by lay interviewers. *Psychological Medicine*, 22, 465–486.

Thompson, C. (1989) *The Instruments of Psychiatric Research*. Chichester: Wiley.

World Health Organisation (1992) *The International Classification of Diseases and Related Health Problems* (ICD-10). Geneva: WHO.

Wing, J.K., Babor, T., Brugha, T. et al (1990) SCAN Schedules of Clinical Assessment in Neuropsychiatry. *Archives of General Psychiatry*, 47, 589–593.

Part II

Consumers of research

Chapter 9

Influencing practice at primary care level

Paul Walters and Andre Tylee

Introduction

Primary health care is in a unique position. It is often the first point of contact between patients and health services, and it offers continuity of care and coordinates a patient's care (Horton, 1999). In the UK, primary care now consists of multidisciplinary teams. Teams often consist of the general practitioner (GP) together with practice nurses, health visitors, occupational therapists, social workers, counsellors, psychologists and dietitians. More recently, there are also graduate mental health workers, gateway workers and 'star' workers. Increasingly, service users are playing an important role. In England, Primary Care Trusts (PCTs) are responsible for overseeing and funding the provision of care, and are also responsible for purchasing secondary care services. In considering influences on primary care practice, we will discuss serious mental illness, depression and the role of education in the primary care setting, and consider why there have been changes in the primary care management of people suffering from severe mental illness but little change in the management of those suffering from depression.

Influencing practice in primary care – what works?

The types of evidence that have salience in primary care differ between the organisational aspects of care delivery and care delivered by individual practitioners. At PCT level, evidence-based medicine takes precedence. PCTs are responsible for auditing and monitoring primary care services. In order to achieve this, service delivery and standards need to be measured against quantifiable benchmarks. Clinical and best practice guidelines, usually derived from evidence-based systematic reviews, allow PCTs to monitor and audit the provision of primary care. PCTs can also use guidelines to determine which services should be provided and by whom, and set targets that primary care services must meet. Guidelines used by PCTs are often derived from nationally produced guidelines modified to meet local needs.

This can result in a tension between the PCT and primary care practitioners. The uses of evidence are very different between these groups. PCTs use the evidence for population and economic outcomes, whereas GPs treat individual patients who often do not conform to the populations of patients studied in clinical trials and from which much of the evidence is derived (Rosser, 1999).

For evidence to have an influence on practice at the level of primary care professionals, they must have the knowledge, skills and motivation to adopt the evidence, organisational support to help adopt the evidence, and support from colleagues. Moreover, it is crucial that the evidence is acceptable to patients.

Tomlin et al (1999) examined reasons why GPs had made recent changes to their practice. They found the three main factors that accounted for the changes GPs had made in practice were contact with or observation of hospital practice and doctors, journal articles and scientific meetings. Faced with clinical uncertainty, GPs sought help from colleagues or hospital doctors rather than from scientific literature. Mayer and Piterman (1999) found similar results among Australian GPs. They examined GPs attitudes to evidence-based medicine and found that GPs often felt their clinical experience was more influential than research evidence. They also found that local specialists, opinion leaders and hospital practice had a great influence on GPs' practice. If there was a conflict between local practice and the research evidence, they found that GPs would discuss the matter with local colleagues and local specialists rather than critically appraise the evidence base.

Allery et al (1997) used a critical incident methodology to explore why GPs and hospital consultants made changes to their clinical practice. They found the most important driver of practice change in GPs was the organisational need to change. This was followed by contact with other professionals, education and then clinical experience. The most important organisational factors to promote change were economic, while GP colleagues and respected hospital consultants were the most influential contacts in promoting change. GPs thought that meetings were the most important educational influences on practice change. In particular, refresher courses and postgraduate meetings were rated as highly influential. Interestingly, medical newspapers, rather than scientific journals, were found to be the most salient literature for influencing change.

Armstrong (1997) examined GPs' reasons for changing prescribing behaviour and described three different models in which GPs were influenced to change. The accumulation model of change depended upon the weight of pressure of evidence in a certain direction, such as following the practice of a trusted and respected hospital consultant or respected GP colleague, letters, articles and talks. They also found that the GPs' personal experience was an important factor in influencing change. The second model they proposed was the challenge model of change. In this model, changes in practice tended to be rapid, and were often in response to critical incidents. However, rapid change was also found to occur after the success of a treatment about which the GP had doubts. The last model of change they proposed was the continuity model. This model suggests that change is a function of a GP's 'preparedness to change' and the congruence between the possible change and the GP's approach to practice. Factors which had an effect on GPs' preparedness to change were cost pressures and whether the change personally 'made sense' to them.

Preparedness to change has been defined according to how quickly GPs adopt a change. Five categories of change 'adopters' have been defined by the rapidity with which they take up innovations: innovators, early adopters, early majority, late majority and laggards (Rogers, 1983; Haines & Jones, 1994). Innovators tended to have extensive friendship networks and were defined as opinion leaders by their colleagues.

Haines and Jones (1994) described strategies for implementing change. Patient-centred approaches involved educating patients about evidence for effectiveness of interventions, to change GPs' behaviour. Educational approaches included continuing medical education activities to encourage implementation of evidence. Administrative and economic strategies included changes to save on costs or remuneration for instituting changes. However, as the authors point out, no individual strategy is likely to be successful.

Case study of academic research that has influenced practice – the primary care management of severe mental illness

Up to a quarter of people with schizophrenia in the UK are seen in primary care alone (King, 1992). Patients with schizophrenia and other severe mental illnesses (SMI) consult their GP more often than patients with chronic physical disorders, although, until recently, their care tended to be unstructured (Kendrick et al, 1991; King & Nazareth, 1996). People suffering with schizophrenia have twice the mortality rate of the normal population from physical illness, cardiovascular and respiratory disease being the main cause of the increased mortality (Allebeck, 1989). Diabetes also appears to be more common in patients with schizophrenia (Jeste et al, 1996; Goldman, 1999). In the light of this evidence, there has been concern that the needs of patients with schizophrenia and other severe mental illnesses are not being adequately met in primary care. Over the past 5 years, there have been changes in the primary care management of this patient population to ensure that their needs are adequately met. The care of patients with SMI is being restructured, so that an increasing number of practices have registers of patients with SMI, allowing regular follow-up and ensuring their mental and physical health care needs are addressed. Many practices now work more closely with secondary mental health services to ensure patients are followed up and have regular health checks.

A number of factors are probably important to account for this recent change in the management of patients with SMI in the primary care setting. These include both top-down and bottom-up approaches.

Of particular importance in changing the agendas of mental health service provision in the UK is the National Service Framework for Mental Health (NSF for Mental Health), introduced by the Department of Health in 1999 (Department of Health, 1999c). The NSF for Mental Health in England has set out the national standards that services delivering mental health care must meet. The NSF for Mental Health has seven standards, and covers both primary and secondary care. Standards two and three relate directly to primary care and access to specialist services for anyone who may have a mental health problem. Standards four and five cover effective services for people with severe mental illness. The NSF for Mental Health has been instrumental in promoting primary care mental health provision and raising the profile of mental health in the primary care setting.

Also important in this context is the National Institute for Clinical Excellence (NICE). NICE has been established to produce evidence-based guidelines that can then be promulgated for local use. It has thus far produced a number of mental health guidelines, including self-harm, anxiety disorders, post-traumatic stress disorder and depression (www.nice.org.uk). The first mental health clinical guideline produced was on the management of schizophrenia in primary and secondary care (National Institute for Clinical Excellence, 2002b).

Complementing the work of NICE, the National Institute for Mental Health in England (NIMHE), as part of the Modernisation Agency of the Department of Health, has developed a Primary Care Programme (Department of Health, 2002c; Tylee, 2003). This programme has an important role in aiding the dissemination and implementation of guidelines in primary care working within its aims of improving the fundamentals of primary mental health care and facilitating innovative practice. The programme has five proposed areas consistent with current policy to address the agendas of the NHS Plan and NSF for Mental Health. These programme areas are staff development, commissioning and developing effective partnerships, developing the primary care user perspective, integrating care for people with severe mental health problems, and research and development.

In determining how best to incorporate top-down approaches, local Primary Care Trusts play an important role in determining how best to implement evidence to meet local needs. Primary Care Trusts are also important in driving organisational change that may be necessary to incorporate improvements in care. These top-down approaches can be influential, but they are usually not sufficient to ensure grass-roots change. 'Bottom-up' approaches are also required.

At a local level, the Care Programme Approach for patients with SMI has meant that the community mental health team have a responsibility to keep the GP informed of a patient's current health status together with a detailed plan of management and the responsibilities of each professional involved in the patient's care. It is likely that this formalised arrangement has improved communication between GP and specialist. As has been discussed, the relationship between the hospital specialist and the GP is an important factor that influences practice change. Changes in the structure of mental health service provision are also likely to have an influence on practice. Increasingly, multidisciplinary primary care mental health teams are being established. Primary care liaison psychiatric nurses are becoming more common, increasing the primary care professional's exposure to mental health workers and secondary care professional's exposure to primary care.

Economic factors are important in promoting or hindering practice change in primary care. In the UK, a new GP contract has been renegotiated. The new General Medical Services contract (GMS) awards payments for attaining quality indicators in certain areas of health care, such as the prevention of coronary heart disease, hypertension and diabetes. The new GMS contract includes mental health indicators. However, mental health attracts only 41 out of a total of 550 points. These points are awarded for having a practice register of patients with psychotic illness, arranging physical health checks on these patients and organising the care of patients on lithium. The contract also allows for 'enhanced services' for people with mental health problems, and these can include services for depression, although the details are yet to be developed. Interestingly, enhanced care could be provided by GPs, practices, primary care organisations, mental health trusts or voluntary organisations, and bids may also be collaborative.

This gradual change in the primary care management of patients with serious mental illness is unlikely to be due to any single 'type' of 'evidence' but a combination of top-down and bottom-up initiatives. It could be argued that the real success lies in the evidence base, or interpretation of it, being sufficient to convince contract negotiators to allocate points to the management of severe mental illness for remuneration.

Case study of non-academic evidence –
'Trailblazers'

Education and training are vital if the mental health skills of primary care professionals are to be improved. However, evidence suggests that traditional educational activities may do little to change practice (Davis et al, 1995; Oxman et al, 1995). The Workforce Action Team Special Primary Care Report concluded that, currently, 'there is a shortfall in the provision of education and training' in mental health for primary care professionals, and that 'all staff in primary care need support, education and training to deliver effective mental health care' (Workforce Action Team, 2001).

Clinical leadership and opinion leaders are important influences on practice change. This has been recognised by the NHS modernisation agency as key to engaging the field in policy reform.

However, in the UK, there is organisational, professional and cultural separation between primary and specialised services (Workforce Action Team, 2001). Indeed, research has shown that a vital part of interventions that have improved care of patients with mental health problems is a fluid and accessible relationship between primary and secondary care (Von Korff & Goldberg, 2001). The interface between primary and secondary care is therefore of key importance. Different models have evolved to address this, but, ultimately, training and education across the interface is important to promote organisational, professional and cultural integration (Gask et al, 1997; Cohen & Paton, 1999).

Mental health training programmes therefore need to be multiprofessional, take into account the local needs of practices and primary care organisations, develop leadership capabilities allowing the cascade of knowledge and experience to local colleagues, teach core mental health skills, and cross the primary/secondary care interface, promoting integration between services. The national Trailblazers courses have developed over the past 10 years to meet these requirements. The courses are recognised by the National Institute for Mental Health (England) as an early national project to be promoted within its primary care programme.

The courses have been extremely successful in changing local practice in line with evidence-based medicine. Their success has been measured in the number of course graduates now involved in primary care mental health education and as primary care organisation mental health leads. To date, over 300 health-care professionals have been through the courses. Experience has shown that participants develop an interconnecting network, active locally, regionally and nationally. Course evaluations have demonstrated a wide variety of practice changes that have been attributable to the courses. These have included, for instance, severe mental illness registers, antidepressant prescribing audits, mental health initiatives for post-partum mothers, plans for routine mental health checks for the elderly, and organisational change.

We must then ask why these courses, although not evidence based, appear to be so successful at changing local practice. Part of the success of the courses is their use of adult learning methodologies, allowing learning to be self-directed and in response to learning need. Many GPs often prefer this as a learning style (Campion-Smith et al, 1998). Kaufman (2003) has summarised adult learning theory as follows:

- establishing an effective learning climate, where learners feel safe to express themselves

- involving learners in mutual planning of curricula
- having learners diagnose their own needs
- encouraging learners to formulate their own learning aims and objectives
- encouraging learners to identify resources and devise strategies to use the resources to meet their objectives
- supporting learners in carrying out their plans
- involving learners in evaluating their own learning.

Using this method to help professionals change their practice allows them to be independent and self-directing, and to use the professional experience they have accumulated, integrating their learning into practice. They are also motivated to learn by individual drives rather than external ones. This allows education to be relevant to the complex work setting of primary care and the experience and expertise of the learner.

The courses emphasise collaboration between paired professionals, one from primary care and one from specialist mental health services, in working together. They are unique in bringing together pairs of colleagues from primary and secondary mental health services to define and meet their local learning and service development needs. This allows primary and secondary care professionals to learn from one another as well as facilitating the wider primary or secondary care teams that provide opportunities for individuals to change their practice.

The courses to date have tended to recruit the 'innovators' from primary and secondary care; that is, professionals keen to change practice in line with the current evidence base. The courses encourage individuals to pass on their skills and expertise to others through personal coalitions and collaborative networks, broadening their professional networks both within and between primary and secondary care. This facilitates the diffusion of innovations (Haines & Jones, 1994) to both primary and secondary care services. The courses have a primary care focus within a whole mental health system context supporting primary care development and whole system redesign. In parallel, several supporting primary care mental health networks have become established, such as PriMHE, the Yorkshire Trailblazers Network, and the West Midlands Primary Mental Health Network. There is also increasing international interest in developing the courses in the USA, Australia and New Zealand.

Top-down approaches to changing practice alone are unlikely to be successful, as demonstrated by the Defeat Depression Campaign in the UK (Paykel et al, 1998; Rix et al, 1999). The Trailblazers course allows participants to develop local bottom-up initiatives that incorporate current evidence. Being locally relevant increases the likelihood of evidence influencing change.

Although there is as yet a dearth of evidence to validate the usefulness of the Trailblazer approach, the success of the courses and the changes participants have made at local levels suggest that this is a useful format of education which brings together the main drivers found to be important in promoting evidence-based practice change.

What types of evidence have low saliency in primary care?

Allery et al (1997) found medicolegal factors to be the least likely to change GPs' practice, followed by information from pharmaceutical companies and factors associated with waiting lists. Traditional educational activities also appear to have little direct impact on improving professional practice, despite GPs feeling their practice is influenced by continuing educational activities (such as conferences) (Davis et al, 1995; Allery et al, 1997).

The saliency of evidence-based medicine to primary care is controversial. McColl et al (1998) examined GPs' attitudes to evidence-based medicine. Overall, they found that GPs felt practising evidence-based medicine would improve patient care, and most thought the best way to practise evidence-based medicine was to follow evidence-based guidelines. Similar results were found among Australian GPs (Mayer & Piterman, 1999). However, the use of guidelines in primary care has had disappointing results (Kendrick, 2000; Thompson et al, 2000).

The debate continues about whether all recommendations made by GPs should be based on evidence-based medicine, or whether randomised, controlled trials (RCTs) should be the reference standard in determining practice in primary care (Horton, 1999; Rosser, 1999; Culpepper & Gilbert, 1999; Mant, 1999; van Weel & Knottnerus, 1999; Kernick, 1999, 2000; Little, 2002). The use of evidence-based practice needs to take into account the quality of the evidence, the context within which the evidence is to be applied and the values of practitioners and patients (Rosser, 1999). Culpepper and Gilbert (1999) have argued that generalising the outcomes of RCTs to primary care should be questioned. RCTs are conducted in rarefied populations (often in secondary care or tertiary care), which usually bear little or no resemblance to patients in primary care elsewhere (van Weel & Knottnerus, 1999). The results of such trials may not, therefore, be appropriate to generalise to different settings.

Evidence, from clinical trials, for example, is accumulated from populations. This often conflicts with primary care, in which the personal dimension predominates (Sweeney et al, 1998; van Weel & Knottnerus, 1999). It has been argued that guidelines derived from the evidence base fail to take into account the doctor–patient relationship, and that evidence-based medicine may distort this relationship (Culpepper & Gilbert, 1999). The reductionism inherent in evidence-based medicine therefore sits uncomfortably within the values-based medicine of primary care.

Patient-centred primary care means the values of individuals, their social and personal context, and the doctor–patient relationship are of paramount importance. Guidelines to promote evidence-based practice all too often neglect or relegate these in favour of particular clinical decisions for particular illnesses. Patient preference is usually ignored. If evidence-based care is to be delivered in general practice, it must take account of these problems.

Case study of academic research that has failed to affect practice: depression guidelines in primary care

Clinical guidelines have been promoted as a way to improve the quality and consistency of care received by patients in general practice. There is evidence from the general medical setting that guidelines lead to a change in clinical practice and improve patient outcomes (Grimshaw & Russell, 1993). In primary care, a multitude of guidelines have been produced to encourage GPs to follow evidence-based practice. Some commentators have complained about the quantity of guidelines descending on primary care. Hibble et al (1998) sampled 65 practices and found 855 different guidelines, 'a pile 68 cm high weighing 28 kg'.

There have also been numerous guidelines for mental health. Early primary care mental health guidelines were developed for the management of depression, as a joint campaign organised by the Royal College of Psychiatrists and the Royal College of General Practitioners in 1992 (Paykel & Priest, 1992). Primary care guidelines have since been produced on dementia (Eccles et al, 1998), deliberate self-harm (Bennewith et al, 2002) and schizophrenia (National Institute for Clinical Excellence, 2002b). Littlejohns et al (1999) surveyed depression guidelines developed between 1991 and 1996 and found considerable differences in quality, although many were derived from those of the Defeat Depression Campaign. More recently, NICE have produced depression management guidelines for use in primary and secondary care (www.nice.org.uk). These guidelines were developed with the most up-to-date evidence available.

However, the initial optimistic trust in the ability of clinical guidelines to improve the management of mental health in primary care (Effective Health Care, 1993) has not been realised in practice (NHS Centre for Reviews and Dissemination, 2002). Although the use of guidelines has been shown to have an impact on the management of some conditions, such as diabetes and possibly asthma (Feder et al, 1995), their influence alone on the management of mental health problems in primary care has been less successful.

Studies that have examined the effectiveness of clinical guidelines often combine the implementation of guidelines with educational initiatives. Rutz et al (1989) showed that suicide rates decreased and antidepressant prescription increased in Gotland, Sweden after an educational programme for GPs consisting of a 2-day course delivered by psychiatrists. However, the study was small, with no control group, and the benefits had disappeared at 2 years (Rutz et al, 1992). Upton et al (1999) evaluated the ICD-10 primary health care mental health guidelines in improving the detection and management of depression in primary care. They found that the guidelines had no impact on the overall detection of mental disorders, accuracy of diagnosis or prescription of antidepressants, and concluded that the success of guidelines in effecting change is uncertain. More recently, the Hampshire Depression Project was designed to assess whether a Gotland-style approach would work with British GPs. They examined the effects of a clinical practice guideline for depression and an educational programme on the detection and outcome of depression in the primary care setting. The guidelines were extensive and included advice on practice organisation, roles of non-medical professionals, and useful general and local information. The educational initiatives included seminars, video teaching, small-group discussions and role-play. Despite this, no differences were found between the intervention and the control group in terms of recognition rates or patient outcomes (Thompson et al, 2000).

It has been argued that to be successful, efforts should be directed toward implementation of guidelines rather than the production of yet more guidelines (Littlejohns et al, 1999). Grol et al (1998) found that specific attributes of guidelines determine whether or not they are used in practice. They found that evidence-based recommendations are more likely to be followed than those without a scientific basis, and that there needs to be precise definitions of recommended performance. Guidelines should be compatible with GPs' value sets, not demand too much change to existing practice and have specific advice on management in specific situations. It could be argued these attributes mean there is very little room for clinical guidelines to do other than recommend what is usual practice for GPs. A small study by Freeman and Sweeney (2001) examined qualitatively the reasons why GPs do not implement evidence-based guidelines of best practice. They identified six main themes that acted as barriers to implementation. These included the doctor–patient relationship, the GPs' feelings about the evidence in relation to their patients, the GPs' personal and professional experiences, and the logistics of implementation.

In primary care, there appears to be three levels that affect the implementation of mental health guidelines:

1   the quality and attributes of the guidelines
2   the organisational investment in the guidelines
3   the individual characteristics of the primary care professional.

Improving clinical outcomes in primary care through the use of clinical guidelines is therefore a complex process. Not only does the guideline have to be of the highest quality, using the most up-to-date evidence available, but it also has to conform to specific attributes, and even then may remain unimplemented if there is a failure to take into account organisational obstacles or the context of the doctor–patient relationship and personal experiences of the GP.

It is interesting to compare this with the case for SMI. Although there are numerous evidence-based guidelines for depression, the evidence base does not appear to have been sufficient to influence negotiations between the GP contract negotiators and the Department of Health. The depression guidelines developed by NICE should redress this.

Conclusions

The complexities of influencing primary care practice mirror the complexities of primary care itself. The values-based, patient-centred approach of primary care often appears incompatible with that of evidence-based medicine. However, the ethos of evidence-based care dictates 'the conscientious, explicit and judicious use of current best evidence' (Sackett et al, 1996). Thus, the patient's context and patient–doctor relationship are important considerations within this model. Changes in practice are rarely due to one influence or another but rely on the complex interaction of the quality of the evidence, the sources of the evidence, organisational factors, economic factors, factors relating to the individual professional, the doctor–patient relationship and, above all, the patient. To influence change in primary care practice reliably therefore requires a multifaceted approach, taking all these into consideration. It will be interesting to see how much further development there will be in the management of patients with severe mental illness in primary care and whether this will lead to a reduction in their mortality rates. Equally, because the multitude of depression guidelines have arguably led to a vagueness about the management of depression in primary care, this could, in contrast, lead to little change in practice. It remains to be seen whether the recently produced NICE depression guidelines will be able to deliver where others have failed.

Chapter 10

Influencing community mental health team practice to improve care outcomes

Tom Burns

Introduction

The move to a more community-based mental health service is often described in terms of deinstitutionalisation and the overall reduction in inpatient bed numbers. This has been paralleled with the development of community-based services to serve the varied and complex needs both of those patients discharged from hospital but also, equally importantly, of all those patients who, because of these services, either never get to hospital or spend only brief periods in them.

The early development of community services has varied internationally. Among the best known are the US community mental health centre movement launched by Kennedy's New Deal for Mental Health (Talbott et al, 1987), the French '*secteur*' approach (Kovess et al, 1995), catchment area teams in the UK (Johnson & Thornicroft, 1993) and the later dramatic developments in Italy in response to Law 180 in 1978 (Tansella, 1987). The US community mental health centre experience was less than satisfactory and essentially was superseded by developments in case management and assertive community treatment (ACT), and the French interest in the *secteur* has faded somewhat from attention (Verdoux & Tignol, 2003).

The UK generic multidisciplinary community mental health team (CMHT) and its Italian counterpart have endured and are remarkably similar. They share common radical intellectual roots despite differences in presentation with a tendency to be antiauthoritarian and 'casual' in their internal relationships. Both emphasise pragmatism and teamwork characterised by role blurring and role overlap; both strive for continuity of care across the community/inpatient boundary; both are explicitly territorial, serving a defined geographic population. Both also prioritise the needs of the severely mentally ill, although this is more explicit in Italy. CMHTs have evolved rather than been prescribed. As a result, their composition and practices vary at the edges. Writing about them draws on clinical practice and consensus rather than research findings or strict definitions.

What types of evidence have salience for mental health teams?

UK CMHTs have undergone enormous changes in their structure and practice in the last 10 years. Much of this has simply been a refining of good practice in an increasingly managerial age (greater clarity about internal accountability and about accessibility, explicit statements about the range and content of treatments offered, and requirements for audit). However, more fundamental changes have been driven by a series of national policy documents, such as the National Service Framework (Department of Health, 1999c) and the NHS Plan (Department of Health, 2000a), and refined in a series of detailed and prescriptive policy implementation guides (Mental Health Policy Implementation Guide, 2001a).

These policy documents have emphasised that their proposals are 'evidence-based' and even prescribe a ranking of the different forms of evidence from case reports up to meta-analyses. Broadly, the evidence draws on two types of study:

- studies of specific interventions applied and assessed at individual patient level
- studies of service organisations, applied at team level and assessed at the individual level.

The former studies are generally randomised, controlled trials (RCTs) of pharmacological or psychological treatments with their outcomes compared in terms of relapse in severe mental illness (e.g. clozapine treatment (Kane et al, 1988), behavioural family management for schizophrenia (Leff et al, 1990), and early warning sign monitoring in bipolar disorder (Perry et al, 1999)). The latter are mostly studies of one team structure compared with local practice (treatment as usual (TAU)). Many of these have been of differing forms of providing community care (Burns et al, 1993; Dean et al, 1993; Thornicroft et al, 1998), with increasing emphasis on assertive outreach of one form or another (Mueser et al, 1998) of which the most influential is the Madison study (Stein & Test, 1980).

The methodological quality of the treatment studies is, almost invariably, superior to the service structure studies. However, they have had little impact on CMHTs. Penetration of these evidence-based treatments into practice has been remarkably low. Clozaril, for instance, is still prescribed at much lower levels than research evidence available for almost two decades would indicate. Even more striking, despite the generous provision of training in psychological and psycho-social interventions provided through Thorn courses (Gournay & Birley, 1998), very few teams offer the psycho-social interventions at all, and certainly not routinely. While practice has undoubtedly been enriched by skills and approaches acquired on these courses, few of those trained offer interventions following the prescribed forms.

The methodologies of many of the 'team structure' studies are subject to several criticisms – most tellingly, the failure to take account of different qualities of control services or the impact of product champions (Coid, 1994), the repetition of small-scale, short-term studies, and the unreflecting translation of results to entirely different health-care contexts (Burns, 2000). Their results are also, often misleadingly, presented as consistent (Mosher, 1983) when they have, in fact, been highly variable and often contradictory (Catty et al, 2002). They have, however, been responsible for driving the major upheaval observed in UK services.

There seem to be two main reasons for this disproportionate impact. Firstly, they have caught the attention of government and policy makers, who have mandated them. Investment and structure, unlike professional behaviour, can be altered rapidly by political will. Secondly, there has been enthusiasm for change within the professions, and these high-profile structural alterations can be achieved promptly and relatively simply. The investment of energy is over a short period, and the results (in terms of process, though not of individual patient outcome) are immediate and obvious.

An academic study that has been influential on CMHT practice

The Madison study of ACT by Stein and Test (1980) has been arguably one of the most influential studies for recent CMHT practice. Its impact is evidenced by its being mandated for the care of the severely mentally ill in many states of the USA and Canada, and now in many parts of Australia and New Zealand and several European countries, including the UK. However, its impact goes beyond the setting up of ACT teams. It has been influential in stimulating long overdue attention to team processes and structure, which has influenced all CMHTs, not just ACT teams.

The Madison study was simple and elegant and arose out of dissatisfaction with local community care at the time (associated with high rates of relapse and readmission). It was also opportunistic in that it was the closure of a ward and redeployment of the staff that allowed the researchers to test their approach. Essentially, they deployed the staff to work as intensive case managers for patients who would otherwise be admitted to the hospital. With strictly limited caseloads of only 10 patients each, the team worked collaboratively and flexibly to support and stabilise their patients. They 'did whatever was necessary' in terms of both practical help and emotional support as well as treatments. What was revolutionary about their service was that they eschewed clinics and offices and did virtually all their work with patients and families in their own homes and neighbourhoods. There was a clear commitment to ensuring compliance with antipsychotic medication (including daily delivery and supervision). Team practice was organised to avoid overintense relationships by encouraging familiarity and involvement between most patients and most staff.

Outcome was assessed across a range of measures – hospitalisation (number and duration), drop-out, social and vocational functioning, symptoms, and patient and family satisfaction. A detailed economic analysis was also conducted (Weisbrod et al, 1980). The results were overwhelmingly positive for the experimental service. Hospitalisation was halved, and social and vocational functioning was improved, as were symptoms and satisfaction. Depending on how the analysis was conducted, the experimental service was either cost neutral or saved money because of reduced hospital care.

An unexpected outcome

The rationale behind the approach (originally called 'training in community living' (TCL)) reflected a sophisticated social skills training model. The authors viewed psychoses as lifelong disorders, and their intention was to train patients intensively how to survive in the community with their disorders. It was seen as a short-term intervention, and the home-based '*in vivo*' focus reflected preoccupations about transfer of learning in rehabilitation. Money for the service ran out earlier than expected, however. Although the research team had funding for 3 years, the clinical team was disbanded with a follow-up of only 14 months. Stein and colleagues continued to follow up their patients for a further 14 months and noted that their gains diminished inexorably. This forced a rethink about their approach. They realised that the service was not a training programme but a very successful community support system. As a consequence, they changed the name from TCL to ACT and introduced the requirement for open-ended treatment ('no-close policy') into their service description.

Impact of the Madison study

Stein and Test's work has been enormously influential for two main reasons. Firstly, the sheer size of the therapeutic effect: few other mental health service studies can have found such clinically large and statistically significant benefits in virtually all of their outcome domains. The clinical reader does not have to conduct complex trade-offs in evaluating the study, such as symptom improvement at the cost of social deterioration, or reduced hospitalisation at the cost of decreased satisfaction. All the outcomes moved in the same direction, and the cost-effectiveness seems uncontestable. It is not surprising that it was published in such a high-impact journal and benefited from having all three comprehensive papers (Stein & Test, 1980; Test & Stein, 1980; Weisbrod et al, 1980) published together.

Its success is also due to the clarity of the service description. Unusually for community psychiatry research papers, the authors were able to give a brief but eloquent description of their innovation (see boxes). This covered both the main principles of the approach along with the core practice features. As a result, it would be possible to set up a similar team with considerable confidence without extensive further reading and research.

PACT* programme principles

- Assertively keep patients involved
- Individually tailor programmes
- *In vivo* (at home) services
- Capitalise on patients' strengths
- Titrate support
- Patients as responsible citizens
- Crisis stabilisation (24 hours)

* PACT: programme of assertive community treatment

PACT core practices

- Low caseloads (1:10–1:15)
- Frequent contact (weekly to daily)
- *In vivo* (home and neighbourhood)
- Emphasis on medication
- Multidisciplinary/shared caseload
- Flexibility, crisis stabilisation (24/7)
- Not time limited

Following these principles and practices, most clinicians were able to replicate the ACT approach relatively faithfully. There have been concerns that some of the process components (e.g. the frequency of visits, emphasis on medication) are more likely to drift from optimal practice than the structural ones (e.g. case load sizes, multidisciplinary work). Some scales of model fidelity have been developed (Teague et al, 1998), and these have been used to support the contention that greater adherence to the model delivers more consistent results (McHugo et al, 1999).

An influential non-academic study

One of the most significant changes in CMHT practice in the UK in the last 15 years has been the introduction of the care programme approach (CPA)

(Department of Health, 1990). Its introduction can teach us much about the sources of 'evidence' that change practice. It was introduced in a government circular in 1990 and arose in response to mounting concern about the coordination of care for the severely mentally ill in large cities.

The CPA required that all patients taken on for care by the secondary mental health services should have a single, identifiable document that recorded their problems (referred to as 'needs') and the interventions that were proposed to meet those needs. It also required the identification of an individual who was to be responsible for organising (and to a greater or lesser extent providing) that care – initially their key worker, but the term has gone through various changes before ending up as 'care coordinator'. The document was to be dated, the various individuals responsible for specific interventions were to be identified, and there was to be a date for review set. The plan was that this document (the 'care plan') would be negotiated with the patient and relevant professionals and family members. It was to be then circulated to all involved – patient, family, GP, social services, etc. Just to make things easy, it was proposed to have different 'levels' of CPA to reflect complexity.

Government directives about mental health practice were not infrequent during the 1990s! Indeed, they fairly rained down on practitioners and many of the more recent ones have had specific funding attached to them. Few have had much effect and most have simply faded away. CPA has, despite having no funding attached to it and considerable initial professional opposition (Burns & Leibowitz, 1997), become a cornerstone of current practice. It has altered the language (clinical review meetings are often referred to as CPA meetings), and is the building block of audit practice and internal monitoring and statistics.

Over the last 10 years, its role and influence have been consolidated as the vehicle for developments in carer involvement, risk assessment, the enabling of structured clinical and social outcome measures, the collection of a mini mum data set, and the focus on substance abuse and vocational and social therapeutic goals. It is so much a feature of clinical practice and performance management that it is hard to recall how much resistance it faced at its introduction.

Why, then, did it come to be taken up by teams and become so influential in practice? Although CPA was legislated for in 1990, it took several years before it began to be adopted. Its fate was sealed by the impact on the profession of the first of the independent inquiries into homicides by individuals under the care of the mental health services, the seminal 'Clunis Report' (Ritchie, 1994).

Christopher Clunis was a young, homeless, psychotic man, who, acting on delusions, murdered a complete stranger in an unprovoked attack on a London underground station. Ritchie's report catalogued a long history of fragmented and uncoordinated care during a period of mounting severity of dangerous and threatening behaviour. Each clinical assessment in various psychiatric units and accident and emergency departments across the capital was conducted without knowledge of the past history – not even the immediately preceding developments. The result was judgements based on a series of clinical snapshots by various doctors unaware of the clear and ominous pattern of accelerating danger.

The Ritchie report benefited from being exceptionally well written and clinically well informed. It was without the naive and often political tone that has diminished so many of her successors' products. Ritchie outlined the mistakes that were made and the inevitable tragedy with a balance and understanding that ensured they could neither be ignored nor explained away. Even the many psychiatrists who felt that homicide inquiries were fundamentally unfair could not fail to acknowledge the failure of care recorded. A bullish defence was not viable.

The two outstanding failures of Christopher Clunis' care that emerge from the report were the willingness of hospitals and services to wash their hands of seriously ill patients as soon as they moved out of their areas and the absence of sensible, accessible information. CPA proposals were then languishing with middle management in most services, being experimented with in some, and being ignored by most (along with much of the avalanche of meaningless bureaucracy current then which has now found well-deserved obscurity).

The CPA proposals targeted precisely the two failings highlighted in the Ritchie report. The moral force of the proposals was immeasurably strengthened by the report and as a consequence was soon adopted as standard practice. Their force reflects their face validity rather than any evidence available for an improvement in outcome resulting from their use. They underline the power of heuristic models in affecting practice. The CPA 'made sense' to practitioners, and this appears to be more influential than the results of many outcome studies. The explanation is similar to why psychodynamic counselling and psychotherapy continue to occupy a significantly greater proportion of mental health practitioner time than does cognitive behaviour therapy (CBT) despite its much stronger evidence base.

What types of evidence have low salience for mental health teams?

The impact of service structure research is in direct contrast to the experience with psychological treatment interventions, such as behavioural family management for schizophrenia or CBT for persistent delusions. Although mental health professionals support the aspirations of a public health approach to their disciplines and acknowledge the long-term nature of their work, research evidence on treatments without an immediate, proximal outcome is less likely to influence their practice.

In these highly researched and structured interventions, consistent change in practice is required for results that are probabilistic – a reduced rate of relapse over the next year or so. The results are not obvious, and there is no immediate positive feedback. In many, the level of investment required is very high (e.g. 5–7 courses of behavioural family management to avoid one relapse (Mari & Streiner, 1994)). Staff are also exposed to a perverse feedback – they become aware only when the treatments fail (the patient relapses), not when they are successful.

As well as being very demanding of time, some of these interventions are stressful and dependent on high levels of compliance from patients and families. With CBT, there is growing evidence of the importance of therapist competence as a factor in successful outcome. As the results are not immediate, it has proved difficult to sustain commitment to providing these interventions to acquire that level of skill.

In recognition of these problems, the UK Department of Health is attempting to 'prescribe' such interventions in documents such as the NICE guidance on schizophrenia (National Institute for Clinical Excellence, 2002a). It will be interesting to see how successful this approach is in treatments where quality cannot be externally assessed and ensured.

An academic study that failed to be influential

It has been proposed above that, in the UK, research focusing on longer-term quality outcomes has generally less salience. Practice seems more to be driven by evidence-based treatments with immediately observable outcomes and with avoidance of adverse outcomes. In community psychiatry, relapse and hospital admission are the outcomes which seem to have maximal salience. Have there been high-profile studies where significant improvements in such outcomes have been demonstrated and yet which have not been translated into practice?

The failure of the Manchester Acute Day Hospital study (Creed et al, 1990, 1991) to translate into routine practice has recently been highlighted (Marshall, 2003). In their study, Creed and colleagues demonstrated that a significant proportion (about 40%) of patients bound for inpatient care could successfully be managed in an acute day hospital. This approach was clearly preferred by patients and their families and seemed also to be associated with a somewhat reduced rate of admission over a year's follow-up (suggesting that those involved had learnt an alternative strategy to cope with relapse).

Marshall (2003) asks why these findings have not been put into practice more. Although the original authors raise issues about burden shifting to families and the need for well-functioning services, these do not seem to have interfered with the take-up of the PACT approach, to which they are equally relevant.

Two possible reasons immediately present themselves. Firstly, Creed and colleagues published a second paper (Creed et al, 1991) comparing two day hospitals about 20 miles apart. Although both found that day hospitals were able to divert patients from inpatient care, the second hospital was successful in engaging only 54% of the day hospital subjects (as opposed to 80% in the Manchester day hospital). The authors acknowledged that staffing difficulties and attitude significantly restricted the efficacy of the second day hospital. This very open reporting of differences may play into a common reservation that clinicians have about such studies, that they run on exceptional commitment from staff and are not reproducible (Coid, 1994). High-profile successful studies need to be replicated in less prestigious surroundings before they will carry sufficient conviction.

Secondly, the study required a clinical decision about suitability for day hospital care to be made, excluding compulsorily detained patients and those who posed substantial risks or were isolated and unsupported. In short, the default option remains the traditional admission to inpatient care. The decision to try day care may have to be made during a stressful assessment while the benefits are still problematical.

Conclusions

The nature of medical training has changed enormously within the last two to three decades. What used to be essentially an apprenticeship has acquired a genuinely academic dimension. It is no longer adequate simply to emulate your teacher – doctors have to keep abreast of recent innovations and research literature. In mental health care, this has involved not just a significant improvement in the quality of research design to answer increasingly complex questions but also an awareness of evidence from around the world.

Mental health practice is, however, still very dependent on societal attitudes and constraints. The major changes in UK CMHT practice in the last 15 years have been driven by factors other than research. CPA has been influential, not because of research but because it relieved an overwhelming professional embarrassment. Similarly, although ACT was launched with an excellent research study, its introduction into UK services reflected more a dissatisfaction with current generic CMHT practice than the strength of evidence for its benefits – evidence that is, indeed, increasingly questionable (Burns et al, 2002).

However, the status of evidence in driving clinical practice has risen markedly during this time. Even the proposition that the National Service Framework is based on evidence (Department of Health, 1999c) must be seen as a significant step forward. Knowledge about research evidence is now widespread and attitudes toward its importance have become more positive. As with most human activities, changes in knowledge and attitudes precede by some time changes in behaviour. The next 15 years is likely to see real developments in practice driven by research evidence.

Chapter 11

Influencing the public perception of mental illness

Vanessa Pinfold and Graham Thornicroft

Introduction

In this chapter, we shall focus on how public perceptions of mental illness have been shaped by different types of research evidence and the way programmes to challenge stigma have adapted in response to persistent negative global public views of people living with mental health problems. We are interested in how 'the public' respond to different types of academic research and other evidence sources, but we need to consider this population in groups rather than as a heterogeneous whole. The public en masse are a grouping with diverse perceptions and experiences of both mental health and mental illness, and therefore 'the public' have varied mental health information requirements and will react to new information using a range of different response mechanisms. Disseminating any information to influence public opinion and belief systems is known to be best facilitated through market segmentation principles, as the strategies of political campaigners, public health specialists and marketing departments in commercial companies clearly demonstrate.

To provide some contextual background to work on public perceptions of mental illness, we will briefly review some recent developments in studies and projects tackling prejudice, discrimination, social exclusion and stigma in the mental health field. Mental illnesses are common, accounting for about 12.3% of the global burden of disease, and this will rise to 15% by the year 2020. Considering disability alone, the impact of neuro-psychiatric conditions is starker still, as they account for 31% of all years lived with disability (World Health Organisation, 2001). However, despite advances in medical and psycho-social interventions, the stigma and discrimination associated with mental illness often make it much more difficult for mental health service users and their families to benefit fully from these new treatments thus hindering recovery (Kinderman & Cooke, 2000; Link & Phelan, 2001; Dickerson et al, 2002). There are few mental health service users or family carers who do not have a story to share about the social disability of mental illness on their lives.

In recent years, the public health problems associated with psychiatric stigma have become prominent worldwide health concerns (US Department of Health and Human Services, 1999; World Psychiatric Association, 2000; World Health Organisation, 2001). In the UK, a reduction in discrimination and social exclusion of vulnerable groups, and mental health promotion for all, forms standard one of the National Service Framework for Mental Health (Department of Health, 1999a) and discrimination is a core theme in the UK Social Exclusion Unit report on mental health (2004).

Studies across the western world that have addressed public perceptions of mental illness report various attitude constructs, such as fear and exclusion, social control and goodwill (Taylor & Dear, 1981). Factors influencing public attitudes are known to include age, gender, social class, family structure, educational attainment (Wolff, 1997) and personal experience of mental illness (Corrigan et al, 2001b). Opinion formation toward people with different types of mental illness also varies, for example, the public reveal more sympathetic views of people with dementia, an organic illness, than of people with drug and alcohol addiction or schizophrenia (Crisp et al, 2000). The most damaging stereotype associated with people with severe mental illness is one linking high risk of violent and dangerous behaviour with psychiatric illness, which persists despite contradictory evidence (Tayor & Gunn, 1999), a point we shall return to later in this chapter.

An increased profile has been given to psychiatric stigma and disability rights over the last 10 years in the UK. There have been a number of specific campaigns e.g. See Me Campaign (www.seemescotland.org), groups have lobbied for legislative change e.g. Disability Discrimination Act (www.drc.org.uk) and the Mental Health Act Alliance high-profile opposition to the proposed new mental health act legislation centre on civil liberty concerns (www.mind.org). In addition to these national initiatives, there have been a proliferation of activities at a local level for example through mental health education work (Pinfold, 2003), user training programmes (www.openuptoolkit.net), media volunteer schemes (www.rethink.org) and community empowerment projects (Mentality, 2003).

The growth of practical initiatives on the ground have been matched by an increase in research on psychiatric stigma (see reviews by Hayward & Bright, 1997; Crocker et al, 1998; Link & Phelan, 2001; Byrne, 2001; Corrigan & Watson, 2002). We know that promoting positive contacts between the target audience and people with experience of mental distress is the most effective way of affecting changes in emotional and practical responses to people with mental health problems (Sayce, 2000; Corrigan et al, 2001a; Couture & Penn, 2003; Alexander & Link, 2003). We know that mental health lessons can have a positive impact on young people's perception of mental illness (Rahman et al, 1998; Schulze et al, 2002a; Pinfold et al, 2003a), and short educational sessions can also affect adults (Penn et al, 1994; Holmes et al, 1999). However, despite these advances, the recent Department of Health report comparing attitudes between 1993 and 2003 disappointingly showed that public views between 1993 and 2000 stayed the same, but between 2000 and 2003 they became less positive (Department of Health, 2003). Are 'we' (the mental health community) not very good at putting our message across? Are our messages mixed and confused? Do the public not believe our 'evidence' and prefer to believe popular mythology dominated by the belief that mental illness is a weakness and the mentally ill are unreliable, violent and dangerous?

In this chapter, we look at various types of information and 'research evidence' shaping public opinion on issues related to mental illness, and consider why our campaigns and programmes have had such a low impact on reshaping views over time. We write from the experience of working with local antidiscrimination education projects across England (Pinfold, 2003; Pinfold et al, 2003a,b; Pinfold et al, 2005). It is important to note that structured mental health education is only one strategy for addressing stigma and discrimination on the grounds of mental illness; others include reform of mental health services, user and carer empowerment initiatives, public mental health promotion advertising campaigns, race awareness initiatives, community social inclusion programmes; and mental health promotion activities.

Positive public response: evidence that makes an impact

In considering evidence that has a high impact on public perceptions of mental illness, the research hierarchy that is used in academic circles to assess the reliability and validity of findings (Department of Health, 1999a) is inverted. Whereas systematic reviews and randomised, controlled trials are reference standard research evidence in science, the lay public look to expert opinion for most first-level evidence material, and a proportion will follow up accounts from experts with their own research into relevant information sources. For example, in a recent survey by the mental health charity Rethink, severe mental illness carers indicated where they obtained information to support their caring role. From 1000 responses, 60% obtained information through carer support networks (carer experts) and 43% from mental health professionals (practitioner experts) compared to 10% direct from books, magazines and journals, and 21% from the Internet (Pinfold & Corry, 2003). Evidence that has high salience with the public is information delivered by people with direct experience of what they are talking about – the human element – who are well respected and credible sources.

As indicated in our introduction, both research studies and large bodies of anecdotal evidence show that people with mental health problems are themselves integral to the success of antidiscrimination work plans (see also www.likeminds.govt.nz). There are some additional provisos: research also shows that the public respond far more to lay understanding of mental illness than to a delivery based on the biomedical model (Walker & Read, 2002), consistent with a lowering of public confidence in science and, to some extent, medical professionals following a series of negligence cases, new technological innovations and public health scares (Millstone & van Zwanenberg, 2000; Royal College of Medicine, 2001). Moreover, one-off initiatives are of limited value whereas sustained multilevel and multifaceted programmes are far more effective (Link, 2001), and presenting evidence that is low in conflict to existing belief systems will also produce better outcomes (Warner, 2001).

Antidiscrimination initiatives can share statistics, provide definitions of mental illnesses, list signs of illness, and describe coping strategies to protect mental health, but it is the voices of people managing depression or psychosis who deliver the messages and also share their stories that make an impact. This is why television soap dramas, magazine and newspaper interview reports, and films are so powerful in shaping public opinion, sometimes positively, but far too often they use cultural stereotypes to perpetuate public fears and misconceptions from an early age (Wilson et al, 2000). Putting a message across in mental health is challenging because even within the mental health field there are active debates over the 'facts' relating to mental illness and mental distress. But what the public responds to is evidence based on human stories that are credible, informative and emotive, and having evoked a response in the target group, the researchers, trainers or campaigners must then motivate and support the audience to follow up an emotional response with antidiscrimination actions (Palmer & Fenner, 1999; Corrigan & Lundin, 2001).

Research damaging public perceptions of mental illness

Not only are popular conceptions of mental disorder often profoundly damaging to people with mental health problems, but professional models can also have seriously detrimental consequences. One example of ideas with stigmatising consequences originating from clinical/research sources is the 'schizophrenogenic mother' concept. Emerging in the mid-1950s (Jackson et al, 1958), the 'schizophrenogenic mother' concept that developed within American psychiatry is of particular interest in relation to stigma (Hartwell, 1996). The idea is that dysfunctional forms of mother–child interaction may increase the likelihood that a child will later develop schizophrenia. In particular, a dominant, overprotective but basically rejecting maternal style was incriminated as a causal influence on the development of schizophrenia (Parker, 1982).

A series of inconclusive studies attempted to validate the concept in relation to performance on psychological tests (Meyer & Karon, 1967; Mitchell, 1969). By the 1960s, the concept of the schizophrenogenic mother had been scientifically discredited. For example, Brown et al (1966: 78) wrote: 'None of the theories which have been put forward to explain the genesis of abnormal family relationships seems to have sufficient empirical foundation to be useful in planning services.' Indeed, they argued that it was at least as plausible that interaction with a person with schizophrenia may be enough to explain the observed interactional abnormalities of some parents.

In 1978, Wing referred to this view as an approach that 'labelled the relatives in a particularly insulting way as incompetent' (Wing, 1978: 131). Interestingly, during that period, research was also being undertaken to develop valid and reliable measures of such family interactions (Rutter & Brown, 1969). What this work went on to show is that such abnormal patterns of communication are common in families with a person suffering from schizophrenia, and are associated not with the onset of the condition, but with its course and outcome. This line of investigation went on to provide invaluable insights that were the basis for new forms of family intervention, later shown to reduce the relapse rate in schizophrenia (Kuipers, 1979; Leff, 1994; Mari & Streiner, 1994; Barrowclough & Hooley, 2003).

In relation to stigma, early versions of this family interaction model (Siegler & Osmond, 1976) clearly saw the contemporary family as a pathogenic institution, capable of contributing to the onset of schizophrenia. Within this context, the mother of the affected person attracted particular odium when described as 'schizophrenogenic'. Thus, in addition to the other difficulties experienced by parents of people with schizophrenia, they were also asked to bear some blame for the cause of the condition itself (Wasow, 1983). The uptake of such ideas of blame by the wider community have contributed to the reluctance of some parents to disclose details about their child's mental disorder to others (Phelan et al, 1998; Tsang et al, 2003).

In the clinical domain, such ideas may have greater longevity than their scientific standing warrants, and it is still common for family members and other carers of people with schizophrenia not only to feel excluded from care planning and services, but also to receive the distinct impression from staff that they have in some way contributed to the genesis of the disorder (Warner, 1999; Struening et al, 2001). The theory of the schizophrenogenic mother therefore provides a salutary example of non-evidence-based ideas which have been positively harmful in increasing stigmatisation.

Sources of speculation: the power of the popular press

When we consider non-academic evidence that has influenced public perceptions of mental illness, the press, and the tabloids in particular, are the main candidate for attention primarily because they reflect, and some would argue fuel, the public's preoccupation with the link between 'risk' or violence and mental health problems. In addition to reporting news stories that influence public opinion, the press media are also an important outlet for the dissemination of peer-review published research findings. Editors regularly translate key research findings for the lay public, but not enough is known about the kinds of news coverage that is in the best public interest or the extent to which the lay public appreciates how a single journal article rarely provides definitive evidence warranting changes in behaviour (Entwistle et al, 1995; Department of Health, 2002a). A recent example would be the powerful role of the media reporting Dr Andrew Wakefield's research findings on autism and the MMR vaccine (Hargreaves et al, 2003), which coincided with increased public fears over the safety of MMR, and reduced uptake of the vaccine, while the research community debated the findings from such research programmes.

Newspapers are only one of many media sources available to the public, but their importance is borne out in the latest newspaper circulation figures. In January 2004, 10,026,507 copies of tabloid papers were sold daily, compared to 2,497,445 broadsheets, equivalent to nearly one in two homes across the UK having access to a copy of a tabloid. For mental health, and other issues concerned with social justice and antidiscrimination, this is challenging, because the tabloid press has a poor record of portraying a balanced view of mental illness (see Wahl, 1995; Philo, 1996).

The recent government attitudes to mental illness survey asked where the public hear publicity about mental health or mental illness. Although 69% of respondents reported that, recently, they could not recall any publicity, the most commonly reported source described was the newspapers (Department of Health, 2003). In Australia, a 12-month media-monitoring project 2000–1 analysed how journalists portray suicide and mental illness. They found 17,151 items, the nature of reporting was highly variable, and inappropriate language was a central concern (www.mentalhealth.govt.aus).

In considering the influence of tabloid 'evidence' about mental illness, it is also important to investigate whether there is any correlation between what is reported in the press and public perceptions of mental illness. In other words, does reading about violent acts committed by one person with a mental health problem influence one's general view of mental illness? In Germany, a study analysing the influence on public attitudes of forensic cases in the news surveyed the content of the tabloid *Bild-Zeitung* for 9 months (Angermeyer & Schulze, 2001). Only 0.7% of news related to mental illness, but, of those stories appearing, 51% were about crime and mental illness compared to 3% on advice, 6% on suicide and 19% reporting information such as new discoveries on Alzheimer's disease. The authors also analysed surveys of public opinion after the assassination attempts on two politicians and the stabbing of Monica Seles, the tennis champion. They found that the public were generalising the behaviour of a few as the likely actions of the majority. For example, aversion to having a neighbour with schizophrenia doubled from 19% in April 1990 to 36% in December of the same year. These are similar to findings in the UK from a study assessing public attitudes before and after the murders at Hungerford, which received considerable coverage in the media (Appleby & Wessely, 1988).

We are not suggesting that tabloid stories about rare violent acts committed by a 'psychiatric patient' or a 'care in the community case' are always trans-lated into beliefs about people across the UK that will experience some form of mental health problems at some time in their lives. The public are critical readers of information and will be influenced by other factors, including cultural heritage, personal knowledge and experience, and peer pressures. Unfortunately, however, it is not only the media that perpetuate the associ-ations between violence, dangerousness and the mentally ill in the public eye. For the past 10 years, the public protection risk agenda has been the driving force behind mental health policy development and funding priorities (Szmukler & Holloway, 2000), fuelled, it could be argued, by sustained media coverage of high-profile homicides by people with mental health problems and the subsequent inquiries. Thus, the mental health community invests enormously in persuading the press to place positive mental health stories and awarding good practice through an annual awards ceremony hosted by Mental Health Media in London. This work is crucial, if the public atti-tude to the majority of people with mental health problems is to become disentangled from the mythology generated by media stereotyping.

Lies, damned lies and statistics

In this section, we consider the types of evidence that have low salience for public opinion formation and methods that are least likely to affect public views of mental illness. We focus on the use of statistical information and challenge the use of 'facts' to address stigma and discrimination. In the men-tal health field, discovering the 'facts' about mental illness is no exact science, as shown by debates over the existence and nature of mental health problems. In a study addressing the impact on attitudes to mental illness of education sessions with college tutors, one participant addressed this point in his ques-tionnaire and challenged: 'Why should I have an opinion on these statements when people within psychiatry can't agree on the causes of mental illness.' Mental health is a richly contested arena in terms of practical solutions to problems and theoretical explanations of mental 'illness'.

Attitude surveys consistently report public fears of dangerous behaviour, violence and the unpredictability of people with severe mental illness (Crisp et al, 2000; Stuart and Arboleda-Florez, 2001; Gaebel et al, 2002). Mental health promotion organisations and mental health campaigners attempt to counteract public fears by reporting positive mental health messages, helping people with mental health problems to recover a meaningful quality of life – themselves counteracting negative associations through their own actions – and underscoring the rare occurrence of homicides by people with severe mental illness. Statistics are used to highlight the far more frequent victimisation or self-harming behaviour prevalent in this group and to address rates of 'common' mental disorders in the community. 'One in four' is often quoted for both the number of people experiencing mental health problems in a lifetime as well as the number with mental health problems in any given year – which is correct? In practice, public suspicion of the validity and reliability of statistical information, the subject of several publications in the USA (Best, 2001), makes it a weak tool in the fight again stigma.

Popular mythology across the world supports the idea that people with mental problems particularly those with severe mental illness – schizophrenia, manic depression, drug-induced psychosis – are a danger to other people because they may behave violently. Every year, about 3500 people are killed on the roads in the UK and, although there are pressure groups lobbying for safer transport, the reaction, by comparison, is barely visible. Compare this to the coverage of homicides committed each year by the mentally ill in the UK, estimated at 35–55. Can we use statistics more effectively to influence public attitudes?

Some statistical approaches used to address the incidence of violent acts recorded by people with mental health problems include:

1   Relative risk for perpetrators – are people with schizophrenia more likely to be violent than members of the general population?
2   Relative risk for victims – are you more likely to be killed in a road accident or by a person with a diagnosis of schizophrenia?
3   Absolute 'attributable' risk – to what extent do people with schizophrenia contribute to societal violence?

The answer to the first question until recently was a resounding 'no', but new epidemiological evidence has changed this view, studies reporting that there is a moderate but significant association between schizophrenia and violence (Stueve & Link, 1997; Arboleda-Flórez et al, 1998; Angermeyer, 2000; Walsh et al, 2001). This is not surprising, considering the symptoms and treatment of schizophrenia and the impact the illness can have on people's lives. Relative risk of violence also increases when dual and complex problems of psychosis and substance misuse are present, but the overwhelming majority of people with severe mental illness are not violent (Hiday et al, 2001). When you consider *whom* people with severe mental illness are most likely to be violent toward, strangers are in a low-risk group, but this message gets lost in the headlines such as 'Maniac freed . . . to kill again' (*The Express*, 11/10/03), 'Monster works in shopping mall' (*News of the World*, 30/11/2003), 'Psychopath who was given bypass on the NHS' (*Daily Mail*, 1/4/2004). Mental health staff and family members are the most common 'victims' of violent behaviour by people with severe mental illness (Department of Health, 1999d).

When risk of violence is considered in societal terms, however, the proportion of risk of violence attributable to schizophrenia and other psychoses is low, as illustrated in the car accident statistics above. In an opinion paper on homicide inquiries, Szmukler (2000) estimated the risk of being killed by a stranger with psychosis to be around the same as that of being killed by lightning – about 1 in 10 million. Taking into account the statistical relationship between schizophrenia and violence, a recent review provides the following warning to researchers:

> To prevent unnecessary stigmatisation of the seriously mentally ill, it is the duty of researchers to present a balanced picture. . . . Risk is generally presented in terms of odds ratios, yet research has shown that people find it difficult to digest such measures. Better ways are required for presenting risk magnitudes in a digestible form . . . if communities are grouped into roughly logarithmic clusters (e.g. individual (1), family (10), village (1000), etc), then such a classification allows individuals to think in terms of levels of risk to themselves, their family, their town and so forth.
>
> (Walsh, 2001, p. 494)

The presentation of statistical information, and education of the public to understand statistical figures and explanations, is crucial if the lay public are to be able to make an informed judgement based on a combination of personal experiences and statistical trends. However, the widespread public scepticism toward the presentation of statistical information by governments, academic researchers and the media means that it is unlikely that the problems of people with mental health problems, in terms of social inclusion and reduced discrimination, will be solved by relying on factual data alone.

Failing to make a difference: the persistence of stigma and discrimination

For people with mental health problems, accessing employment opportunities, improving relationships with neighbours and the local community, being valued as experts by mental health professionals in decisions regarding their own care and treatment and the removal of the mental illness 'taboo' in society will follow from improvements in public mental health literacy and attitudes to mental illness. Currently, many people with mental health problems feel like second-class citizens, excluded, devalued and marginalised by the views, based upon ignorance and fear, that many in society share. Despite hundreds of academic studies in the past 10 years and several UK campaigns – Defeat Depression (Paykel et al, 1998), the Changing Minds Campaign by the Royal College of Psychiatrists, the Respect Campaign by MIND, and the government's Mind Out for Mental Health Initiative in England and See Me in Scotland – we are failing to make a significant impact on 'stigma' and discrimination. The failure is particularly acute where double discrimination is experienced, as in race and mental health or sexuality and mental health. Progress is noted in some areas, particularly where campaigns are tied to action in local areas, such as community-empowerment projects, advocacy schemes or user-led education projects, but, compared to New Zealand and

Australia, a lack of investment in mental health promotion, prevention and antidiscrimination activities is a severe limitation in the UK.

Are lessons being learnt from our campaign failures? Unfortunately, few antidiscrimination programmes have the resources to evaluate their actions thoroughly in the UK. There is a very weak evidence base supporting interventions that work, with most of the existing evidence originating from the USA; for example, see www.stigmaresearch.org. Research limitations in many studies include inadequate follow-up periods, social biasing within attitude measurements, few measures of behaviour change and overreliance on self-reporting rather than observational evidence.

Assembling evidence from across the globe for the National Institute of Mental Health England (see www.nimhe.org), three organisations (Mentality, Mental Health Media and Rethink) recommended the following six principles for successful programmes:

1   User and carers (experts by experience) should be involved throughout the design, delivery, monitoring and evaluation of the programme (www.likeminds.govt.nz).
2   National programmes supported by local activities demonstrate the most potent combination – the multilevel, multifaceted approach (www.openthedoors.com).
3   Programmes should address behaviour change with solutions that adopt both 'stick' and 'carrot' strategies, such as litigation and education (Sayce, 2003).
4   Clear, consistent messages should be delivered in targeted ways to specific target audiences. This includes developing models for antidiscrimination work; for example, rights-based approaches, instead of individual growth models (Sayce, 2000).
5   Programmes should be appropriately monitored and evaluated.
6   Long-term planning and funding underpins programme sustainability.

Our failure to collate 'good practice' evidence and disseminate lessons from campaigns means that valuable resources are being wasted, as new initiatives replicate the failures of past campaigns. Getting people to change behaviour – both in terms of emotional responses and practical actions, requires a clear dissemination strategy underpinned by models that harness individual 'readiness to change' approaches from education, management studies, sociology and psychology. What many experts are agreed upon is our need to reach people early, and that means setting up comprehensive mental health promotion programmes in our schools. We also need to pay more attention to the dissemination mechanisms and media required to affect public attitudes.

Chapter 12

Influencing the media[1]

Sophie Petit-Zeman

Declaring an interest

As a neuroscientist who came to medical writing and journalism via research and biomedical project management in mental health, I am familiar with the processes of both rigorous scientific enquiry, and what makes headlines – or at least a paragraph on an inside page, or a mention at the end of a news programme.

Currently writing on science, health and social care for broadsheets, occasionally tabloids, many specialist journals, the NHS, and broadcast media, I am also lead journalist for the government-funded Mind Out for Mental Health campaign (www.mindout.net). This involves devising and delivering workshops, primarily for journalism students, which promote open-minded media coverage of mental health and illness (www.mindout.net/p/mindshift.pdf).

This chapter thus reflects my experience, but its contents are my personal views. It aims to help those working in mental health, especially researchers, understand the media machine and how to harness it most usefully to disseminate their work. And 'useful' is crucial: 60% of psychiatric service users blame media coverage for the daily discrimination that they face (MIND, 2000), and 40% of the general public associate mental illness with violence, because the media tell them of this association (Philo, 1997).

As a freelancer who sells editors stories that I think are worth telling, I risk biting hands that feed me by highlighting such criticisms. Mental health media coverage is not all bad, but much is. You need to find ways to be confident that, if your work attracts media attention, or if you want it to, it contributes to real knowledge rather than the sensational spin of psycho stories.

1 Written December 2003.

Making news

What types of evidence have high salience for the media?

Newspaper pioneer Lord Northcliffe defined journalism as 'A profession whose business it is to explain to others what it personally does not understand.' Most journalists are not scientists, mental health stories which include that all-appealing element – violence – are often dealt with by crime correspondents, and the media's bottom line is sales or audience figures. However good your research, however fascinating to you and your peers, it needs the 'CFM [cor, f*** me] factor' (White et al., 1993 – an excellent practical guide) to make the media grade.

There are many types of media and many types of salience. Food for tabloid headlines may not whet the appetite of a broadsheet features editor, and the stuff of good radio may be very different, in style, content or both, from strong visual images which lend themselves to television. And, of course, the Internet has opened up valuable avenues for global information exchange as well as providing an undiscerning superhighway spreading junk further and faster than ever before.

This chapter focuses on the national 'lay' media and is illustrated with examples from print and broadcast, setting out general principles which apply to both. Local media have much the same requirements, although here, of course, local stories with a strong community angle appeal most.

What has salience for the media has a lot to do with who or what shouts loudest. Editors are bombarded with ideas and suggestions – press releases, gossip around the coffee machine, keen freelancers, dinner parties, their own personal interests – so the efficiency of the 'machine' behind a research team, the centre where they work or the journal which publishes them, is very relevant in influencing what makes it to the top of the pile. And, of course, if a member of your team has already cultivated a media profile, or has a grand title, or you can get someone of this ilk to comment on your work, it helps.

Invaluable are skilled press officers used to getting press releases (there is evidence that newspapers do pick up on these; www.ama-assn.org/public/ peer/7_15_98/jpv80001.htm.) to the relevant editors (this matters: a story about electroconvulsive therapy will not interest even the most broad-minded fashion editor just because she was in charge of health last week) and pursuing them through to print or broadcast. You will make their lot far easier if you are actively keen to raise your public profile, and able to provide lay explanations of your work, sound bites, human interest angles, and often all this at five o'clock on a Sunday afternoon.

Your willingness may in turn be determined by pragmatic motives: where are you in the promotion race, or the quest for funding? Or perhaps you simply know that your research matters and should be shared.

Journalists, editors or programme makers meanwhile ask themselves: will my audience like this story? While what makes the grade for news and features may be different, it is arguable that both will reflect public concerns and consciousness, although this climate may be one which the media themselves have generated.

The medium's audience in turn influences a story's salience. A broadsheet may run a story on stress among university students, while a paper whose readers encompass a lower proportion of those who attend university will not.

But some mental health issues stand a stronger chance of cutting the mustard whatever the outlet's core audience: personal stories or a 'consumer' angle – the implications for you – or celebrity gossip, often do the job.

Consultant psychiatrist Mark Salter wrote in his excellent review of the pitfalls and possibilities of the relationship between psychiatry and the media (2003, 124): 'For the media, the content of all accounts of mental illness, even those with an explicit educational intent, are subsidiary to another question: is it interesting?'

While interest remains subjective (try reading the *Guardian* if you normally choose the *Sun*, or hearing 'Gardener's Question Time' when you thought it would be the 'News Quiz'), common elements outlined above help to push mental health stories up the media agenda (Byrne, 2003).

It is worth remembering, too, that stories can be interesting for very different reasons: being totally in accord with what is known, or totally new: miracle cures or amazing facts. In the first case, in mental health, this too often means stories that reinforce negative beliefs or stereotypes. When American journalist Alexander Cockburn defined the first law of journalism as being 'to confirm existing prejudice, rather than contradict it', he could have been throwing down the gauntlet so readily picked up by some journalists who choose to tackle mental health and illness along these lines.

Making a splash

Academic research which received wide media reporting: why was it influential?

In July 2003, a study linking the risk of developing depression to a mutation in a single gene was reported in *Science* (Caspi et al, 2003), a journal with a reputation for publishing high-quality research and with an efficient machinery for getting that information out to the mass media – simply getting published here rather than in a lesser known journal with less clout certainly helped. The story appeared widely across the UK media, from broadsheets to tabloids to broadcast.

The story combined research from internationally renowned centres in the UK, the USA and New Zealand, with two topics which had already captured public interest. The WHO had singled out depression as a major and growing contributor to global disability, while decoding the genetic 'book of life' was coming along apace, and said to be virtually complete just 3 months before this work was published (http://news.bbc.co.uk/1/hi/sci/tech/2940601.stm).

Here was fertile ground on which a study about an inherited basis of depression could take root in the lay media, a story with, or easily adapted to have, many media-friendly elements.

Apparently, the finding could help elucidate why some people succumb while others are resistant to what *Metro* called 'traumatic events', and the *Guardian*, 'life's assaults' and 'stresses'. Trauma and stress are easy, catchy concepts familiar to journalists and their audiences alike.

The reports also latched on to the consumer angle – what it might one day mean for *you*. The researchers raised the possibility that a test for vulnerability to depression could follow, while the BBC (quoting Marjorie Wallace, chief executive of the mental health charity SANE) pointed out that such studies might aid the development of individually tailored treatments (http://news.bbc.co.uk/1/hi/health/3066065.stm).

So here, with consumer interest icing the salience cake, new research injected new life into ongoing media preoccupations. For the more ambitious journalist, another aspect of the research lent itself quite readily to coverage: the genetic finding could be explained in simple terms. While the original paper is predictably complex, journalists could latch on to the fact that having the 'short' version of a gene left you vulnerable to depression, while the long version was apparently protective.

Here was a straightforward concept which did not require explanation of chromosomes, mutations, dominance and recession. Furthermore, the gene in question was linked to the brain's serotonin system, and, again, long-standing media interest in antidepressant drugs such as Prozac, that interact with this system, allowed the story to build on an existing public knowledge base, or at least familiarity with terms.

Not all research has such handy topical tie-ins (the media call them 'hooks'), but, as explained later in this chapter, look hard enough and they are often there.

So, you have done the work, and the media are interested. Who will get the credit? Sometimes it is clear who should be interviewed, and it could be you. However, evidence suggests that, for most journalists, a mental health story means ask a psychiatrist, even if this ignores the valuable contribution of other mental health professionals, from clinical psychologists to outreach workers. I have often been glad to bypass the person running the show, first name on the paper, and get to whoever did the work. If you did it, shout about it.

Finally, while the compelling nature of the human interest angle has been discussed earlier, and the limitations of anecdote covered in following sections, it often appears at second hand. According to Mental Health Media (2001), only 6.5% of articles about mental health contained the voices of current or former service users.

I have heard too many stories of service users being told their view does not count precisely because they have or do use services. The mindshift guide (www.mindout.net/p/mindshift.pdf) hopefully explains why such prejudice may leave journalists without exactly the expert angle they need, and why the experiences of service users are so often ignored, while the journalist moves swiftly on to something less challenging. If you know someone who wants to speak from this perspective on your story, on *their* story, openly or anonymously, help ensure their voice is heard.

Why the excitement?

Non-academic research which received wide media reporting: why was it influential?

Medical journals publish countless 'case reports' which are valuable in drawing attention to rare events or recording approaches to treating common ones. Scientific research (when it is good) does not draw big conclusions from individual events. The media do.

As Simon Lawton-Smith, senior policy adviser at the King's Fund, says, 'Violence is always a good basis for a "nutter" story'. He adds, 'It's cynical but not wholly untrue to suggest that the media don't let the truth get in the way of a good story.'

A much-praised BBC 'Panorama' programme in October 2002 about the antidepressant Seroxat prompted a media feeding frenzy. The drug was linked with violence, addiction, suicide and self-harm. People's own accounts were distressing, it was important to hear them, and the drug company was hauled over the coals. It was compelling television, and a follow-up programme was made.

According to a BBC press release (www.bbc.co.uk/pressoffice/press-releases/stories/2003/05_may/11/panorama_seroxat.shtml):

> Feedback to the programme was unprecedented with 67,000 calls to the BBC helpline and almost 1,400 emails to Panorama.
>
> Charles Medawar, a drug safety expert, and world renowned pharmacologist Dr Andrew Herxheimer were commissioned to analyse the emails.
>
> Their report published this week in the *International Journal of Risk and Safety* reveals that from the emails alone Seroxat is believed to be linked to:
> - 16 accomplished suicides;
> - 47 cases of attempted suicide;
> - 92 cases of people who had thoughts of harming themselves or others;
> - 19 cases of children who had suffered serious side effects.

So the 'evidence' (but see below) was being analysed and reported, and Medawar and co-authors called for greater user involvement in drug monitoring. But few of the reports which mentioned this study told of perhaps its most salient findings.

The media were still almost uniformly portraying Seroxat as devilish, yet the emails to 'Panorama' found that while 48% categorised the drug as negative, 17% found it positive, and a further 812 emails 'were predominantly critical, not so much of the drug as about how it was promoted, recommended, tested and described'.

Here was a story which could set the 'Panorama' debate in a new, balanced context. Responsible journalism would indeed draw attention to the medical profession's tendency to dole out drugs rather than try to find out what else might help (or, to be fair, to a system that often makes this impossible), expose the failings of drug testing and licensing systems, and in turn feed into informed decisions about whether or not to take a drug in part by listening to the experiences of those who do. Yet much of the media persisted in slanting the story to fit the negative agenda; the newshounds' noses mostly failed to twitch as the 'evidence' emerged, and they slunk off to simpler stories. Could this one day happen to the fruits of your labour?

The eminent biologist Professor Lewis Wolpert (personal communication) was appalled by the programmes. He says: 'The evidence against Seroxat seems mainly anecdotal and thus very poor science. One should be very wary of those looking for something to blame for their depressive state and suicidal tendencies. These are the nature of depression. If only Seroxat was a plant everyone would love it.'

That Wolpert himself suffers from depression, and takes Seroxat, leaves him as he says, 'prejudiced'. His own experience may of course have coloured his views, and is no more 'evidence' than other anecdotes, but they do highlight the fact that most stories have at least two sides.

The Seroxat saga may be good media fodder in part because it is unbalanced. It is a more complicated challenge (for media and audience alike) to take it further – seek out the silent people's views – those who get on OK with things tend to say little about them – and compare them with stories that people are more eager to tell.

Who were the self-selected group that responded to the programme? Did those who fared worst shout loudest? What were the rates of suicide or self-harm among a comparable group of people with depression on other, or no, medication?

The tragic Seroxat suicides, its grotty side-effects for some, made good drama, but was only half a script.

The press release about the follow-up programme stated: 'Andy Bell, Panorama producer, said: "The response to the first Panorama investigation was unprecedented with many of the viewers saying that watching October's programme was the first time they had made a link between their unhappy experiences and Seroxat." '

And the *Sunday Times* (11 May 2003, 'Critic's Choice') commented, 'The new material is substantial and amounts to a significant body of evidence: the response of viewers to the original film, which consisted of 67,000 calls to the helpline and 1,400 e-mails. Analysed by two experts, the latter link 16 suicides and 47 attempted suicides to Seroxat. Many patients had not connected their own or their loved ones' problems to the drug until they saw the Panorama report.'

Challenging drug companies is vitally important: around this time, Seroxat's makers amended the patient information leaflet, and the use of Seroxat in children was revisited and advised against. But an article in the *Scotsman* (19 May 2003) perhaps illustrates an important point: 'Here is a riveting programme, to which thousands responded, and immediately patterns can be recognised.'

Just as it has been argued that public fears about the MMR vaccine causing autism spiralled because the possibility received media attention, might the media at least in part have manufactured a Seroxat scare?

Interest in the story simmers on (see, for example, www.socialaudit.org.uk/5111-006.htm) – there is little like a strong polemic, especially one that challenges villains, from pharma giants to regulators, for grabbing and holding attention.

Seroxat may turn out to be a mistake, but meanwhile millions of people presumably take it because it makes them feel better. And not only better from some problem manufactured by drug companies to extend their products' life and scope, but better enough to cope.

For everyone on Seroxat who feels suicidal, how many are there who have depression and are not on Seroxat, who feel suicidal too? For everyone on Seroxat who says they feel terrible, how many could tell you it saved their life? It's an evidence base that would take working at, and require a move away from these anecdotes. Perhaps the challenge of taking the debate forward now seems to be leaving the media cold for just these reasons?

Not worth knowing?

What types of evidence have low salience for the media?

The media clearly like stories which come from credible academic sources, contain human interest – someone prepared to talk and, ideally, be photographed, a consumer angle – something readers can do, even if only get excited that one day there might be a 'test' for depression, or clamour against a dodgy drug being doled out by irresponsible GPs under pressure from evil drug barons. If a celebrity will say they have been depressed, or the story be amenable to being linked with some other media-friendly topic, such as drug abuse, sexual proclivity or, that old favourite, violence (see later), then it may well make the grade.

Take the items on this list in reverse order, and we have the recipe for low salience. As Oscar Wilde said: 'The public have an insatiable curiosity to know everything. Except what is worth knowing. Journalism, conscious of this, and having tradesman-like habits, supplies their demands.'

A rigorous research study, however important its implications, will rarely alone be enough. White et al (1993, 8) write of the 'So what?' test that 'every story, wherever it originates, has to pass . . . science stories, more than most, because they are less immediately understandable than a murder, political row or pop star's divorce'.

The three rules of journalism, *make it juicy, make it brief, make it up*, apply here. There is no turn off for an editor or hack as reliable as a complicated story without an immediate human angle and through which even the most creative writer will find it tricky to weave the wow factor.

Good work, bad news

Academic research which failed to receive wide media reporting: why was it not influential?

With as many as 300 press releases landing on any one journalist's desk each week, or, more often now, pinging into their electronic in-boxes, it is unsurprising that researchers who know they have something incredibly important to tell the world are frequently disappointed by the world's failure to recognise their genius.

In late 2002, I was offered exclusive access to the results of a peer-reviewed study of peer review. This time-honoured process by which what gets into the journals, and in turn into the lay media and public awareness, is decided – so quite important really – was apparently seriously flawed.

While this finding potentially overturned not only how the world of scientific and medical publishing works, but also cast doubt on wider issues such as how grants are awarded (if peer review does not work, how can anyone know what is high quality and rigorous?), I heard the collective shrug of shoulders as I tried to sell the story to my broadsheet editors, and they asked, 'So what?'

To me, it was exciting stuff, yet it turned out to be one of the most difficult to place (Petit-Zeman, 2003). And I understand why: If you do not know that peer review is the way that science gets out of the laboratory and into the clinic, you are unlikely to care that peer review may be bunk.

There are countless examples of such difficulties in mental health. As Deborah Hart, Head of External Affairs and Information Services at the Royal College of Psychiatrists, points out (personal communication) 'Much of the research from our journals is good, solid science with fascinating findings, but the media just don't get excited. For instance, a recent study that looked at psychological and behavioural problems in people with learning disabilities who had been sexually abused wasn't picked up at all.'

If the story lacks the wow factor, however scientifically rigorous, it will not make the media. The more mundane aspects of severe mental illnesses such as schizophrenia or manic depression, the reality of daily life for those who have them, their friends or relatives, are far less appealing to mass media than are the shock horror rarities, the violent or bizarre acts.

And this unfortunate irony feeds the cycle of media perpetuation of stigma against those with mental illness: it may be the sheer novelty of the link between violence (at least, that toward others rather than misery that becomes self-directed) and mental illness which makes it news. Yet for those who repeatedly read, see or hear about mental illness set in such contexts, it easily becomes the apparent reality, however far they know, at heart, it is from the boring, distressing truth that touches most people's lives at some time. With luck, the media may be losing the battle to keep the nutters in a different box, pretending that it is somewhere they have never been and will never go.

When the Office of National Statistics published a survey of 200 people aged 16–74 who had a psychotic disorder asking about their daily lives at home – their patterns of seeing their GP, of hospital attendance, of medication, of how life really was for them, it passed virtually unnoticed (Stationery Office/ ONS, 2000). It was not apparently press-released (www.statistics.gov.uk) despite containing important information about medication use, what people found difficult and whether their needs were being met. Did the researchers behind the work perhaps not want their findings widely publicised? Did the media know about it but just found it too dull? Did it fall foul of the topicality test? Trends, whims and climate certainly influence what makes the media. As we saw earlier, genetics is hot, and will probably stay so for a while, and depression has had celebrity boosts (from Alistair Campbell to Frank Bruno), so the next depression gene story may still pack a punch.

Working one summer to fill the health feature pages of a broadsheet, I found myself writing about the danger of drowning after getting your hair trapped in a swimming pool filter. Why? Because (a) it was unusually hot and pools were popular, and (b) the editor knew someone who knew someone to whom this might have happened and was preoccupied by it. I had a tough job finding anyone who knew anything about swimming pools to say that the magnitude of this risk was other than miniscule. Salience sometimes has the strangest of triggers, so even if you doubt your story will make the grade, it might, for reasons you could not begin to imagine.

The comedian Ronnie Shakes said: 'After twelve years of therapy my psychiatrist said something that brought tears to my eyes. He said, "No hablo ingles." '

Speaking different languages may not foster understanding, and while journalists may not speak science, researchers sometimes find it hard to make their findings comprehensible. With mutual effort, media and mental health might, and none too soon, become better bedfellows.

Acknowledgements

Grateful thanks to Simon Lawton-Smith, Deborah Hart and Lewis Wolpert.

Chapter 13

Influencing policy in the United Kingdom

Frank Holloway

Evidence and UK mental health policy

Contemporary mental health policy in the UK is very firmly devolved to its constituent countries, and their parliaments and assemblies. While England and Wales share a Mental Health Act, Northern Ireland[1] and Scotland operate under quite distinct legislation. The process of deinstitutionalisation and the development of community care has been markedly quicker in England than in Scotland and Northern Ireland. Wales had not adopted the care programme approach (CPA) a decade after it became the core of mental health policy and practice in England. Accordingly, this chapter reflects the making of mental health policy in England. Readers are assumed to have a working knowledge of the current structure of health and social care provision in England.

The past

There is a long history of overtly evidence-based policy making in England. Prior to the passing of the 1845 Lunatics Act, which required local authorities to build asylums for pauper lunatics, a Select Committee of the House of Commons received a range of evidence (Scull, 1982). This included data showing that a high percentage of patients who were admitted to an asylum within 6 months of the onset of their illness were subsequently discharged 'cured' or 'relieved'. Those admitted to asylums more than a year after the onset of illness were very unlikely to be discharged, and remained a call upon the public purse. It would seem that the Select Committee was persuaded that an expansion of asylum care was a good investment.

The expansion of the asylum system during the nineteenth century can be criticised from a postmodern perspective. It can be argued that the decision,

---

1 At the time of writing, the Northern Ireland Assembly is suspended and policy making is in the hands of the Northern Ireland Office.

rather than being a rational response to a social problem, reflected the undue influence of interest groups, notably, in this case, the asylum doctors, who stood to gain from an expansion in the number of asylums. Policy making may have involved the selective use of evidence by ignoring, for example, the quite well-documented voice of people who had been incarcerated by 'mad-doctors' (although it is worth noting that the original data on good outcomes for the early asylum was in fact replicated internationally (Bockhoven, 1954)). Scull (1982) has argued that the Lunatics Act was a manifestation of larger-scale social forces relating to the management of an expanding population of the urban poor. Similar sorts of criticisms could be levelled against any contemporary policy initiative.

Kinds of evidence

Biomedical scientists are taught to place meta-analyses of randomised, controlled trials at the top of an evidential pyramid. This is a very limited perspective, and Part I of this book outlines the variety of empirical evidence that might usefully inform policy making. However, solid empirical evidence of whatever form is but one of a wide variety sources that we all draw from in making decisions. Additional kinds of evidence include 'folk wisdom' (what my mother told me), current popular beliefs (the water-cooler effect), personal experience (what *I* know, have seen with my own eyes or been told by convincing witnesses), what the media tells me, received wisdom from the government bureaucracy, and the weight of professional opinion. The media have, of course, taken a particular interest in the more lurid aspects of mental health care, potentially distorting the perceptions of both the general public and politicians.

Many actors are involved in the formulation of social policy: government, policy-making elites, civil society (including particular interest groups), industry, the media and academia. In a democracy, policy is ultimately determined by elected politicians, who are seeking solutions to perceived political or practical problems (see Levin, 1999, for a series of case studies in the implementation of social policy in the late 1980s and early 1990s). Politicians will only rarely have the technical expertise required to come to an independently informed opinion in their area of responsibility. They are quite specifically and peculiarly affected in their decision making by the media, the concerns of their constituents, their own personal experience, what they are told by their political advisers and officials, and what they choose to hear from interest groups. Implementation of policy is in the hands of an increasingly politicised bureaucracy and may throw up unexpected problems that in turn require solutions (the law of unintended consequences).

Policy and practice in the National Health Service (NHS): what is policy?

The NHS is a huge organisation. Its policy is manifested through primary legislation, regulation, guidance, exhortation and a variety of executive acts, which include setting the administrative structures within which health-care organisations work, defining professional tasks and roles, controlling their financial allocations and managing performance. At the time of writing, performance management in the NHS is through the Local Delivery Plan, which reflects the local health economy's response to governmental must-do's and must-must-do's. In addition, health-care organisations must meet quality targets defined by the Health Care Commission. Failure to meet targets may lead the chair and chief executive of a trust to lose their jobs.

The broad outlines of mental health policy in England under New Labour were set out in a Green Paper and further refined by the National Service Framework for Mental Health (NSF-MH) and the NHS Plan (Department of Health, 1998, 1999, 2000a). An impressive range of guidance has followed that can be accessed through the website of the National Institute for Mental Health in England (www.nimhe.org.uk).[2] The more significant policy documents come with ministerial forewords (from the Prime Minister, in the case of the NHS Plan). An overview of progress toward achieving mental health policy objectives in England has recently been published (Appleby, 2004).

Health policy has also required the development of evidence-based guidance and guidelines by or on behalf of the National Institute for Clinical Excellence (NICE) (www.nice.org.uk). Health-care commissioners, providers and practitioners must take account of NICE recommendations. NICE Guidelines relating to mental illnesses and deliberate self-harm have potentially profound implications for mental health services in England. Health policy documents are couched in an evidence-based language and, for a professional audience, have an academic apparatus. However, like the workings of the Health Care Commission and NICE publications, they are not subject to external peer review.

The relationship between research evidence and policy

The logical relationship between empirical evidence and policy could be defined thus:

1   There is no evidence and no policy.
2   Policy exists in the absence of evidence.

---

2 From April 2005, NIMHE, formerly part of the NHS Modernisation Agency, became part of CISP. The brand name has been retained.

3   There is evidence but there is no policy.
4   There is both evidence and evidence-based policy.
5   Policy and empirical evidence actively contradict each other.

It is worth noting that a subset of 2, is that policy may be in *advance* of good evidence: policy makers may go beyond existing knowledge but later be shown to be correct.

This chapter will present three case studies of the impact of evidence of all kinds on contemporary mental health policy. These come with a health warning – the author has a particular perspective on both what represents policy and the research evidence. A brief conclusion attempts to draw some lessons on the often troubled relationship between policy makers and those tasked with providing the evidence base.

The rise of assertive outreach: evidence-based policy?

The NSF-MH proposed the setting up of 170 Assertive Outreach Teams (AOTs) across the country, a figure increased to 220 in the NHS Plan. The Policy Implementation Guide (PIG) (Department of Health, 2001a) set out a detailed description of the AOT and a number of other so-called functional mental health teams. Local health economies have been given very detailed targets for the introduction of these 'functional' teams and the caseloads that they are to carry. The result has, in policy terms, been a spectacular success: Appleby (2004) reports that, by March 2004, 263 AOTs were in place. Some AOTs have been developed as a result of additional investment made in mental health services under the NHS Plan. In other areas, targets have been met by taking resources from existing well-established services, notably generic community mental health teams and rehabilitation/outreach teams.

Role and function of the AOT

The AOT is a multidisciplinary team that is designed to offer care to 'hard-to-engage' patients with severe mental health problems (in practice, psychotic illnesses) who are heavy users of services. Such hard-to-engage patients, whose illness career is characterised by repeated admissions and recurrent rejection of community services, have long been a preoccupation of policy makers. The CPA was introduced in 1990 to ensure that all potentially vulnerable patients were followed up on discharge from hospital. (The policy was introduced following the recommendations of a well-publicised inquiry into the homicide of a social worker by her former mentally ill client (Spokes, 1988).) The introduction of AOT can be seen as a response to the perceived failure of the CPA for a subgroup who actively avoided follow-up, and was recommended in *Keys to Engagement*, an influential report by the Sainsbury Centre for Mental Health, published in 1998.

The service description provided in the PIG draws heavily on a well-established American service model, the Programme for Assertive Community Treatment (PACT). This in turn is based on the pioneering work of Stein and Test (1980), who carried out a controlled trial of a team providing an alternative to inpatient admission and subsequent intensive community support for people with psychosis. Scales have been developed to measure the fidelity of a service to the PACT model, which emphasises low caseloads, teamwork, assertive engagement with clients, *in vivo* work focusing on enhancement of skills and 24-hour availability (Burns & Firn, 2002, pp. 34–44). AOTs are not a cheap option. A team supporting 120 individuals requires more staff than would traditionally be available to provide a generic community mental health team offering comprehensive care to a catchment area of 40,000 people.

Evidence base

PACT is very thoroughly researched: by 2001, 25 controlled trials had been reported (Phillips et al, 2001). The Cochrane Collaboration meta-analytic review is unequivocally positive that implementation of PACT results in savings in bed days, lower rates of drop-out from care and improved clinical outcomes on some, but not all, parameters (Marshall & Lockwood, 1998). The success of PACT contrasts with the failure of other forms of 'case management' (a generic term for the allocation of responsibility for arranging or providing community care to a team or individual). These have not been shown to reduce admissions or improve outcomes, although they do reduce loss to follow-up (Marshall et al, 1998). One practice, 'care management', which was introduced by the Conservative government as part of their community care reforms, has been shown to be particularly ineffective (as could have been predicted by anyone who had understood the relevant literature available at the time (Holloway, 1991)).

However, there are limitations to the evidence base, which is largely made up of studies from the USA. Reviewers come to differing conclusions about the effect of PACT and case management on key outcome variables, such as symptoms and social functioning (Marshall & Lockwood, 1998; Marshall et al, 1998; Mueser et al, 1998; Ziguras & Stuart, 2000). Implementation of PACT or PACT-like services in Europe has been significantly less successful (Burns et al, 2001). An important study, the UK700, demonstrated no evidence of efficacy compared with standard community mental health team care (Burns et al, 1999). Critics argue that the study is not one of true PACT, although ratings of fidelity to the PACT model were high. One aspect of PACT orthodoxy, a 'no-discharge' policy, is plainly impossible in the English context, given the resources PACT/AOT demands. Another aspect, the team approach to care, is directly at odds with the requirement for all mental health patients to have a named care coordinator. A general difficulty with the mental health research literature can also be encountered in the PACT debate – studies tend to be of demonstration projects at a relatively early stage of their lives and tend to use a control condition that does not reflect best orthodox practice. In other words the efficacy of PACT in the USA may have been established. Its effectiveness when applied to the real world in a European context is not clear.

Commentary: why AOT captured the policy high ground

The development of the AOT throughout England is an example of the adoption of a policy with a strong evidence base within a high-profile, large-scale reform to the overall health service in England, the NHS Plan. Implementation has required very considerable investment of scarce staffing and financial resources, and has been successfully achieved (at least in terms of numbers of teams following the required pattern).

A number of factors have contributed to this success. Firstly, AOTs seek to address a very long-standing policy concern, the failure of mental health services in the era of community care to follow up vulnerable patients with severe mental illness appropriately and effectively. This failure is perceived to have resulted in well-publicised tragedies and, more pragmatically, to have produced the 'revolving door' syndrome of the expensive patient that is repeatedly admitted to hospital. By implication, implementation of AOT promises to eliminate unacceptably poor outcomes and reduce pressure on inpatient psychiatric beds. Secondly, AOT was adopted after other simpler and cheaper measures had apparently failed, in this case the CPA and the expansion of the generic community mental health team model across the country. Thirdly, AOT is a local version of an internationally recognised form of service provision that has a very clear and easily explained rationale. Fourthly, key interest groups with high credibility and influence on policy, most notably, in this case, the Sainsbury Centre for Mental Health, were persuaded of the value of the AOT approach. Proponents of PACT and the other 'functional' teams have an evangelical zeal that has proven highly persuasive: sceptics can become victims of scorn and abuse (see, for example, Rosen & Teesson, 2002). Fifthly, measures of fidelity to the model are available (important in the contemporary delivery culture), and convincing research evidence in its favour can be cited, including health-economic data. Finally, introduction of AOT has been intensively performance managed by novel mechanisms of central control.

The rise of the risk industry: policy without adequate evidence?

Risk and mental illness

It is a truism that we live in a society obsessed with risk, risk avoidance and the attachment of blame when bad things happen (Prins, 1999). Doctors have always had a role in the assessment and care of individuals who have harmed others while mentally ill: the management of the risky offender lies at the core of the speciality of forensic psychiatry. There is a strong popular perception that people with mental illness, particularly schizophrenia, represent a risk to the community due to a propensity to unprovoked violence, and that this risk has increased materially since the adoption of community care policies. The first proposition is true, although only a very modest proportion of societal violence can be attributed to schizophrenia, and much of this excess is associated with co-morbid substance misuse (Walsh & Fahy, 2002; Taylor & Estroff, 2003). The second proposition is false: a clear example is found in the risk of homicide by a person with a mental illness in the UK, which has remained unchanged over 50 years, while the overall number of homicides has increased very markedly (Taylor & Gunn, 1999).

Psychiatric patients have a markedly elevated standardised mortality ratio (Santhouse & Holloway, 1999). Part of this excess mortality is due to the very high suicide rate in certain mental illnesses, some to the increased rates of death from accidental injury and a small proportion to the direct toxic effects of psychotropic medication. The largest proportion of this excess in death is caused by increased physical morbidity experienced by patients (who tend to be physically inactive, poor, unemployed and smokers). Patients are potentially vulnerable to self-neglect and exploitation. Increasingly, as people with a severe mental illness become parents, there is concern over the welfare of their children.

Policy response

The real (and imagined) risks associated with mental illness have provoked an increasingly intense policy response since the early 1990s. Reduction in suicide, which is the leading cause of death among young adults, has been a priority since the publication of the Public Health White Paper, *Health of the Nation* (Department of Health, 1991). Most recently, a *National Suicide Prevention Strategy*, which seeks to be evidence-based, has been published (Department of Health, 2002b). The concerns over physical health issues resulted in GPs receiving modest remuneration for undertaking physical health checks on their severely mentally ill patients under the new General Medical Services contract.

The defining moment in policy and public perception of risk to others from people with a mental illness occurred in December 1992 (Holloway, 1996). Christopher Clunis, who had a long history of psychosis that had resulted in multiple contacts with London's mental health services, stabbed a stranger to death on an underground platform. A flurry of policy making ensued within the Department of Health, resulting in the publication of a 10-point plan aimed at reducing the risk. One element of the plan was a commitment to change the law to allow compulsory community treatment. The perception that mental health services were unsafe and required reform to ensure public safety was carried over into the subsequent Labour administration, which included a commitment to reform the Mental Health Act in its first mental health policy document (Department of Health, 1998). One proposed aspect of this reform was to ensure that people with a 'dangerous severe personality disorder' (DSPD), which does not appear in any psychiatric nosology, could be detained in hospital, even if they had not yet been convicted of a crime and were not felt to be treatable.

Throughout the 1990s and subsequently, there has been an increasing emphasis on the importance of mental health services carrying out risk assessments in order to prevent adverse outcomes. Revised CPA guidance included a highly prescriptive account of the form of risk assessments to be undertaken by staff (Department of Health, 2000b). Policy has been increasingly informed by the National Confidential Inquiry into Suicide and Homicide and Suicide by People with Mental Illness, published under the title *Safety First* (Appleby et al, 2001), which identified 'twelve points to a safer service', including mandatory training every 3 years for mental health staff in risk assessment and the development of AOTs. Meeting the requirements of *Safety First* has been assertively performance managed.

Where policy contradicts the evidence

There are many aspects of the policy response to the perceived risks to themselves and others by people with a mental illness that are clearly evidence based, notably the public health responses put in place to reduce further suicide rates (Department of Health, 2002b). Others are not. There is no evidence that risks are increasing, and therefore no obvious rationale for emphasising the assessment and management of risk over other aspects of mental health care. The suicide rate in England is both low internationally and has been declining over recent decades (Department of Health, 2002b). As noted above, the risk of being killed by a mentally ill person is unchanged in absolute terms and has declined markedly in relative terms over the past 50 years (Taylor & Gunn, 1999).

There is good reason to believe that placing risk assessment at the heart of psychiatric care is, at best, a distraction from the task of reducing the adverse consequences of mental illness. This is because, thankfully, serious adverse outcomes are rare. The mathematics of risk mean that it is not possible to predict adverse events unless the base rates are high, as be the case in some aspects of forensic practice, but is not true in general adult psychiatry (Szmukler, 2003). It is quite clear that the epidemiologically robust risk factors for suicide are of no value in identifying who will kill themselves as an inpatient (Powell et al, 2000). Similarly, although with vigorous use of hindsight a proportion of homicide inquiries identify the homicide as preventable, the event is rarely if ever in any real sense predictable (Munro & Rumgay, 2000). It is highly probable that the most effective way mental health services can reduce the risk of severe adverse consequences is by providing optimal treatment for the underlying mental disorders that increase risk. In any case, avoiding risk is a very poor basis for decision making compared with an assessment of the benefits that might flow from effective treatment.

At worst, the preoccupation with risk will have severely negative consequences for mental health care. The introduction of compulsory community treatment may have the perverse effect of driving people in need away from the mental health care system, resulting in overall worse outcomes (Szmukler, 2003). The experience of the investigation of children potentially at risk is disturbing. Here an obsession with risk has paralysed the system, demoralising staff and sucking much of the available resource for child welfare into the investigative process. This has been at the expense of services that would be of benefit to children and families, including those where the child is at risk (Munro & Rumgay, 2000).

Commentary: why the obsession with risk?

A number of factors can be identified in the rise of the risk industry in psychiatry. The general risk-averse trend in society has already been mentioned. With this has gone a culture of investigation and inquisition into the causes of adverse events that has revealed deficiencies in mental health services (Spokes, 1988; Ritchie et al, 1994; Appleby et al, 2001). Recommendations made by inquiries for improved risk assessment and other measures, such as the 'twelve points to a safer service', have face validity, particularly when they come from influential actors in the policy arena. Policy developments to address fears of harm to others gain legitimacy from the ever-expanding literature on risk (e.g. Taylor & Estroff, 2003). However, they are largely a political response to media coverage of very rare, highly newsworthy events, such as the case of Clunis and the murder of members of the Russell family by Michael Stone, which precipitated the dangerous and severe personality disorder (DSPD) policy stream.

The forgotten illnesses: evidence in search of an effective policy?

Specialist mental health services in England are required to focus their attention on people with severe and enduring mental illness, which in practice means people with psychotic illnesses, more severe forms of depression and severe personality disorder. These disorders result in the vast majority of admissions in adult mental health, and hence the bulk of the direct costs of secondary mental health care. However, the bulk of psychiatric morbidity (and hence disability and societal distress) is experienced by people suffering from non-psychotic disorders, such as anxiety, less severe depression, somatisation and adjustment disorder as well as substance misuse disorders (Andrews, 2000). Those who seek help do so from primary care and, increasingly, complementary practitioners. Primary care staff are, by definition, generalists. Few have specific training in mental health and fewer still the skills required to provide evidence-based treatments for 'minor' psychiatric disorders, although handbooks are available to support them (e.g. Mynors-Wallis et al, 2002). The needs of individuals with 'minor' disorders may fall between two stools, primary care that lacks the relevant skills and secondary care that is already fully saturated with demand to treat, support and manage people with identified severe mental illnesses.

Policy response

The NSF-MH, in Standard 2, stated that service users presenting with a 'common mental health problem' should both have their needs assessed and be offered effective treatment and referral to specialist services (Department of Health, 1999a). The evidence base suggests that the treatment of choice for common mental disorders is specific psychological treatment, generally cognitive behaviour therapy, delivered by an appropriately trained and supervised therapist (Department of Health, 2001a; NICE, 2004a,b). Appleby (2004, pp. 12–15) describes rather slow progress in recruitment of 'graduate' primary care workers to deliver brief psychological treatments, the elaboration of shared care protocols for common mental disorders and a modest increase in investment in psychological therapies based in primary care. The gap between aspiration and reality is palpable.

Commentary

There are grounds for cautious optimism that the obvious public health need to respond effectively to so-called minor psychiatric morbidity (Andrews, 2000) is at last being taken seriously at a policy level. Progress remains slow compared with the lightning development of AOTs and the rapid penetration of risk assessment as a core aspect of mental health services. There are a number of plausible explanations for the relative lack of emphasis on what is, objectively, a major public health problem. 'Minor' psychiatric morbidity does not hit the headlines, and sufferers and their carers have little public voice. Its direct costs are low compared with severe mental illness (although the indirect costs are much higher). Because of the structure of health care in England, which has relied heavily on primary care gatekeeping, specialists have largely been able to ignore the problem. Mental health remains a very marginal concern for primary care, which in any case has relatively little impact on policy making. The potential solution to the problem, a massive investment in skilled talking therapy, represents a daunting financial, educational and logistical problem for the NHS.

Conclusion

Policy is never made without evidence. The introduction of AOT in England is based on a great deal of solid scientific data, although, infuriatingly for the policy maker, not all experts agree on how one should interpret the data. There is very strong evidence relating to the risks that people with a mental illness represent to themselves and others. The policy response as to how to manage these risks has gone beyond the evidence base, and indeed may well, perversely, result in increased societal harms. Here policy makers have been responding to other kinds of evidence, notably headlines in the tabloid press, to ensure that *something is being done*. Sometimes we have good evidence, such as the massive morbidity associated with 'minor' psychiatric morbidity and the potentially effective interventions that can be deployed, but a policy commitment to address the problem is not forthcoming.

There is a great deal of mental health policy in England at the moment (see Appleby, 2004, for an abbreviated summary). Policy makers must be congratulated in seeking to base their efforts on the best available evidence. The research community is challenged both to provide policy-relevant evidence and ensure that implemented policy is thoroughly and dispassionately evaluated.

Chapter 14

Influencing policy in Germany

Bernd Puschner, Heinrich Kunze and Thomas Becker

Evidence in a German context

In the 1970s, about 20 years later than in other Western European countries and the USA, a major reform process of the psychiatric service system began in Germany.[1] It was inspired by the Psychiatrie-Enquête (Psychiatrie-Enquête, 1975), which itself was an expression of a general atmosphere of social reform that characterised the Federal Republic of Germany (FRG) during that time.[2] A commission of 23 experts and a range of international and national advisers contributed. The commission presented a report to the West German parliament which was based on extensive data collection on all branches of the psychiatric service system. It was concluded that the condition of care for the mentally ill was in a horrifying state; that is, their needs were neglected and many of them were occupying long-term custodial institutions with substandard care and inhumane living conditions, at times including low staffing levels. Even though this had been known for more than a decade (Bauer et al, 2001), it obviously took a long time to convince the majority of mental health professionals and their organisations that things were no longer tolerable. These were turbulent times characterised by often fierce ideological disputes between 'old-school' psychiatrists, some of whom

---

1 This text deals with psychiatric reform in West Germany, that is, the Federal Repubic of Germany of pre-1990 (before reunification). It does not address the complex psychiatric reform process in the German Democratic Republic (GDR), which is discussed in Bauer et al (2001) and Thom and Wulff (1990). There was an autonomous psychiatric reform movement in East Germany, and the book *Social Psychiatry in Socialist Society* provides a landmark reference in both practical and academic terms (Schwarz et al, 1971). In spite of the Iron Curtain, there were contacts and mutual influences of psychiatric reform in East and West Germany, particularly between academic institutions in Leipzig and Hannover (Thom & Wulff, 1990). The history of psychiatric reform in the GDR has been addressed by some authors (e.g. Schmiedebach et al, 2000), but both this topic and East–West interactions in the reform process need to be explored in detail.

2 In the GDR, the 'Rodewisch Theses' of 1963 had provided a similar stimulus to psychiatric reform (Rodewischer Thesen, 1965; Waldmann, 1998).

had been involved in the systematic extermination of the mentally ill during the Nazi era, and reformers, who were partly influenced by the civil rights and political protest movement (Bauer, 2003).

The Enquête's recommendations included the following (Häfner, 2001):

1 development of a needs-based, community-oriented psychiatric service system, including outpatient and complementary services
2 coordination and cooperation between service providers and catchment areas
3 development of outpatient services and psychiatric departments at general hospitals.

Given the decentralised nature of the German health service system (see below), the Enquête's recommendations did not become binding principles, as might have been the case in the UK, where the National Health Service (NHS) has substantial regulative power. Instead, they turned out to be compelling but non-mandatory guidelines to clinicians and administrators, leading to remarkable changes in the psychiatric service system. However, their practical meaning was open to interpretation; thus, implementation varied widely within and between parts of the service system, including political institutions. Two selected areas in which an evidence base has been accumulated according to the Enquête's suggestions that subsequently also affected service provision will be outlined.

Dehospitalisation

Many patients who earlier would have spent most of their lives in hospital were discharged, resulting in an overall massive reduction in length of stay (LOS). The number of psychiatric hospital beds was reduced from 1.8 to 0.8 per 1000 inhabitants in West Germany between 1970 and 1990 (Kunze, 1999), and is still being further reduced (0.6 in 2002) (Häfner, 2003). At the same time, average LOS was drastically reduced from 210 days in 1975 to 27.8 days in 1998, while the number of office-based psychiatrists increased enormously during that time, from 1 per 68,000 to 1 per 17,173 inhabitants (Fritze & Schmauß, 2001). However, this reduction was not always achieved by sending patients to their communities, where they would receive adequate care. Rather, large numbers of long-stay patients were labelled differently ('nursing cases') and thus removed from the responsibility of psychiatry and placed in other institutions, mostly remote sheltered homes with a poor social environment (Kunze, 1985). Today, the number of psychiatric patients in sheltered homes is about the same as the number of psychiatric inpatient beds (Brill, 2000), while there is a striking lack of evidence on the effect of the supposedly poor social environment in sheltered homes on their inhabitants.

Further evidence for this was provided by the Berlin Dehospitalisation

Study, which showed that 68% of 422 middle-term and long-term inpatients were still in institutional settings 2 years after discharge (Kaiser et al, 1998) while only 31% of the subjects were estimated to be in need of special protective measures. The Hessian Dehospitalisation study (Franz et al, 2001) showed that, of 266 schizophrenic, long-stay patients, only 60 (22.6%) were discharged during a 4-year period. Apart from the most evident reasons against discharge (risk to self and/or others), hardly any differences were found between discharged patients and those who stayed at the hospitals. Similarly, Vieten et al (1996) found that duration of hospitalisation for 220 severely mentally ill patients did not affect the decision to discharge. Moreover, Meyer et al (2002) showed that poor social adaptation was unrelated to likelihood of discharge.

However, there seems to be a considerable group of patients who prefer to stay in institutional settings. For example, Hoffmann et al (1997) found that long-stay patients' overall satisfaction with treatment was high, even though some of them were hardly satisfied with regard to the likelihood of staying in the hospital for a long time. Furthermore, even though most discharged patients reported that living in the community brought about a substantial improvement of their quality of life, they expressed dissatisfaction with regard to their financial situation and family contacts (Ropers et al, 1999).

On the one hand, this evidence indicates that much larger numbers of (long-stay) patients could be discharged, but, on the other hand, it could also mean that a hospital stay – sometimes even an extensive one – is indicated (and preferred by the patients) in some cases. Furthermore, as already outlined in the 'three hospitals study' (Wing & Brown, 1970), reluctance to leave is not an uncommon attitude to discharge. Research still has to provide data which could aid the clinician in deciding, together with the patient and his or her family, when to discharge a person with severe mental illness and to which setting.

Day hospitals

Following the Enquête's recommendations, large numbers of the then limited day hospitals were put into service. Today, almost every psychiatric hospital or department provides a day-care unit (Eikelmann, 1999a), even though there is still a sizeable shortage of day-treatment options for patients with substance abuse problems and geriatric patients. In the beginning, day hospitals were the only institutions which also treated the severely and/or chronically mentally ill outside the hospital. Given the lack of adequate complementary institutions – such as halfway houses – many patients kept going to the day hospital even after actual treatment had been terminated (Reker, 1999). During the last years, the function of day hospitals shifted from rehabilitation to merely providing a place to go for more acute care.

Although proponents of day treatment/partial hospitalisation frequently claim that this treatment form is at least as effective as full-time hospital treatment (Eikelmann, 1999b), evidence is sparse. Although some studies in the USA, the UK and the Netherlands (summarised in (Marshall et al, 2004a) showed that day-hospital care reduced relapse and improved outcome, there is only one relevant study in Germany (Eikelmann, 1991), which also showed that day-hospital treatment was effective in terms of reduction of symptom impairment and vocational reintegration. While proponents of day-hospital treatment suggest that up to 40% of patients in need of full-time inpatient care can be treated in day-hospital settings (Albers, 1999), this goal has been only partially met in Germany. In regions with a highly developed service system, it is estimated that up to 20% of patients otherwise in need of inpatient care are treated in day hospitals.

There is still a lack of knowledge on the effectiveness of day-hospital treatment in acute care, and information which could be put to use for treatment planning and selecting patients suitable for day-hospital treatment is sparse. Only now, is relevant evidence being accumulated in a multicentre European study (Kallert et al, 2002).

Decentralised organisation of psychiatric service provision in Germany

As in most other countries, during the last three decades, there has been a massive reduction in length of inpatient stays, but the provision of community services is still far from optimal (Becker & Vazquez-Barquero, 2001). The reason for the comparably slow rate of change in service structures is above all the decentralised organisation of the German health-care system. While in the UK the (mental) health service system is organised 'top-down', with the NHS as the institution with extraordinary directive power, the system in Germany can be characterised as 'multicentre'; that is, there is no central organisation with overall responsibility, let alone power, to plan service provision. The German government can provide only a legal framework and define overarching goals. Specific responsibilities are shared between federal authorities, the 16 states, local authorities, and semistatutory organisations.

Although at an organisational level, many of the Enquête's demands have been met, evidence on its effects on outcome was accumulated with great delay and is still sparse. Mental health service research, in Germany, needs to address questions beyond treatment efficacy and aim at providing knowledge useful for clinicians faced with the question of which treatment is best suited for which patient at what time in local service settings.

Academic research which has substantially affected policy

International research and theories also affected the rather isolated German psychiatric community – which had also lost some of its most talented members to emigration before World War II – with some delay. Before the 1970s, evidence from outside was only sporadically taken note of, as in Freudenberg's 1962 review paper, 'Das Anstaltssyndrom und seine Überwindung' ('The institutional syndrome and how to overcome it'), which appeared in the influential German periodical *Nervenarzt*. In this paper, Freudenberg described changes at Netherne Hospital, such as new drugs, open hospital, rehabilitation workshops, paid work, multiprofessional teams and mixed-sex wards, and their effects on outcome.

A milestone was the publication of a book edited by Michael von Cranach and Asmus Finzen (1972), which translated and presented international – mainly UK and US – social psychiatric research, such as the concepts of hospitalism and institutionalism, Goffmann's ideas on the mental hospital as a 'total institution', Wing and Brown's research on institutionalism and schizophrenia, Russell Barton's work on institutional neurosis, and the work of Cumming and Cumming and Leona Bachrach. This led to a system view of deinstitutionalisation. This kind of research had a slow but long-lasting effect on many clinicians that were, on the one hand, convinced that the custodial approach of the German system was harmful to the patients, but, on the other hand, were unsure about how adequately to change provision of services. Here, they found descriptions and systematic evaluations of laborious, but mostly successful efforts toward dehospitalisation, and day-hospital and day-care treatment, as well as rehabilitation and rich conceptual material.

Multidisciplinary outpatient clinics

'Institutsambulanzen', that is, multidisciplinary outpatient clinics, have a pivotal place in the German psychiatric service system, since, although the number of office-based psychiatrists is high, they are often ill-prepared to treat the severely and/or chronically mentally ill (Eikelmann, 1998). Above all, these clinics provide continuity of care for patients with the highest level of care needs just after discharge, via multiprofessional teams (psychiatrists, psychologists and social workers). Consequently, multidisciplinary outpatient clinics are confronted with difficult-to-treat and often severely impaired patients – most with diagnoses of schizophrenia, major depression and severe personality disorder (Spengler, 2003).

The widespread introduction of multidisciplinary outpatient clinics ('Institutsambulanzen') at psychiatric hospitals started in the mid-1970s (Spengler, 1991). In 1988, already 40 of 115 general psychiatric hospitals provided an outpatient treatment service, and today there is hardly an inpatient care institution which does not offer this service; it is estimated that, in 2001, almost 175,000 people with mental illness were treated in such multidisciplinary outpatient clinics (Spengler, 2003). About 21% of all schizophrenic patients are treated in these services (Besthehorn et al, 1999). In the year 2000, federal legislation created the framework for setting up such multidisciplinary outpatient clinics also at general hospital psychiatric units.

The work of the Institutsambulanzen is in some ways comparable to community mental health teams in other countries, although the level of inpatient/outpatient service integration is limited. Unfortunately, evidence on the quality and outcome of patients treated in Institutsambulanzen has not been collected until now. Thus, the results of the introduction of a documentation system for all outpatient clinics in Bavaria (Welschehold & Berger, 2002) are eagerly awaited.

Case study of 'non-academic' evidence which has affected policy

Before the Enquête, staffing indices in psychiatric hospitals were defined solely as average medical and nursing staff numbers per bed, ignoring patients' severity of illness and needs. This regulation provided little incentive to hospitals to discharge long-stay patients who needed little care but – through fixed per diem funding – constituted a constant source of income. On the basis of three groups of patients in adult psychiatry and six subgroups according to needs, the federal staffing directive, for inpatient and day care, enacted in 1990, recommended 18 staff resource allocation groups (Kunze & Kaltenbach, 2003). This directive served as a binding standard for health insurers and hospital management committees. As a result, between 1990 and 1995, staffing increased by 24% across all professional groups, that is, psychiatrists, psychologists, social worker, occupational therapists and nurses (Aktion Psychisch Kranke, 1998).

Furthermore, the federal staffing directive indirectly contributed to the reduction of psychiatric hospital beds and was an incentive for structural change, since budget cuts were foreseen for psychiatric hospitals that did not fulfil their mandatory share of patient care (in order to avoid selection of 'easy-to-treat' patients). Thus, inpatient treatment was further intensified and oriented more toward treatment rather than long-term care with custodial aspects. This was accentuated by financial pressure in the hospital funding system favouring 'acute care' categories over 'rehabilitation' categories. Consequently, LOS was reduced while admission rates increased; that is, more and more patients in need of intensive aftercare were discharged, and this, in turn, stimulated the implementation of community services such as Institutsambulanzen.

Types of evidence which have low salience for policy

Avenues to care and GP psychiatry

As in other countries, the prevalence of mental disorders in Germany in GP practices (Hausarztpraxen) is high (27%) (Linden et al, 1999), and although GPs care for about 80% of mentally ill patients, there is scepticism as to their qualification to detect and treat adequately mental disorders. For instance, it was found that there is only about 60% agreement between CIDI-based ICD-10 diagnoses and their recognition by the physician (Linden et al, 1996), although recent evidence suggests that recognition rates, at least for major depression, has increased in recent years (from about 50% to 75%) (Wittchen et al, 2000). Still, the failure of GPs to detect less severe disorders is a cause for concern since – compared to chronic somatic diseases – the negative social and medical consequences already of any (and including mild) depression are notable (Kühn et al., 2002).

Moreover, the analysis of avenues to care in Germany is a difficult task, since free choice of doctor is one of the basic principles of the German system; that is, there has always been unrestrained access to specialist care, unlike most other countries, where patients are obliged to visit a GP as a 'gatekeeper' that decides on the referral to a specialist (such as a psychiatrist). Only recently, is evidence on avenues to care in Germany being presented, as by Linden et al (2003), who found that first contact for patients in a gate-keeper system, such as that of the Netherlands, is almost exclusively with the GP (95%), while in the German open access system, this rate is much lower (69%). Still, the relevance of such findings for psychiatric service provision is not obvious, and further research, including not just primary but also secondary care populations, is necessary.

Elsewhere, especially in the UK, research on avenues of care, such as the Goldberg–Huxley model (Goldberg et al, 2001), which suggests five levels of psychiatric morbidity, that is, in the community, for primary care attenders (total and subgroup conspicuous psychiatric morbidity), and in mental illness services (total and hospitalised), has already affected mental health service planning, leading to increased involvement of psychiatrists in primary care and increased follow-up of treatment success (Goldberg, 1999).

Nevertheless, in Germany, the recognition of the importance of data on avenues to care has been delayed by about 20 years, probably also due to the segmentation of psychiatric services not just between outpatient and inpatient sectors, but also within outpatient care, that is, between clinicians responsible for primary (GPs) or secondary (office-based psychiatrists) care. Only in recent years have professional organisations of GPs and psychiatrists started communicating about models of cooperation and curricula for the continuing education of GPs (Richter-Kuhlmann, 2004).

Academic research which has failed to affect policy: case study

Case management

Case management aims at the coordination of an individual's treatment as well as psychosocial needs in the community and is widely implemented in the USA and the UK (Marshall et al, 2004b) but to a lesser extent in Germany. For Germany, one study (Rössler et al, 1992), with 162 patients discharged from psychiatric hospitals who received case management from four social-psychiatric services, found no significant effects of case management on the rate of rehospitalisation nor on length of time in hospital. Research in other countries yielded similar results; that is, while case management increased contact with services, it approximately doubled the rehospitalisation rate and consequently also did not save treatment costs (Marshall et al, 2004b). Thus, one could argue that, even though the decision not to introduce case management into psychiatric care in Germany is in concordance with the evidence, the reason not to introduce it was more likely its limited practical value in a highly defragmented and decentralised German health-care system.

Nevertheless, the need to move toward a needs-led and person-centred approach in psychiatric service provision has been acknowledged by the introduction of an expert commission to improve care planning and staff allocation in community care for patients with chronic mental illness (Kauder & Aktion Psychisch Kranke, 1997). It was recognised that patients living on their own in need of more intensive treatment were too easily admitted to hospital because the system could otherwise not provide adequate care, and, vice versa, that patients too often stayed in the institution even though less intense (or less institutionally focused) treatment would suffice. Thus, as in the UK's 'Care Programme Approach' (Department of Health, 1990), the commission established patient-related and goal-oriented staff time budgets to be used by different providers of community mental health care covering various treatment needs including social care, general health care, self-care at home, social contacts, work and education, as well as specific professional interventions (Kunze et al, 2004). This approach is intended as an incentive to the different agencies to focus on patient needs rather than on the provider organisation's interests and to become more cooperative and flexible. Unfortunately, due to lack of funding, the feasibility and effects of these guidelines has not been evaluated so far.

Sociotherapy

Originating from a model project, a programme to implement and evaluate 'sociotherapy' was developed (Melchinger & Giovelli, 1999). Sociotherapy is a needs-oriented intervention aiming at the rehabilitation of mentally ill people and could be seen as an attempt to realise case management under the conditions of the German psychiatric service system. Treatment goals include improvement of basic skills (nutrition, personal hygiene, finances, work), social skills, utilisation of health service system, and coping with chronic psychiatric and somatic illness. The evaluation study (N = 186) showed that sociotherapy in outpatient/community settings is feasible and effective; that is, subjects showed improved social competence and global functioning, and a reduction of psychosocial distress, relapse and treatment costs. Thus, in 2000, a law was passed requiring the public health insurance companies to offer outpatient sociotherapy throughout Germany as a reimbursable treatment option. Nevertheless, until now, its implementation failed; that is, office-based clinicians and community-based psychiatric services hardly applied it, supposedly because of peculiarities of financing in the German health system. This must be seen against the background of a total budget agreed upon between the health insurance companies and provider agencies. Ironically, if sociotherapy were successful in reducing readmissions, it could lead to underfunding in the inpatient care segment, and additional costs would have to be covered (intervention plus loss of inpatient funding due to underutilisation). Since no agreement was reached as to the financing of outpatient sociotherapy, reimbursement policy was restricted drastically, and thus implementation failed almost entirely – much to the disappointment of many researchers and practitioners (Melchinger & Machleidt, 2003), who saw this intervention as a viable change to provide continuity of care.

Conclusions

Psychiatric reform in Germany has led to substantial progress in mental health care. Ideas on social politics and inclusion-oriented discussion (common in Europe during the last quarter of the twentieth century), as well as international (mostly Anglo-American) research evidence on community care, have had a substantial impact on the reform process. Academic research within the country, however, has had a limited impact on the reform process. Some major initiatives in the political and administrative sphere have left a mark on the reshaping of mental health services. There is still a lack of integration in the psychiatric care system, but funding levels have been relatively high, and a broad range of services is being provided. On the whole, the German case study underlines the role of broad cultural trends, political consensus and enlisting international trends in health service research in reshaping mental health care planning and management. Some serious attempts at 'mapping' services (Enquête, expert commission), combined with professional, political and administrative consensus (psychiatric staffing directive), local enthusiasm and flexible service models across the country, have contributed to a rich system of services with sufficient similarity across regions. Reform is local and regional, but the broad lines of the process have been national (and close to the general trend across Europe).

Chapter 15

Influencing policy in Italy

Lorenzo Burti

Introduction

On the night of 7 January 1610, from his university location in Padua, Galileo Galilei aimed his home-made telescope at Jupiter and observed three nearby brilliant stars on a line parallel to the ecliptic.[1] The following nights, he was surprised to note that the three stars had swiftly changed their positions with respect to Jupiter and to one another: it became clear that they were not background stars, but natural satellites orbiting Jupiter. On 8 March, these findings had already been published in the *Sidereus Nuncius,* and provided empirical evidence that Copernicus was right.

Every schoolchild knows what happened next: scientific method had to strive long and hard to become accepted as a sophisticated form of evidence and meanwhile it almost doomed its own inventor. The ingredients of a dramatic clash of doctrines were all present: a momentous scientific revolution was marching against a universal view of the world that had defied the centuries and could count on the full support of an undisputed religion, which, in turn, had an equally undisputed influence on the state. The times as well were the least propitious: the conflict between the Reformation and the Catholic Counter-Reformation was harsh and contributed to increase the power of the Inquisition, a permanent institution in the Roman Catholic Church charged with the eradication of heresy, supervised by a group of consultants, the Holy Office. In 1616, these consultants condemned Copernicus's theory as heretical and in 1633 tried Galileo for supporting it; he saved his life but had to remain under house arrest until his death in 1642.

During the following centuries, science has brought unfathomable changes to human life and the environment, both physical and cultural, yet mankind has remained the same biologically and, perhaps, psychologically. Therefore, we may expect a mixture of primitive and novel attitudes to empirical evidence, especially when it implies important or even crucial individual and communal decisions.

1 The plane of planets' orbits.

Following the editors' guidelines to the authors of this volume, I restricted the scope of this enquiry to my own country, Italy, and in order to collect themes and opinions on this topic, I interviewed persons both in academic and non-academic psychiatry. Here are the resulting facts and opinions.

The Italian deinstitutionalisation movement and the psychiatric reform law: a case of non-academic evidence with high salience for policy

By far, the most important initiative in mental health policy in Italy took place in 1978, when a radical, nationwide reform of the whole psychiatric delivery system was enacted. By looking at that momentous initiative, one may possibly find some hints on the kind of *evidence* that was instrumental in setting it in motion. This is, somehow, a reverse way to try to answer the initial question: what is the relationship between evidence and mental health policy making in Italy?

When a formerly academic psychiatrist with a phenomenological orientation, Franco Basaglia, and his colleagues took over the state hospital of Gorizia, a small city in northeastern Italy, in 1961, they were profoundly shocked by the terrible conditions of the inmates. It was the *direct evidence* of these inhumane conditions that struck those workers and convinced them of the need for a concrete change. They published a book that soon became a bestseller (Basaglia, 1968) and brought this kind of evidence to a wide audience, including professionals, politicians and lay persons. The personal experience of such evidence is well described by Basaglia: 'I got my degree 25 years ago, but I understood what my duty was as a psychiatrist when I was assigned to this mental hospital as superintendent' (p. 266).

One of the key persons I consulted defined this kind of evidence as one derived from ethics, or indignation at the inhumane conditions of the mental hospital. However, while those professionals, the founders of the movement, were struck by this kind of evidence, whatever its definition may be, and were initially determined to embark on a completely different, irrevocable course, they needed another set of evidence to move on concrete grounds. It was a turning point that made them effective in remodelling the whole system instead of remaining confined to philosophical or small-scale antipsychiatry, as occurred to others elsewhere. They capitalised on Maxwell Jones' (1953) work with the therapeutic community in Scotland to rearrange the mental hospital of Gorizia and transform it into a therapeutic community *Italian style*. This same group of professionals had to provide evidence that would attract laypersons and politicians, that is, successful improvement of human conditions within the hospital (ethical evidence, as it was termed above) and successful discharge of inmates to the community (clinical evidence). Recognition among the public and the support of political, especially left-wing, parties were instrumental in transforming Basaglia's original initiative into a movement that eventually resulted in the nationwide psychiatric reform of 1978, whose principles were the following:

- A ban on all admissions to mental hospitals. Readmissions were also banned, but existing inpatients were not discharged en masse and abandoned in the community: prevention of institutionalisation rather than deinstitutionalisation was the principal aim of the reform.
- The development of community-based services in charge of all kinds of psychiatric interventions for the adult population.
- The use of voluntary and involuntary hospitalisations only in urgent situations, when community treatment has already been applied in vain. Hospitalisation may occur only in small general-hospital units (15 beds maximum). Both inpatient and outpatient services must cooperate conjointly for prevention and rehabilitation, besides providing integrated treatment.

The initial progress of the reform was slow and patchy, in view of the lack of funds and staffing, with delays in the development of community alternative services and consequent dissatisfaction. Such dissatisfaction fed the opposition, and soon proposals to repeal the reform were brought to the parliament. However, these same proposals were deferred and eventually dropped for economic reasons: no funds were available to establish the new mental hospitals proposed by the opponents of the reform. Finally, in the mid-1990s, a comprehensive network of community, residential and hospital-based services all over the nation became a reality. This made it possible for the services to follow up in the community practically *all psychotic* people, including those severely ill who used to become long-term mental hospital inmates, offering *continuity of care* on a regular basis. The commitment to serve primarily the most severe cases in the community is common practice in the Italian mental health system. At the same time, services provide increasing attention to patients with milder conditions and to new types of psychiatric discomfort both directly, by an increasing offer of outpatient interventions, and through integration with primary health care. In 1994, a national mental health plan was eventually passed that confirmed and integrated the reform by defining standards to operate and finance the services. The plan prescribed local umbrella administrative organisations, departments of mental health (DMH), to integrate all the services that had to be provided for a given population of about 150,000. The following services were prescribed in each catchment area: a community mental health centre (CMHC) in charge of outpatient care and serving as hospital gatekeeping; a general hospital psychiatric ward (GHPW) with one bed per 10,000 population; semiresidential facilities (day hospitals and day centres), with one bed per 10,000 population; residential facilities with at least one bed per 10,000 population; and group homes. Other plans were issued in the following years, stressing the better integration of health and human services. The termination of state hospitals was accomplished in 1998, when a Fiscal *law* mandated their closure by definitely cutting the funds for their maintenance. It is ironic that the economic recession and a consequential new concern for health costs accomplished a process that had been initiated decades before, for completely different reasons. Economy provides a most effective form of evidence!

All in all, one may say that the 1978 reform has been pragmatically success-ful in demonstrating that it is possible to replace the mental hospital with alternative services. However, the initial radical spirit and attitudes that guided the Italian deinstitutionalisation movement of the 1960s had to come to terms with the medical model since the times of the reform itself. In spite of its revolutionary characteristics, Law 180 represented a compro-mise between two worlds: radical psychiatry and the medical establishment. General hospital units have adopted the medical model *tout court,* and are generally locked facilities where the use of physical restraints is decided by the doctor on duty; although the Founders of deinstitutionalisation had *started* their work by banning locked wards and restraints as a humanitarian, clini-cal, ideological and political choice. Community services are also directed by medical doctors and basically rely on paramedical staff. Since the early reports of the mid-1980s, a considerable proportion of them use approaches based on a less than ideal balance between medication and psychosocial interventions (Mosher and Burti, 1994).

It is routine to express regret that the implementation of the Italian reform, to date, has not been adequately studied, but this is not really true (Burti, 2001). It was certainly true in the beginning and for several years to come. The movement was generally unable to provide convincing evidence to a number of domestic and international scientists that, for years, remained generally sceptical and critical. Only decades later, with the complete imple-mentation and dissemination of community-based services and relevant good research, was the reform awarded positive appraisal by both the scientific community and official organisations (World Health Organisation, 2001).

What one may learn from the Italian mental health reform law of 1978 is that major policies, especially momentous, nationwide ones, arise because of changes in public opinion, concomitant acknowledgement of a problem as urgent and cultural, and political pressure in favour of reform. Only later, a lack of more sound evidence, including the empirical kind, is perceived as a serious lack when the initial enthusiasm gives way to a more thoughtful attitude to change already accomplished, and the dissatisfied demand facts rather than values and beliefs. In an ideal world, societal awareness, research, policy making and practice go hand in hand for the best possible timing and integration. Of course, Italy is not an ideal world. Its psychiatric reform was hampered by delays and moved on a rough path, but it was eventually satis-factorily implemented and still stands as a unique example of the application of a radical, nationwide mental health policy. The game is not over, yet: after the political success of the Right in 2001, new proposals to repeal or modify the 1978 reform were discussed. A special commission worked hard to prepare a combined proposal aimed at facilitating involuntary admissions and establishing hospital-based departments for medium and long-stay patients. After long debate, based on old and new forms of evidence brought forward by rival factions, the proposal was eventually dropped, basically for economic reasons. Recently (winter 2005–2006), the Ministry of Health announced that a new proposal is on the drawing board, but the climate of political uncertainty preceding the national elections of next April is likely to slow-down the initiative.

Academic research succeeds in affecting policy: the Italian medication inventory case

In 1993–4, a national commission of experts was established to revise the medication inventory of the Italian national health service, that is, the Italian national formulary. The commission based its selection on available evidence of efficacy. Listed drugs were subdivided into three classes according to their relevance for treatment and the corresponding ranks of reimbursement by the health service: class A preparations (those for life-threatening or chronic illness) almost completely free of charge; class B, 50% paid for by the patient; and class C, non-reimbursable. Since resistance to the initiative was expected, the commission was given extraordinary decision power without the involvement of all stakeholders: a choice that made the reform faster but laid the ground for future, still unresolved disputes. Such revision was long overdue, since the previous formulary was hopelessly redundant and included *many* ineffective or possibly dangerous drugs. Nevertheless, years of stagnation had passed while new drugs were accumulated. However, it was a need for cost reduction that set the initiative in motion. Therefore, the lesson we may learn from this process is that *economic* evidence played a basic role in launching the policy, while *scientific evidence* provided directions to implement it. In addition, *cost-effectiveness* was an important aspect of the kind of evidence considered. The operation was successful: by *considerably* decreasing the number of drugs in class B (partially reimbursable), while judiciously increasing the number of drugs in class A (fully reimbursable), both considerable savings were made (almost 30% of total expenses between 1992 and 1994), and patients with severe or chronic illness had access to medication they needed practically for free (Garattini, 1995). The formulary has been annually reviewed ever since.

As to what concerns mental health, the impact on psychopharmacology of the initial revision and of all subsequent ones was substantial. Interestingly, the debate has grown hotter in recent years about second-generation psychotropic drugs. The commission, basing its judgement on evidence derived from comparative clinical trials, repeatedly rejected the inclusion of selective serotonin-release inhibitors (SSRIs) and second-generation antipsychotics in class A preparations. Atypical antipsychotics are still subject to strict criteria of reimbursement based on registered indications: a decision that is overtly challenged by current clinical practice, the steep rise in their consumption that boosts costs, and criticism among professionals and some researchers. Therefore, on the one hand, this represents a successful example of evidence, based on solid experimental data, influencing medical (and, consequently, mental health) policies. On the other hand, this same example effectively represents the complexities of relationships between scientific evidence, other kinds of evidence, costs and professional practice. In other words, this same example illustrates a case of academic research that has actually *succeeded* in affecting policies, but *may fail* to affect practice in the long run, since the use of new antipsychotics is growing exponentially, in spite of the still poor empirical evidence of their superiority to traditional ones and the emerging evidence of their side effects. Curiously, also this important reforming initiative was initially driven by a cultural shift in public opinion after a scandal of corruption in drug registration (Garattini, 1995).

The Di Bella case: scientific evidence wins at last, but at what price!

A few years ago, Italy set the stage for a deplorable, but sociologically interesting, national medical case. Although it does not pertain to psychiatry, but to oncology, I decided to describe it here as a case study because its kaleidoscopic, even grotesque, facets dramatically illustrate what a weird mixture of primitive gullibility and cutting-edge science makes up our contemporary social attitudes to medicine and health. The case was systematically studied, and reports were published in the international literature (Simini, 1998; Ramuzzi and Schieppati, 1999).

In 1997, Luigi Di Bella, an 85-year-old Italian physiologist, who had been treating cancer patients with a mixture of somatostatin, vitamins, melatonin and other drugs, announced unsupported claims of cures by the thousands without the side effects of orthodox antineoplastic treatment. Di Bella received great media coverage when his patients formed an association to support the new treatment and submitted applications for reimbursement (up to US$5000 per patient per month: the *money factor* again) from the national health service. The Minister of Health rejected the application and prohibited the use of Di Bella's treatment in public medical facilities. This aroused unparalleled denunciations by the public, the media and the right-wing political opposition of the leftist ruling government. Eventually, the Minister of Health had disgracefully to surrender to the mob, after a court order, and to devise phase II trials of Di Bella's treatment regimen subsidised by public funds, under the supervision of an international board of specialists. Meanwhile, patients had their hopes raised by the media and flocked to receive the new treatment. Applicants (7000) far outnumbered the slots available for the trials; 964 patients were eventually enrolled, while somatostatins and the other treatment drugs were stolen, smuggled and sold on the black market. Hysteria swept the nation, while doctors and experts who called for caution were marginalised and ridiculed.

The story ended as one may anticipate: the trials showed that Di Bella's treatment does not cure cancer and is not without side effects, as originally maintained: of 386 patients with a 3-month follow-up, none showed complete remission, three showed partial remission, 12% had stable disease, 52% progressed and 25% died. Some 40% of patients suffered side effects, 26% of a severe degree (Italian study group for the Di Bella multitherapy trials, 1999). Research costs amounted to US$20 million, an unusually generous funding for a nation always accused of stinginess by Italian researchers and their institutions.

In order to study such a disconcerting phenomenon that aroused dangerous feelings of uncertainty and confusion among the patients and their families, the physicians and the public, a group of oncologists collected the opinions of more than 1000 patients with an ad hoc questionnaire (Passalacqua et al, 1999). The questionnaire was distributed in 13 oncology centres across the nation when the public controversy was at its climax, but before the beginning of the trials. Results showed that 85% of respondents knew about the Di Bella treatment, the greatest majority having derived the information from the media, and only 5% from a doctor. Just 1% believed the treatment was ineffective, 42% thought it was effective and 57% were uncertain. In addition, 53% declared their hopes had increased, and 63% that they would try unproven treatments in the hope of a cure. The authors conclude by emphasising the role of the media in feeding patients' tendency to believe in promises that increase hope, the incapacity of the scientific community to educate the general public, and the lack of doctor–patient communications. All in all, it seems that the choice of treatment depends more on patients' trust in their doctors than on scientific grounds. Old Di Bella, who was presented as ostracised by the medical establishment, but offered hope, was perceived as *the* doctor who can be trusted.

Scientific evidence with low salience: the case of alternatives to hospitalisation

One key person I interviewed asserted that *no* academic research *ever* had an impact on Italian mental health policies. While such a pessimistic conclusion sounds extreme, it has a number of supporters among Italian researchers who share a disheartened attitude to funding and careers in the scientific arena in general, and in medicine in particular, in Italy.

A convenient example of empirical evidence that, with a few exceptions mentioned below, had almost no salience in Continental Europe, including Italy, is the use of alternatives to acute hospitalisation and low-dose or no neuroleptic treatment of newly identified psychotic persons. The Soteria project (Bola & Mosher, 2003) compared an alternative psychosocial treatment of early-episode, schizophrenia-spectrum psychosis in a home-like residential community with the standard, hospital-based one as control. Experimental subjects received no antipsychotic medication, or very low doses, while 100% of control subjects received high doses of antipsychotic medication. The original projects have been replicated both in the USA and in Europe. McAuliffe House, a Washington-based therapeutic community modelled on Soteria, was also the site of a random assignment study to compare alternative treatment with the usual, hospital-based one. Both programmes proved equally effective in terms of symptom reduction, but the alternative cost less (Fenton et al, 1998). The Swiss replication, 'Soteria Bern', which has been in operation for 20 years, had similar results. The outcome of experimental subjects treated in the house with low doses of antipsychotics did as well as those admitted to the hospital and exposed to high doses of drugs. In addition, in the experimental sample, subjects with lower doses seemed to fare better. These studies have confirmed that a properly organised social environment can offer a viable alternative to hospitalisation and virtually eliminate the need for the rapid introduction of drugs into the treatment of acute psychosis. A psychosocial, albeit non-residential, approach to treat first-episode psychosis with minimal antipsychotic regime has had some diffusion in Finland (Lehtinen et al, 2000) and has generated projects elsewhere in Scandinavia (Cullberg et al, 2002), but is far from being implemented to its full potential, as shown by existing empirical research. It is especially intriguing to learn why it was not implemented in Italy, where a substantial network of residential, home-like facilities already exists (de Girolamo & Cozza, 2000) for medium- to long-term stays and could be easily adjusted to admit patients with acute cases. Possible reasons for this are the prevailing medical orientation in the care of acute patients, including early psychotic ones; excessive reliance on standard community care in the prevention of chronic psychosis; and lack of incentives to divert funds from hospitals to alternative, community-based, treatment programmes and facilities. A more general reason has to do with what one can define as *critical mass*. Model programmes, whose success is supported by evidence, have to grow in number and dissemination beyond a critical point to warrant shared recognition, and then become routine services. There must be enough professionals trained by these alternative programmes to seed the model elsewhere and enough converted administrators next door to reassure local ones that the professionals' proposals are practical and feasible.

Concluding remarks

There seem to be universal basic mechanisms between various kinds of evidence and health policies in general, and mental health ones in particular, but their interplay may vary from country to country and from time to time. Recent Italian history shows that cultural, ideological and political evidence has been instrumental in bringing about major changes in mental health policies. Media seem to play an increasing role, especially when emotionally charged decisions are made, while economic reasons maintain a final say. In spite of scholars' wishes and commonplace academic pride, scientific evidence alone is not enough to provide broad-based support for or against an initiative, or science may even be under siege, as the Di Bella case demonstrated. Poor scientific education in Italian primary and secondary schools has been blamed for the little grasp of science by the public (Passalacqua et al, 1999). In any case, this is an area of study badly in need of more extensive empirical investigation on the complex relationships between available knowledge and individual and public decisions on mental health.

Acknowledgements

I am indebted for relevant information and advice to Mario Maj, Loren R. Mosher and Giuseppe Guido Pullia.

Chapter 16

Influencing policy in Sweden

Lars Hansson

Types of evidence with high and low salience for mental health policy

This chapter will make some reflections on different types of influences and evidence that have had an impact on changes in mental health policy in Sweden. It will focus on some factors of importance for the transformation of services toward community-based services as well as changes in the content of services on an intervention level. This task is complicated by the fact that a number of types of evidence and other influences are simultaneously affecting mental health policy in a way which makes it hard to distinguish their specific contribution. Broadly, we might find three hypothetical sources of influences. The first is concerned with the implementation of scientific evidence of efficacy and effectiveness, manifested in the movements of evidence-based medicine and evidence-based care. The second, less clear-cut group of influences stem from what may be labelled 'clinical evidence', which includes the history of personal or local experiences of treating people with mental illness, although not systematically analysed. The third group of factors, which have been growing in importance, are related primarily to ethical or humanitarian views or ideologies of different stakeholders in psychiatric services. Obviously, the development of the user movements is of great importance in this context. However, these influences might be different or vary in strength depending on whether we look at the patient intervention level, local service level or national level. A fourth factor is that these influences also probably differ in importance depending on what aspect of treatment or mental health policy we are looking at.

In comparison to other mental health interventions, the scientific evidence from randomised, controlled studies probably plays a more important role in psychopharmacological treatment, although this evidence is underpinned by the substantial marketing forces from the medical companies. An example of this is the rapid introduction and widespread use of the new atypical antipsychotic drugs. In contrast, the implementation of evidence-based psychosocial interventions during the last decade has not been substantial. A number of research reviews on severe mental illness has shown strong evidence of specific family interventions, social skills training, supported employment and cognitive or cognitive-behavioural therapy as elements of rehabilitation work (Lehman & Steinwachs, 1998; Dickerson, 2000; Crowther et al, 2002; Pharaoh et al, 2002). Based on this evidence, none of these interventions have been systematically implemented in psychiatric services in Sweden. We may find local services which have partially implemented family interventions in terms of patient and family education programmes, often based on a local influence from the users' movements. We may find local services using social skills-training programmes, but the use is scattered, and it is the work of local staff with an interest in developing the quality of services. Supported employment programmes are greatly lacking, and there seem to be no professional or public opinion to support their implementation. Cognitive therapy is to some extent used for people with severe mental illness, which to a great extent is the tribute to the pioneering work of the late Professor Carlo Perris (Svensson, 1999). If we look at system-level case management, this intervention model with a scientifically established efficacy has not been widely used until the last few years; this will be expanded on below. On a national policy level, there is knowledge of the evidence for these interventions. A recently published guideline for treatment and rehabilitation of people with schizophrenia included all these interventions in its guidelines (National Board of Health and Welfare (NBHW), 2003). One striking difference between psychopharmacological and psychosocial interventions is the lack of commercial potential in the latter. If there was profit in selling family interventions or social skills training, might the picture be radically different. This introduces the role of the market economy and the influence of profit-making opportunities as an important and salient factor for the actual implementation and use of different interventions, which might strongly contrast with mental health policy documents and official policies.

Case study of academic research which has substantially affected policy

There has been a vast and increasing number of international intervention studies demonstrating the efficacy and effectiveness of various models of case management, and the assertive community treatment model in particular. This has not been the incentive for an implementation of case management services in Sweden. A few local pilot services (Aberg-Wistedt et al, 1995) have been set up, but nothing more on a large scale happened until the last few years. What is, then, the background of this radical change?

Since the 1960s, the transition of the psychiatric services has followed a pattern similar to other western countries. One outcome of this was the introduction of sectorised psychiatric services as a national policy, fully implemented in the mid-1980s. This development will be expanded on in the next section of this chapter. However, in Sweden, as well as in other countries, the deinstitutionalisation process has been linked to evidence that care and support for people with severe mental illness was not adequate in the new community-based services. A parliamentary commission of 1992, the Committee on Psychiatric Care, concluded that the psychiatric and social services for people with a severe mental illness in a number of ways were still largely inadequate and not provided in a satisfactory manner (Ministry of Health and Social Welfare, 1992). The parliamentary commission resulted in a mental health care reform, which went into effect in 1995. The reform was directed toward individuals suffering from severe and long-standing mental illness. As part of this reform, pilot services testing case management were introduced. Ten services throughout the country were implemented and financed by state grants. These services were to be in operation during a 3-year period and were subject to an evaluation, and an academic doctoral thesis. Patient outcome was investigated with regard to changes in use of services, needs of care, psychosocial functioning, social network, psychopathology, quality of life, and satisfaction with the case-management service. The evaluation also included an analysis of the content of the case managers' work with regard to type of interventions and support, and the life domains of the patients involved. The results from an 18-month follow-up showed that there were major reductions in the use of psychiatric inpatient services, and this was corroborated by a randomised, controlled trial performed in conjunction with the main evaluation study. Patients were also highly satisfied with the services, and more satisfied than patients receiving standard care. A reduction in need for care was also identified. This study was published by the NBHW in 1999, as part of the evaluation of the mental health care reform (NBHW, 1999), and in 2000 as a doctoral thesis (Björkman, 2000). Three conditions interacted at this moment to cause a marked change in national policy concerning case management. Beside the academic evidence of effectiveness of case management as implemented in the 10 pilot services, there was an influence from the users' movement, which strongly promoted the implementation of case management. There was also a political willingness and readiness by the government to implement case management on a national level. The political readiness was linked to financial support in terms of state subsidies to case-management services. In the year 2000, the Ministry of Health and Social Affairs decided to grant money for this purpose (NBHW, 2000). Case management were to be implemented in all the 300 Swedish municipalities, under the responsibility of the local social services. From the year 2001, the sum of around 9 million euros per year was allocated for this purpose. This has enabled a major change in implementation of case management in Sweden. At the end of 2003, around 100 case-management services has been implemented in 235 (80%) municipalities. Around 300 case managers have been employed, and during the 3 years of operation, around 4000 clients have been in contact with these services (NBHW, 2003).

We must admit that several decades of scientific evidence of the effectiveness of case management based on international studies did not have any influence on mental health policy in this respect in Sweden. Then a single Swedish study of 10 pilot services in a short period of time enabled the introduction of case management on a national scale. This would of course never have happened if, at the same time, there had not been strong ethical/ humanitarian-based support for this development from the users' movement, or if, in the aftermath of the mental health reform, there had not been a political and financial readiness to support the aspects of this reform which had shown a positive outcome.

Case study of non-academic evidence which has substantially affected policy

In Sweden, there has been a process of deinstitutionalisation, similar to that in all other western countries, although the pace has varied in different countries. In 1967, there were nearly five psychiatric hospital beds per 1000 inhabitants, and alternative psychiatric treatment in ambulant or community-based services was very rare. In 1992, around 1.4 beds per 1000 inhabitants were available, and the figure for 2002 is 0.6 beds per 1000 inhabitants. During the late 1960s, some pioneer services had developed, along with trial day-care wards and independent day hospitals for psychiatric care. A number of the principles guiding this general development, such as normalisation, integration, prevention, accessibility and availability of care, were subsumed under the principles of sectorisation. During the 1970s and 1980s, a number of policy documents were published by the NBHW to guide the progression from hospital-based services toward community-based care.

A policy document of the Swedish NBHW published in 1973 aimed to reinforce outpatient services and reduce hospitalisation for the mentally ill (NBHW, 1973). An enlargement of the professional composition of outpatient services was also encouraged. Psychiatric nurses, psychologists and professionals from social services were included in the teams. Liaison psychiatry and preventive measures were to be included in addition to regular psychiatric treatment in wards or outpatient services. These services were to be situated in residential areas within the catchment area. Sectorised psychiatric services, with one comprehensive organisation responsible for all in- and outpatient care within a delimited catchment area, were established throughout Sweden between 1975 and 1985. At the end of this period, 135 psychiatric sectorised services had been established according to the principles of the NBHW. Although this development was outlined in several policy documents in the early 1970s, the implementation of sectorised services took around 15 years. Furthermore, the impetus for this development was not Swedish academic research or other scientific studies. Instead, the policy documents were based on the same mixture of ideological, humanitarian and financial arguments as in the rest of the western world, although the US community mental health centre movement was a primary source of inspiration. One recurring theme in these policy documents, which are still today under debate, was how to define the distribution of responsibility for care and support between the psychiatric services and the local social services. During the process of implementation, sectorisation was not the subject of a particularly intense scientific interest, although it had a vast impact on the organisation and content of the psychiatric services. The results of the few studies performed were also rather discouraging and generally not supportive of the further development of sectorised services. One pioneer service in Luleå, a town in northern Sweden, where a catchment area-based outpatient service had been established, was especially criticised. According to the researchers, this service had not replaced the old hospital-based service but had, rather, attracted a new group of socially privileged persons with mental illness suitable for psychotherapeutic treatment (Eliasson & Nygren, 1981, 1982).

The first comprehensive psychiatric service organised according to the principles of sectorisation was the so called Nacka project. The catchment area for this service was one of the suburbs of Stockholm, with a population of around 70,000. This service became a model service for the later expansion of sectorised services in Sweden. Evaluations of this service showed a reduction in use of inpatient services and a marked increase in outpatient services (Spri, 1978), which was probably a reflection of a redistribution of resource allocation. A later study of the Nacka project showed that people with severe mental illness, such as schizophrenia, in a number of respects did not receive satisfactory support and treatment, primarily social support (Stefansson & Cullberg, 1986; Stefansson et al, 1990).

In the mid-1980s, another sectorised service in Stockholm was the subject of an academic thesis (Lindholm, 1983). This was a matched control study with a 1-year follow-up, which showed no differences between control and experimental catchment areas with regard to use of inpatient services. Experimental patients used more outpatient services and were less satisfied with inpatient care. No cost differences between experimental and control conditions were detected.

Despite some scientific evidence of drawbacks and inferiority of the new sectorised psychiatric services, sectorisation was national policy in 1985 and onward, although, in recent years, we have seen development from general sectorised services toward more specialised, non-catchment area-based services. This shows that other influences and forces were given a higher priority. Although no uniform picture of these influences exists, a major influence has been the steady stream of policy documents from the NBHW, which was integrating all the influences we have seen in this perspective on the international scene (Hansson, 1996, 2001).

Chapter 17

Influencing policy in the United States

John S. Lyons and Whitney P. Witt

Introduction

While discussions of evidence-based practices are a predominant trend in the USA, mental health policy can not yet be characterised as data-driven. However, over the past decade, there have been increases in the translation of such research into mental health policy at the federal, state and local levels. Part of that progress has come from a greater understanding by researchers of the kind of information that policy makers can use and from a greater trust among policy makers in the relevance, accuracy and utility of empirical data.

Characteristics of research that has high policy salience

There are three classes of empirical data that appear to have particular salience for mental health policy making in the USA at present. The first class is the randomised clinical trial (RCT). These data mimic the research that drives the introduction of new medications through the Federal Drug Administration, albeit no such federal authority exists for identifying and certifying effective psychosocial interventions. Generally speaking, the accepted criterion for credibility of data from RCTs has been the presence of multiple studies completed by different research groups in different locales. Examples of treatment approaches whose dissemination and implementation have been enhanced through the publication of multiple and diverse RCTs include assertive community treatment (ACT) (Drake et al, 2000; Mueser et al, 2003) and multisystemic treatment (MST) (Henggeler et al, 1997). Generally, these studies begin as academic research, often with federal funding from the National Institute of Mental Health (NIMH), the National Institute on Alcohol Abuse and Alcoholism (NIAAA), the National Institute on Drug Abuse (NIDA) or the Substance Abuse and Mental Health Service Administration (SAMHSA). The results of the RCTs are generally published in widely read research journals, and those publications are used essentially to 'advertise' the availability of a treatment that works. Following such publication, some form of enterprise is created by the original researchers to support the dissemination of the treatment product.

The second class of data that has demonstrated policy relevance and impact is the carefully designed and completed epidemiological study that can be generalised nationally. The classic example of this type of study is the epidemiological catchment area (ECA) study (Robins & Regier, 1991), which will be discussed in detail later. However, other national studies of the epidemiology of service need, access and use have a policy impact. These studies share a common attention to careful sampling to ensure meaningful generalisations.

The third class of data that has demonstrated its utility in informing the policy programme is individualised research that has addressed specific policy-relevant questions by methods developed within the framework of outcomes-management approaches. These studies are nearly always commissioned by the individuals in control of the policy-making process, and, as such, results from these studies are less accessible to wider audiences, unless sharing the findings is in the best interest of the policy process. Thus, this approach is generally funded internally with minimal incentive for dissemination outside the immediate policy-making group. Sometimes these studies are performed by academic researchers; however, just as often, they are conducted by policy 'think-tank' groups or consultants. Generally, they are accomplished by states, counties, or municipalities. A national study of this type would likely be too burdensome and expensive. The time frames for this type of research are much shorter, as they must fall within the US political cycle. All state governors serve 4-year terms. Often, the first year is involved in establishing or re-establishing staff. The last year is spent running for re-election. That leaves a 2-year window for substantive policy work; thus, the time window for the application of data to policy making is short.

Case study of academic research which has had substantial impact on mental health policy in the USA

The ECA study (Robins & Regier, 1991) and the US National Comorbidity Study (NCS) (Kessler et al, 1994) are arguably the two most important pieces of academic mental health epidemiology and services research to date. This iterative research has had a substantial impact on US mental health policy in several important ways; it characterises the burden of mental illness and helps identify and treat individuals with mental health problems.

Prevalence

In 1978, the report of the President's Commission on Mental Health and Illness identified a need for population-based data on the prevalence of mental illness. At the time, no diagnostic instrument existed to measure population-based prevalence. In response to this paucity of an instrument, the NIMH funded the development of the Diagnostic Interview Schedule (DIS) (Robins et al, 1981). The DIS was first fielded in the ECA, a ground-breaking study of more than 20,000 respondents in five areas across the USA.

Findings from the ECA suggested that approximately 16% of the respondents had a mental health or addiction disorder over a 1-month period, and 28% reported a disorder over 1 year (Regier et al, 1993). This study was a milestone in mental health services research, because the results better characterised the magnitude of the problem of mental illness and resources required to address the need for mental health services.

Nationally representative data

Ten years after the ECA, the NIMH funded the NCS to address some of the methodological shortcomings of prior research (Kessler et al, 1997). The methodological advances of the NCS, specifically the sampling and measurement, made the findings from this research especially policy relevant. First, the NCS is the only nationally representative survey documenting the prevalence of mental health disorders and associated utilisation of services. This collaborative study was based on a national household sample of 8098 respondents aged 15–54. Second, the NCS used a modified version of the Composite International Diagnostic Interview (CIDI), a structured psychiatric diagnostic survey, to measure the prevalence of mental health disorders. The UM-CIDI asked additional symptom questions to allow diagnoses based on the *Diagnostic and Statistical Manual of Mental Disorders* (3rd edition, revised) (DSM-III-R) and the *International Statistical Classification of Diseases and Related Health Problems* (10th revision) (ICD-10). This contrasted with the DIS, which could only map onto the DSM-III-R. This difference allowed important cross-cultural comparisons (Kessler et al, 1997).

Building on the ECA, the NCS offered important new information about the prevalence and risk factors for psychiatric disorders. Results from the NCS indicated that the most frequent disorders in the USA included major depressive episode, alcohol dependence, social phobia and simple phobia. Almost half of respondents reported at least one lifetime disorder, and 29% had at least one disorder over the past year. For individuals with a lifetime disorder, less than 40% ever received professional treatment. In addition, less than 20% of respondents who reported a recent mental health disorder had received treatment over the last year (Kessler et al, 1997). Most of the lifetime disorders were comorbid disorders (Kessler et al, 1994), indicating opportunities to prevent secondary conditions.

The NCS also provided, for the first time, national estimates of unmet need for mental health care. In fact, for individuals with any lifetime disorder, about 40% ever received any professional treatment. In addition, less than

20% of respondents who reported a recent mental health disorder had received any treatment over the last year.

Over the last several decades, the ECA and the NCS have informed mental health policy by providing critical information about the disparities, burden and undertreatment of disorders in the USA. These results have been used for better allocatation of research and programmatic funding, further improvement of efforts at identification and prevention, and ensuring the quality of treatment of mental health disorders among vulnerable populations (van der Feltz-Cornelis et al, 1997; Lyons et al, 1998).

A case study of a non-academic project that has had substantial impact on mental health policy in the USA

The best examples of non-academic empirical studies that have had substantial policy impact are exemplars of the second class of projects mentioned earlier. This class of research is evaluative in nature and does not rise to the methodological level of RCTs or what is traditionally considered to be research in behavioural sciences. That does not mean, however, that the findings are not reliable or valid. Rather, the research model is field research, which capitalises on those quasi-experimental methods that have been developed within the framework of what is generally called outcomes management.

As mentioned previously, these projects often are tailored for very specific audiences and, therefore, are less widely known than their academically based counterparts. Therefore, we selected our case example from projects we have directly participated in, not because they are necessarily the best examples, but because they were ones with which we were intimately familiar. We have selected the first in a series of projects involving the reform of child serving systems (Olin & Mednick, 1996), because it builds a methodological approach that has led to rather different policy decisions in various applications (Lyons, 2004). This first project involved a reinvestment strategy while the second involved a new investment strategy.

Community reinvestment strategy

The project was a community reinvestment project in the Illinois Department of Children and Family Services (IDCFS). In the mid-1990s, the DCFS had a budget of $1.5 billion, of which $450 million was spent on various forms of behavioural health care. While this is not an overall resource issue, the problem was that about 80% of these funds were tied up in long-term residential treatment and psychiatric hospitalisation. This left too few resources for wards of the state living in foster homes or homes of relatives, where the unmet need is the highest (Burns et al, 2004). At the time, the state was in a budget crisis, and the new director of the DCFS could not even be confirmed due to negative stories about the agency. Therefore, the only way to fix the problem was a community reinvestment strategy (Olin & Mednick, 1996). The strategy would work only if there were children in residential treatment facilities who did not need to be there and who could be moved safely to community placements.

The initial strategy was to ask residential treatment centres (RTC) to identify children who were candidates for return to the community. This process was a disaster and had to be abandoned, as RTCs identified children that were not being helped rather than children that had stabilised. In one particularly tragic case, a 16-year-old boy was identified as a step-down candidate despite his recent violence and complex psychiatric presentation. He was placed with his grandparents and he murdered them both. Clearly, having residential providers identify which children to remove from their care was not a workable strategy.

At that point, I was invited to become involved in the process and asked to design a decision-support model for determining which children to step down. To accomplish this objective, I met with representatives of many perspectives, including parents, therapists, case managers, teachers and youth, and had focus groups to identify what information people thought should ideally direct decision making about the level and intensity of care. Three dimensions were identified: symptom guide decisions about the nature of treatment, risk behaviour guide decisions about the setting and intensity of treatment, and the capacity of the caregiver to modify the impact of these other characteristics. From this model, the Childhood Severity of Psychiatric Illness (CSPI) was created (Lyons, 1997).

The next step was to complete a needs-based planning study in which a stratified random sample of children currently in residential treatment were reviewed and assessed with the CSPI (Lyons et al, 1998). More than 300 children were assessed, by a retrospective file review method, at two time points: at admission into the placement and for the past 30 days. Analyses of these reviews revealed that 13% of children in the sample had never engaged in significant high-risk behaviours (i.e. suicide, violence, absconding, other delinquent behaviour or sexual aggression). Another 20% had engaged in these behaviours historically, but not in the period prior to the current admission. Thus, about one-third of all admissions into residential treatment did not have any recent concerns about high-risk behaviours. These children would be the best candidates for return to the community and future prevention by placement.

Based on the findings of this study, a decision-support algorithm was created and used for placement review (e.g. managing the front door) and step-down (e.g. managing the back door). Only by controlling both admissions and discharges would it be possible to reduce the number of children in residential treatment. If only admissions are controlled, lengths of stay would be expected to increase. If only discharges are controlled, admissions would be expected to increase. By controlling both, the number of children in residential treatment placements was reduced by one-third within an 18-month time frame, saving the state tens of millions of dollars, which could be reinvested in community-based services. A re-review of a stratified random sample 3 years later demonstrated that the initiative did have the intended effect of preventing children without high needs from being placed in residential treatment centres.

An interesting aspect of this example is that, as one of the side effects of the community reinvestment initiative, a number of residential treatment centres actually closed. Public reforms are often derailed by special interests which might be harmed by the initiative. Residential treatment centre executives and boards can put pressure on governors and legislatures to save their businesses, even if it is not in the best interest of children in the state. This did not happen in this case. In fact, several facilities voluntarily decided either to close their doors or to evolve into agencies that provide more intensive, community-based treatment alternatives. While it is impossible to know why this project went so smoothly, I believe that part of the reason was that, thanks to the outcomes-management approach, which is based on the needs of children in the system, the project always remained about doing the right thing for children. It never became a discussion of who gets the money. The issue was which children need an intensive and expensive treatment and which children do not.

Impact in other states

In the past few years, we have replicated this method, among other projects, to design a bundled rate method for Florida Medicaid, to guide new children's public mental health investments in New York State, to evaluate a special programme for children with psychotic disorders in Illinois, and to design a decision-support strategy for the New Jersey Partnership for children. These projects have led to notable policy shifts. For example, in New York State, despite considerable political pressure to increase the number of residential beds, the study supported the successful new investment of $50 million on an expansion of community-based services.

From the original CSPI work, the 'child and adolescent needs and strengths' approach (Lyons, 2004; Lyons et al, 2004) was created, which is now used in various child-serving systems in 28 US states and several other countries. These applications continue to support system evolution that is directed by reliable data on children and families.

What types of evidence have low salience for mental health policy in the USA?

At present, the majority of behavioural research falls into the category of low salience. The vast bulk of scientific research does not have a great deal of salience in terms of influencing policy. A part of this lack of salience comes from the historical irrelevance of data to the policy process; however, there are some characteristics of research that lead directly to its low relevance.

Investigator-initiated research

First and foremost, research with the primary intent to answer questions of importance to researchers but not to policy makers tends to have little impact. At times, researchers can be somewhat like bodybuilders. Bodybuilders commit an enormous amount of time and focus to perfecting the musculature of their bodies. They compete with each other about the number of 'cuts' in their abdominal muscles. Most of us are not so interested, and at times we look at the focus of bodybuilders as somewhat strange. Similarly, researchers can get tied up with the nuances of research questions that people outside the research enterprise feel is 'counting how many angels can dance on the head of a pin'.

Treatment efficacy studies

Research on the efficacy of specific treatments is critical to understanding the performance and safety of a mental health treatment. These studies are the building blocks for identifying evidence-based treatments. In general, this body of research shows that most mental health disorders are treatable through prescription medications (Berber, 1999) and psychotherapy (Yamagami, 1998; Segal et al, 2002).

However, because of limited generalisability, these studies are of relatively low importance in crafting mental health policy. Efficacy studies typically examine treatment under ideal conditions and are commonly based on RCTs. As these studies maximise internal validity, they do not offer information about whether treatment produces beneficial results in actual clinical practice (Norquest et al, 1999). There is a need to translate findings from efficacy research into community-based practice settings.

The salient policy-relevant questions are related to the effectiveness of mental health treatments in population-based samples. Specifically, more research is needed on the barriers to and quality of treatment – particularly the issues surrounding limited access to care, inadequate dosing of medications and lack of appropriate psychotherapy. This information would help us understand why there are very low rates (only 10%) (Hirschfeld et al, 1997) of effective treatment among those affected.

Convenience samples

Studies that draw solely upon clinical populations or convenience samples should be strongly scrutinised for use in policy making. These studies are systematically biased, since individuals who use health and mental health care are quite different from those who choose not to interface with the system or encounter barriers to care (Berkson, 1946; Jenkins, 2003). While such studies may be helpful in monitoring services, this research has limited external validity in constructing population-based estimates of mental health-care need in the USA.

Mixed substantive and methodological models of effectiveness research

The strengths and limitations of efficacy trials and observational research call for integrating these study designs to improve the quality of effectiveness research. Thus, some researchers have moved to extending the use of RCTs in real-life situations for better understanding of effectiveness, in contrast to purely observational studies, which suffer from limited internal validity (Hotopf et al, 1999; Hotopf, 2002).

The examination of effectiveness on many levels will be another important area for policy formation. There is a need to know whether mental health treatments are feasible and effective on all levels – from the system as a whole, to providers, and patients and their family members.

Case study of a low-salience academic study

One of the lowest impact, large-scale academic studies has been the Collaborative Depression Study (Elkin et al, 1989). In this study, patients were randomly assigned to one of four groups: imipramine, cognitive-behavioural therapy, interpersonal therapy and a check-in placebo intervention that involved a 20-minute supportive contact with a psychiatrist. The authors found no real differences between groups over the course of the study, although the patients treated with imipramine, who were more severely depressed, might have benefited somewhat more than those in the other arms of the study (Elkin et al, 1989).

The following reasons explain why this multimillion dollar, federally funded study had little or no impact on mental health policy besides the fact that it had very limited results:

- The sample inclusion/exclusion ruled out most patients with a coexisting condition, including suicidality and 'need for immediate treatment'. As such, the actual sample bears little resemblance to any sample of patients with major depressive disorder that one might encounter in actual clinical practice.

- The choice of which pharmacotherapy agent to include became rapidly dated. When the study was originally conceptualised, imipramine was the best practice medication. By the time the study was reviewed, funded, implemented and finally published, serotonin reuptake inhibitors had become the pharmacotherapy of choice for depression.
- About one-third of patients in the placebo condition showed a reliable clinical response. This means either that the sample was quite suggestive or that the placebo had an active treatment component imbedded.
- Many patients did not actually finish a full trial of whatever treatment they were assigned.
- The randomisation process failed to stratify on clinical variables that might predict differential response to the treatments. As such, the rules of interpreting these trials prevent the investigators from confidently presenting the findings of secondary analyses that might have added to the information value to the overall study.

In sum, despite the significant financial investment, this study contributed little to the treatment research on depression and less to mental health policy in the USA. Furthermore, it exposed the limitations of large-scale projects that take years to design and implement to study time-sensitive questions.

Conclusion

The USA is moving toward greater use of empirical data, collected through both quantitative and qualitative methods, in guiding mental health policy. The interest in identifying and implementing evidence-based practices is one indicator of this movement. In general, good science informs good policy. However, the timeliness of the science has enormous impact on the relevance of the work to the policy process. For this reason, many have advocated creating total clinical outcome-management platforms that allow for the real-time collection of relevant clinical, demographic and treatment information (Manderscheid, 2001; Lyons, 2004) to balance the need for quality research with the need for timely information.

Part III

Generating high-impact research

Chapter 18

The evidence context in mental health research

Joan Busfield

Introduction

As its title suggests, this volume on mental health services research is concerned with the generation of research evidence and its impact. The papers it contains are broadly of two types. The early chapters outline the details of the various methods utilised in the production of evidence in mental health research. The later chapters examine the influence of mental health research on policy making in several countries and on key groups such as the media and the public. The aim of this chapter is to introduce and apply some sociological ideas that can help to deepen our understanding of the character and impact of mental health services research and the evidence it generates by focusing on some wider questions. Why do certain types of research and certain types of evidence predominate? Why do some types of research have more impact than others? To answer questions like these, we need to consider who is producing the research evidence and the groups to which they belong, along with the group's power, influence and methodological traditions, as well as the social processes that lead others to assign factual status to certain ideas and evidence.

I want to draw on two main sets of sociological ideas to help to understand the production, reception and impact of mental health services research. First, I use insights from Bruno Latour's work on the construction of science to explore the social processes involved in the development of mental health research and in its acceptance and influence. Second, I use the framework provided by Donald Light to identify the key groups involved in such research – in both its generation and use – and to consider issues of power, since the power of these groups, particularly if they act in alliance, affects their capacity to shape the research and its reception, as well as to influence changes in policy and practice.

Theoretical underpinnings

Latour, in his influential text, *Science in Action* (1987), drew on empirical studies of scientists' work in laboratories to examine the tactics they use to develop and support their ideas in the process of what he calls 'fact making'. He argues that fact making is a collective process, and the response of other actors determines whether particular claims start to take on the status of facts.[1] Scientific facts are those ideas that have come to be accepted by the scientific community as supported by good evidence, and are unchallenged, at least for the time being – they are placed in the scientific black box, a box not normally opened until a major challenge is made to the facts because of new evidence.[2] Latour analyses the contests and controversies involved in scientific fact making, the publication of research findings, the use of 'inscription devices' such as graphs and figures to present data and arguments, the use of citation, the struggles between competing researchers, and the crucial building of alliances.[3] Consequently, we can see the collection of data and the way it is presented in research papers as 'strategies of communication' (Porter, 1995) that are vital to scientific fact making: the aim is to convince the audience of the scientific nature of the research and the validity of its claims. Echoing Latour's arguments about inscription devices, Porter argues that numbers, graphs and formulae have taken on a special status in claims about validity and objectivity: quantitative data that are apparently shorn of subjectivity can be readily communicated across the world, and can be trusted in a way that other data cannot. Hence the use of numbers and their power to facilitate fact making. Here I use Latour's approach to help to understand the predominance of particular research methods in mental health research.

Although Latour uses the language of alliances and dynamic struggles in his analysis of the construction of science and pays attention to issues such as resources, he offers no explicit examination of power. Yet, power is an essential component in any analysis of the production of mental health service research and of its influence and impact, as of any research. Here Light's (1995) concept of countervailing powers, first introduced by J.K. Galbraith (1952), is valuable. Countervailing powers are powers that stand in a dynamic relation to one another, the increasing power of one group leading to the possibility of resistance and the reassertion of power by another. The concept is particularly useful in exploring relationships – the struggles and alliances – between a wider range of groups, not just binary relationships.

1　He uses the word 'actor' to refer to things or persons.
2　Latour comments 'The word *black box* is used by cyberneticians whenever a piece of machinery or a set of commands is too complex. In its place they draw a little box about which they need to know nothing but its input and output' (1987, pp. 2–3).
3　An inscription device is 'any set-up, no matter what its size, nature and cost, that provides a visual display of any sort in a scientific text' (1987, p. 68).

Light identifies four major political, social and economic groups involved in health care:

1   the state (governments)
2   the medical profession – in the case of mental health services, mainly the psychiatric profession
3   the medico-industrial complex, that is, the private companies involved in providing health care, health insurance or health-care technologies, such as drugs or medical equipment
4   patients.

Figure 18.1 portrays this framework when applied to the mental health services.
    In the section that follows, I look briefly at each group.

The major countervailing powers

Governments are major actors in relation to mental health services. On the one hand, they grant legal powers to psychiatrists and other medical professionals, such the powers to prescribe and to detain patients compulsorily; they also determine the extent and character of the regulation of mental health services and practice, including the regulation of the pharmaceutical industry. On the other hand, they can have an important role as funders or providers of mental health services and as policy makers, sometimes basing policy on research evidence, sometimes responding to external pressures such as media furores, and sometimes pursuing their own political agendas. They may also fund mental health research either directly or indirectly.

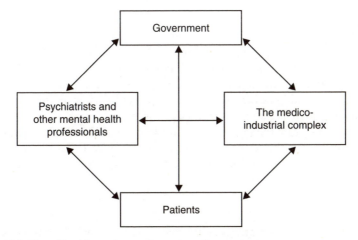

Figure 18.1 Mental health services and countervailing powers.

Psychiatrists have considerable power within the mental health system and still head the hierarchy of mental health professionals, notwithstanding post-war commitments to team working. Their power vis-à-vis governments varies. Historically, the medical profession has had considerable autonomy, but in many countries governments have increasingly sought to control professionals, not least in order to contain costs. As members of the medical profession, psychiatrists have used the natural sciences and a focus on body as the source of claims to expertise and professional power. This has helped to shape their methodological traditions (see below, and the weight given to different types of research evidence. Some, mostly those employed as academics, carry out research; others are primarily clinicians but may be involved in research by providing patients for clinical trials or producing data for a research study. There is, however, a tension between clinical demands, with the need to focus on the individual's interests, and the demands of scientific research, where the focus is on producing generalisations, and treatment may need to be withheld as part of a trial. Other mental health professionals – psychologists, psychotherapists, nurses and social workers – are typically less powerful than psychiatrists. Psychologists, who try to maintain independence from psychiatrists, are the most important vis-à-vis research since they generate research data as well as using it to inform their own work. Psychology's ideal typical research model is the experiment, but psychologists working in clinical contexts use a broader range of research methodologies.

Both voluntary and commercial groups contribute to mental health services, the extent of commercialisation varying across time and place. The same applies to private health-care insurers. In the USA, private providers and insurers, such as the Health Maintenance Organisations (HMOs), are very powerful and can play a similar role to governments in trying to control professional power and keep costs down. The pharmaceutical industry is also a major player in the medico-industrial complex. Drug treatments are an important weapon in doctors' therapeutic armoury and an even more important feature of psychiatric practice. The industry is powerful and is dominated by a small number of leading companies that make the bulk of their profits from patented drugs, including psychotropic medicines (Busfield, 2003).[4] Drugs tend to be heavily marketed, with industry spending on marketing almost as high as on research and development.

Patients constitute the fourth group in Light's model and are generally the least powerful – as the connotations of the term suggests. However, patients may form user groups and through collective action can increase their power,

---

4 Ten companies have over half of the pharmaceutical market measured by sales revenue. One or more psychotropics usually feature in the list of the top 10 'blockbuster' drugs.

in some cases funding research and producing their own publicity, selecting from the evidence that is available those data that support their case.

Drawing on both Latour's and Light's ideas, we can explore how the struggles and alliances between different groups affect the production and impact of mental health research by considering their relation to some of the specific methods used. I focus on three methods, all discussed in more detail in earlier chapters – randomised, controlled trials (RCTs), epidemiological studies and case studies (although the latter cover several types of approach).

RCTs

The RCT nowadays constitutes the reference standard of health service research (see Chapter 6). The method, first developed by doctors and statisticians, is squarely grounded in the experimental tradition of the natural sciences, sciences fundamental to medicine's claims to expertise. The RCT has two marked quantitative features: the statistical randomisation in the selection of treatment and control groups, which allows somewhat smaller samples to be used; and the calculation of statistical significance of the findings generated – both features that undoubtedly contribute to the trust often placed in the findings, even though there are important ethical and methodological problems in carrying out RCTs.[5]

RCTs were developed before World War II, first with animals and then humans, and came to be widely used in the context of drug evaluation (see Healy, Chapter 4). Their spread and acceptance resulted from a combination of activities and circumstances that generated an alliance between the medical profession, the pharmaceutical industry and government, all powerful and important actors in their own right. In the early post-war period, an increasing number of doctors began to recognise the method as a scientific way of evaluating treatment interventions, although there were debates about the value of different types of trial.[6] The thalidomide tragedy of the early 1960s then transformed the situation by making mandatory the use of RCTs in the evaluation of drugs. The public scandal led governments in many countries to tighten the regulation of the industry; in particular, to require more rigorous evaluation of safety and effectiveness before a drug could be released onto the market. Prompted and strengthened by public concern, governments used their power to regulate an industry that was itself becoming more powerful and important within health care, and backed a method of

---

5 One of these is the high-drop out rates that can arise in clinical trials, especially of medicines with more severe side effects as, for instance, with antipsychotic medications (see NHS Centre for Reviews and Dissemination, 1999).

6 For instance, whether the control group should be given a placebo or an active substance for the same condition already on the market.

evaluation, the RCT, to which many of the medical profession were already sympathetic. The result was that the industry accepted the RCT as a necessary and routine procedure in drug evaluation, and it became the model for the evaluation of other forms of treatment, even though RCTs of interventions, such as psychotherapy, or of service developments, such as the use of community mental health teams or crisis services, are more difficult to carry out. Moreover, some argue that there is 'a danger of trivializing science by throwing up statistically significant values [on effectiveness] that in real life are insignificant' (Healy, 1997, p. 107). It is also the case that the method is relevant only to a specific set of questions concerning effectiveness, and not to many other issues, such as causation or professional–patient relationships. Nonetheless, since psychotropic medication constitutes the most common form of service intervention in the mental health field, drug evaluations involving RCTs provide the evidence that underpins the bulk of psychiatric interventions.

The pharmaceutical industry, far larger and more powerful than in the 1960s, now funds most of the expensive drug evaluation necessary for a drug's release onto the market. The companies often employ their own pharmacologists to carry out and oversee their research prior to a drug's approval, even though the evidence indicates that studies carried out by industry researchers tend to be more positive about the drugs evaluated than studies carried out by independent researchers (Kjaegard & Als-Neilson, 2002; Lexchin et al, 2003). Companies can also choose how to present the evidence on safety and effectiveness to the approval agencies. Consequently, they tend to have the upper hand in the alliance of government, industry and profession over the generation and use of data from RCTs. Moreover, regulatory approval from a governmental agency, if secured, is an official stamp of approval on a new drug, providing a point of closure, at least for a while, on the scientific black box (Busfield, forthcoming), even though subsequent research, including meta-analyses (see Chapter 7) may challenge earlier findings. Approval transforms a company's claims about a drug into facts that are largely hidden away until other evidence, which needs to be clear-cut and involve a large number of cases, is strong enough to challenge the findings.

In the post-approval stage, the industry is still powerful since psychiatrists depend heavily on drug treatments, so the alliance between industry and profession is largely sustained. However, some psychiatrists play a more a more active role in drug evaluation, setting up further RCTs, which may produce more nuanced or more critical findings, though a fuller evaluation of a drug may take many years. Such evidence may generate clear struggles around the value of a particular drug, as has happened with the antidepressant, Seroxat, and in some cases a drug may be withdrawn. However, these struggles are acted out against a backdrop of a broad alliance between profession, industry and government. Alternatively, patients and patient groups may start to challenge claims about a particular drug, and this may lead to new advice about its effectiveness or dangers, as happened in the late 1970s and 1980s, when the benzodiazepines, librium and valium, widely used to treat anxiety and depression, were found to have addictive properties.

In addition, governments may be concerned to carry out wider assessments of a drug's cost-effectiveness, a tendency encouraged by the new emphasis on evidence-based medicine that has developed since the 1990s. Here the method-ological strategy frequently invoked is that of cost-benefit analysis, in which reliance is placed on costs that can be quantified. In Britain, the National Institute of Clinical Excellence (NICE) collects evidence to deter-mine whether particular drugs should be used within the NHS. For instance, NICE initially supported the use of Aricept as drug to treat Alzheimer's disease. However, following new studies that showed little impact on overall social functioning despite some positive effects on memory (AD2000 Col-laborative Group, 2004), NICE issued draft guidance in 2005 that it should not be widely prescribed in the NHS. Similarly, HMOs produce guidance or constraints on treatment, including prescribing, thereby limiting the power of psychiatrists and other doctors (Scheid, 2001). Government policy making prompted by cost concerns does not of course necessarily depend on evidence derived from RCTs. For instance, the initial establishment of asylums was encouraged by medical and philanthropic claims about how the new asylums would provide a therapeutic environment that would cure madness and so reduce the burden of dependency.

Epidemiological research

Epidemiological studies have somewhat similar attractions to RCTs as quanti-tative and properly scientific. Here the focus is on the distribution and causes of illness, although by extension such studies can be used to look at the distribution of treatments and service provision. Epidemiological research first developed in the nineteenth century and again resulted from collaborative work between medical practitioners and statisticians. During the twentieth century the studies often involved social scientists working alongside clini-cians, and focused on social factors such as class, gender and ethnicity, as well as the physical causes of illness. The method involves the utilisation of what can be viewed as a natural experiment – that is, the observation of the out-comes of some change or difference that arises or exists without intervention from the researcher, and requires comparison between at least two groups – a familiar example involves comparing the health of smokers and non-smokers. Counting, measurement and statistical analysis are essential to the method, and epidemiological studies tend to be large-scale.

Given the size of the studies usually needed, epidemiological research is expensive and is often funded by governments, either directly or indirectly. The classic study in psychiatric epidemiology, *Social Class and Mental Illness*

(1958), by A.B. Hollingshead (a sociologist) and F.C. Redlich (a psychiatrist), was funded by the US National Institute of Mental Health at a time when it was seeking to support research into social factors and mental health. The study involved a large team of researchers and showed that mental illness was concentrated in the lowest social class, a finding repeated in a range of studies across a range of societies. The NIMH also funded the Epidemiologic Catchment Area Survey in the early 1980s (Robins & Regier, 1991). Similarly, in Britain, the Office of Population Censuses and Surveys carried out a household survey of mental illness in the community in the early 1990s (Meltzer et al, 1995b). The willingness of governments to fund epidemiological research is usually less a matter of seeking to understand causation than of generating evidence to assess health needs and the adequacy of service provision, and so facilitate service planning.

The scale of the epidemiological research funded by governments contributes to its status, and it has a high standing as a methodology. For instance, its use by social scientists can help to ensure that their work carries more weight with the medical profession than if other methods are used, as in the case of Brown and Harris's influential study *Social Origins of Depression* (1978). However, the associations yielded by such research are not uncontested, since they depend on the sampling and the measures used. For instance, claims about the prevalence of mental illness depend on the instruments used, and high prevalence rates may be a function of broad definitions of mental illness operationalised through symptom checklists (Busfield, 1996, pp. 82–90). Pharmaceutical companies do not usually fund epidemiological research, but may use evidence of undetected or untreated illness to help generate demand for their products, publicising such data through press releases as well as in material sent to doctors.

Case studies

The case study falls at the other end of the spectrum from epidemiological research in terms of size and the use of quantification. As clinicians, psychiatrists have a long tradition of writing up one or several individual cases as part of their research endeavour, transforming their clinical observation and data collection into research papers. While such research does not meet the canons of quantitative research, under certain circumstances it may be viewed as reasonably scientific because of the reliance on systematic observation, and can be influential in generating new ideas and avenues for research. Moreover, techniques such as the single-case experiment (see Chapter 2) introduce new ways of making individual case studies approximate more closely to natural scientific models. Certainly, the reporting of systematic observations by clinicians of a limited number of individual cases is still common. Psychoanalysis, for instance, which initially developed within the framework of medical practice, still places major emphasis on the in-depth study of the individual case, focusing on observing mental processes rather than bodily functioning.

Small-scale qualitative research in psychology, sociology or anthropology follows a similar model when it focuses on the in-depth study of a small number of individual cases, often through the use of interviews, and, like psychoanalysis, typically receives a less favourable reception from those whose methodological traditions are grounded in the natural sciences. Moreover, in some instances, there has been an important shift from observation to the reporting of subjective experience. The classic medical case depended on observation and, where possible, on the measurement of bodily functioning. Individuals' symptom reports might provide one source of data, but the doctor's observation was central. Increasingly, some social scientists have focused on illness narratives (Kleinman, 1988), considering what the patient thinks and feels as highly pertinent to their treatment. Significantly, this has coincided with a new emphasis on listening to users' voices and the growth of user movements, partly prompted by the civil rights movements of the 1960s and the focus on the rights of marginal groups. This pressure has had some impact on government policy and has, arguably, generated a somewhat greater recognition of the value of more qualitative research.

The power and potential fascination of the individual case (although usually not an academic report of a clinical case) is recognised by the media and is also sometimes used by politicians. And governments may be provoked to action by publicity surrounding a single case, such as a killing by a mental health patient. However, such cases, when widely reported, can distort public perceptions, creating a view that persons with mental illness are more dangerous than epidemiological evidence indicates (Monahan, 1992).

A case study of a specific institution or organisation and its practices, or of a community rather than of individuals, is a methodological strategy widely used by sociologists and anthropologists. Here the emphasis is usually on observation, although interviews focusing on subjective experience may also be deployed. Perhaps the example most pertinent to mental health services is Erving Goffman's (1961) famous study, *Asylums*, in which he used participant observation of a single mental hospital in the USA to develop an argument about the ways in which patients were treated within the institution. This example reveals the influence such studies can have when evidence is presented through a convincing and powerful conceptual framework that generates new ways of understanding.

Conclusion

Since the 1990s, there has been an increasing emphasis by governments and other health-care providers on the value of evidence-based medicine, including decisions about care and treatment within the mental health services. What counts as good evidence, and whether a particular piece of research is seen as generating new facts about mental health or mental health services, depends on a wide range of factors. Traditions of how to do good research develop over time, and research that falls outside the accepted canons is more likely to be dismissed as unscientific and its findings ignored. Disciplinary traditions are important, and psychiatry, along with other branches of medicine, now relies heavily on the natural sciences and the status given to the experimental tradition and to quantification as the source of 'good' evidence. However, the adoption of the RCT as the reference standard owes much to the power of governments and the pharmaceutical industry, and the desire for better evaluation of drugs, although the bulk of the research is designed to secure drug approval and leaves out a range of issues of wider relevance to clinical practice. Similarly, epidemiological research has depended heavily on the support of governments, not least for funding, but also as a reflection of government needs for data that will facilitate service planning. Case studies are smaller in scale and often perceived as less scientific, but they can generate new insights and understandings.

We can fully understand the character and impact of mental health research only by considering the dynamics of power between the different groups involved in its production and reception.

Chapter 19

A service-user perspective on evidence

Peter Beresford

Introduction

It would be misleading to suggest that there is one 'service-user' view on 'evidence' or the 'production of evidence'. Even the term 'service user' is contentious and lacking agreed definition. It is associated with not only mental health service users/survivors, but also a wide range of people who are or have been long-term users of health and social care. This includes people with learning difficulties, older people, people with physical and sensory impairments, people living with HIV/AIDS and so on. These groups have their own movements and organisations. Such organisations themselves vary considerably in their nature and purpose, from self-help to campaigning organisations, as well as innovative organisations which combine both roles (e.g. Campbell & Oliver, 1996; Campbell, 1999; Wallcraft et al, 2003). Many service users who take part in mental health debates and developments are affiliated to such organisations, although some are not. There are now local, regional, national, European and international service-user organisations. There are also links and overlaps between different groups of service users, so that, for example, some mental health service users/survivors are also involved in disabled people's organisations, and there are discussions and shared learning between different service user constituencies (Beresford et al, 2002).

However, while it is important to make clear that service users generally, and indeed mental health service users/survivors specifically, are not monolithic groups, there do seem to be some areas of agreement among them in relation to issues of evidence, research and knowledge formation. These provide a helpful starting point for exploring service-user approaches to 'evidence' and the 'production of evidence'.

Service users and the idea of 'evidence'

An initial point to make clear is that many service users and much service-user discussion fights shy of the idea of 'evidence'. Few people are likely to take exception at face value to the government's view, which found early expression in its Health Care White Paper (1997), that the 'services and treatment that patients receive across the NHS should be based on the best evidence of what does and does not work, and what provides best value for money' (para. 75). However, what has concerned many service users is that the notion of evidence embodied in leading discussions about 'evidence-based practice' is a very narrow one, based on particular understandings of what counts as evidence. This tends to privilege systematic reviews and randomised, controlled trials (RCTs), both approaches associated with science and medicine, and both deemed to be the most objective approaches and to attach less value to qualitative research and the views of service users. Such a hierarchical approach to evidence, is, for example, embodied in the government's National Services Framework for Mental Health (Department of Health, 1999a, p. 6) as a means of grading and synthesising the evidence (Table 19.1).

However, this approach has been criticised both by service users and others. RCTs and meta-analysis have not been shown to be more reliable than other approaches. They can answer only limited questions and they do not include other non-statistical forms of knowledge (Cohen et al, 2004). Critics have questioned the way in which data and information are presented as 'evidence' without elaboration on how they may actually serve as such. Service users have therefore been critical of the ruling approach to understanding 'evidence'-based services, which tends to gloss over the process whereby information or data actually become evidence and the attribution of different degrees of legitimacy and credibility to different evidence sources. Both of these disadvantage service users.

Service users, knowledge and research

Service users tend to frame their own discussions instead in terms of *knowledge*-based policy and practice. Their emphasis is on knowledge, not

Table 19.1 A hierarchy of evidence

Hierarchy	Type of evidence
Type I	At least one good systemic review, including at least one RCT
Type II	At least one good RCT
Type III	At least one well-designed intervention study without randomisation
Type IV	At least one well-designed, observational study
Type V	Expert opinion, including the views of service users and carers

evidence, and they highlight the contribution of service-user knowledge (Oliver & Barnes, 1998). Furthermore, service users tend to see research as only one way of generating knowledge. They also place value on the knowledge created by service users' individual experience and the collective knowledge that is generated through their organisations and movements. All of these are seen as having validity and a role to play in the development of knowledge-based policy and provision. In recent years, mental health service users have developed their own discourse, based largely on their shared learning from being involved in collective action. Research has played only a small, if nonetheless significant, role in this. Many service users see little benefit in research that only 'tells us what we already know'. They tend to be especially suspicious where they feel that validity is attributed to their experience only if it is reinforced by findings from conventional research. This represents another expression of the devaluing of their perspectives and understanding.

However, it is perhaps in mental health service users' own research that we can find the most developed discussion of their views about knowledge, knowledge-based policy and practice and research. They have not only increasingly become involved in mainstream mental health research, but they have also developed their own 'survivor'- or 'user-controlled' research approach. Mental health service users have done a lot in a relatively short time. Writing in 1997, one could say that most survivor research was small scale, sometimes unfunded and almost entirely based on qualitative research approaches (Beresford & Wallcraft, 1997). By 2005, there were a number of large-scale, user-led research projects, major quantitative as well as qualitative research projects, schemes equipping service users with research skills, a national network of survivor researchers and a dedicated research hub in the government's Mental Health Research Network, run by service users with a brief to support user involvement in research and user-controlled research across the network (the Service User Research Group England (SURGE)). There is now a significant canon of work by mental health service users/survivor researchers, reported in international peer review journals and mainstream texts as well as in service users' own publications, reports and newsletters.

While the mental health service users' focus has been on knowledge rather than evidence, and they have not seen research as the only route to knowledge production, they have also seen the purpose of research as being much more than the production of knowledge. A new review of user-controlled and survivor research (Turner & Beresford, 2005), based on a review of literature, individual interviews and group discussions with service users and service user researchers, reports the following range of aims and characteristics that tend to be associated with such research:

- the empowerment of service users and the improvement of their lives (through both the process and purpose of research)

- being part of a broader process of making social and political change
- a changed more equal relations of research production
- being based on social models of understanding and interpretation (as in the social model of disability).

The following key values and principles are associated with user-controlled research:

- empowerment
- emancipation
- participation
- equality
- antidiscrimination.

Making change, for the individual, the group and in society, is the aim at the heart of survivor/user-controlled research. While it has largely developed separately from the emancipatory disability research pioneered by the disabled people's movement, it is very similar to it. Emancipatory disability research emphasises all of the following:

- equalising the social relations of research production
- commitment to the empowerment of disabled people
- achieving broader social and political change rather than solely the accumulation of knowledge
- being based on a social model of disability developed by disabled people (e.g. DHS, 1992; Barnes & Mercer, 1997; Mercer, 2002; Barnes 2003, 2004).

Survivor research also emphasises service users, rather than other interests or groups, being in control of research that relates to them (Turner & Beresford, 2005). Both these research approaches are also indebted to 'new paradigm' research approaches, including feminist research, Black research and research associated with community education and liberatory educationalist (Reason & Rowan, 1981).

User involvement and user-controlled research

It is perhaps helpful at this point to draw a distinction between service-user involvement in research and survivor/user-controlled research. User involvement in research has recently received considerable support and priority from government, statutory and non-statutory research funders, and the wider research community, and it is increasingly becoming a requirement for research proposals. User-controlled research can be seen as an expression of user involvement, one end of a continuum that starts with no service-user involvement and is most fully developed in user control. On the other hand, though, not only is user-controlled research still marginal in scale and proportion as part of research overall (Turner & Beresford, 2005), but it also raises different and frequently fundamental issues for research that are not necessarily posed by user involvement in research. User involvement in research may mean no more than the admission of service-user perspectives to the research process. User-controlled research, that is to say, research which reflects the concerns and commitments of service users themselves, raises much more substantial issues for research, knowledge formation and understanding of knowledge-based policy and practice. This is because it represents a different research paradigm, with, as we have seen, a different ideological base.

The defining characteristic of such research is that it is based on the prioritising of experiential knowledge; that is, knowledge derived from service users' direct experience. Service users' own knowledge (whether generated through research or collective action) is seen as the basis for developing effective policy and practice. This has been a theme of the growing body of survivor research, whether its focus is policy, services, evaluation, crisis or spirituality (Faulkner & Layzell, 2000; Rose, 2001; Nicholls et al, 2003; User Focused Monitoring, 2004).

This takes us back to our earlier discussion about the hierarchising of evidence in conventional discussions about 'evidence-based policy and practice'. Such a hierarchy has followed from traditional research values of 'objectivity', 'neutrality' and 'distance'. A golden rule of many standard textbooks is that research should be 'objective'. This is based on the view that things exist as meaningful entities independent of consciousness and experience, and that rigorous, scientifically based research can discover that objective truth and meaning (Crotty, 1998, p. 5). Such an 'objectivist' approach to research highlights the need for and possibility of research that is 'neutral', 'unbiased' and 'distanced' from its subject. The unbiased, value-free position of the researcher is a central tenet of such research. By the claim to eliminate the subjectivity of the researcher, the credibility of the research and its findings are maximised. Research can therefore be replicated by other researchers in similar situations and always offer the same results. Research that does not follow these rules and that is not based on this value set tends to be seen as inferior, providing results which are less valid and reliable.

Competing research values and principles

Judged by such criteria, service-user research seems unlikely to score highly, with its explicitly political commitment to change, allegiance to the rights of service users, emphasis on control by service users and valuing of subjectivity. But service users argue that research has historically served sectional interests, and they are merely seeking to redress the balance. Not only service users, but, for some time, also researchers more generally have been raising questions about whether neutrality is actually possible in research. This is based on the view that, as researchers, we come to human beings as other human beings, with attitudes and emotions. How we understand how people live, and why they do what they do, is affected by our judgements and values. This affects what is seen as important to research and why people behave as they do. Should people behave like this? What is there about them that they behave as they do? We come to research through our senses and feelings – through what we have learnt and experienced – through our 'subjectivity' as fellow human beings. Service-user/survivor researchers equate medicalised psychiatric research values of neutrality, objectivity and distance with traditional positivist, Enlightenment approaches to research, which they call into question. They are critical of discourse about evidence-based policy and practice that leaves the political relations of research and the policy process unexamined.

Thus, service users/survivors not only acknowledge the subjectivity of their own (and other research) approaches, but they have also begun to challenge positivist assumptions about the helpfulness of being 'distanced' from their 'subject'. They not only challenge traditional beliefs about the deficiencies of service users designing questions and interviewing research participants, but they also identify gains in doing this, as for instance, in terms of these making more sense to the participants and eliciting different, fuller responses (Rose, 2001). Now, both implicitly and explicitly, the advocates of such research approaches are questioning both the possibility of 'neutrality' and 'distance' in research, and whether what have been seen as their 'merits' may actually be deficiencies (Beresford, 2003).

An additional insight on this is offered by considering the historical role of service users in mental health research and indeed medical and social research more generally. At least three stages can be identified historically in this relationship between such research and people on the receiving end of the policies and social problems it has studied, informed, described and analysed. These stages can be summed up in terms of people being:

1   ignored
2   surveyed
3   involved.

First, the views of service users were ignored. Researchers were interested in the problems they saw them as representing, but not their views or experience. They offered their own 'scientific' findings about them. Second, people's views and experiences were sought. They were seen as a valid and helpful data source to be collated and analysed by researchers as the basis for producing quantitative (and sometimes qualitative) research findings. This approach is still perhaps the predominant one. Third, as we have seen, an interest has developed in 'service-user involvement' in research. Generally, however, the analysis and interpretation of data provided by service users remain with professional, non-service-user researchers. User-controlled research perhaps represents a fourth stage in this process. With this, service users are in control of the research, and it is *their* interpretations of their experience which become central to the process of research, rather than those of non-service users, as has traditionally been the case. Thus, instead of seeing it as a virtue for the interpretation of experience to be distanced from that experience, service users see it as having strengths and advantages to be more closely connected to it (Beresford, 2003).

Furthermore, service users have highlighted potential problems with researchers being 'distant' from the experience that they interpret. This can lead to the distortion and misunderstanding of such experience, for the following reasons:

- unequal power relationships between researcher and research partici-pant, resulting in either hostile or paternalistic understandings
- inadequate awareness on the part of 'distanced' interpreters of their own position in relation to other people's experience, culture and perspectives
- separation of people or groups by discrimination relating to class, race, gender and other forms of difference
- commitments to ideologies, agendas and values that pull people away from valuing or being able to appreciate other persons and their experience
- socialisation into and reliance on models of understanding which sub-ordinate and pathologise people (for example, medical models of 'mental health' (Beresford, 2004).

An historically significant example of the problems inherent in such 'dis-tance' was the Miller and Gwynne study of institutionalised disabled people in the 1970s. Disabled people's reaction against this research played a key part in the development of emancipatory disability research. This study rejected the experiential knowledge of disabled research participants, who said that they wanted to and could live with appropriate support 'independ-ently in their own homes'. It asserted instead that this was 'unrealistic' and that they were inherently 'parasitic' (Miller & Gwynne, 1972). Subsequent changes in thinking, policy and practice, based on the experiential knowledge of disabled people, have fundamentally disproved this argument.

Challenges for the future

More recently, a range of gains from researchers being 'closer' to the issue under study have been identified, and the benefits of researchers getting closer to the experience with which they are concerned have been explored.

A number of ways in which researchers (without shared experience with research participants) can do this have also been suggested (Mercer, 2002; Beresford, 2003). These include:

- listening to what people say
- seeking to develop empathy with the perspectives and situations of others, sympathy being unlikely to be wanted
- working toward being open-minded and non-judgemental and challenging discrimination in oneself and others
- valuing rather than devaluing direct experience
- acknowledging the possibility of there being knowledge (that one may not fully understand) other than one's own
- being prepared to act on knowledge that is based on direct experience and to work with service users to bring about change (active knowledge)
- involving people with direct experience (such as service users) in the development and provision of professional education and training
- recognising the value of the direct experiences of service users to the provision of health and social care, and commitment to the recruitment of service users as workers
- making available research training for people with direct experience (for example, as service users) and supporting their involvement in research structures and processes to influence the process of knowledge production.

Judging by mental health service-user research itself, service users not only question conventional understandings of 'evidence', but they also place significantly different values on different kinds of knowledge and research than does much conventional research discussion. Service-user research breaks down conventional divisions between research production and consumption. It raises major questions about different knowledge claims. It rests on a view of research and development as inseparable. It is an intellectual arm of broader collective action. It signals a collision of cultures in the field of mental health research. Wherever we are located in this arena – as researcher or non-researcher; service user or non-service user – we are likely to see our values and assumptions challenged. Big issues are raised, and it is not yet clear how far they are resoluble or negotiable. What will be needed is safe space to discuss these issues, and opportunities and resourcing for survivor/ user-controlled research to be developed and for its principles and potential to be evaluated.

Chapter 20

Postmodern mental health services

Pat Bracken and Phil Thomas

Introduction

We are very grateful to the editors, Mike Slade and Stefan Priebe, for the opportunity to contribute to this book. As we understand it, our role is to provide a broad overview of the relationship between the dynamics of postmodernism and questions concerning mental health research. The focus of the book is evidence: how it is gathered and how it is used. The editors write that their approach is rooted in 'postmodern epistemology' and question the idea that 'evidence' is an absolute concept, something that can be evaluated separately from background context. The central theme is that there are different sorts of 'research consumers' in the field of mental health, and each may require evidence produced by different research approaches. The range of chapters reflects this approach to an extent. Our contribution will develop some of the themes raised by Peter Beresford in Chapter 19.

While we broadly agree with the approach of the editors, we believe that moving to a 'postmodern epistemology' involves something more complex than simply asserting the validity of multiple research methodologies. We shall argue that the main questions raised by postmodern theory deal with the relationship between these different methodologies, the people who use them, the people who are subjected to them, and the contexts in which they are used. This leads us to consider the issues of power and interest that influence what we consider to be admissible as evidence in the first place. We believe that developing a postmodern approach to knowledge also involves an attempt to move beyond the Enlightenment quest, which aimed to establish 'facts' as things that are separable from values. Postmodern thought involves an attempt to come to terms with the uncomfortable idea that such a separation is never really possible. This is actually implicit in the approach of the book. In their introductory chapter, the editors outline their reasons for focusing on the 'type of audience which the researcher is seeking to influence'. Scientists are never only involved in an attempt to reveal the nature of things, but are also always involved in 'seeking to influence' some audience or other. The production of knowledge is never completely detached and disinterested. In many ways, postmodern thought involves a coming-to-terms with the problems thrown up by this. In this chapter, we aim to do the following:

1   briefly outline a broad typology of the 'postmodern'
2   argue that most mental health researchers are still working to a modern-ist agenda with a strong commitment to a concept of progress centred on scientific evidence and technology
3   raise the possibility that positive change in the field of mental health has not been generated, to any great extent, by the application of scientific research evidence, but has rather been promoted by changing political, cultural and ethical values and priorities
4   describe briefly the limitations of the approach adopted throughout this text, and consider the implications of this for our understanding of evidence.

The idea of postmodernism

The term 'postmodern' has a wide spectrum of related but different refer-ences. Bradley Lewis, a psychiatrist based in New York, presents an excellent overview of 'Psychiatry and Postmodern Theory' in the *Journal of Medical Humanities* (Lewis, 2000). In this paper, he attempts to bring some order to the many meanings of the term 'postmodern'. He argues that there are three basic ways in which the concept is used:

1) postmodern art, literature, or architecture (referring to creative works showing distinctive breaks from their modernist heritage, such as the work of Andy Warhol),
2) postmodern culture (referring to recent explosion in world cultures of mass media influence, global village cosmopolitanism, and transnational capitalism), and
3) postmodern theory (referring to recent continental philosophy critiques of Enlightenment philosophy).

(Lewis, 2000, p. 76)

These ways of using the term overlap. Overly 'neat' definitions of the term 'postmodern' are inappropriate and self-contradictory. Indeed, one theme common to many postmodern thinkers is a profound suspicion of any simple, binary distinctions.

In reality, there are no clear separations along the spectrum of use. At one end, the word 'postmodernity' is often used to refer to a contemporary social, cultural and political *condition*, something we simply find ourselves living through. Like the term 'Victorian', it points to a cultural idiom, something associated with a particular set of socio-economic developments. We find ourselves in the midst of these developments. In this sense, our postmodern culture is not something we *choose*. Rather, it is something we have to come to terms with for good or bad. We might not like the postmodern world of the 'global village' with its myriad lifestyles and identities, but we cannot deny that it exists. We might not like the sort of post-industrial consumerist society we have developed, but it is there and we have to struggle with it. A number of analysts have related the culture of postmodernity to underlying economic developments. For example, Frederic Jameson (1991) argues that postmodernism is the 'cultural logic of late capitalism'.

At the other end of the spectrum, the term 'postmodern' is used to denote a particular *way of reflecting* upon the world and our place within it. This corresponds with Lewis's notion of 'postmodern theory'; it implies a much more conscious and deliberate phenomenon. We can *choose* to embrace a postmodern philosophical framework or instead reject it and assert alternative values and viewpoints. The central organising principle involved is an acceptance that the worlds we inhabit are more complex than previously realised. With this comes an acceptance that no single framework will ever be able to explain everything. Jean-François Lyotard famously declared: 'I define postmodern as incredulity toward metanarratives' (1984, p. xxiv).

In this way, postmodern thought represents a sort of anti-foundationalism. The insights produced by metanarratives such as psychoanalysis or Marxism are not denied, but any claims that they have the ability to explain everything (or even close to everything) are rejected.

Along this spectrum from cultural condition to philosophical viewpoint lie other uses of the term. Somewhere in the middle are those artistic and aesthetic productions that incorporate a postmodern perspective. Whatever the context, what is common to all these positions is a sense of moving beyond 'modernity' or the 'modern'. Postmodern thought, culture and ethics involve a coming to terms with the downside of the modernist Enlightenment dream: a world ordered according to the dictates of reason; a world shaped by science, technology and the primacy of efficiency and effectiveness.

From our point of view, postmodern thinking does not involve a *rejection* of Enlightenment values and ideals. Instead, it reflects a concern to understand their *limitations*; it is about understanding that there has been a serious downside to modernity. When it comes to the question of epistemology (the search for knowledge and truth), a postmodern approach posits the idea that there are truths (plural) and different paths to attain these. However, it also involves a questioning of whether it is possible easily to separate facts from values. Since the publication of Thomas Kuhn's *The Structure of Scientific Revolutions* in 1958, there has been a growing realisation that what shows up as a 'fact' in any particular scientific discourse is, to a large extent, dependent on the theoretical assumptions of that discourse. Facts and theories do not exist as separate elements. And different theories involve different ways of looking at the world. In turn, these involve different priorities, assumptions, ontologies and values. To us, a postmodern approach to evidence is about coming to terms with this realisation. It involves a recognition that our assumptions and values 'set up' a realm in which debates about 'evidence' and 'truth' can take place. As Foucault puts it (1984, p. 73), there are 'regimes of truth' in which it becomes possible to talk about what is true, what is false and what will count as evidence.

A postmodern approach to evidence highlights the 'messy' way in which facts and values are intertwined. It works to show that the technological attitude to human life through which our suffering shows up as something that can be easily defined, measured and manipulated is not without its negative side. It questions forms of research that claim to be simply about the 'collection of facts'; instead, it promotes research that engages actively with the ways in which the worlds of both researcher and researched are layered with assumption and values.

As the editors point out in Chapter 1, this is not a flight from scientific rigour in the field of mental health, but a realisation that the application of such rigour should be seen as happening as a *secondary* event. We need to position a democratic debate about values, perspectives, assumptions and priorities as the *primary* event in a science of mental health. From this debate will emerge the questions to be asked, the methodologies to be used, and decisions about who will carry out the research and in what context.

Mental health and the modernist approach to progress

One of the central themes of modernity is the quest for progress: the idea that through the application of our human reason, properly trained and educated, we can solve many of the problems that face us as human beings. Through science, we can become more effective, more productive and more in control of our destinies. For example, from a modernist viewpoint, agriculture is essentially about efficiency: how the greatest yield can be generated with the least expenditure of effort. In the modernist understanding of the world, our problems show up as technical issues: with the right form of research and analysis, the correct intervention can be identified.

Modernist mental health shares a central concern with efficiency and effectiveness. This emerges in some of the chapters in this book. In Chapter 2, Barbara A. Wilson, writing on single case experimental designs, asserts that: 'The basic question facing all clinicians is, "Is this patient changing and, if so, is the change because of my intervention or would it have happened anyway?"' (p. 10).

Progress means developing services that use only those interventions scientifically proven to work. It is also about making sure that we use our resources in a non-wasteful manner. Psychiatry (like the rest of medicine) is understood to be essentially a set of technical interventions that can be compared scientifically; hence, the current importance attached to double-blind studies. In relation to randomised, controlled trials, Simon Wessely maintains in Chapter 6 that we just 'need more trials, bigger trials and better trials' (p. 97).

We make progress in mental health to the extent that the results of these scientific studies are applied in clinical encounters. In Chapter 10, in the context of Community Mental Health Teams, Tom Burns bemoans the fact that 'Mental health practice is . . . still very dependent on societal attitudes and constraints. The major changes in UK CMHT practice in the last 15 years have been driven by factors other than research' (p. 238).

He looks forward to a time when research evidence is in the driving seat.

The way forward will be mapped out by experts: white-coated scientists based in universities and research centres. Debates about assumptions, values, ethics and philosophies are not to be dismissed, but they are very much *secondary* concerns. The *primary* focus has to be on developments in areas such as clinical trials, the technology of family interventions, and cognitive psychology. Clinical encounters are essentially about the application of discoveries in these fields to the problems of our patients.

Is progress in mental health about scientific evidence?

All this suggests that there is a gulf between what researchers and what service users consider to be important. In a book entitled *Community Mental Health Care*, published by the Royal College of Psychiatrists, Christine Dean (1993) provides a useful summary of the needs that service users themselves identify:

> The type of needs expressed by service users at stakeholder conferences are for 24-hour, 7-days-week availability of help, meaningful occupation or employment, friendship, to be recognised and treated as an individual, not to be stigmatised, to have local accessible services, a satisfactory standard of living in terms of a home, food, information, availability of respite, safety/security (at times), and transport.
>
> (Dean, 1993, p. 100)

This provides a clue about the real concerns of service users. If progress in mental health means anything, surely it involves a move toward the fulfilment of these sorts of needs. But this list does not involve a demand for more science, technology or research evidence. Most of these needs are actually very similar to those that we all seek and, for the most part, take for granted. They concern social role, acceptance and inclusion. In other words, they are about 'citizenship' (Sayce, 2000). It can be argued that loss of social position is the single greatest burden experienced by people with mental health problems. Real progress is about overcoming social exclusion (Office of the Deputy Prime Minister, 2004).

Such improvements as have been made in the field of mental health are more the result of changing *social attitudes* toward people with mental health problems and the resulting developments in *social policy*. Positive change has not been the result of developments in the *science* of psychiatry. It has been driven more by factors such as changes in social policy, changes in the legal framework around mental illness, improved welfare rights, a more vocal and active voluntary sector, special housing provision and political decisions about ending the role of large institutions. In turn, as Peter Beresford has pointed out, these factors have been predicated upon a wider discourse about disability, concerned with issues such as values, meanings and social position.

Implications

We have seen that postmodern theory involves a critical reflection on the limitations of science and positivism. We may choose whether or not we engage in such reflection, and whether or not we face up to the many challenges that confront us should we do so. However, we have no choice in living out our lives within the context of postmodern culture, or the 'postmodern condition'. So, as mental health service researchers and practitioners in the twenty-first century, we have to engage with some difficult questions. The issue of risk raised in Chapter 1 is such an issue, but there are others that have not been dealt with. Our analysis has raised the matter of human interest in research. Commentators both inside and outside the profession of psychiatry have expressed serious concerns about the issue of interest and research, raising the importance of transparency. Joanna Moncrieff (2003) has drawn attention to the enormous power of the pharmaceutical industry. It is very much in the industry's financial interest to support and encourage research in mental health that suits its financial interests, even though this research may be in, say, psychosocial interventions for schizophrenia. Such interventions go hand in glove with the view of schizophrenia as a medical disorder requiring treatment with drugs. Indeed, it is commonly the case that people entered into studies that evaluate cognitive-behaviour therapy in psychosis are required to take neuroleptic medication during the course of the study. All this points to a way of framing evaluative research in psychiatry that serves the interests of the pharmaceutical industry.

But interest also operates at a personal level. This happens in ways that are so obvious that we rarely think about them. We overlook the fact that, as researchers, our lives are dependent on our engagement in research in fundamental ways. We write here as we reflect on our own positions as clinicians, psychiatric researchers and writers of academic papers. Our research has kept us in employment. It has fed and clothed us, and kept roofs over our heads. It has been a powerful source of self-esteem. Our papers, chapters in books, books, attendance at conferences to deliver papers, etc., have helped us to believe that we are valued as researchers, as doctors and as psychiatrists. They have made us feel important and valued, bringing influence, prestige and power. But it is salutary for us to reflect that in our field of mental health research, the great majority of people whom we have studied, the people on whom we depend for the results of our efforts, are not valued. The great majority of mental health service users, those who are the subjects of psychiatric research, are drawn from the most disadvantaged quarters of our society: people from black and minority ethnic (BME) communities, the unemployed, those living in our inner-city areas, the elderly and women. When we consider these *political* distances and differences between research subjects and ourselves as researchers, we believe that it is no longer acceptable for us to wander carelessly into the lives of individuals and communities, taking what we want and leaving nothing in return. It is no longer possible for us to justify our involvement in the type of 'distant' and 'objective' science that characterises the vast majority of research undertaken in psychiatry and the field of mental health. Looked at in this way, evidence-based medicine is not only incapable of handling the ethical and moral aspects of 'gathering evidence', but it is actually a part of the problem. In addition, it is incapable of responding to different interpretations of emotional distress and psychosis, and the values and interests that underpin these (Faulkner & Thomas, 2002). We believe that the problem of human interest in science is ontological and thus inescapable; it colours and shapes our interpretation of knowledge and what we mistakenly believe to be objective truths and facts. If research to improve mental health services is to be conducted by academics and mental health professionals, it must be done in ways that are sensitive to these issues, and that can engage with them. We therefore need approaches that make these issues explicit, and that place the question of ethics before the question of technology. One such approach is participatory action research (PAR).

PAR is not so much a research methodology as a style of research, and, as such, it encompasses a wide variety of research methodologies, both quantitative and qualitative. Hart and Bond (1995) describe four main types of PAR, experimental, organisational, professionalising and empowering. These are not strict typologies, and to an extent they overlap. The service-user-led research described by Peter Beresford (Chapter 19) is an excellent example of empowering action research. Another is the project, Sharing Voices Bradford (SVB), a community-development project working with Bradford's BME communities, currently being undertaken jointly by the Sainsbury Centre for Mental Health, the Community Development Foundation and the Centre for Citizenship and Community Mental Health at Bradford University (Seebohm et al, 2004). Both these examples are user-controlled, seeking to shift the balance of power in society and to achieve structural change. From our point of view, the vital feature of PAR is that its participatory and democratic nature (Meyer, 2000) means that all research questions are framed within the human contexts in which the research is to take place.

Consequently it is well placed to deal with issues of inequality and social exclusion that we have referred to. It does this by clearly blurring the distinction between researchers and research subjects. For example, the SVB participatory action research project is working with people from Bradford's BME communities who have experienced emotional distress or psychosis. It has supported them as community researchers. They have chosen the research questions that are important to them and identified subjects for interview, including themselves. Thus, they are both researchers and research subjects. The evaluation has made it possible for isolated and socially excluded people, such as a group of Pashtun women, or unemployed, young South Asian men, to describe how they understand their experiences of distress, and what they have found helpful or unhelpful in coping with these. The outputs of such research may include conventional papers describing a piece of qualitative research undertaken as part of the study, or dance, performance, creative writing and music, depending upon which consumer group the output is aimed at.

If those who are developing mental health services are to engage seriously with the lessons of postmodern theory and the postmodern condition in which we live, there has to be a careful engagement with the lives and social realities of those who use mental health services. As we said earlier, postmodern critiques do not entail rejecting the benefits of science, but, in our view, we can retain the benefits of science only if the main interest being served is that of service users and the community. PAR makes it possible to undertake high-quality, well-designed social science research (quantitative or qualitative) within a framework that recognises the epistemological and ethical shortcomings of more traditional research.

Chapter 21

Research production and consumption

Stefan Priebe and Mike Slade

Introduction

The book has described the state of the art of methods in mental health service research. The wider context of such research was outlined, including its impact on the media, the public, mental health policies, service development, and clinical practice. By considering research consumption and the impact of research on the 'real world' one leaves the ivory tower of academic research, and instead must consider the metalevel perspective of the relationship between research production and consumption. We have argued that such a perspective might be helpful for the different stakeholders in mental health service research, particularly when it comes to decisions on research methods.

Choice of research method

How should researchers select the best research method? Barbara A. Wilson (Chapter 2) points out: 'There is no right or wrong way to carry out research. It depends on the question to be answered' (p. 13). We agree, and would add that there are aspects other than the nature of the question to be considered in deciding what research methodology to select. Some of these aspects have been mentioned in the chapters of the book, but often more implicitly than explicitly, and are pragmatic rather than conceptual in nature. Some of these considerations are shown in Box 21.1.

First, there are the background and personality of individual researchers. They may have a particular interest in applying specific methods, and their talent and style might not be suited to use all methods equally well. For whatever reasons, researchers are likely to prefer some methods over others and are entitled to choose a method that makes them enjoy their work.

The experience and expertise of the researcher in working with a methodology are also relevant. It may take a long time to acquire the necessary skills and competence to apply the given method with sufficient rigour and quality. The call for methodological pluralism does not diminish the need

---

Box 21.1 Some considerations in choosing research methodology

Scientific interests of researcher
Preference of researcher for a particular method
Expertise of researcher in a particular method
Current popularity of research method
Relevance of method to target audience

---

for uncompromising quality in whatever methodology is used. Individual researchers and research groups have to have a focus and cannot develop expertise in every single research methodology at the same time. When working with a method for a long time, individuals and groups may change or specify their interest and amend or further develop a method. In this, methodological experience beyond a very specific approach might be beneficial. What the best balance is between focus on one method and wider experience with different methods may vary, and depend on factors such as size and background of the research group, available resources, research environment, personalities and type of research. This balance and the exact combination of methods that a group has expertise in might influence to what extent a research group can be innovative by either significantly advancing a research method or applying an established methodology in a new way. In any case, level of existing expertise is certainly a major aspect to be considered when deciding on a methodology.

Researchers are not necessarily more altruistic than other people in modern societies. Like everyone else, they need a salary and like to have a prospect for their future. Subsequently, their choice of methodology has to consider the chances to generate funding and promote their own career – and almost always does. This may be lamentable, particularly as the peer review system for funding and publishing research is likely to favour mainstream research rather than innovation and creativity. Yet, the need to compete in a changing academic world will affect methods and research dissemination. Academic institutions are in an increasingly globalised competition for the best research output and reputation, and have to position themselves accordingly. What counts are publications of international relevance, and not of only local interest. Ignoring this makes survival in an academic environment rather difficult. At the same time, there have been attempts to evaluate research on the basis of its impact on service development. For instance, the NHS in England provides funding for mental health service research and requires researchers to outline whether their research – directly or indirectly – has had such an impact. Claims that single studies and publications had a substantial impact on service development are not easy to substantiate, and so far the impact factor that is widely used to assess the standing of scientific journals in the field has not been matched by an equally established 'policy impact factor' or 'practice impact factor'. Establishing metrics which capture the impact of research at these more complex levels will not be straightforward. Although dissemination to an academic audience may be more easily measured (through scientific journal impact factors), we agree with the quote attributed to Robert McNamara that the challenge is to make the important measurable, not the measurable important.

Research production and research consumption

The contributors to Part II have emphasised the complexity of the link between research on the one hand and policies and practice on the other. For example, Frank Holloway (Chapter 13) touched on historical developments in the nineteenth century. A historical perspective might be helpful to reflect on the role of research and academia on service development. The twentieth century saw several innovations in mental health care that – more or less successfully – initiated attempts of major reforms. To illustrate, in the early 1920s, Kolb developed the model of 'open care' in Germany and widened the activities of care beyond the walls of asylums. Not much later in the Netherlands, Querido effectively reduced hospital admissions through delivering care in the community including the patients' homes. In the 1940s, Jones developed the model of 'therapeutic communities' in the UK, which represented a new approach to care of patients with severe illnesses. In Italy, Basaglia worked to abolish an unacceptable form of hospital care and had a major influence on Law 180, which was passed by parliament in 1978. None of these reforms were initiated because of seminal research publications on the subject, and none of the mentioned reformers even held a significant academic position at the time of the reforms. Thus, psychiatric research and academia rarely played a central role in mental health reforms in the history of psychiatry. More recently, this picture may have become more positive, but still varies internationally, as the contributions on the impact of research on policy in four European countries (Chapters 13–16) and in the USA (Chapter 17) illustrate. The historical and cultural reasons for this marked difference cannot be analysed here, but their existence is important as a reflection on the role of research in service development.

In all countries, researchers may feel frustrated because scientific evidence is not translated into policies. For example, Rachel Jenkins and colleagues highlight in Chapter 8 that insufficient attention is paid to national survey data in planning mental health services, and Lorenzo Burti in Chapter 15 considers the possibility that no academic research has ever affected Italian mental health policy. Yet, politicians who are responsible for political decisions understandably have a different agenda – most notably to get re-elected – which may or may not fit with the implementation of new ideas for mental health care. While this principle applies in all countries, the interest of politicians in taking notice of and being informed by evidence from mental health service research varies. In the UK, there is at least a debate at political and managerial levels on the evidence for certain service models, such as assertive outreach. In Germany, as noted by Bernd Puschner and colleagues in Chapter 14, researchers do not find open ears of politicians, and there is more widespread cynicism among researchers about the chance to influence policies. This of course hinders the development of mental health service research. Mental health researchers are probably in a better position when health care is a remit of the government, as in the nationalised health service in the UK. In such systems, governmental agencies are likely to have a (possibly ambivalent) interest in research evidence, are pressed to provide transparency for the reasons of their decisions, and have the financial means to fund research on service models. In a more privatised and decentralised health-care system, it is less clear who has an interest in research evidence and a responsibility to fund research studies.

Guidelines as the connection point between research and practice

One major reason for a stronger impact of research on service development is the establishment of the National Institute of Clinical Excellence (NICE) in the UK, a model that is widely seen as so successful that other countries are establishing similar institutes. The scope of NICE was initially restricted to evaluating the effectiveness and efficiency of therapeutic interventions, and favoured the type of evidence provided by randomised, controlled trials (RCTs) and systematic reviews/meta-analyses based on RCTs. However, RCTs are not free from limitations, as outlined by Simon Wessely in Chapter 6. As Simon Gilbody explains in Chapter 7, systematic reviews and subsequent guidelines can also consider the types of evidence provided by other methods, including qualitative approaches such as those outlined by Rosemarie McCabe (Chapter 3), Dave Harper (Chapter 4) and Karen Henwood (Chapter 5). Beyond these technical considerations of what type of evidence each method produces, Peter Beresford points out in Chapter 19 that 'privileging' certain types of research (such as RCTs and systematic reviews) over others is a value-based as well as a scientific decision.

Overall, this points to the need to use multiple types of evidence to develop clinical guidelines. However, synthesising the findings generated by different methods is a new challenge. At present, such synthesis is the exception in developing guidelines, but might be more widely used in the future. If and when that happens, guidelines will have an even more important function in connecting research production with care practice than they already have today. The degree to which research findings are used in generating guidelines might be seen as a measure of practical relevance. Such a measure could be used to evaluate research, alongside or instead of more traditional academic criteria of the impact factor.

A second challenge will then be to formulate guidelines in a way which promotes the intended behaviour change. Paul Walters and Andre Tylee (Chapter 9) usefully outline some factors which affect implementation of mental health guidelines at primary care. However, Tom Burns indicates in Chapter 10 that other contextual factors, such as societal attitudes and impending embarrassment for a profession, are also influential. The need for a 'wow factor' is discussed by Sophie Petit-Zeman (Chapter 12) in relation to media reporting of research, but may also be relevant to implementing guidelines – the proposed change needs to make sense to the target audience. In other words, the purpose and need for the guidelines must be made very clear, and the goals made explicit. The difficulties in introducing routine use of standardised outcome measures in England (National Institute for Mental Health in England, 2005) illustrate the point that unless there is a visible, clear and agreed purpose, there is unlikely to be consistent implementation. On the other hand, Vanessa Pinfold and Graham Thornicroft in Chapter 11 highlight the implications of a media focus on violence and mental ill-health, which arises from overemphasising the wow factor. The same concerns need to be considered in formulating clinical guidelines; that is, the need to balance what is doable (i.e. sufficiently close to current professional values and concerns) with what is needed (i.e. of benefit to patients, whether or not it fits with professional values and concerns).

Messages from research

The contributions in Part II highlight that it is not possible to produce a simple taxonomy of the association between research methods and their success in producing findings that are noticed and acted upon by different stakeholders. The link between research and changes in the real world is complex, and influenced by various factors. The reputation of research methods and the 'fashion' in research can change over time. For example, the relative weight ascribed to the three types of evidence identified by Lars Hansson in Chapter 16 – scientific, clinical and ethical – will vary over time. Literature searches will easily provide information on what methods 'worked' to get published, yet they are by definition outdated when it comes to decisions on methods for future studies. There always is a time gap between designing a study and the publication of results. Thus, while a literature search can give an accurate picture of research that was 'fashionable' at the time when decisions on funding were taken, this will be different some time later. Therefore, judging the reputation, standing and impact of research methods, both within the scientific community and beyond, is problematic.

Answers to research questions can be relatively straightforward or more complicated, and for that reason alone the findings may have a different likelihood of influencing practice. For instance, if a study clearly shows that drug A is strongly superior to drug B on a simple and sensible outcome criterion, the finding is more likely to be published, read and remembered than a more complicated message, such as that drug A has a small probability of being superior to drug B, but only for a subgroup of patients, and that the benefit on one criterion comes with negative outcomes on other criteria such as side effects. A health service research example from a recent study on assertive outreach (AO) teams in London illustrates the point. In the original service model, AO teams were required to provide out-of-hours service rather than restricting their operation to normal office hours. Because of the 'extra' costs incurred, the notion that out-of-hours service provision is really necessary for the efficacy of the teams was repeatedly challenged. Therefore, service managers were interested in research evidence on the subject. The Pan-London Assertive Outreach Study assessed whether existing teams did or did not provide out-of-hours service, and tested the association with outcome – in this case, rehospitalisation within a 9-month follow-up period. Analysis showed that out-of-hours service provision was actually associated with poorer patient outcomes, suggesting it might be detrimental rather than helpful. However, when the influence of other factors, such as weekend working, was controlled for, the result changed into its opposite: weekend working always predicted poorer outcome, and out-of-hours working now predicted more positive outcome. Statisticians will have no problem in explaining what is behind such results, but this may not help service managers to decide what matters to them: should AO teams work out of hours or should they not? The study was intended to provide a comprehensive and practice-relevant answer, but the answer is not straightforward and requires longer explanations. No matter how valid this research finding is, it is unlikely to have an irresistible impact on service development.

All research methods described in this book face the challenge not just to provide interesting and clear results to get published in respectable journals and generate further funding, but also to produce brief and understandable messages that can be disseminated more widely, are taken notice of by relevant audiences, and are included in, or at the least inform, guidelines.

The credibility of messages based on different methods will depend on the audience and the context. Qualitative methods often illustrate their findings with real comments from real people, and the resulting message may have an intuitive appeal that is often missing in the numerical reporting of quantitative approaches. Parts of the research community and clinicians may be more familiar with quantitative research reports, and therefore more inclined to accept the provided evidence.

Expectations and different types of research

The perception and use of research will also be influenced by expectations. The term 'research' is not copyrighted, but can be defined as all forms of 'systematic investigation to discover facts or collect information', as well as the process to 'carry out investigations'. In mental health care, such definition can encompass at least three different activities:

1   the routine documentation of patient characteristics, service activities and – possibly – outcomes, such as the Minimum Data Set in England or the Basis Dokumentation in Germany
2   audits that investigate whether service delivery is in line with guidelines based on research evidence or common sense
3   scientific research that contributes to the generation of guidelines.

These three categories overlap with the proposal by John S. Lyons and Whitney P. Witt (Chapter 17) that there are three types of credible scientific evidence in the USA: RCTs, epidemiological studies and outcomes management approaches.

This definition of scientific research implies that each result – at best – feeds into a worldwide base of research evidence. This global body of knowledge will later inform local practice, as through guidelines. Such a definition may be disputed, but helps to distinguish research from local quality-management and quality-improvement processes in services with the aim of maintaining or improving performance in specific services. For local quality management, other methods than scientifically rigorous research are likely to be more appropriate. By contrast, research has the aim of informing more widely than the setting in which it is conducted. This, of course, does not mean that methods, such as RCTs and meta-analyses, which purport to have external validity (i.e. to generalise to other settings) are superior – local audits, qualitative investigations, routinely collected data aggregated to the national level, and national survey data are all potential sources of information for generating guidelines.

However, stakeholders sometimes expect that research should be directly relevant to local practice, and will produce results that have an immediate impact on service configuration and care practice. Such expectations are understandable and legitimate, but unlikely to be met by scientific research, which often produces results that are complex and can be interpreted only in the context of all other existing research evidence. These expectations are more realistic for quality-management processes, and mixing quality management with scientific research is probably not helpful. In a more postmodern concept of research, quality management and scientific research may overlap more than in traditional academic concepts of research, and in practice the two are not mutually exclusive. In any case, researchers and research funders should be explicit and unequivocal about the aim of the research activities, to avoid mutual disappointment of the commissioner and the producer of the study.

Moreover, expectations of stakeholders often have a different time scale than research can deliver on. Politicians are after an answer to a question that they face now, and not in 3 years' time when a new RCT on the issue might be completed. Politicians in England decided to introduce AO on the basis of the evidence that existed at the time. Commissioning new trials on the efficacy of AO within the context of NHS and waiting for the results before taking a decision would have paralysed the political process of funding new services. The results of such trials, now coming in, question the efficacy of AO, and political decisions on service funding and targets may or may not be amended as a result of the findings. The fact that research can often not deliver in line with time scales in political life is important to understand when considering the function of methodologically rigorous research for service development. In Chapter 18, Joan Busfield outlines some of the forms of power which politicians have at their disposal, such as granting legal powers, establishing regulatory frameworks and, most directly, funding research. Ignoring these considerations (for instance, by refusing to engage in short-term research) risks further marginalising the role of research in informing mental health policy.

Beyond the ivory tower

Do researchers have a responsibility to consider the effects and impact of their research? The philosophical and ethical dimensions of this question have been addressed extensively elsewhere. For instance, Dürrenmatt showed in his play *The Physicists* the inner conflicts of physicists involved in the development of nuclear weapons technology. By comparison, findings in mental health service research are less earth shattering, and run the risk of being ignored rather than misused (although the latter might happen occasionally).

Yet, this is not a book about research ethics – it is about the concept of evidence, which varies between and within modern – or postmodern – societies. How can we understand the role that research and evidence, as provided by specific research methods, play within those societal processes that determine how people with mental health problems are being treated? The answer requires considering research consumption in deciding on the research method. The choice of method should be influenced by the target audience and intended use of the research. We therefore propose a framework, for scientific enquiry, shown in Figure 21.1, in which the links between research production and consumption are made more explicit.

This framework is intended to improve on the traditional scientific model of enquiry, shown in Figure 1.1 in Chapter 1. The chapters in Part I provide

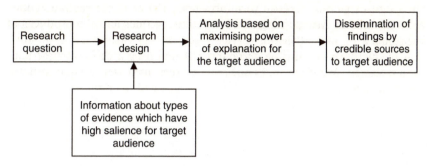

Figure 21.1 Proposed model of scientific enquiry.

many examples of research methods that have worked in the context in which the research has been conducted. They also identify limitations of both research methods and the relevance to different audiences, from the perspective of the researcher. The relevance to practice and policy is then considered in Part II from the perspective of the potential users of the research evidence.

Neither Part I on research methods nor Part II on the impact of evidence are exhaustive. More research methods may raise claims to be included as important, and there are more relevant audiences and obviously many more countries. However, we are confident that the chapters provide a good and relatively systematic description of the association between research methods, audiences and countries. Taken together, these are intended to provide the information needed to implement the model of enquiry shown in Figure 21.1.

Ivory tower research in the field of mental health will probably continue to exist, and might be rewarded in parts of the scientific community. However, it should be in the interest of all researchers as well as of society at large to maximise the relevance of research to society. This will involve a dialogue between researchers and stakeholders in mental health care, including the media, the wider public, patients, their relatives, practitioners, politicians, insurance companies and service managers. This statement does not contradict the tradition of psychiatry, and we agree with Pat Bracken and Phil Thomas in Chapter 20 that postmodern thinking does not involve a *rejection* of Enlightenment values and ideals. On the contrary, it re-emphasises the reasons for the rise of scientific endeavours within the Enlightenment period, and the subsequent wide establishment of academic institutions in the industrialising world.

A postmodern perspective may help us to understand why evidence has become a challenged and more variable concept. It may also cast light on the societal processes that determine the perception and consumption of research in the twenty-first century, and that will have implications for research production. However, the challenge of getting research into practice (and, as we have argued, getting practice to inform research) does not require a post-modern critique. Maintaining and strengthening the societal relevance and importance of mental health service research will involve understanding how the methods, production and consumption of research in mental health are associated. We hope this book will be seen as a step toward such an understanding.

References

Aberg-Wistedt, A., Cressell, T., Lidberg, Y., et al (1995) Two-year outcome of team-based intensive case management for patients with schizophrenia. *Psychiatric Services* 46, 1263–1266.

AD2000 Collaborative Group (2004) Long-term donepezil treatment in 565 patients with Alzheimer's disease (AD 2000); randomised double-blind trial. *Lancet*, 363, 2105–2115.

Adams, C. E., Power, A., Frederick, K. et al (1994) An investigation of the adequacy of MEDLINE searches for randomized controlled trials (RCTs) of the effects of mental health care. *Psychological Medicine*, 24, 741–748.

Agency for Health Care Policy Research (1993) *Depression in Primary Care.* Washington, DC: US Department of Health and Human Services.

Aitken, G., Burman, E. (1999) Keeping and crossing professional and racialised boundaries. Implications for feminist practice. *Psychology of Women Quarterly*, 23, 277–297.

Aktion Psychisch Kranke (1998) *Bundesweite Erhebung zur Evaluation der Psychiatrie-Personalverordnung [Nationwide Assessment in Order to Evaluate the Psychiatric Staffing Directive].* Baden-Baden: NOMOS.

Albers, M. (1999) Kosten und Nutzen der tagesklinischen Behandlung [Cost and utility of day hospital treatment]. In B. Eikelmann, T. Reker, M. Albers (eds), *Die psychiatrische Tagesklinik* (pp. 113–120). Stuttgart: Thieme.

Alderman, N., Ward, A. (1991) Behavioural treatment of the dysexecutive syndrome: reduction of repetitive speech using response cost and cognitive overlearning. *Neuropsychological Rehabilitation*, 1, 65–80.

Alexander, L., Link, B. (2003) The impact of contact on stigmatising attitudes towards people with mental illness. *Journal of Mental Health*, 12, 271–289.

Allebeck, P. (1989) Schizophrenia: a life-shortening disease. *Schizophrenia Bulletin*, 15, 81–89.

Allen, R., Nairn, R.G. (1997) Media depictions of mental illness: An analysis of the use of dangerousness *Australian and New Zealand Journal of Psychiatry*, 31, 375–381.

Allery, L.A., Owen, P.A., Robling, M.R. (1997) Why general practitioners and consultants change their clinical practice: a critical incident study. *British Medical Journal*, 314(7084), 870–874.

Altman, D.A., Schulz, K.F., Moher, D., et al. (2001) The revised CONSORT statement for reporting randomized trials: explanation and elaboration. *Annals of Internal Medicine*, 134, 663–694.

Andrews, G. (2000) Meeting the unmet need with disease management. In G. Andrews, S. Henderson (eds), *Unmet Need in Psychiatry* (pp. 11–36). Cambridge: Cambridge University Press.

Andrews, K. (1991) The limitations of randomized controlled trials in rehabilitation research. *Clinical Rehabilitation*, 5, 5–8.

Angermeyer, M. (2000) Schizophrenia and violence. *Acta Psychiatrica Scandinavica*, 102 (9S407), 63–67.

Angermeyer, M., Schulze, B. (2001) Reinforcing stereotypes: how the focus on forensic cases in news reporting may influence public attitudes towards the mentally ill. *International Journal of Law and Psychiatry*, 24, 469–486.

Anon. (1990) Flawed Study's Mixed Effects. *Hospital Doctor*, 18 Oct.

Antaki, C., Billig, M., Edwards, D., Potter, J. (2003) Discourse analysis means doing analysis: a critique of six analytic shortcomings. *Discourse Analysis Online*, 1 (1) <http://www.shu.ac.uk/daol/articles/v1/n1/a1/antaki2002002-paper.html> (accessed 15 Feb 2004).

Antaki, C., Young, N., Finlay, M. (2002) Shaping clients' answers: departures from neutrality in care-staff interviews with people with a learning disability. *Disability and Society* 17, 435–455.

Antman, E., Lau, J., Kupelnick, B. et al (1992) A comparison of results of meta-analyses of randomized controlled trials and the recommendations of clinical experts. *Journal of the American Medical Association*, 268, 240–248.

Appleby, L. (2004) *The National Service Framework for Mental Health – Five Years On*. London: Department of Health.

Appleby, J., Shaw, J., Sherratt, J. et al. (2001) *Safety First: Five-Year Report of the National Confidential Inquiry into Homicides and Suicides by People with a Mental Illness*. London: Department of Health.

Appleby, L., Wessely, S. (1988) Public attitudes to mental illness: the influence of the Hungerford massacre. *Medicine, Science and Law*, 28, 291–295.

Arboleda-Flórez, J., Holley, H., Crisanti, A. (1998) Understanding causal paths between mental illness and violence. *Social Psychiatry and Psychiatric Epidemiology*, 33, S38–S46.

Armstrong, E. (1997) Do practice nurses want to learn about depression? *Practice Nursing*, 8, 21–26.

Atkinson, J.M., Heritage, J. (1984) *Structures of Social Action*. Cambridge: Cambridge University Press.

Baddeley, A.D., Wilson, B.A. (1994) When implicit learning fails: amnesia and the problem of error elimination. *Neuropsychologia*, 32, 53–68.

Banister, P., Burman, E., Parker, I. et al (1994) *Qualitative Methods in Psychology: A Research Guide*. Buckingham: Open University Press.

Banks, M.H., Jackson, P.R. (1982) Unemployment and risk of minor psychiatric disorder in young people: cross sectional and longitudinal evidence. *Psychological Medicine*, 12, 789–798.

Barbour, R. (2003) The new found credibility of qualitative research? Tales of techno-logical essentialism and co-option. *Qualitative Health Research*, 13, 1019–1030.

Barker, C., Pistrang, N., Elliott, R. (2002) *Research Methods in Clinical and Counselling Psychology* (2nd edn). Chichester: Wiley.

Barnes, C. (2003) Reflections on doing emancipatory disability research. In J. Swain, S. French, C. Barnes et al (eds) *Disabling Barriers – Enabling Environments* (pp. 47–53). London: Sage.

Barnes, C. (2004) What a difference a decade makes: reflections on doing 'emancipatory' disability research. *Disability and Society*, 18, 3–17.

Barnes, C., Mercer, G. (eds) (1997) *Doing Disability Research*. Leeds: Disability Press.

Baron, R.M., Kenny, D.A. (1986) The moderator-mediator variable distinction in social psychological research: conceptual, strategic and statistical considerations. *Journal of Personality and Social Psychology*, 51, 1173–1182.

Barrett, R.J. (1988) Clinical writing and the documentary construction of schizophrenia. *Culture, Medicine and Psychiatry*, 12, 265–299.

Barrowclough, C., Hooley, J.M. (2003) Attributions and expressed emotion: a review. *Clinical Psychology Review*, 23, 849–880.

Barrowclough, C.H.G., Tarrier, N., Lewis, S.W. et al (2001) Randomized controlled trial of motivational interviewing, cognitive behaviour therapy, and family intervention for patients with comorbid schizophrenia and substance use disorder. *American Journal of Psychiatry*, 158, 1706–1713.

Basaglia, F. (1968) *L'istituzione negata*. Torino: Einaudi.

Baszanger, I. (1997) Deciphering chronic pain. In A. Strauss, J. Corbin (eds), *Grounded Theory in Practice* (pp. 1–34). London: Sage.

Bauer, M. (2003) *Reform als soziale Bewegung: Der 'Mannheimer Kreis' und die Gründung der 'Deutschen Gesellschaft für Soziale Psychiatrie' [Reform as social movement: The Mannheim Circle and the foundation of the German Society for Social Psychiatry*. In F.-W. Kersting (ed.), *Psychiatriereform als Gesellschaftreform* (pp. 155–164). Paderborn: Ferdinand Schöningh.

Bauer, M., Kunze, H., von Cranach, M. et al (2001) Psychiatric reform in Germany. *Acta Psychiatrica Scandinavica*, 104, 27–34.

Bebbington, P.E., Hurry, J., Tennant, C. et al (1981) Epidemiology of mental disorders in Camberwell. *Psychological Medicine*, 11, 561–580.

Beck, U. (1986) *The Risk Society*. London: Sage.

Becker, T., Vazquez-Barquero, J.L. (2001) The European perspective of psychiatric reform. *Acta Psychiatrica Scandinavica Supplementum*, 8–14.

Bennewith, O., Stocks, N., Gunnell, D. et al (2002) General practice based intervention to prevent repeat episodes of deliberate self-harm: cluster randomised controlled trial. *British Medical Journal*, 324(7348), 1254–1257.

Berber, M.J. (1999) Pharmacological treatment of depression. Consulting with Dr Oscar. *Canadian Family Physician* 45, 2663–2668.

Beresford, P. (2003) *It's Our Lives: A Short Theory of Knowledge, Distance and Experience*. London: Citizen Press in association with Shaping Our Lives.

Beresford, P. (2004) Where's the evidence?: comparing user controlled with traditional research. *Mental Health Today*, 31–34.

Beresford, P., Wallcraft, J. (1997) Psychiatric system survivors and emancipatory research: issues, overlaps and differences. In C. Barnes, G. Mercer (eds) *Doing Disability Research*, Leeds: The Disability Press.

Beresford, P., Harrison, C., Wilson, A. (2002) Mental health service users and disability: implications for future strategies. *Policy and Politics*, 30(3): 387–396.

Bergmann, J. (1992) Veiled morality: notes on discretion in psychiatry. In P. Drew, J. Heritage (eds), *Talk at Work*. Cambridge: Cambridge University Press.

Berkson, J. (1946) Limitations of the application of fourfold table analysis to hospital data. *Biometrics Bulletin*, 2, 47–53.

Bero, L., Grilli, R., Grimshaw, J. et al (1998) The Cochrane Effective Practice and Organisation of Care Group (EPOC) Module. *Cochrane Library*, Issue 4. Oxford: Update Software.

Best, J. (2001) *Damned Lies and Statistics: Untangling Numbers from the Media, Politicians, and Activists*. Berkeley, CA: University of California Press.

Besthehorn, M., Tischer, B., Glaser, P. et al (1999) Repräsentative Studie zur Verteilung schizophrener Patienten auf medizinische Versorgungseinrichtungen in Deutschland [Representative study on the distribution of schizophrenic patients utilizing medical health care services in Germany]. *Fortschritte in Neurologie und Psychiatrie*, 67, 487–492.

Billig, M. (1997) Rhetorical and discursive analysis: how families talk about the royal family. In N. Hayes (ed.), *Doing Qualitative Analysis in Psychology*. Hove: Psychology Press.

Björkman, T. (2000) Case management for individuals with severe mental illness. A process-outcome study of ten pilot services in Sweden. Doctoral dissertation, Lund University.

Black, N. (2001) Evidence-based policy: proceed with care. *British Medical Journal*, 323, 275–279.

Blackman, L. (2001) *Hearing Voices: Embodiment and Experience*. London: Free Association Books.

Blumer, H. (1954) What is wrong with social theory? *American Sociological Review*, 19, 3–10.

Blumer, H. (1969) *Symbolic Interactionism*. Englewood Cliffs, NJ: Prentice-Hall.

Bockhoven, J.S. (1954) Moral treatment in american psychiatry. *Journal of Nervous and Mental Diseases*, 124, 167–194.

Bola, J.R., Mosher L.R. (2003) Treatment of acute psychosis without neuroleptics: two-year outcomes from the Soteria project. *Journal of Nervous and Mental Diseases*, 191, 219–229.

Bola, M., Drew, C., Gill, R. et al. (1998) Representing ourselves and representing others: a response. *Feminism and Psychology*, 8, 105–110.

Bolger, E.A. (1999) Grounded theory analysis of emotional pain. *Psychotherapy Research*, 9, 342–362.

Bolton, D., Hill, J. (1996) *Mind, Meaning and Mental Disorder*. Oxford: Oxford University Press.

Boring, E. (1950) *A History of Experimental Psychology*, 2nd edn. New York: Appleton Century Crofts.

Boyd, E.A. (1998) Bureaucratic authority in the 'company of equals'. The interactional management of medical peer review. *American Sociological Review*, 63, 200–224.

Boyle, M. (1990) *Schizophrenia: A Scientific Delusion?* London: Routledge.

Boyle, M. (1998) Endnote: reflections on 'promoting the interchange'. *Clinical Psychology Forum*, 114, 34–35.

Boyle, M. (2002) It's all done with smoke and mirrors. Or, how to create the illusion of a schizophrenic brain disease. *Clinical Psychology*, 12, 9–16.

Boyle, M. (2003) The dangers of vulnerability. *Clinical Psychology*, 24, 27–30.

Bracken, P., Thomas, P. (2001) Postpsychiatry: a new direction for mental health. *British Medical Journal*, 322, 724–727.

Brill, K.E. (2000) Zum Stand komplementärer Angebote [The state of complementary services]. *Psychosoziale Umschau*, 4, 4–7.

British Psychological Society Division of Clinical Psychology (2000) *Recent Advances in Understanding Mental Illness and Psychotic Experiences.* Leicester: British Psychological Society.

Britton, A., McKee, N., Black, N. et al. (1998) Choosing between randomised and non-randomised studies: a systematic review. *Health Technology Assessment*, 2.

Broca, P. (1861) Nouvelle observation d'aphémie produite par une lésion de la moité postérieur des deuxième et troisième circonvolutions frontales. *Bulletin de la société anatomique de Paris*, 36, 398–440.

Brown, G., Bone, M., Dalison, B. et al (1966) *Schizophrenia and Social Care.* London: Oxford University Press.

Brown, G.W., Davidson, S., Harris, T. et al (1977). Psychiatric disorder in London and North Uist. *Social Science and Medicine*, 11, 367–377.

Brown, G.W., Harris, T. (1978) *Social Origins of Depression.* London: Tavistock.

Bryman, A. (2001) *Social Research Methods.* Oxford: Oxford University Press.

Buck, N., Gershuny, J., Rose, D. (1994) *Changing Households.* ESRC Research Centre on Micro-Social Change. Colchester: University of Essex.

Bulmer, M. (1979) Concepts in the analysis of qualitative data. In M. Bulmer (ed.), *Sociological Research Methods* (pp. 241–262). London: Macmillan.

Burman, E. (1995) Identification, subjectivity and power in feminist psychotherapy. In J. Siegfried (ed.), *Therapeutic and Everyday Discourse as Behavior Change: Towards a Micro-Analysis in Therapy Process Research.* New York: Ablex.

Burman, E. (2004) Discourse analysis means analysing discourse: some comments on Antaki, Billig, Edwards & Potter 'Discourse analysis means doing analysis: a critique of six analytic shortcomings'. *Discourse Analysis Online.*

Burman, E., Parker, I. (eds) (1993) *Discourse Analytic Research: Repertoires and Readings of Texts in Action.* London: Routledge.

Burns, B.J., Phillips, S.D., Wagner, R.H. et al. (2004) Mental health need and access to mental health services by youth involved with child welfare: a national survey. *Journal of the American Academy of Child and Adolescent Psychiatry*, 43, 960–970.

Burns, T. (2000) Models of community treatments in schizophrenia: do they travel? *Acta Psychiatrica Scandinavica*, 102, 11–14.

Burns, T., Beadsmoore, A., Bhat, A.V. et al (1993) A controlled trial of home-based acute psychiatric services. I. Clinical and social outcome. *British Journal of Psychiatry*, 163, 49–54.

Burns, T., Catty, J., Watt, H. et al (2002) International differences in home treatment for mental health problems. Results of a systematic review. *British Journal of Psychiatry*, 181, 375–382.

Burns, T., Creed, F., Fahy, T. et al (1999) Intensive versus standard case management for severe psychotic illness: a randomised trial. *Lancet*, 353, 2185–2189.

Burns, T., Fioritti, A., Holloway, F. et al. (2001) Case management and assertive community treatment in Europe. *Psychiatric Services*, 52, 631–636.

Burns, T., Firn, M. (2002) *Assertive Outreach in Mental Health.* Oxford: Oxford University Press.

Burns, T., Leibowitz, J. (1997) The Care Programme Approach: time for frank talking. *Psychiatric Bulletin*, 21, 426–429.

Burr, V. (2003) *Social Constructionism* (2nd edn). London: Routledge.

Burti, L. (2001) Italian psychiatric reform 20 plus years after. *Acta Psychiatrica Scandinavica Supplementum*, 41–46.

Busfield, J. (1996) *Men, Women and Madness: Understanding Gender and Mental Disorder*. London: Macmillan.

Busfield, J. (2003) Globalization and the pharmaceutical industry. *International Journal of Health Services*, 33, 581–605.

Busfield, J. (2006) Pills, power, people: sociological understandings of the pharmaceutical industry. *Sociology*, 40(2), 297–314.

Buston, K., Parry-Jones, W., Livingston, M. et al (1998) Qualitative research. *British Journal of Psychiatry*, 172, 197–199.

Byar, D. (1978) Sound advice for conducting clinical trials. *New England Journal of Medicine*, 297, 553–554.

Byrne, P. (2001) Psychiatric stigma. *British Journal of Psychiatry*, 178, 281–284.

Byrne, P (2003) Psychiatry and the media. *Advances in Psychiatric Treatment*, 9, 135–143.

Camic, P., Yardley, L., Rhodes, J. (eds) (2003) *Qualitative Research in Psychology: Expanding Perspectives and Methods*. Washington, DC: American Psychological Association.

Campbell, J., Oliver, M. (1996) *Disability Politics: Understanding Our Past, Changing Our Future*. Basingstoke: Macmillan.

Campbell, P. (1999) *The Service User/Survivor Movement. This is Madness: A Critical Look at Psychiatry and the Future of Mental Health Services*. Ross-on-Wye: PCCS Books.

Campion-Smith, C., Smith, H., White, P. et al. (1998) Learners' experience of continuing medical education events: a qualitative study of GP principals in Dorset. *British Journal of General Practice*, 48, 1590–1593.

Caspi, A., Sugden, K., Moffitt, T.E. et al (2003) Influence of life stress on depression: moderation by a polymorphism in the 5-HTT gene. *Science* 18, 291–293.

Catty, J., Burns, T., Knapp, M. et al (2002) Home treatment for mental health problems: a systematic review. *Psychological Medicine*, 32, 383–401.

Caudle, L. (2002) An unhealthy alliance: a discourse analytic study of general practitioners and pharmaceutical representatives, gifts and samples. Unpublished thesis, Department of Psychology, University of Adelaide. *Healthy Skepticism International News*, 20, 8–10.

Chalmers, I. (2001) Comparing like with like: some historical milestones in the evolution of methods to create unbiased comparison groups in therapeutic experiments. *International Journal of Epidemiology*, 30, 1156–1164.

Chalmers, I., Altman, D.G. (eds) (1995) *Systematic Reviews*. London: BMJ.

Chalmers, T., Celano, P., Sacks, H. et al (1983) Bias in treatment assignment in controlled clinical trials. *New England Journal of Medicine*, 309, 1358–1361.

Chamberlain, P., Camic, P., Yardley, L. (2004) Qualitative analysis of experience: grounded theory and case studies. In D. Marks, L. Yardley (eds), *Research Methods for Clinical and Health Psychology*. London: Sage.

Charlton, J., Kelly, S., Dunnell, K. et al (1993) Suicide deaths in England and Wales. II. Trends in factors associated with suicide. *Population Trends*, 71, 34–42.

Charmaz, K. (1990) Discovering chronic illness: using grounded theory. *Social Science and Medicine*, 30, 1161–1172.

Charmaz, K. (1995) Grounded theory. In J. Smith, R. Harre, L. van Langenhove (eds), *Rethinking Methods in Psychology*, 27–49.

Charmaz, K. (2000) Grounded theory: objectivist and subjectivist methods. In N. Denzin, Y. Lincoln (eds), *Handbook of Qualitative Research* (2nd edn. pp. 509–535). London and Thousand Oaks, CA: Sage.

Clare, L., Wilson, B.A., Breen, E.K. et al (1999) Errorless learning of face-name associations in early Alzheimer's disease. *Neurocase*, 5, 37–46.

Clare, L., Wilson, B.A., Carter, G. et al (2001) Long-term maintenance of treatment gains following a cognitive rehabilitation intervention in early dementia of Alzheimer type: a single case study. *Neuropsychological Rehabilitation*, 11, 477–494.

Cochrane, R., Stopes-Roe, M. (1980) Factors affecting the distribution of psychological symptoms in urban areas of England. *Acta Psychiatrica Scandinavica*, 61, 445–458.

Cohen, A., Paton, J. (1999) *A Workbook for Primary Care Groups*. London: Sainsbury Centre for Mental Health.

Cohen, A.M., Stavri, P.Z., Hersh, W.R. (2004) A categorization and analysis of the criticism of evidence-based medicine. *International Journal of Medical Informatics*, 73, 35–43.

Coid, J. (1994) Failure in community care: psychiatry's dilemma. *British Medical Journal*, 308, 805–806.

Collins, R., Peto, R., Gray, R. et al (1996) Large scale randomized evidence: trials and overviews. In D. Weatherall, J. Ledingham, D. Warrell (eds), *Oxford Textbook of Medicine* (pp. 21–32). Oxford: Oxford University Press.

Cooper, C.L. (1998) *Theories of Occupational Stress*. Oxford: OUP.

Cooper, H., Hedges, L.V. (1994) *The Handbook of Research Synthesis*. New York: Russell Sage Foundation.

Cooper, J.E., Kendell, R.E., Gurland, B.J. et al. (1972) *Psychiatric Diagnosis in New York and London: A Comparative Study of Mental Hospital Admissions*. London: Oxford University Press.

Corrigan, P., Green, A., Lundin, R. et al (2001a) Familiarity with and social distance from people who have serious mental illness. *Psychiatric Services*, 52, 953–958.

Corrigan, P.W., Lundin, R. (2001) *Don't Call Me Nuts: Coping with the Stigma of Mental Illness*. Champaign, IL. Recovery Press.

Corrigan, P.W., River, L.P., Lundin, R.K. et al (2001b) Three strategies for changing attributions about severe mental illness. *Schizophrenia Bulletin*, 27, 187–195.

Corrigan, P.W., Watson, A.C. (2002) Understanding the impact of stigma on people with mental illness. *World Psychiatry*, 9, 16–20.

Couture, S., Penn, D. (2003) Interpersonal contact and the stigma of mental illness: a review of the literature. *Journal of Mental Health*, 12, 291–305.

Cox, B.D., Blaxter, M., Buckle, A.L.J. et al (1987) *The Health and Lifestyle Survey*. Cambridge: Health Promotion Research Trust.

Coyle, A. (2000) Discourse analysis. In G.M. Breakwell, S. Hammond, C. Fife-Shaw (eds), *Research Methods in Psychology* (2nd edn). London: Sage.

Coyle, A., Rafalin, D. (2000) Jewish gay men's accounts of negotiating cultural, religious and sexual identity: a qualitative study. *Journal of Psychology and Human Sexuality*, 12, 21–48.

Creed, F., Black, D., Anthony, P. et al (1990) Randomised controlled trial of day patient versus inpatient psychiatric treatment. *British Medical Journal*, 300, 1033–1037.

Creed, F., Black, D., Anthony, P. et al (1991) Randomised controlled trial of day and in-patient psychiatric treatment. II. Comparison of two hospitals. *British Journal of Psychiatry*, 158, 183–189.

Crisp, A.H., Gelder, M.G., Rix, S. et al (2000) Stigmatisation of people with mental illnesses. *British Journal of Psychiatry*, 177, 4–7.

Crocker, J., Major, B., Steele, C. (1998) Social stigma. In D. Gilbert, S. Fiske, G. Lindzey (eds), *The Handbook of Social Psychology* (pp. 504–553). Boston, MA: McGraw-Hill.

Crotty, M. (1998) *The Foundations of Social Research. Meaning and Perspective in the Research Process*. London: Sage.

Crowther, R., Marshall, M., Bond, G. et al (2002) Vocational rehabilitation for people with severe mental illness (Cochrane Review). In *Cochrane Library*, Issue 1, Oxford: Update Software.

Cullberg, J., Levander, S., Holmqvist, R. et al. (2002) One-year outcome in first episode psychosis patients in the Swedish Parachute Project. *Acta Psychiatrica Scandinavica*, 106, 276–285.

Culpepper, L., Gilbert, T.T. (1999) Evidence and ethics. *Lancet*, 353(9155), 829–831.

Cutliffe, J.R. (2000) Methodological issues in grounded theory. *Journal of Advanced Nursing*, 31, 6, 1476–1484.

Davies, B., Harré, R. (1990) Positioning: the discursive production of selves. *Journal for the Theory of Social Behaviour*, 20, 43–63.

Davis, D.A., Thomson, M.A., Oxman, A.D. et al (1995) Changing physician performance. A systematic review of the effect of continuing medical education strategies. *Journal of the American Medical Association*, 274, 700–705.

Dean, C. (1993) Identifying the mental health needs of local populations. In C. Dean, H. Freeman (eds), *Community Mental Health Care. International Perspectives on Making It Happen*. London: Gaskell.

Dean, C., Phillips, J., Gadd, E.M. et al (1993) Comparison of community based service with hospital based service for people with acute, severe psychiatric illness. *British Medical Journal*, 307, 473–476.

De Girolamo, G., Cozza, M. (2000) The Italian psychiatric reform. A 20-year perspective. *International Journal of Law and Psychiatry*, 23, 197–214.

Denzin, N., Lincoln, Y. (eds) (2000) *Handbook of Qualitative Research* (2nd edn). Thousand Oaks, CA: Sage.

Department of Health (1990) *The Care Programme Approach for People with a Mental Illness Referred to the Specialist Psychiatric Services*. HC(90)23/LASSL(90)11. London: Department of Health.

Department of Health (1991) *Health of the Nation: Key Area Handbook* (2nd edn). London: Department of Health.

Department of Health (1995) *Building Bridges: A Guide to Arrangements for Inter-agency Working for the Care and Protection of Severely Mentally Ill People*. Wetherby: Department of Health.

Department of Health (1996) *The Spectrum of Care: Local Services for People with Mental Health Problems*. London: Department of Health.

Department of Health (1997) *The New NHS: Modern, Dependable*. London: Department of Health.

Department of Health (1998) *Modernising Mental Health Services. Safe. Sound. Supportive*. London: Department of Health.

Department of Health (1999a) *National Service Frameworks for Mental Health: Modern Standards and Service Models*. London: HMSO.

Department of Health (1999b) *Effective Care Co-ordination in Mental Health*. London: Department of Health.

Department of Health (1999c) *Modern Standards and Service Models: Mental Health National Service Framework*. London: Department of Health.

Department of Health (1999d) *National Confidential Inquiry into Homicides and Suicides*. London: HMSO.

Department of Health (2000a) *The NHS Plan. A Plan for Investment. A Plan for Reform*. London: Department of Health.

Department of Health (2000b) *Effective Care Co-ordination in Mental Health*. London: Department of Health.

Department of Health (2001a) *Mental Health Policy Implementation Guide*. London: Department of Health.

Department of Health (2001b) *Treatment Choice in Psychological Therapies and Counselling. Evidence-Based Clinical Practice Guideline*. London: Department of Health.

Department of Health (2002a) *Evaluating the Role of the Media in Promoting Uptake of Research Findings*. www.dh.gov.uk.

Department of Health (2002b) *National Suicide Prevention Strategy for England*. London: Department of Health.

Department of Health (2002c) *First Year Strategy for NIMHE. 2002*. Leeds: NIMHE/Department of Health.

Department of Health (2003) *Attitudes to Mental Illness 2003: Report*. London: HMSO.

Des Jarlais, D.C., Lyles, C., Crepaz, N. (2004) The TREND Group. Improving the reporting quality of non-randomized evaluations of behavioral and public health interventions: the TREND Statement. *American Journal of Public Health*, 94, 361–366.

Dey, I. (2004) Grounded theory. In C. Seale, G. Gobo, J.F. Gubrium et al (eds), *Qualitative Research Practice*. London: Sage.

DHS (1992) *Special Issue: Researching Disability. Disability, Handicap and Society*, 7, 99–203.

Dickerson, F.B. (2000) Cognitive behavioral psychotherapy for schizophrenia: a review of recent empirical studies. *Schizophrenia Research*, 43, 71–90.

Dickerson, F., Sommerville, J., Origoni, A. et al. (2002) Experiences of stigma among outpatients with schizophrenia. *Schizophrenia Bulletin*, 28, 143–155.

Dickerson, P., Rae, J., Stribling, P. et al (2005) Autistic children's co-ordination of gaze and talk: re-examining the 'asocial autist'. In P. Seedhouse, K. Richards (eds), *Applying Conversation Analysis*. London: Palgrave Macmillan.

Dixon-Woods, M., Fitzpatrick, R. (2001) Qualitative research in systematic reviews. *British Medical Journal*, 323, 765–766.

Dohrenwend, B.P., Dohrenwend, B.S. (1974) Psychiatric disorders in urban settings. In G. Caplan (ed.), *American Handbook of Psychiatry* (2nd edn, vol. 2). New York: Basic Books.

Doll, R. (1998) Controlled trials: the 1948 watershed. *British Medical Journal*, 317, 1217–1220.

Drake, R.E., Mueser, K.T., Torrey, W.C., et al. (2000) Evidence-based treatment of schizophrenia. *Current Psychiatry Reports*, 2, 393–397.

Drew, P. (2003) Comparative analysis of talk-in-interaction in different institutional settings; a sketch. In P.J. Glenn, C.D. LeBaron, J. Mandelbaum (eds), *Studies in Language and Social Interaction: In Honour of Robert Hopper*. Mahwah, NJ: Erlbaum.

Drew, P., Chatwin, J., Collins, S. (2001) Conversation analysis: a method for research into interactions between patients and health-care professionals. *Health Expectations*, 4, 58–70.

Drew, P., Heritage, J. (1992) *Talk at Work*. Cambridge: Cambridge University Press.

Drummond, M.F., Jefferson, T.O. (1996) Guidelines for authors and peer reviewers of economic submissions to the BMJ. *British Medical Journal*, 313, 275–283.

Eaton, W.W., Kessler, L.G. (1985) *Epidemiologic Field Methods in Psychiatry: The NIMH Epidemiologic Catchment Area Program*. Orlando, FL: Academic Press.

Eccles, M., Clarke, J., Livingstone, M. et al. (1998) North of England evidence based guidelines development project: guideline for the primary care management of dementia. *British Medical Journal*, 317(7161), 802–808.

Edgington, E.S. (1982) Nonparametric tests for single-subject multiple schedule experiments. *Behavioral Assessment*, 4, 83–91.

Edwards, D. (1995) Two to tango: script formulations, dispositions, and rhetorical symmetry in relationship troubles talk. *Research on Language and Social Interaction*, 28, 319–350.

Edwards, D., Ashmore, M., Potter, J. (1995) Death and furniture: the rhetoric, politics and theology of bottom line arguments against relativism. *History of the Human Sciences*, 8, 25–49.

Edwards, D., Potter, J. (1992) *Discursive Psychology*. London: Sage.

Effective Health Care (1993) *The Treatment of Depression in Primary Care. Bulletin no. 5*. Leeds: University of Leeds.

Egger, M., Davey Smith, G., Altman, D.G. (eds) (2000) *Systematic Reviews in Health Care*. London: BMJ Books.

Eikelmann, B. (1991) *Gemeindenahe Psychiatrie: Tageskliniken und Übergangseinrichtungen [Community Psychiatry: Day Hospitals and Transitional Institutions]*. München: Urban und Schwarzenberg.

Eikelmann, B. (1998) *Sozialpsychiatrisches Basiswissen [Basic Knowledge in Social Psychiatry]*. Stuttgart: Enke.

Eikelmann, B. (1999a) Zur Geschichte der psychiatrischen Tagesklinik [The history of psychiatric day hospital treatment]. In B. Eikelmann, T. Reker, M. Albers (eds), *Die psychiatrische Tagesklinik* (pp. 35–40). Stuttgart: Thieme.

Eikelmann, B. (1999b) Zur Evaluation psychiatrischer Tagesbehandlung [The evaluation of psychiatric day hospital treatment]. In B. Eikelmann, T. Reker, M. Albers (eds), *Die psychiatrische Tagesklinik* (pp. 107–112). Stuttgart: Thieme.

Eliasson, R., Nygren, P. (1981) *Psychiatric Service. I. Society – Outlook on People and Modern Mental Health Care* (in Swedish). Stockholm: Prisma.

Eliasson, R., Nygren, P. (1982) *Psychiatric Services. II. Experiences of Psychotherapy* (in Swedish). Stockholm: Prisma.

Elkin, I., Shea, M.T., Watkins, J.T. et al (1989) National Institute of Mental Health Treatment of Depression Collaborative Research Program: general effectiveness of treatments. *Archives of General Psychiatry*, 46, 971–982.

Elliott, R., Fischer, C., Rennie, D.L. (1999) Evolving guidelines for publication of qualitative research studies in psychology and related fields. *British Journal of Clinical Psychology*, 38, 215–229.

Elliott, R., Fischer, C.T., Rennie, D.L. (2000) Also against methodolatry: a reply to Reicher. *British Journal of Clinical Psychology*, 39, 7–10.

Ellwood, P. (1988) Outcomes management – a technology of patient experience. *New England Journal of Medicine*, 318, 1549–1556.

Elwyn, G., Gwyn, R. (1999) Narrative-based medicine. Stories we hear and stories we tell: analysing talk in clinical practice. *British Medical Journal*, 318, 186–188.

Emmerik, A., Kamphuls, J., Hulsbosch, A. et al (2002) Single session debriefing after psychological trauma: a meta analysis. *Lancet*, 360, 736–741. empirical studies. Schizophr Res 43, 71–90.

Entwistle, V. (1995) Reporting research in medical journals and newspapers. *British Medical Journal*, 310, 920–923.

Evans, J.J., Emslie, H., Wilson, B.A. (1998) External cueing systems in the rehabilitation of executive impairments of action. *Journal of the International Neuropsychological Society*, 4, 399–408.

Everitt, B., Wessely, S. (2004) *The Randomised Controlled Trial in Psychiatry*. Oxford: Oxford University Press.

Farrell, M., Bebbington, P., Brugha, T. et al. Substance misuse and dependence: its relationship to social deprivation. *British Journal of Psychiatry*, in press.

Faulkner, A., Layzell, S. (2000) *Strategies for Living: A Report of User-Led Research into People's Strategies for Living with Mental Distress*. London: Mental Health Foundation.

Faulkner, A., Thomas, P. (2002) User-led research and evidence based medicine. *British Journal of Psychiatry*, 180, 1–3.

Fechner, G.T. (1860) *Elemente der Psychophysik*. Leipzig: Breitkopf und Härtel.

Feder, G., Griffiths, C., Highton, C. et al (1995) Do clinical guidelines introduced with practice based education improve care of asthmatic and diabetic patients? A randomised controlled trial in general practices in east London. *British Medical Journal*, 311(7018), 1473–1478.

Feinstein, A.R. (1995) Meta-analysis: statistical alchemy for the 21st century. *Journal of Clinical Epidemiology*, 48, 71–79.

Fenton, W.S., Mosher, L.R., Herrel, J.M. et al (1998) Randomized trial of general hospital and residential alternative care for patients with severe and persistent mental illness. *American Journal of Psychiatry*, 155, 516–522.

Fiander, M., Burns, T., McHugo, G.J. et al (2003) Assertive community treatment across the Atlantic: comparison of model fidelity in the UK and USA. *British Journal of Psychiatry*, 182, 248–254.

Foreman, S., Dallos, R. (1992) Inequalities of power and sexual problems. *Journal of Family Therapy*, 14, 349–369.

Foucault, M. (1984) Truth and power. In P. Rabonow (ed.), *The Foucault Reader*, Harmondsworth: Penguin.

Fox, D.R., Prilleltensky, I. (eds) (1997) *Critical Psychology: An Introduction*. London: Sage.

Franz, M., Meyer, T., Ehlers, F. et al (2001) Schwer chronisch kranke schizophrene Langzeitpatienten. Welche Merkmale beeinflussen den Prozess der Enthospitalisierung? Teil 4 der Hessischen Enthospitalisierungsstudie [Severely and chronically ill schizophrenic long-term patients: which factors determine the process of deinstitutionalization? Part 4 of the Hessen Deinstitutionalization Study]. *Krankenhauspsychiatrie*, 12, 95–100.

Freeman, A.C., Sweeney, K. (2001) Why general practitioners do not implement evidence: qualitative study. *British Medical Journal*, 323(7321), 1100–1102.

Freudenberg, R. (1962) Das Anstaltssyndrom und seine Überwindung [The institutional syndrome and how to overcome it]. *Nervenarzt*, 33, 165–172.

Frith, C. (1992) *The Cognitive Neuropsychology of Schizophrenia*. London: Lawrence Erlbaum Associates.

Fritze, J., Schmauß, M. (2001) Psychiatrische Versorgung in Deutschland: Personalprobleme? [Psychiatric services in Germany: staffing problems?]. *Nervenarzt*, 72, 824–827.

Frosh, S., Burck, C., Strickland-Clark, L. et al (1996) Engaging with change: a process study of family therapy. *Journal of Family Therapy*, 18, 141–161.

Fulford, K.W.M. (1989) *Moral Theory and Medical Practice*. Cambridge: Cambridge University Press.

Fuller, T.D., Edwards, J.N., Vorakitphokatorn. S. et al (1996) Chronic stress and psychological well-being: evidence from Thailand on household crowding. *Social Science and Medicine*, 42, 265–280.

Gabbay, J. (1982) Asthma attacked? Tactics for the reconstruction of a disease concept. In P. Wright, A. Treacher (eds), *The Problem of Medical Knowledge: Examining the Social Construction of Medicine*. Edinburgh: Edinburgh University Press.

Gaebel, W., Baumann, A., Witte, A.M. et al. (2002) Public attitudes towards people with mental illness in six German cities. *European Archives of Psychiatry*, 252, 278–287.

Galbraith, J.K. (1952) *American Capitalism: The Concept of Countervailing Power*. New York: Houghton Mifflin.

Garattini, S. (1995) Cultural shift in Italy's drug policy. *Lancet*, 346, 5–6.

Garfinkel, H. (1967) *Studies in ethnomethodology*. Cambridge: Polity Press.

Gask, L., Sibbald, B., Creed, F. (1997) Evaluating models of working at the interface between mental health services and primary care. *British Journal of Psychiatry*, 170, 6–11.

Geddes, J., Harrison, P. (1997) Closing the gap between research and practice. *British Journal of Psychiatry*, 171, 220–225.

Georgaca, E. (2000) Reality and discourse: a critical analysis of the category of 'delusions'. *British Journal of Medical Psychology*, 73, 227–242.

Georgaca, E. (2003) Analysing the interviewer: the joint construction of accounts of psychotic experience. In L. Finlay, B. Gough (eds), *Reflexivity: A Practical Guide for Researchers in Health and Social Sciences*. Oxford: Blackwell Science.

Georgaca, E. (2004) Factualization and plausibility in 'delusional' discourse. *Philosophy, Psychiatry and Psychology*, 11, 13–23.

Gergen, K.J. (1985) The social constructionist movement in modern psychology. *American Psychologist*, 40, 266–275.

Gianutsos, R., Gianutsos, J. (1987) Single case experimental approaches to the assessment of interventions in rehabilitation psychology. In B. Caplan (ed.), *Rehabilitation Psychology* (pp. 453–70). Rockville, MD: Aspen.

Gilbert, G.N. (1980) Being interviewed: a role analysis. *Social Science Information*, 19, 227–236.

Gilbody, S.M., House, A.O., Sheldon, T.A. (2001) Routinely administered question-naires for depression and anxiety: a systematic review. *British Medical Journal*, 322, 406–409.

Gilbody, S.M., Song, F., Eastwood, A.J. et al (2000) The causes, consequences and detection of publication bias in psychiatry. *Acta Psychiatrica Scandinavica*, 102, 241–249.

Gilbody, S.M., Wahlbeck, K., Adams, C.E. (2002a) Randomised controlled trials in schizophrenia: a critical review of the literature. *Acta Psychiatrica Scandinavica*, 105, 243–251.

Gilbody, S., Whitty, P., Grimshaw, J.G. et al (2002b) *Improving the Recognition and Management of Depression in Primary Care*. York: University of York.

Gilbody, S., Whitty, P., Grimshaw, J. et al (2003) Educational and organizational interventions to improve the management of depression in primary care: a system-atic review. *Journal of the American Medical Association*, 289, 3145–3151.

Gill, R. (1995) Relativism, reflexivity and politics: interrogating DA from a feminist perspective. In S. Wilkinson, C. Kitzinger (eds), *Feminism and Discourse*. London: Sage.

Gillett, G. (1997) A discursive account of multiple personality disorder. *Philosophy, Psychiatry and Psychology*, 4, 213–222.

Gist, R. (2002) What have they done to my song? Social science, social movements and the debriefing debates. *Cognitive and Behavioral Practice*, 9, 273–279.

Glaser, B. (1978) *Theoretical Sensitivity: Advances in the Methodology of Grounded Theory*. Mill Valley, CA: Sociology Press.

Glaser, B. (1992) *Emergence Versus Forcing: Basics of Grounded Theory Analysis*. Mill Valley, CA: Sociology Press.

Glaser, B., Strauss, A. (1964) *Awareness of Dying*. Chicago: Aldine.

Glaser, B., Strauss, A. (1967) *The Discovery of Grounded Theory*. New York: Aldine.

Glass, G.V. (1976) Primary, secondary and meta-analysis. *Educational Research*, 5, 3–8.

Glisky, E.L., Schacter, D.L., Tulving, E. (1986) Computer learning by memory impaired patients: acquisition and retention of complex knowledge. *Neuropsycho-logia*, 24, 313–328.

Godlee, F., Smith, R., Goldmann, D. (1999) Clinical evidence. *British Medical Journal*, 318, 1570–1571.

Goffman, E. (1961) *Asylums*. Harmondsworth: Penguin.

Goldberg, D. (1999) The management of anxious depression in primary care. *Journal of Clinical Psychiatry*, 60, 39–42.

Goldberg, D., Huxley, P. (1980) *Mental Illness in the Community – the Pathway to Psychiatric Care*. London: Tavistock.

Goldberg, D., Huxley, P. (1992) *Common Mental Disorders: A Biopsychosocial Approach*. London: Routledge.

Goldberg, D., Mann, A., Tylee, A. (2001) Primary care. In G. Thornicroft, G. Szmukler (eds), *Textbook of Community Psychiatry* (pp. 409–417). Oxford: Oxford University Press.

Goldberg, D.P. (1972) *The Detection of Psychiatric Illness by Questionnaire GHQ* (Maudsley Monograph 21). London: Oxford University Press.

Goldman, L.S. (1999) Medical illness in patients with schizophrenia. *Journal of Clinical Psychiatry*, 60(Suppl 21), 10–15.

Gough, B., Lawton, R., Madill, A. et al. (2003) *Guidelines for the Supervision of Undergraduate Qualitative Research in Psychology*. Report and Evaluation Series No. 3. York: LTSN Psychology.

Gournay, K., Birley, J. (1998) Thorn: a new approach to mental health training. *Nursing Times*, 94, 54–55.

Greatbatch, D., Luff, P., Heath, C. et al. (1993) Interpersonal communication and human–computer interaction: an examination of the use of computers in medical consultations. *Interacting with Computers*, 5, 193–216.

Hurwitz, B., Greenhalgh, T., Skultans, V. (eds) *Narrative Research in Health and Illness*. London: BMA Books.

Griffiths, L. (2001) Categorising to exclude: the discursive construction of cases in community mental health teams. *Sociology of Health and Illness*, 23, 678–700.

Grimshaw, J., Wilson, B., Campbell, M. et al (2001) Epidemiological methods. In N. Fulop, P. Allen, A. Clarke et al (eds), *Studying the Organisation and Delivery of Health Services*. London: Routledge.

Grimshaw, J.M., Russell, I.T. (1993) Effect of clinical guidelines on medical practice: a systematic review of rigorous evaluations. *Lancet*, 342(8883), 1317–1322.

Grol, R., Dalhuijsen, J., Thomas, S. et al. (1998) Attributes of clinical guidelines that influence use of guidelines in general practice: observational study. *British Medical Journal*, 317(7162), 858–861.

Gupta, S. (1999) The fourth national survey of ethnic minorities. In D. Bhugra, V. Bahl (eds), *Ethnicity: An Agenda for Mental Health*. London: Gaskell.

Haakana, M. (2001) Laughter as a patient's resource: dealing with delicate aspects of medical interaction. *Text*, 21, 187–219.

Haakana, M. (2002) Laughter in medical interaction: from quantification to analysis, and back. *Journal of Sociolinguistics*, 6, 207–235.

Häfner, H. (2001) Die Psychiatrie-Enquete – historische Aspekte und Perspektiven [The 'Psychiatrie-Enquête' – historical aspects and perspectives]. In Aktion Psychisch Kranke (ed.), *Tagungsband: 25 Jahre Psychiatrie-Enquete* (pp. 72–102). Psychiatrie-Verlag: Bonn.

Häfner, H. (2003) Die Inquisition der psychisch Kranken geht ihrem Ende entgegen: Die Geschichte der Psychiatrie-Enquête und Psychiatriereform in Deutschland [The inquisition of the mentally ill approaches its end: the history of the 'Psychiatrie-Enquête' and of psychiatric reform in Germany]. In F.-W. Kersing (ed.), *Psychiatrie als Gesellschaftsreform* (pp. 113–140). Paderborn: Schöningh.

Haines, A., Jones, R. (1994) Implementing research findings. *British Medical Journal*, 308, 1488–1492.

Hallam, R.S. (1994) Some constructionist observations on 'anxiety' and its history. In T.R. Sarbin, J.I. Kitsuse (eds), *Constructing the Social*. London: Sage.

Hammersley, M. (1989) *The Dilemma of Qualitative Method: Herbert Blumer and the Chicago Tradition*. London: Routledge.

Hansson, L. (1996) Sectorized services outcome research. In H.C. Knudsen, G. Thornicroft (eds), *Mental Health Service Evaluation*. Cambridge: Cambridge University Press.

Hansson, L. (2001) Sectorization. In G. Thornicroft, G. Szmukler (eds), *Textbook of Community Psychiatry*. Oxford: Oxford University Press.

Hardy, M., Bryman, A. (eds) (2004) Handbook of Data Analysis. London: Sage.

Hare, E.H., Shaw, G.K. (1965) *Mental Health on a New Housing Estate: A Comparative*

Study of Health in Two Districts in Croydon (Maudsley Monographs No. 12). London: Oxford University Press.

Hargreaves, I., Lewis, J., Speers, T. (2003) *Towards a Better Map: Science, the Public and the Media*. London: Economic and Social Research Council.

Harper, D. (1998) Discourse analysis and psychiatric medication. *Clinical Psychology Forum*, 114, 19–21.

Harper, D. (1999) Tablet talk and depot discourse: discourse analysis and psychiatric medication. In C. Willig (ed.), *Applied Discourse Analysis: Social and Psychological Interventions*. Buckingham: Open University Press.

Harper, D. (2002) When the drugs don't work. *Open Mind*, 114, 8.

Harper, D. (2003) Developing a critically reflexive position using discourse analysis. In L. Finlay, B. Gough (eds), *Reflexivity: A Practical Guide for Researchers in Health and Social Sciences*. Oxford: Blackwell Science.

Harper, D., Mulvey, R.M., Robinson, M. (2003) Beyond evidence-based practice: rethinking the relationship between research, theory and practice. In R. Bayne, I. Horton (eds), *Applied Psychology: Current Issues and New Directions*. London: Sage.

Harper, D.J. (1994a) Histories of suspicion in a time of conspiracy: A reflection on Aubrey Lewis's history of paranoia. *History of the Human Species*, 7(3), 89–109.

Harper, D.J. (1994b) The professional construction of 'paranoia' and the discursive use of diagnostic criteria. *British Journal of Medical Psychology*, 67, 131–143.

Harper, D.J. (1995) Discourse analysis and 'mental health'. *Journal of Mental Health*, 4, 347–357.

Harper, D.J. (1996) Deconstructing 'paranoia': towards a discursive understanding of apparently unwarranted suspicion. *Theory and Psychology*, 6, 423–448.

Harper, D.J. (2004a) Storying policy: constructions of risk in proposals to reform UK mental health legislation. In B. Hurwitz, T. Greenhalgh, V. Skultans (eds), *Narrative Research in Health and Illness* (pp. 397–413). London: BMJ Books/Blackwell Publishing.

Harper, D.J. (2004b). Delusions and discourse: moving beyond the constraints of the modernist paradigm. *Philosophy, Psychiatry and Psychology*, 11, 55–64.

Harré, R. (2004) Staking our claim for qualitative research as science. *Qualitative Research in Psychology*, 1, 3–14.

Harré, R., Moghaddam, F. (eds), *The Self and Others: Positioning Individuals and Groups in Personal, Political, and Cultural Contexts*. Westport, CT: Praeger.

Harré, R., Secord, P. (1972) *The Explanation of Social Behaviour*. Oxford: Blackwell.

Harré, R., Van Langenhove, V. (1991) Varieties of positioning. *Journal for the Theory of Social Behaviour*, 21, 393–407.

Harré, R., Van Langenhove, V. (1999) *Positioning Theory: Moral Contexts of Intentional Action*. Oxford: Blackwell.

Hart, E., Bond, M. (1995) *Action Research for Health and Social Care: A Guide to Practice*. Buckingham: Open University Press.

Hartwell, C.E. (1996) The schizophrenogenic mother concept in American psychiatry. *Psychiatry*, 59, 274–297.

Hayward, P., Bright, J.A. (1997) Stigma and mental illness: a review and critique. *Journal of Mental Health*, 6, 435–454.

Healy, D. (1997) *The Antidepressant Era*. Cambridge, MA: Harvard University Press.

Heath, C. (1986) *Body Movement and Speech in Medical Interaction*. Cambridge: Cambridge University Press.

Heath, C. (1992) The delivery and reception of diagnosis in the general practice consultation. In P. Drew, J. Heritage (eds), *Talk at Work*. Cambridge University Press: Cambridge.

Heenan, C. (1998) Discourse analysis and clinical supervision. *Clinical Psychology Forum*, 114, 19–21.

Henggeler, S.W., Rowland, M.D., Pickrel, S.G. et al (1997) Investigating family-based alternatives to institution-based mental health services for youth: lessons learned from the pilot study of a randomized field trial. *Journal of Clinical Child Psychology*, 26, 226–233.

Henwood, K.L. (1993) Women and later life: the discursive construction of identities within family relationships. *Journal of Aging Studies*, 7, 303–319.

Henwood, K.L. (1996) Qualitative inquiry: perspectives, methods and psychology. In J.T.E. Richardson (ed.), *Handbook of Qualitative Research Methods for Psychologists and the Social Sciences* (pp. 25–42). Leicester: BPS Books.

Henwood, K.L. (2004) Reinventing validity: reflections on principles from beyond the quality-quantity divide. In Z. Todd, B. Nerlich, S. McKeown et al (eds.), *Mixing Methods in Psychology*. London: Taylor & Francis.

Henwood, K.L., Nicolson, P. (eds) (1995) *Qualitative Approaches in Psychology*. Special Issue of *Psychologist*, 8(3), 109–129.

Henwood, K.L., Pidgeon, N.F. (1992) Qualitative research and psychological theorizing. *British Journal of Psychology*, 83, 97–111.

Henwood, K.L., Pidgeon, N.F. (1994) Beyond the qualitative paradigm: a framework for introducing diversity in qualitative psychology. *Journal of Community and Applied Social Psychology*, 4, 225–238.

Henwood, K.L., Pidgeon, N.F. (2001) Talk about woods and trees: threat of urbanisation, stability and biodiversity. *Journal of Environmental Psychology*, 21, 125–147.

Henwood, K.L., Pidgeon, N.F. (2003) Grounded theory in psychological research. In P. Camic, L. Yardley, J. Rhodes (eds), *Qualitative Research in Psychology*. Washington, DC: American Psychological Association Press.

Hepburn, A. (2003) *An Introduction to Critical Social Psychology*. London: Sage.

Hepburn, A., Potter, J. (2003) Discourse analytic practice. In C. Seale, D. Silverman, J. Gubrium et al (eds), *Qualitative Research Practice*. London: Sage.

Hepworth, J. (1999) *The Social Construction of Anorexia*. London: Sage.

Heritage, J. (1984) *Garfinkel and Ethnomethodology*. Cambridge: Polity Press.

Heritage, J. (1997) Conversation analysis and institutional talk. In D. Silverman (ed.), *Qualitative Research: Theory, Method and Practice*. London: Sage.

Heritage, J. (2004) Conversation analysis and institutional talk. In D. Silverman (ed.), *Qualitative Research: Theory, Method and Practice* (2nd edn). London: Sage.

Heritage, J., Boyd, E., Kleinman, L. (2001) Subverting criteria: the role of precedent in decisions to finance surgery. *Sociology of Health and Illness*, 23, 701–728.

Heritage, J., Maynard, D. (in press) *Practising Medicine: Structure and Process in Primary Care Encounters*. Cambridge: Cambridge University Press.

Heritage, J., Stivers, T. (1999) Online commentary in acute medical visits: a method of shaping patient expectations. *Social Science and Medicine*, 49, 1501–1517.

Hersen, M., Barlow, D.H. (1976) *Single Case Experimental Designs: Strategies for Studying Behavior Change*. Elmsford, NY: Pergamon Press.

Hibble, A., Kanka, D., Pencheon, D. et al (1998) Guidelines in general practice: the new Tower of Babel? *British Medical Journal*, 317(7162), 862–863.

Hiday, V., Swanson, J., Swartz, M. et al (2001) Victimisation: a link between mental illness and violence? *International Journal of Law and Psychiatry*, 24, 559–572.

Hirschfeld, R.M., Keller, M.B., Panico, S. et al (1997) The National Depressive and Manic-Depressive Association consensus statement on the undertreatment of depression. *Journal of the American Medical Association*, 277, 333–340.

Hoffmann, K., Priebe, S., Isermann, M. et al (1997) Lebensqualität, Bedürfnisse und Behandlungsbewertung langzeithospitalisierter Patienten. Teil II der Berliner Enthospitalisierungsstudie [Quality of life, needs and treatment evaluation of long-term hospitalized patients. Part II of the Berlin Deinstitutionalization Study]. *Psychiatrische Praxis*, 24, 221–226.

Hollingshead, A.B. Redlich, F.C. (1958) *Social Class and Mental Illness*. New York: Wiley.

Holloway, F. (1991) Case management: looking at the evidence. *International Journal of Social Psychiatry*, 38, 2–11.

Holloway, F. (1996) Community psychiatric care: from libertarianism to coercion. 'Moral panic' and mental health policy in Britain. *Health Care Analysis*, 4, 235–243.

Hollway, W. (1989) *Subjectivity and Method in Psychology: Gender, Meaning and Science*. London: Sage.

Holmes, P., Corrigan, P., Williams, P. et al (1999) Changing attitudes about schizophrenia. *Schizophrenia Bulletin*, 25, 447–456.

Horder, J. (1983) The Alma Ata declaration. *British Medical Journal*, 286, 191–194.

Horton, R. (1999) Evidence and primary care. *Lancet*, 353(9153), 609–610.

Horton, R. (2001) The clinical trial: deceitful, disputable, unbelievable, unhelpful, and shameful – what next? *Controlled Clinical Trials*, 22, 593–604.

Horton-Salway, M. (2001) The construction of M.E.: The discursive action model. In M. Wetherell, S. Taylor, S. Yates (eds), *Discourse as Data: A guide for analysis* (pp. 147–188). London: Sage

Hotopf, M. (2002) The pragmatic randomised controlled trial. *Advances in Psychiatric Treatment*, 8, 326–333.

Hotopf, M., Churchill, R., Lewis, G. (1999) Pragmatic randomised controlled trials in psychiatry. *British Journal of Psychiatry*, 175, 217–223.

Hotopf, M., Normand, C. (1997) Putting trials on trial – the costs and consequences of small trials in depression: a systematic review of methodology. *Journal of Epidemiology and Community Health*, 51, 354–358.

Houston, H.R., Venkatesh, A. (1996) The health care consumption patterns of Asian immigrants: grounded theory implications for consumer acculturation theory. *Advances in Consumer Research*, 23, 418–423.

Hunt, M. (1997) *How Science Takes Stock*. New York: Russell Sage Foundation.

Hutchby, I., Wooffitt, R. (2003) *Conversation Analysis*. Cambridge: Polity Press.

Institute of Medicine (2001) *Neurological, Psychiatric and Developmental Disorders: Meeting the Challenge in the Developing World*. Washington, DC: National Academy Press (www.iom.edu).

Italian study group for the Di Bella multitherapy trials. (1999) Evaluation of an unconventional cancer treatment (the Di Bella multitherapy): results of phase II trials in Italy. *British Medical Journal*, 318, 224–228.

Jackson, D., Block, J., Block, J.H. et al (1958) Psychiatrists' conceptions of schizophrenic parents. *Archives of Neurology and Psychiatry*, 79, 448–459.

Jameson, F. (1991) *Postmodernism, or, The Cultural Logic of Late Capitalism*. Durham, NC: Duke University Press.

Jefferson, G. (1984) On the organization of laughter in talk about troubles. In J.M. Atkinson, J. Heritage (eds), *Structures of Social Action*. Cambridge: Cambridge University Press.

Jefferson, G., Lee, J.R.E. (1992) The rejection of advice: managing the problematic convergence of a 'trouble-stelling' and a 'service encounter'. In P. Drew, J. Heritage (eds), *Talk at Work*. Cambridge: Cambridge University Press.

Jenkins, R. (1985a) Minor psychiatric morbidity in employed young men and women, and its contribution to sickness absence. *British Journal of Industrial Medicine*, 42, 147–154.

Jenkins, R. (1985b) Minor psychiatric morbidity and labour turnover. *British Journal of Industrial Medicine*, 42, 534–539.

Jenkins, R. (2003) Making psychiatric epidemiology useful: the contribution of epidemiology to government policy. *International Review of Psychiatry*, 15, 188–200.

Jenkins, R., Bebbington, P., Brugha, T.S. et al (1998) British Psychiatric Morbidity Survey. *British Journal of Psychiatry*, 173, 4–7.

Jenkins, R., Griffiths, S., Wylie, I. et al (1994) (eds) *The Prevention of Suicide*. London: HMSO.

Jenkins, R., MacDonald, A., Murray, J. et al (1982) Minor psychiatric morbidity and the threat of redundancy in a professional group. *Psychological Medicine*, 12, 799–807.

Jenkins, R., Meltzer, D. (2003) A decade of national surveys of psychiatric epidemiology in Great Britain: 1990–2000. *International Review of Psychiatry*, 15, nos 1 and 2.

Jenkins, R., Scott, J. (1998) The medical staffing crisis in psychiatry. *Psychiatric Bulletin*, 22, 239–241.

Jenkins, R., Singh, B. (2000) Policy and practice in suicide prevention. *British Journal of Forensic Psychiatry*, 2, 3–11.

Jenkins, R., Strathdee, G. (2000) The integration of mental health care. *International Journal of Law and Psychiatry*, 23, 277–291.

Jeste, D.V., Gladsjo, J.A., Lindamer, L.A. et al (1996) Medical comorbidity in schizophrenia. *Schizophrenia Bulletin*, 22, 413–430.

Joffe, H., Yardley, L. (2004) Content and thematic analysis. In D. Marks, L. Yardley (eds), *Research Methods for Clinical and Health Psychology*. London: Sage.

Johansson, H., Eklund, M. (2003) Patients' opinion on what constitutes good psychiatric care. *Scandinavian Journal of Caring Sciences*, 17, 339–346.

Johnson, S., Thornicroft, G. (1993) The sectorisation of psychiatric services in England and Wales. *Social Psychiatry and Psychiatric Epidemiology*, 28, 45–47.

Jones, M. (1953) *The Therapeutic Community*. New York: Basic Books.

Kaiser, W., Hoffmann, K., Isermann, M. et al. (1998) Behandlerprognosen und Entlassungen nach zwei Jahren. Teil III der Berliner Enthospitalisierungsstudie [Treatment prognosis and discharge 2 years later. Part III of the Berlin Deinstitutionalization Study]. *Psychiatrische Praxis*, 25, 67–71.

Kallert, T.W., Schützwohl, M., Nawka, P. et al (2002) Efficacy of psychiatric day hospital treatment: review of research findings and design of a European multicentre study. *Archives of Psychiatry and Psychotherapy*, 2, 55–77.

Kane, J., Honigfeld, G., Singer, J. et al (1988) Clozapine for the treatment-resistant schizophrenic. A double-blind comparison with chlorpromazine. *Archives of General Psychiatry*, 45, 789–796.

Kaptchuk, T. (1998) Intentional ignorance: a history of blind assessment and placebo controls in medicine. *Bulletin of the History of Medicine*, 72, 389–433.

Karp, D., Tanarugsachock, V. (2000) Mental illness, care giving and emotion management. *Qualitative Health Research*, 10, 6–25.

Kasl, S.V., Gore, S., Cobb, S. (1975) The experience of losing a job: reported changes in health, symptoms and illness behaviour. *Psychosomatic Medicine*, 37, 106–122.

Katon, W., Von Korff, M., Lin, E. et al (1997) Population-based care of depression: effective disease management strategies to decrease prevalence. *General Hospital Psychiatry*, 19, 169–178.

Kauder, V., Aktion Psychisch Kranke (1997) *Personenzentrierte Hilfe in der psychiatrischen Versorgung [Person-Centred Help in Psychiatric Service Provision]*. Bonn: Psychiatrie-Verlag.

Kaufman, D.M. (2003) Applying educational theory in practice. *British Medical Journal*, 326(7382), 213–216.

Kazdin, A.E. (1982) *Single-Case Research Designs: Methods for Clinical and Applied Settings*. New York: Oxford University Press.

Kellett, J.M. (1985) Crowding and territoriality – a psychiatric view. In H.L. Freeman (ed.), *Mental Health and the Environment*. London: Churchill Livingstone.

Kellett, J.M. (1989) Health and housing. *Journal of Psychosomatic Research*, 33, 255–268.

Kelly, S., Charlton, J., Jenkins, R. (1995) Suicide deaths in England and Wales, 1982–1992; the contribution of occupation and geography. *Population Trends*, 80, 16–25.

Kendall, J. (1999) Axial coding and the grounded theory controversy. *Western Journal of Nursing Research*, 21, 743–757.

Kendrick, T. (2000) Why can't GPs follow guidelines on depression? We must question the basis of the guidelines themselves. *British Medical Journal*, 320(7229), 200–201.

Kendrick, T., Sibbald, B., Burns, T. et al (1991) Role of general practitioners in care of long term mentally ill patients. *British Medical Journal*, 302(6775), 508–510.

Kernick, D.P. (1999) Evidence and primary care. *Lancet*, 353(9164), 1622.

Kernick, D.P. (2000) Muddling through in a parallel track universe. *British Journal of General Practice*, 50(453), 325.

Kessler, R.C., Anthony, J.C., Blazer, D.B. et al (1997) The US National Comorbidity Survey: overview and future directions. *Epidemiologia e Psichiatria Sociale*, 6, 4–16.

Kessler, R.C., McGonagle, K.A., Zhao, S. et al (1994) Lifetime and 12-month prevalence of DSM-III-R psychiatric disorders in the United States. Results from the National Comorbidity Survey. *Archives of General Psychiatry*, 51, 8–19.

Kinderman, P., Cooke, A. (2000) *Recent Advances in Understanding Mental Illness and Psychotic Experiences*. London: British Psychological Society.

King, M., Nazareth, I. (1996) Community care of patients with schizophrenia: the role of the primary health care team. *British Journal of General Practice*, 46, 231–237.

King, M.B. (1992) Management of patients with schizophrenia in general practice. *British Journal of General Practice*, 42, 310–311.

King, N. (1998) Template analysis. In G. Symon, C. Cassell (eds), *Qualitative Methods and Analysis in Organisational Research*. London: Sage.

Kirk, J., Miller, M.L. (1986) *Reliability and Validity in Qualitative Research*. London: Sage.

Kjaegard, L.L., Als-Neilson, B. (2002) Association between competing interests and author's conclusions: epidemiological study of randomised clinical trials published in the BMJ. *British Medical Journal*, 325, 249–252.

Kleijnen, J., Gotzsche, P., Kunz, R. et al (1997) So what's so special about randomisation? In A. Maynard, I. Chalmers (eds), *Non-random Reflections on Health Services Research: On the 25th Anniversary of Archie Cochrane's Effectiveness and Efficiency* (pp. 93–106). London: BMJ Publishing.

Kleinman, A. (1988) *The Illness Narratives: Suffering, Healing and the Human Condition*. New York: Basic Books.

Kogan, S.M., Gale, J.E. (1997) Decentering therapy: textual analysis of a narrative therapy session. *Family Process*, 36, 101–126.

Kovess, V., Boisguerin, B., Antoine, D. et al (1995) Has the sectorization of psychiatric services in France really been effective? *Social Psychiatry and Psychiatric Epidemiology*, 30, 132–138.

Krishef, C. (1991) *Fundamental Approaches to Single Subject Design and Analysis*. Melbourne, FL: Krieger.

Kühn, K.U., Quednow, B.B., Barkow, K. et al (2002) Chronifizierung und psychosoziale Behinderung durch depressive Erkrankungen bei Patienten in der Allgemeinarztpraxis im Einjahresverlauf. Ergebnisse aus einer Studie der Weltgesundheitsorganisation [Chronicity and psychosocial disability in depressed patients in primary care: 1-year follow-up]. *Nervenarzt*, 73, 644–650.

Kuhn, T. (1962) *The Structure of Scientific Revolutions*. Chicago: Chicago University Press.

Kuipers, L. (1979) Expressed emotion: a review. *British Journal of Social and Clinical Psychology*, 18, 237–243.

Kunz, R., Oxman, A. (1998) The unpredictability paradox: review of empirical comparisons of randomised and non-randomised clinical trials. *British Medical Journal*, 317, 1185–1190.

Kunze, H. (1985) Rehabilitation and institutionalisation in community care in West Germany. *British Journal of Psychiatry*, 147, 261–264.

Kunze, H. (1999) Personenzentrierter Ansatz in der psychiatrischen Versorgung in Deutschland [The person-centred approach in psychiatric service provision in Germany]. *Psycho*, 25, 728–735.

Kunze, H., Becker, T., Priebe, S. (2004) Reform of psychiatric services in Germany: hospital staffing directive and commissioning of community care. *Psychiatric Bulletin*, 28, 218–221.

Kunze, H., Kaltenbach, L. (2003) *Psychiatrie-Personalverordnung [Psychiatric Staffing Directive]* (4th edn). Stuttgart: Kohlhammer.

Landauer, T.K., Bjork, R.A. (1978) Optimum rehearsal patterns and name learning. In M.M. Gruneberg, P.E. Morris, R.N. Sykes (eds), *Practical Aspects of Memory* (pp. 625–632). London: Academic Press.

Langner, T.S. (1962) A twenty-two item screening score of psychiatric symptoms indicating impairment. *Journal of Health and Human Behaviour*, 3, 269–276.

Latour, B. (1987) *Science in Action*. Cambridge, MA: Harvard University Press.

Lavin, D., Maynard, D. (2001) Standardization vs. rapport: respondent laughter and interviewer reaction during telephone surveys. *American Sociological Review*, 66, 453–479.

Leason, K. (2002) News analysis of opposition to mental health bill. *Community Care*, 22–28 August, 20–21.

Leff, J. (1994) Working with the families of schizophrenic patients. *British Journal of Psychiatry*, 164 (Suppl 23), 71–76.

Leff, J., Berkowitz, R., Shavit, N. et al (1990) A trial of family therapy versus a relatives' group for schizophrenia. Two-year follow-up. *British Journal of Psychiatry*, 157, 571–577.

Lehman, A.F., Steinwachs, D.M. (1988) Translating research into practice: the Schizophrenia Patient Outcomes Research Team (PORT) treatment recommendations. *Schizophrenia Bulletin*, 24, 1–10.

Lehtinen, V., Aaltonen, J., Koffert, T. et al (2000) Two-year outcome in first-episode psychosis treated according to an integrated model. Is immediate neuroleptisation always needed? *European Psychiatry*, 15, 312–320.

Leighton, D.C., Harding, J.S., Macklin, D.B. et al (1963) *The Character of Danger Stirling County Study* (vol. 3). New York: Basic Books.

Levin, P. (1999) *Making Social Policy*. Buckingham: Open University Press.

Levinson, S. (1983) *Pragmatics*. Cambridge: Cambridge University Press.

Lewis, B. (2000) Psychiatry and postmodern theory. *Journal of Medical Humanities*, 21, 71–84.

Lewis, G., Booth, M. (1994) Are cities bad for your mental health? *Psychological Medicine*, 24, 913–915.

Lewis, G., Araya, R. (1995) Is the General Health Questionnaire (12 item) a culturally biased measure of psychiatric disorder? *Social Psychiatry and Psychiatric Epidemiology*, 30, 20–25.

Lewis, G., Pelosi, A., Araya, R. (1992) Measuring psychiatric disorder in the community: a standardized assessment for use by lay interviewers. *Psychological Medicine*, 22, 465–486.

Lewis, S.E. (1995) A search for meaning: making sense of depression. *Journal of Mental Health*, 4, 369–382.

Lexchin, J., Bero, L.A., Djulbegovic, B. et al. (2003) Pharmaceutical industry sponsorship and research outcome and quality: systematic review. *British Medical Journal*, 326, 1167–1173.

Light, D. (1995) Countervailing powers: a framework for professions in transition. In T. Johnson, G. Larken, M. Saks (eds), *Health Professions and the State in Europe*. London: Routledge.

Lincoln, Y., Guba, E. (1985) *Naturalistic Inquiry*. Beverly Hills, CA: Sage.

Linden, M., Gothe, H., Ormel, J. (2003) Pathways to care and psychological problems of general practice patients in a 'gate keeper' and an 'open access' health care system: a comparison of Germany and the Netherlands. *Social Psychiatry and Psychiatric Epidemiology*, 38, 690–697.

Linden, M., Lecrubier, Y., Bellantuono, C. et al. (1999) The prescribing of psychotropic drugs by primary care physicians: an international collaborative study. *Journal of Clinical Psychopharmacology*, 19, 132–140.

Linden, M., Maier, W., Achberger, M. et al. (1996) Psychische Erkrankungen und ihre Behandlung in Allgemeinarztpraxen in Deutschland: Ergebnisse aus einer

Studie der Weltgesundheitsorganisation (WHO) [Psychiatric diseases and their treatment in general practice in Germany: results of a WHO study]. *Nervenarzt*, 67, 205–215.

Lindholm, H. (1983) Sectorized psychiatry. A methodological study of the effects of reorganization on patients treated at a mental hospital. *Acta Psychiatrica Scandinavica Supplement* 304, 67.

Link, B. (2001) Stigma: many mechanisms require multifaceted responses. *Epidemiologia Psichiatria Sociale*, 10, 8–11.

Link, B., Phelan, J. (2001) Conceptualizing stigma. *Annual Review of Sociology*, 27, 363–385.

Link, B., Stueve, A. (1994) Psychiatric symptoms and violent/illegal behaviour of mental patients compared to community schools. In J. Monahan, H.J. Steadman (eds), *Violence and Mental Disorder* (pp. 137–159). Chicago: Chicago University Press.

Little, J.M. (2002) Humanistic medicine or values-based medicine. What's in a name? *Medical Journal of Australia*, 177, 319–321.

Littlejohns, P., Cluzeau, F., Bale, R. et al (1999) The quantity and quality of clinical practice guidelines for the management of depression in primary care in the UK. *British Journal of General Practice*, 49, 205–210.

Lloyd, K., Jenkins, R., Mann, A.H. (1996) The longterm outcome of patients with neurotic illness in general practice. *British Medical Journal*, 313, 26–28.

Long, A., Dixon, P. (1996) Monitoring outcomes in routine practice: defining appropriate measurement criteria. *Journal of Evaluation in Clinical Practice*, 2, 71–78.

Luborsky, L., Singer, B., Luborsky, L. (1975) Comparative studies of psychotherapy: is it true that 'everyone has won and all must have prizes'? *Archives of General Psychiatry*, 32, 995–1008.

Luria, A.R. (1981) *The Man with a Shattered World*. Harmondsworth: Penguin.

Lynch, M. (1985) *Art and Artifact in Laboratory Science: A Study of Shop Work and Shop Talk*. London: Routledge and Kegan Paul.

Lyons, J.S. (2004) *Redressing the Emperor: Improving the Children's Public Mental Health System*. Westport, CT: Praeger.

Lyons, J.S, Kisiel, C.L., Dulcan, M. et al (1997) Crisis assessment and psychiatric hospitalization of children and adolescents in state custody. *Journal of Child and Family Studies*, 6, 311–320.

Lyons, J.S., Mintzer, L.L., Kisiel, C.L. et al (1998) Understanding the mental health needs of children and adolescents in residential treatment. *Professional Psychology: Research and Practice*, 29, 582–587.

Lyons, J.S., Weiner, D.A., Lyons, M.B. (2004) Measurement as communication. The Child and Adolescent Needs and Strengths tool. In M. Mariush (ed.), *The Use of Psychological Testing for Treatment Planning and Outcome Assessment* (vol. 2, 3rd edn). Hillsdale, NJ: Lawrence Erlbaum Associates Inc.

Lyotard, J.-F. (1984) *The Postmodern Condition: A Report on Knowledge*. Manchester: Manchester University Press.

Madill, A., Barkham, M. (1997) Discourse analysis of a theme in one successful case of brief psychodynamic-interpersonal psychotherapy. *Journal of Counseling Psychology*, 44, 232–244.

Madill, A., Jordan, A., Shirley, C. (2000) Objectivity and reliability in qualitative analysis: realist, contextualist and constructionist epistemologies. *British Journal of Psychology*, 91, 1–20.

Madill, A.L., Widdicombe, S., Barkham, M. (2001) The potential of conversation analysis for psychotherapy research. *The Counseling Psychologist*, 29, 413–434.

Madsen, K.M., Hviid, A., Vestergaard, M. et al (2002) A population-based study of measles, mumps, and rubella vaccination and autism. *New England Journal of Medicine*, 347, 1477–1482.

Malson, H. (1997) *The Thin Woman: Feminism, Post-Structuralism and the Social Psychology of Anorexia Nervosa*. London: Routledge.

Manderscheid, R.W., Henderson, M.J., Brown, D.Y. (2001) Status of national efforts to improve accountability for quality. In B. Dickey, L.I. Sederer (eds), *Improving Mental Health Care: Commitment to Quality* (pp. 163–178). Washington, DC: American Psychiatric Publishing.

Mant, D. (1999) Can randomised trials inform clinical decisions about individual patients? *Lancet*, 353(9154), 743–746.

Mari, J.J., Streiner, D.L. (1994) An overview of family interventions and relapse on schizophrenia: meta-analysis of research findings. *Psychological Medicine*, 24, 565–578.

Marks, D. (1992) Decision-making in case conferences: an example from education. *Clinical Psychology Forum*, 45, 14–17.

Marks, D. (1993) Case-conference analysis and action research. In E. Burman, I. Parker (eds), *Discourse Analytic Research: Repertoires and Readings of Texts in Action*. London: Routledge.

Marks, D., Yardley, L. (eds) (2004) *Research Methods for Clinical and Health Psychology*. London: Sage.

Marshall, M. (2003) Acute psychiatric day hospitals. *British Journal of Psychiatry*, 327, 116–117.

Marshall, M., Crowther, R., Almaraz-Serrano, A. et al (2004a) Day hospital versus admission for acute psychiatric disorders (Cochrane Review). *Cochrane Library*, Issue 1. Chichester: Wiley.

Marshall, M., Gray, A., Lockwood, A., Green, R. (1998) Case management for people with severe mental illness. *Cochrane Database of Systematic Reviews*, Issue 2.

Marshall, M., Gray, A., Lockwood, A. et al (2001) Case management for people with severe mental disorders (Cochrane Review). *Cochrane Library*, Issue 2. Oxford: Update Software.

Marshall, M., Gray, A., Lockwood, A. et al (2004b) Case management for people with severe mental disorder (Cochrane Review). *Cochrane Library*, Issue 1. Chichester: Wiley.

Marshall, M., Lockwood, A. (1998) Assertive community treatment for people with severe mental disorders. *Cochrane Database of Systematic Reviews*, Issue 2.

Marshall, M., Lockwood, A. (2001) Assertive community treatment for people with severe mental disorders (Cochrane Review). *Cochrane Library*, Issue 2. Oxford: Update Software.

Mason, J. (1996) *Qualitative Researching*. London: Sage.

Mason, J. (2002) *Qualitative Researching* (2nd edn). London: Sage.

Mayer, J., Piterman, L. (1999) The attitudes of Australian GPs to evidence-based medicine: a focus group study. *Family Practice*, 16, 627–632.

Maynard, D.W. (2003) *Bad News, Good News: Conversational Order in Everyday Talk and Clinical Settings*. Chicago: Chicago University Press.

Mays, N., Roberts, E., Popay, J. (2001) Synthesising research evidence. In N. Fulop, P. Allen, A. Clarke et al (eds), *Studying the Organisation and Delivery of Health Services*. London: Routledge.

McCabe, R. (2004) On the inadequacies of theory of mind explanations of schizophrenia: Alternative accounts of alternative problems. *Theory and Psychology*, 14(5): 738–752.

McCabe, R., Heat, C., Burns, T. et al (2002) Engagement of patients with psychosis in the medical consultation: a conversation analytic study. *British Medical Journal*, 325, 1148–1151 (http://bmj.com/cgi/content/full/325/7373/1148).

McCabe, R., Leudar, I., Antaki, C. (2004) Do people with schizophrenia display theory of mind deficits in naturalistic interaction? *Psychological Medicine*, 34, 401–412.

McCabe, R., Priebe, S. (2003a) Engaging patients with psychosis in consultations: authors' reply. *British Medical Journal*, 326, 549 (http://bmj.com/cgi/content/full/326/7388/549).

McCabe, R., Priebe, S. (2003b) Understanding the un-understandable: communicating about psychotic symptoms in the medical consultation. *Primary Care Mental Health and Education*, 7, 4–6.

McColl, A., Smith, H., White, P. et al (1983) General practitioner's perceptions of the route to evidence based medicine: a questionnaire survey. *British Medical Journal*, 316(7128), 361–365.

McCormick, A., Fleming, D., Charton, J. & OPCS. (1995) *Morbidity Statistics from General Practice: Fourth National Study, 1991–1992*. London: HMSO.

McHugo, G.J., Drake, R.E., Teague, G.B. et al (1999) Fidelity to assertive community treatment and client outcomes in the New Hampshire dual disorders study. *Psychiatric Services*, 50, 818–824.

McKee, M., Britton, A., Black, N. et al (1999) Interpreting the evidence: choosing between randomised and non-randomised studies. *British Medical Journal*, 319, 312–315.

McKenzie, W., Monk, G. (1997) Learning and teaching narrative ideas. In G. Monk, J. Winslade, K. Crocket, D. Epston (eds), *Narrative Therapy in Practice: The Archaeology of Hope*. San Francisco: Jossey Bass.

McLeod, J. (2001) *Qualitative Research in Counselling and Psychotherapy*. London: Sage.

McNamee, S., Gergen, K.J. (eds) (1992) *Therapy as Social Construction*. London: Sage.

Medical Research Council (1965) Clinical trial of the treatment of depressive illness. *British Medical Journal*, i, 881–886.

Medical Research Council (2000) *A Framework for Development and Evaluation of RCTs for Complex Interventions to Improve Health*. London: Medical Research Council.

Melchinger, H., Giovelli, M. (1999) *Ambulante Soziotherapie: Evaluation und analytische Auswertung des Modellprojektes 'Ambulante Rehabilitation psychisch Kranker' der Spitzenverbände der gesetzlichen Krankenkassen [Outpatient Sociotherapy: Evaluation of the Model Project 'Ambulatory Rehabilitation of Mentally Ill']*. Baden-Baden: Nomos.

Melchinger, H., Machleidt, W. (2003) Ambulante Soziotherapie als Kassenleistung – ein Schritt nach vorn in der Psychiatriereform? [Outpatient sociotherapy covered by statutory health insurance – a sustainable contribution to the reform of psychiatry?]. *Krankenhauspsychiatrie*, 14, 107–112.

Meltzer, H., Gatward, R., Goodman, R. et al (2000) *Mental Health of Children and Adolescents in Great Britain*. London: Stationery Office.

Meltzer, H., Gill, B., Petticrew, M. et al (1995a) *OPCS Surveys of Psychiatric Morbidity Report 2. Physical Complaints, Use of Services and Treatment of Adults with Psychiatric Disorders*. London: HMSO.

Meltzer, H., Gill, B., Pettigrew, M. et al. (1995b) *The Prevalence of Psychiatric Morbidity Among Adults Living in Private Households*. London: HMSO.

Meltzer, H., Jenkins, R., Singleton, N. et al (1999) Non-fatal suicidal behaviour among prisoners. London: Office for National Statistics.

Mental Health Media (2001) Mental health and the press, survey. Accessed at www.mhmedia.com/training/report.html

Mentality (2003) *Making It Effective: A Guide to Evidence-Based Mental Health Promotion. Radical Mentalities Briefing Paper One*. London: Mentality.

Mercer, G. (2002) Emancipatory disability research. In C. Barnes, M. Oliver, L. Barton (eds), *Disability Studies Today*. Cambridge: Polity.

Messari, S., Hallam, R. (2003) CBT for psychosis: a qualitative analysis of clients' experiences. *British Journal of Clinical Psychology*, 42, 171–188.

Meyer, J. (2000) Qualitative research in health care: using qualitative methods in health related action research. *British Medical Journal*, 320, 178–181.

Meyer, R.G., Karon, B.P. (1967) The schizophrenogenic mother concept and the TAT. *Psychiatry*, 30, 173–179.

Meyer, T., Franz, M., Gallhofer, B. (2002) Subgruppen und Prognose besonders schwer zu enthospitalisierender schizophrener Langzeitpatienten: Eine Differenzierung des 'harten Kerns'. Teil 2 der Hessischen Enthospitalisierungsstudie [Subgroups and prognosis of difficult-to-place schizophrenic long-term patients: distinguishing the hard core. Part 2 of the Hessian Deinstitutionalization Study]. *Psychiatrische Praxis*, 29, 301–305.

Miles, M.B., Huberman, A.M. (1994) *Qualitative Data Analysis* (2nd edn). Beverly Hills, CA: Sage.

Miller, E.J., Gwynne, G.V. (1972) *A Life Apart*. London: Tavistock and Lippincott.

Millstone, E., van Zwanenberg, P. (2000) A crisis of trust: for science, scientists or for institutions? *Nature*, 6, 1307–1308.

MIND (2000) Counting the Cost: a survey of the impact of media coverage on the lives of people with mental health problems. London: Mind.

Ministry of Health and Social Welfare (1992) *Welfare and Freedom of Choice. Final Report from the Parliamentary Commission on Psychiatric Care*. Swedish Government Official Report 73 (in Swedish).

Misra, G. (1993) Psychology from a constructionist perspective: an interview with Kenneth J. Gergen. *New Ideas in Psychology*, 11, 399–414.

Mitchell, K.M. (1969) Social class and the schizophrenogenic mother concept. *Psychological Reports*, 24, 463–469.

Moher, D., Cook, D., Eastwood, S. et al. (1999) Improving the quality of reports of meta-analyses of randomised controlled trials: the QUOROM statement. *Lancet*, 354, 1896–1900.

Monahan, J. (1992) Mental disorder and violent behaviour: perceptions and evidence. *American Psychologist*, 47, 511–521.

Moncrieff, J. (2003) *Is Psychiatry for Sale? An Examination of the Influence of the Pharmaceutical Industry on Academic and Practical Psychiatry* (Maudsley Discussion Paper). London: Institute of Psychiatry.

Monk, G., Winslade, J., Crocket, K. et al. (eds) (1996) *Narrative Therapy in Practice: The Archaeology of Hope.* San Francisco, CA: Jossey Bass.

Morley, S., Adams, M. (1991) Graphical analysis of single-case time-series data. *British Journal of Clinical Psychology,* 30, 97–115.

Morris, G.H., Chenail, R.J. (eds) (1995) *The Talk of the Clinic: Explorations in the Analysis of Medical and Therapeutic Discourse.* Hove: LEA.

Mosher, L. (1983) Alternatives to psychiatric hospitalisation: why has research failed to be translated into practice? *New England Journal of Medicine,* 309, 1579–1580.

Mosher, L.R., Burti, L. (1994) *Community Mental Health: A Practical Guide.* New York: Norton.

Mueser, K.T., Bond, G.R., Drake, R.E. et al (1998) Models of community care for severe mental illness: a review of research on case management. *Schizophrenia Bulletin,* 24, 37–74.

Mueser, K.T., Torrey, W.C., Lynde, D. et al (2003) Implementing evidence-based practices for people with serious mental illness. *Behavioral Modification,* 27, 387–411.

Muir Gray, J.A. (1999) Postmodern medicine. *Lancet,* 354, 1550–1553.

Mulrow, C.D. (1987) The medical review article: state of the science. *Annals of Internal Medicine,* 106, 485–488.

Mulrow, C.D., Oxman, A.D. (1999) *Cochrane Collaboration Handbook* [updated June 1999]. In T.C. Collaboration (ed.), *Cochrane Library* [database on disk and CDROM]. Oxford: Update Software.

Mulrow, C.D., Oxman, A.D. (2002) *Cochrane Collaboration Handbook* [updated June 2002]. In T.C. Collaboration (ed.), *Cochrane Library* [database on CDROM]. Oxford: Update Software.

Munro, E., Rumgay, J. (2000) Role of risk assessment in reducing homicides by people with mental illness. *British Journal of Psychiatry,* 176, 116–124.

Murphy, E., Dingwall, R., Greatbatch, D. et al (1998) Qualitative research methods in health technology assessment: a review of the literature. *Health Technology Assessment,* 2.

Murray, C.J.L., Lopez, A.D. (1996) *The Global Burden of Disease.* WHO and the World Bank. Boston, MA: Harvard School of Public Health.

Mynors-Wallis, L., Moore, M., Maguire, J. et al. (2002) *Shared Care in Mental Health.* Oxford: Oxford University Press.

National Board of Health and Welfare (1973) *The Aim and Organisation of Psychiatric Health Care* (in Swedish). Stockholm: NBHW.

National Board of Health and Welfare (1999) *Welfare and Freedom of Choice? Final Report from the Evaluation of the 1995 Mental Health Care Reform* (in Swedish with English summary). Stockholm: NBHW.

National Board of Health and Welfare (2000) *State Subsidies to Municipalities for the Development of Case Management Services* (in Swedish). Message from the NBHW 14/2000, Stockholm.

National Board of Health and Welfare (2003) *Care and Support for Patients with Schizophrenia. A Review.* NBHW 2003-110-12, Stockholm.

National Institute for Clinical Excellence (2002a) *Core Interventions in the Treatment and Management of Schizophrenia in Primary and Secondary Care.* London: NICE.

National Institute for Clinical Excellence (2002b) *Computerised Cognitive Behaviour Therapy for Anxiety and Depression.* London: NHS.

National Institute for Clinical Excellence (2004a) Anxiety. *Management of Anxiety (Panic Disorder, With or Without Agoraphobia, and Generalised Anxiety Disorder) in Adults in Primary, Secondary and Community Care.* London: NICE.

National Institute for Clinical Excellence (2004b) *Depression. Management of Depression in Primary and Secondary Care.* London: NICE.

National Institute for Mental Health in England (2005) *Outcomes Measurement Implementation Best Practice Guidance.* Leeds: NIMHE.

Neff, J.A., Husaini, B.A. (1987) Urbanicity, race and psychological distress. *Journal of Community Psychology*, 15, 520–536.

NHS Centre for Reviews and Dissemination (1999) Drug treatment of schizophrenia. *Effective Health Care*, 5, 1–12.

NHS Centre for Reviews and Dissemination (2001a) *Scoping Review on the Effectiveness of Mental Health Services* (CRD report 21). York: University of York.

NHS Centre for Reviews and Dissemination (2001b) *Undertaking Systematic Reviews of Research on Effectiveness: CRD Report 4* (2nd ed). York: University of York.

NHS Centre for Reviews and Dissemination (2002) Improving the recognition and management of depression in primary care. *Effective Health Care*, 7, 1–12.

Nicholls, V., Wright, S., Waters, R., Wells, S. (2003) Surviving User-Led Research: Reflections on supporting user-led research projects. *Strategies for Lining*, London: Mental Health Foundation.

Nightingale, D.J., Cromby, J. (eds) (1999) *Social Constructionist Psychology: A Critical Analysis of Theory and Practice.* Buckingham: Open University Press.

Norquist, G., Lebowitz, B., Hyman, S. (1999) Expanding the frontier of treatment research. *Prevention and Treatment*, 2, 21 March.

Office for National Statistics (2000) *Adults with a Psychotic Disorder Living in Private Households.* London: TSO.

Olin, S.C., Mednick, S.A. (1996) Risk factors of psychosis: identifying vulnerable populations premorbidly. *Schizophrenia Bulletin*, 22, 233–240.

Oliver, M., Barnes, C. (1998) *From Exclusion to Inclusion: Social Policy and Disabled People.* London: Longman.

Oxman, A.D., Guyatt, G.H. (1988) Guidelines for reading literature reviews. *Canadian Medical Association Journal*, 138, 697–703.

Oxman, A.D., Thomson, M.A., Davis, D.A. et al (1995) No magic bullets: a systematic review of 102 trials of interventions to improve professional practice. *Canadian Medical Association Journal*, 153, 1423–1431.

Oxman, T.E., Rosenberg, S.D., Tucker, G.J. (1982) The language of paranoia. *American Journal of Psychiatry*, 139, 275–282.

Palmer, D. (2000) Identifying delusional discourse: issues of rationality, reality and power. *Sociology of Health and Illness*, 22, 661–678.

Palmer, C., Fenner, J. (1999) *Getting the Message Across: Review of Research and Theory About Disseminating Information Within the NHS.* London: Gaskell.

Parker, G. (1982) Re-searching the schizophrenogenic mother. *Journal of Nervous and Mental Diseases*, 170, 452–462.

Parker, I. (1989) *The Crisis in Modern Social Psychology: And How to End It.* London: Routledge.

Parker, I. (1994) Qualitative research. In P. Bannister, E. Burman, I. Parker et al (eds)

Qualitative Research, Qualitative Methods in Psychology: A Research Guide (pp. 1–16). Buckingham: Open University Press.

Parker, I. (ed.) (1998) *Social Constructionism, Discourse and Realism*. London: Sage.

Parker, I. (1999a) Critical reflexive humanism and critical constructionist psychology. In D.J. Nightingale, J. Cromby (eds), *Social Constructionist Psychology: A Critical Analysis of Theory and Practice*. Buckingham: Open University Press.

Parker, I. (ed.) (1999b) *Deconstructing Psychotherapy*. London: Sage.

Parker, I. (2002) *Critical Discursive Psychology*. London: Palgrave-Macmillan.

Parker, I. (2003) Discursive resources in the discourse unit. *Discourse Analysis Online*, 1(1) <www.shu.ac.uk/daol/previous/v1/n1/index.htm> (accessed 15 February 2004).

Parker, I., & the Bolton Discourse Network (1999) *Critical Textwork: An Introduction to Varieties of Discourse and Analysis*. Buckingham: Open University Press.

Parker, I., Georgaca, E., Harper, D. et al (1995) *Deconstructing Psychopathology*. London: Sage.

Parry, G., Watts, F. (eds) (2004) *Behavioural and Mental Health Research*. Hove: Erlbaum.

Passalacqua, R., Campione, F., Caminiti, C. et al (1999) Patients' opinions, feelings, and attitudes after a campaign to promote the Di Bella therapy. *Lancet*, 353, 1310–1314.

Pawson, R., Tilley, N. (1997) *Realistic Evaluation*. London: Sage.

Paykel, E.S., Abbott, R., Jenkins, R. et al (2000) Urban-rural mental health differences in Great Britain: findings from the National Morbidity Survey. *Psychological Medicine*, 30, 269–280.

Paykel, E.S., Hart, D., Priest, R.G. (1998) Changes in public attitudes to depression during the Defeat Depression Campaign. *British Journal of Psychiatry*, 173, 519–522.

Paykel, E.S., Priest, R.G. (1992) Recognition and management of depression in general practice: consensus statement. *British Medical Journal*, 305, 1198–1202.

Peltola, H., Patja, A., Leinikki, P. et al. (1998) No evidence for measles, mumps, and rubella vaccine-associated inflammatory bowel disease or autism in a 14-year prospective study. *Lancet*, 351, 1327–1328.

Pendleton, D. (1983) Doctor–patient communication: a review. In Pendleton, D., Hasler, J. (eds), *Doctor Patient Communication*. London: Academic Press.

Penn, D.L., Guynan, K., Daily, T. et al. (1994) Dispelling the stigma of schizophrenia: what sort of information is best? *Schizophrenia Bulletin*, 20, 567–578.

Peräkylä, A. (1993) Invoking a hostile world: discussing the patient's future in AIDS counselling. *Text*, 13, 291–316.

Peräkylä, A. (1995) *AIDS Counseling: Institutional Interaction and Clinical Practice*. Cambridge: Cambridge University Press.

Peräkylä, A. (1997) Conversation analysis: a new model of research in doctor–patient communication. *Journal of the Royal Society of Medicine*, 90, 205–208.

Peräkylä, A. (1998) Authority and intersubjectivity: the delivery of diagnosis in primary health care. *Social Psychology Quarterly*, 61, 301–320.

Peräkylä, A. (2002) Agency and authority: extended responses to diagnostic statements in primary care encounters. *Research on Language and Social Interaction*, 3, 219–247.

Peräkylä, A. (2004) Reliability and validity in research based on naturally occurring social interaction. In D. Silverman (ed.), *Qualitative Research: Theory, Method and Practice*. London: Sage.

Perry, A., Tarrier, N., Morriss, R. et al (1999) Randomised controlled trial of efficacy of teaching patients with bipolar disorder to identify early symptoms of relapse and obtain treatment. *British Medical Journal*, 318, 149–153.

Persons, J., Silberschatz, G. (1998) Are results of randomized controlled trials useful to psychotherapists? *Journal of Consulting and Clinical Psychology*, 66, 126–135.

Petitti, D.B. (2000) *Meta Analysis, Decision Analysis and Cost Effectiveness Analysis*. Oxford: Oxford University Press.

Petit-Zeman, S. (2003) Trial by peers comes up short. *The Guardian*, 16 Jan.

Petticrew, M. (2001) Systematic reviews from astronomy to zoology: myths and misconceptions. *British Medical Journal*, 322, 98–101.

Petticrew, M. (2003) Why certain systematic reviews reach uncertain conclusions. *British Medical Journal*, 326, 756–758.

Pharaoh, F.M., Mari, J.J., Streiner, D. (2002) Family intervention for schizophrenia (Cochrane Review). In *Cochrane Library*, Issue 1. Oxford: Update Software.

Phelan, J.C., Bromet, E.J., Link, B.G. (1998) Psychiatric illness and family stigma. *Schizophrenia Bulletin*, 24, 115–126.

Phillips, S.D., Burns, B.J., Edgar, E.R. et al (2001) Moving assertive community treatment into standard practice. *Psychiatric Services*, 52, 1394–1395.

Philo, G. (1996) *Media and Mental Illness*. London: Longman.

Philo, G. (1997) Changing media representations of mental health. *Psychiatric Bulletin*, 21, 171–172.

Pidgeon, N.F., Henwood, K.L. (1996) *Grounded theory: practical implementation*. In J.T.E. Richardson (ed.), *Handbook of Qualitative Research Methods for Psychology and the Social Sciences* (pp. 86–101), Leicester: British Psychological Society Books.

Pidgeon, N.F., Henwood, K.L. (2004) Grounded theory. In M. Hardy, A. Bryman (eds), *Handbook of Data Analysis*, 625–648, London: Sage.

Pidgeon, N.F., Turner, B.A., Blockley, D.I. (1991) The use of grounded theory for conceptual analysis in knowledge elicitation. *International Journal of Man-Machine Studies*, 35, 151–173.

Pinfold, V. (2003) *How Can We Make Mental Health Education Work? Example of Successful Local Mental Health Awareness Programme Challenging Stigma and Discrimination*. Report by Rethink Severe Mental Illness and Institute of Psychiatry. London: Rethink Publications.

Pinfold, V., Corry, P. (2003) *Who Cares? The Experiences of Mental Health Carers Accessing Services and Information*. London: Rethink Severe Mental Illness.

Pinfold, V., Toulmin, H., Thornicroft, G. et al (2003a) Reducing psychiatric stigma and discrimination: evaluation of educational interventions in UK secondary schools. *British Journal of Psychiatry*, 182, 342–346.

Pinfold, V., Huxley, P., Thornicroft, G. et al. (2003b) Reducing psychiatric stigma and discrimination: evaluating an educational intervention with the police force in England. *Social Psychiatry and Psychiatric Epidemiology*, 38, 337–344.

Pinfold, V., Thornicroft, G., Huxley, P., Farmer, P. (2005) Active ingredients in anti-stigma programmes in mental health. *International Review of Psychiatry*, 17(2): 123–131.

Pocock, S. (1985) *Clinical Trials: A Practical Approach*. Chichester: Wiley.

Pomerantz, A. (1993) Introduction to 'New Directions in Conversation Analysis'. *Text*, 13, 151–155.

Popay, J., Rogers, A., Williams, G. (1998) Rationale and standards for the systematic review of qualitative literature in health services research. *Qualitative Health Research*, 8, 341–351.

Porter, T.M. (1995) *Trust in Numbers: The Pursuit of Objectivity in Science and Public Life*. Princeton, NJ: Princeton University Press.

Potter, J. (1982) '. . . Nothing so practical as a good theory.' The problematic application of social psychology. In P. Stringer (ed.), *Confronting Social Issues*. London: Academic Press.

Potter, J. (1996) Discourse analysis and constructionist approaches: theoretical background. In J.T.E. Richardson (ed.), *Handbook of Qualitative Research for Psychology and the Social Sciences*. Leicester: BPS Books.

Potter, J. (2003) Discourse analysis. In M. Hardy, A. Bryman (eds), *Handbook of Data Analysis*. London: Sage.

Potter, J., Wetherell, M. (1987) *Discourse and Social Psychology: Beyond Attitudes and Behaviour*. London: Sage.

Potter, J.A. (1998) Qualitative and discourse analysis. In A.S. Bellack, M. Hersen (eds), *Comprehensive Clinical Psychology* (vol. 3). Oxford: Pergamon.

Powell, J., Geddes, J., Deeks, J. et al. (2000) Suicide in psychiatric hospital in-patients. *British Journal of Psychiatry*, 176, 266–272.

Powers, B.A., Knapp, T.R. (1990) *A Dictionary of Nursing Theory and Research*. London: Sage.

Priebe, S., Slade, M. (eds.) (2002) *Evidence in Mental Health Care*. Hove: Brunner-Routledge.

Prince, M., Stewart, R., Ford, T. et al (eds) (2003) *Practical Psychiatric Epidemiology*. Oxford: Oxford University Press.

Prins, H. (1999) *Will They Do It Again? Risk Assessment and Management in Criminal Justice and Psychiatry*. London: Routledge.

Psychiatrie-Enquête (1975) *Bericht über die Lage der Psychiatrie in der Bundesrepublik Deutschland [Report on the State of Psychiatry in the Federal Republic of Germany]*. Bonn: Bundesdrucksache.

Radcliffe, M. (2003) Word power. *The Guardian*, 16 July, 119–120.

Rahman, A., Mubbashar, M.H., Gater, R. et al (1998) Randomised trial of impact of school mental-health program in rural Rawalpindi, Pakistan. *Lancet*, 352, 1022–1025.

Ramuzzi, G., Schieppati, A. (1999) Lessons from the Di Bella affair. *Lancet*, 353, 1289–1290.

Rapley, M. (2004) *The Social Construction of Intellectual Disability*. London: Cambridge University Press.

Reason, P., Rowan, J. (ed.) (1981) *Human Inquiry: A Sourcebook of New Paradigm Research*. Chichester: Wiley.

Reavey, P., Warner, S. (2003) *New Feminist Stories of Child Sexual Abuse: Sexual Scripts and Dangerous Dialogues*. London: Routledge.

Regier, D.A., Narrow, W.E., Rae, D.S. et al (1993) The de facto US mental and addictive disorders service system. Epidemiologic catchment area prospective 1-year prevalence rates of disorders and services. *Archives of General Psychiatry*, 50, 85–94.

Reicher, S. (2000) Against methodolatry: some comments on Elliott, Fischer, and Rennie. *British Journal of Clinical Psychology*, 39, 1–6.

Reker, T. (1999) Die Tagesklinik in der psychiatrischen Versorung [The day hospital in psychiatric service provision]. In B. Eikelmann, T. Reker, M. Albers (eds), *Die psychiatrische Tagesklinik* (pp. 27–34). Stuttgart: Thieme.

Rennie, D. (1992) Qualitative analysis of the clients' experience of psychotherapy: the unfolding of reflexivity. In S. Toukmanian, D. Rennie (eds), *Psychotherapy Process Research: Paradigmatic and Narrative Approaches* (pp. 211–233). Newbury Park, CA: Sage.

Rennie, D., Phillips, J.R., Quartaro, G.K. (1988) Grounded theory: a promising approach to conceptualisation in psychology. *Canadian Psychology*, 29, 139–150.

Rice, P.L., Ezzy, D. (1999) *Qualitative data analysis*. In P.L. Rice, D. Ezzy (eds), *Qualitative Research Methods: A Health Focus*. Oxford: Oxford University Press.

Ritchie, J., Lewis, J. (2003) (eds) *Qualitative Research Practice: A Guide for Social Science Researchers and Students*. London: Sage.

Richter-Kuhlmann, E.A. (2004) Psychische Störungen: Psychiater – Ohne Hausärzte geht es nicht [Mental disorders: psychiatrists – things do not work out without GPs]. *Deutsches Ärzteblatt*, 3, 16.

Ritchie, J.H., Dick, D., Lingham, R. (1994) *The Report of the Inquiry into the Care and Treatment of Christopher Clunis*. London: HMSO.

Rix, S., Paykel, E.S., Lelliott, P. et al (1999) Impact of a national campaign on GP education: an evaluation of the Defeat Depression Campaign. *British Journal of General Practice*, 49, 99–102.

Robins, L.N., Helzer, J.E., Croughan, J. et al (1981) National Institute of Mental Health Diagnostic Interview Schedule. Its history, characteristics, and validity. *Archives of General Psychiatry*, 38, 381–389.

Robins, L.N., Regier, D.A. (1991) *Psychiatric Disorders in America: The Epidemiologic Catchment Area Study*. New York: Free Press.

Robinson, P.W., Foster, D.F. (1979) *Experimental Psychology: A Small-N Approach*. New York: Harper and Row.

Robson, C. (1993) *Real World Research* (2nd edn). Oxford: Blackwell.

Rodewischer Thesen (1965) Internationales Symposium über psychiatrische Rehabilitation vom 23.–25- Mai in Rodewisch im Vogtland [International symposium on psychiatric rehabilitation]. *Zeitschrift für gesellschaftliche Hygiene*, 11, 61–65.

Rogers, E.M. (1983) *Diffusion of Innovation*. New York: Free Press.

Romans Clarkson, S.E., Walton, V.A., Herbison, G.E. et al (1992) Social networks and psychiatric morbidity in New Zealand women. *Australian and New Zealand Journal of Psychiatry*, 26, 485–492.

Ropers, G., Roehl, K.P., Spancken, E. (1999) Gemeindeintegration chronisch psychisch Kranker – Evaluation eines innovativen Enthospitalisierungsprogramms [Integration of the chronically mentally ill in the community: evaluation of an innovative deinstitutionalization program]. In B. Badura, J. Siegrist (eds), *Evaluation im Gesundheitswesen. Ansätze und Ergebnisse* (pp. 363–380). Weinheim: Juventa.

Rose, D. (2001) *Users' Voices: The Perspectives of Mental Health Service Users on Community and Hospital Care*. London: Sainsbury Centre for Mental Health.

Rose, D., Fleischmann, P., Wykes, T. et al (2003) Patients' perspectives on electroconvulsive therapy: systematic review. *British Medical Journal*, 326, 1363–1364.

Rose, N. (1990) Psychology as a 'social' science. In I. Parker, J. Shotter (eds), *Deconstructing Social Psychology*. London: Routledge.

Rose, N. (1996) Psychiatry as a political science: advanced liberalism and the administration of risk. *History of the Human Sciences*, 9, 1–23.

Rosen, A., Teesson, M. (2002) Does case management work? The evidence and abuse of evidence-based medicine. *Australian and New Zealand Journal of Psychiatry*, 36, 731–746.

Rosser, W.W. (1999) Application of evidence from randomised controlled trials to general practice. *Lancet*, 353(9153), 661–664.

Rössler, W., Löffler, W., Fätkenheuer, B. et al (1992) Does case management reduce the rehospitalization rate? *Acta Psychiatrica Scandinavica*, 86, 445–449.

Rost, K., Nutting, P.A., Smith, J. et al (2000) Designing and implementing a primary care intervention trial to improve the quality and outcome of care for major depression. *General Hospital Psychiatry*, 22, 66–77.

Roter, D.L. (1989) Which facets of communication have strong effects on outcome? – a meta analysis. In M.A. Stewart, D.L. Roter (eds), *Communicating with Medical Patients*. Newbury Park, CA: Sage.

Roter, D.L., Hall, J.A., Katz, N.R. (1987) Relations between physicians' behaviours and analogue patients' satisfaction, recall and impressions. *Medical Care*, 25, 437–451.

Roth, W.F., Luton, F.H. (1942) The mental health program in Tennessee. *American Journal of Psychiatry*, 99, 662–675.

Rothwell, P. (1995) Can overall results of clinical trials be applied to all patients? *Lancet*, 345, 1616–1619.

Royal College of Medicine (2001) The changing relationship between the public and medical profession. The Lloyd Roberts lecturer, Sir Donald Irvine CBE. www.gmc-uk.org/news/lloyd_roberts_lecture.htm.

Roy-Chowdhury, S. (2003) Knowing the unknowable: what constitutes evidence in family therapy? *Journal of Family Therapy*, 25, 64–85.

Rutter, M., Brown, G. (1969) The reliability and validity of measures of family life and relationships in families containing a psychiatric patient. In A. Kiev (ed.), *Social Psychiatry* (Vol. 1) (pp. 148–182). New York: Science and Behavior Books.

Rutter, M., Madge, N. (1976) *Cycles of Disadvantage: A Review of Research*. London: Heinemann Educational.

Rutz, W., von Knorring, L., Walinder, J. (1989) Frequency of suicide on Gotland after systematic postgraduate education of general practitioners. *Acta Psychiatrica Scandinavica*, 80, 151–154.

Rutz, W., von Knorring, L., Walinder, J. (1992) Long-term effects of an educational program for general practitioners given by the Swedish Committee for the Prevention and Treatment of Depression. *Acta Psychiatrica Scandinavica*, 85, 83–88.

Ruusuvuori, J. (2001) Looking means listening: coordinating displays of engagement in doctor–patient interaction. *Social Science and Medicine*, 52, 1093–1108.

Sackett, D.L., Haynes, R.B., Guyatt, G.H. et al (1991) *Clinical Epidemiology: A Basic Science for Clinical Medicine*. Boston, MA: Little, Brown.

Sackett, D., Rosenberg, W., Gray, J.A.M. (1996) Evidence-based medicine: what it is and what it isn't. *British Medical Journal*, 312, 71–72.

Sacks, H. (1984) Notes on methodology. In J.M. Atkinson, J. Heritage (eds), *Structures of Social Action*. Cambridge: Cambridge University Press.

Sacks, H. (1996) *Lectures on Conversation*. Cambridge, MA: Blackwell.

Sacks, H., Berrier, J., Reitman, D. et al (1987) Meta-analyses of randomized controlled trials. *New England Journal of Medicine*, 316, 450–455.

Sacks, H., Chalmers, T., Smith, H. (1982) Randomized versus historical controls for clinical trials. *American Journal of Medicine*, 72, 233–240.

Sacks, H., Schegloff, E.A., Jefferson, G. (1974) A simplest systematics for the organization of turn-taking for conversation. *Language*, 50, 696–735.

Sainsbury Centre for Mental Health (1998) *Keys to Engagement*. London: Sainsbury Centre for Mental Health.

Salter, M. (2003) Psychiatry and the media: from pitfalls to possibilities. *Psychiatric Bulletin*, 27, 123–125.

Santhouse, A., Holloway, F. (1999) Physical health of patients in continuing care. *Advances in Psychiatric Treatment*, 5, 455–462.

Sayce, L. (2000) *From Psychiatric Patient to Citizen: Overcoming Discrimination and Social Exclusion*. London: Macmillan.

Sayce, L. (2003) Beyond good intentions: making anti-discrimination strategies work. *Disability and Society*, 18, 625–642.

Schegloff, E.A. (1993) Reflections on quantification in the study of conversation. *Research on Language and Social Interaction*, 26, 99–128.

Schegloff, E.A. (2003) Conservation analysis and communication disorders. In C. Goodwin (ed.), *Conversation and Brain Damage*. New York: Oxford University Press.

Schegloff, E.A., Sacks, H. (1973) Opening up closings. *Semiotica*, 8, 289–327.

Scheid, T.L. (2001) Rethinking professional prerogative: managed mental health care providers. In J. Busfield (ed.), *Rethinking the Sociology of Mental Health*. Oxford: Blackwell.

Schmiedebach, H.P., Beddies, T., Schulz, J. et al (2000). Offene Fürsorge – Rodewischer Thesen – Psychiatrie-Enquete: Drei Reformansätze im Vergleich [Open care – Rodewisch theses – Psychiatrie-Enquête: comparison of three reforms]. *Psychiatrische Praxis*, 27, 138–143.

Schultz, K., Chalmers, I., Grimes, D. et al (1994) Assessing the quality of randomization from reports of controlled trials published in obstetrics and gynaecology journals. *Journal of the American Medical Association*, 272, 125–128.

Schultz, K., Chalmers, I., Hayes, R. et al (1995) Empirical evidence of bias: dimensions of methodological quality associated with estimates of treatments effects in controlled trials. *Journal of the American Medical Association*, 273, 408–412.

Schultz, K., Grimes, D. (2002) Allocation concealment in randomised trials: defending against deciphering. *Lancet*, 359, 614–618.

Schulze, B., Richter-Werling, M., Matschinger, H., Angermeyer, M. (2009) Crazy? So what! Effects of a school project on students' attitudes towards people with schizophrenia. *Acta Psychiatrica Scandinavia*, 106, 1–9.

Schwarz, B., Weise, K., Thom, A. (1971) *Sozialpsychiatrie in der sozialistischen Gesellschaft [Social Psychiatry in Socialist Society]*. Leipzig: VEB Georg Thieme.

Scott, J., Jenkins, R. (1998) Psychiatric disorders specific to women. In: E.C. Johnstone, C.P.L. Freeman, A.K. Zealley (eds), *Companion to Psychiatric Studies* (6th edn, pp. 551–564). Edinburgh: Churchill Livingstone.

Scoville, W.B., Milner, B. (1957) Loss of recent memory after bilateral hippocampal lesions. *Journal of Neurology, Neurosurgery and Psychiatry*, 20, 11–21.

Scull, A. (1982) *Museums of Madness. The Social Organisation of Insanity in Nineteenth-Century England*. Harmondsworth: Penguin Books.

Seale, C., Gobo, G., Gubrium, J.F. et al (eds) (2004) *Qualitative Research Practice*. London: Sage.

Secretary of State for Health (1999) *National Service Framework – Mental Health*. London: HMSO.

Seebohm, P., Thomas, P., Henderson, P. et al (2004) *Sharing Voices (Bradford) Participatory Action Research Evaluation: Early Findings*. London: Sainsbury Centre for Mental Health.

Segal, Z., Vincent, P., Levitt, A. (2002) Efficacy of combined, sequential and crossover psychotherapy and pharmacotherapy in improving outcomes in depression. *Journal of Psychiatry and Neuroscience*, 27, 281–290.

Shakespeare, T. (1998) Social constructionism as a political strategy. In I. Velody, R. Williams (eds), *The Politics of Constructionism*. London: Sage.

Shelton, R.C.K.M., Gelenberg, A., Dunner, D.L. et al (2001) Effectiveness of St John's wort in major depression – a randomized controlled trial. *Journal of the American Medical Association*, 285, 1978–1986.

Sherrard, C. (1997) Qualitative research. *The Psychologist: Bulletin of the British Psychological Society*, 10, 161–162.

Sibbald, B., Roland, M. (1998) Why are randomised controlled trials important? *British Medical Journal*, 316, 201.

Siegler, M., Osmond, H. (1976) *Models of Madness. Models of Medicine*. New York: Harper Colophone.

Silverman, D. (1997) *Discourses of Counseling: HIV Counseling as Social Interaction*. London: Sage.

Silverman, D. (1998) *Harvey Sacks and Conversation Analysis*. Cambridge: Polity Press.

Silverman, D. (2004) *Qualitative Research: Theory, Method and Practice*. London: Sage.

Simini, B. (1998) Frenzy mounts in Italy over assessment of the Di Bella regimen. *Lancet*, 351, 891.

Singh, N.N., Beale, I.L., Dawson, M. (1981) Duration of facial screening and suppression of self-injurious behavior: analysis using an alternating treatment design. *Behavioral Assessments*, 3, 411–420.

Singleton, N., Meltzer, H., Gatward, R. et al (1998) Psychiatric morbidity among prisoners in England and Wales. London: Stationery Office.

Sjogren, T. (1948) Genetic-statistical and psychiatric investigations of a West Swedish population. *Acta Psychiatrica et Neurologica* (Suppl 52).

Skelton, J.R. (2002) Commentary on McCabe et al. Engagement of patients with psychosis in the medical consultation: a conversation analytic study. *British Medical Journal*, 325, 1151 (http://bmj.com/cgi/content/full/325/7373/1151).

Smith, C.J., Kearns, R.A., Abbott, M.W. (1992) Housing and mental health: exploring the relationships in urban New Zealand. *Community Mental Health in New Zealand*, 7, 2–15.

Smith, J.A. (1996) Qualitative methodology: analysing participants' perspectives. *Current Opinion in Psychiatry*, 9, 417–421.

Smith, M.L., Glass, G.V. (1977) Meta-analysis of psychotherapy outcome studies. *American Psychologist*, 32, 752–760.

Social Exclusion Unit (2004) *Mental Health and Social Exclusion: Social Exclusion Unit Report*. London: Office of the Deputy Prime Minister.

Soyland, A.J. (1994) Functions of the psychiatric case summary. *Text*, 14, 113–140.

Soyland, A.J. (1995) Analyzing therapeutic and professional discourse. In J. Siegfried (ed.), *Therapeutic and Everyday Discourse as Behavior Change: Towards a Microanalysis in Psychotherapy Process Research*. Norwood, NJ: Ablex.

Spencer, L., Richie, J., Lewis, J. et al (2003) *Quality in Qualitative Evaluation: A Framework for Assessing Research Evidence*. London: Cabinet Office. <http://policyhub.gov.uk/docs/qqe_rep.pdf> (accessed 15 Feb 2004).

Spengler, A. (1991) *Institutsambulanzen in der psychiatrischen Versorgung [Outpatient Clinics in Psychiatric Service Provision]*. Göttingen: Vandenhoek & Ruprecht.

Spengler, A. (2003) Psychiatrische Institutsambulanzen: Ein Überblick [Psychiatric outpatient clinics: an overview]. *Nervenarzt*, 74, 476–480.

Spitzer, M. (1990) On defining delusions. *Comprehensive Psychiatry*, 31, 377–397.

Spokes, J. (1988) *Report of the Committee of Inquiry into the Care and Aftercare of Sharon Campbell*. London: HMSO.

Spri (1978) *Psychiatry in Transition. The Nacka Project*. Spri report 7–78 (in Swedish). Stockholm.

Squires, E.J., Hunkin, N.M., Parkin, A.J. (1997) Errorless learning of novel associations in amnesia. *Neuropsychologia*, 35, 1103–1111.

Srole, L., Langner, T., Michael, S.T. et al (1962) *Mental Health in the Metropolis*. New York: McGraw-Hill.

Stancombe, J., White, S. (1997) Notes on the tenacity of therapeutic presuppositions in process research: examining the artfulness of blamings in family therapy. *Journal of Family Therapy*, 19, 21–41.

Stansfield, S.A., Marmot, M. (1992) Social class and minor psychiatric morbidity in civil servants: a validated screening survey using The General Health Questionnaire.

Stansfield, S.A., North, F.M., White, J. et al (1995) Work characteristics and psychiatric disorder in civil servants in London. *Journal of Epidemiology and Community Health*, 49, 48–53.

Stefansson, C.G., Cullberg, J. (1986) Introducing community mental health services. *Acta Psychiatrica Scandinavica*, 74, 368–378.

Stefansson, C.G., Cullberg, J., Steinholtz Ekecrantz, L. (1990) From community mental health services to specialized psychiatry: the effects of a change in policy on patient accessibility and care utilization. *Acta Psychiatrica Scandinavica*, 82, 57–164.

Stein, L.I., Test, M.A. (1980) Alternative to mental hospital treatment. I. Conceptual model, treatment program, and clinical evaluation. *Archives of General Psychiatry*, 37, 392–397.

Stewart, M.A. (1984) What is a successful doctor–patient interview? A study of interactions and outcomes. *Social Science and Medicine*, 19, 167–175.

Stiles, W.B. (1993) Quality control in qualitative research. *Clinical Psychology Review*, 13, 593–618.

Stivers, T., Mangione-Smith, R., Elliott, M.N. et al (2003) Why do physicians think parents expect antibiotics? What parents expect vs. what physicians believe. *Journal of Family Practice*, 52, 140–148.

Stone, A.A. (2002) Investigating Psychiatric Abuses. *Psychiatric Times*, 19.

Stoppard, J.M. (1998) Dis-ordering depression in women. *Theory and Psychology*, 8, 79–99.

Stowell-Smith, M., McKeown, M. (1999) Race, psychopathy and the self: a discourse analytic study. *British Journal of Medical Psychology*, 72, 459–470.

Strauss, A. (1987) *Qualitative Analysis for Social Scientists*. Cambridge: Cambridge University Press.

Strauss, A., Corbin, J. (2nd edn) (1990) *Basic of Qualitative Research: Techniques and procedures for developing grounded theory*. New York and London: Sage.

Strauss, A., Corbin, J. (1994) Grounded theory methodology. In N. Denzin, Y. Lincoln (eds), *Handbook of Qualitative Research* (pp. 273–285). Thousand Oaks, CA: Sage.

Strauss, A., Corbin, J. (eds) (1997) *Grounded Theory in Practice*. London: Sage.

Strauss, A., Corbin, J. (1998) *Basics of Qualitative Research* (2nd edn). London: Sage.

Stromgren, E. (1938) *Beitrage zur psychiatrischen Erblehre*. Copenhagen: Munksgaard.

Stuart, H., Arboleda-Flórez, J. (2001) Community attitudes toward people with schizophrenia. *Canadian Journal of Psychiatry*, 46, 245–252.

Struening, E.L., Perlick, D.A., Link, B.G. et al (2001) Stigma as a barrier to recovery: the extent to which caregivers believe most people devalue consumers and their families. *Psychiatric Services*, 52, 1633–1638.

Stueve, A., Link, B.G. (1997) Violence and psychiatric disorders: results from an epidemiological study of young adults in Israel. [Journal article] *Psychiatric Quarterly*, 68(4): 327–342.

Suchman, L., Jordan, B. (1990) Interactional troubles in face-to-face survey interviews. *Journal of the American Statistical Association*, 85, 232–241.

Surtees, P.G., Dean, C., Ingham, J.G. et al (1983) Psychiatric disorder in women from an Edinburgh community: association with demographic factors. *British Journal of Psychiatry*, 142, 238–246.

Sutton, A.J., Abrams, K.R., Jones, D.R. et al (1999) Systematic reviews of trials and other studies. *Health Technology Assessment*, 2.

Svensson, B. (1999) Treatment process and outcome for long-term mentally ill patients in a comprehensive treatment program based on cognitive therapy. Doctoral dissertation, Department of Neuroscience, Lund University, Sweden.

Swann, C.J., Ussher, J.M. (1995) A discourse analytic approach to women's experience of premenstrual syndrome. *Journal of Mental Health*, 4, 359–367.

Swartz, M.S., Hiday, V.A., Wagner, H.R. et al (2001) A randomized controlled trial of outpatient commitment in North Carolina. *Psychiatric Services*, 52, 325–329.

Swartz, S. (1996) Shrinking: a postmodern perspective on psychiatric case histories. *South African Journal of Psychology*, 26, 150–156.

Sweeney, K., McAuley, D., Pereira Gray, D.J. (1998) Personal significance: the third dimension. *Lancet*, 351, 134–136.

Szasz, T. (1961) *The Myth of Mental Illness*. New York: Harper and Row.

Szmukler, G. (2000) Homicide inquiries: what sense do they make? *Psychiatric Bulletin*, 24, 6–10.

Szmukler, G. (2003) Risk assessment. 'Numbers' and 'values'. *Psychiatric Bulletin*, 27, 205–207.

Szmukler, G., Holloway, F. (2000) Reform of the Mental Health Act. Health or safety? *British Journal of Psychiatry*, 177, 196–200.

Talbott, J.A., Clark, G.H. Jr., Sharfstein, S.S. et al (1987) Issues in developing standards governing psychiatric practice in community mental health centers. *Hospital and Community Psychiatry*, 38, 1198–1202.

Tansella, M. (1987) Editorial: the Italian experience and its implications. *Psychological Medicine*, 17, 283–289.

Taylor, L., Chave, S. (1964) *Mental Health and Environment*. London: Longman Green.

Taylor, M., Dear, M. (1981) Scaling community attitudes toward the mentally ill. *Schizophrenia Bulletin*, 7, 225–240.

Taylor, P., Estroff, S.E. (2003) Schizophrenia and violence. In S.R. Hirsch, D. Weinberger (eds), *Schizophrenia* (2nd edn, pp. 591–612). Oxford: Blackwell.

Taylor, P., Gunn, J. (1999) Homicides by people with mental illness: myth and reality. *British Journal of Psychiatry*, 174, 9–14.

Taylor, S.J., Kingdon, D., Jenkins, R. (1997) How are nations trying to prevent suicide? An analysis of national suicide prevention strategies. *Acta Psychiatrica Scandinavica*, 95, 457–463.

Teague, G.B., Bond, G.R., Drake, R.E. (1998) Program fidelity in assertive community treatment: development and use of a measure. *American Journal of Orthopsychiatry*, 68, 216–232.

Ten Have, P. (1990) Methodological issues in conversation analysis. <www2.fmg.uva.nl/emca/mica.htm> (accessed 17 June 2004).

Ten Have, P. (1999) *Doing Conversation Analysis: A Practical Guide*. London: Sage.

Ten Have, P. (2004) *Understanding Qualitative Research and Ethnomethodology*. London: Sage.

Terre Blanche, M. (1997) 'The knowledge that one seeks to disinter': Psychiatry and the discourse of discourse analysis. In A. Levett, A. Kottler, E. Burman et al (eds), *Culture, Power and Difference: Discourse Analysis in South Africa*. London: Zed Books.

Terre Blanche, M., Durrheim, K. (2002a) Social constructionist methods. In M. Terre Blanche, K. Durrheim (eds), *Research in Practice: Applied Methods for the Social Sciences*. Cape Town: University of Cape Town Press.

Terre Blanche, M., Durrheim, K. (eds) (2002b) *Research in Practice: Applied Methods for the Social Sciences*. Cape Town: University of Cape Town Press.

Test, M.A., Stein, L.I. (1980) Alternative to mental hospital treatment. III. Social cost. *Archives of General Psychiatry*, 37, 409–412.

Thom, A., Wolff, E. (1990) *Psychiatrie im Wandel: Erfahrungen und Perspektiven in Ost und West [Psychiatry Undergoing Change: Experiences and Perspectives in the East and in the West]*. Bonn: Psychiatrie-Verlag.

Thompson, A.H., Stuart, H., Bland, R.C. et al (2002) Attitudes about schizophrenia from the pilot site of the WPA world-wide campaign against the stigma of schizophrenia. *Social Psychiatry and Psychiatric Epidemiology*, 37, 475–482.

Thompson, C. (1989) *The Instruments of Psychiatric Research*. Chichester: Wiley.

Thompson, C., Kinmonth, A.L., Stevens, L. et al (2000) Effects of clinical-practice guideline and practice-based education on detection and outcome of depression in primary care: Hampshire Depression Project randomised controlled trial. *Lancet*, 355, 185–191.

Thompson, S. (1995) Why sources of heterogeneity in meta-analysis should be investigated. In I. Chalmers, D.G. Altman (eds), *Systematic Reviews*. London: BMJ Books.

Thornicroft, G., Rose, D., Huxley, P. et al (2002) What are the research priorities of mental health service users? *Journal of Mental Health*, 11, 1–5.

Thornicroft, G., Wykes, T., Holloway, F. et al (1998) From efficacy to effectiveness in community mental health services. PRiSM Psychosis Study 10. *British Journal of Psychiatry*, 173, 423–427.

Thornley, B., Adams, C. (1998) Content and quality of 2000 controlled trials in schizophrenia over 50 years. *British Medical Journal*, 317, 1181–1184.

Todman, G., Dugard, P. (2001) *Single Case and Small-N Experimental Designs: A practical guide to randomization tests*. Hillsdale, New Jersey: Lawrence Erlbaum Associates.

Tomlin, Z., Humphrey, C., Rogers, S. (1999) General practitioners' perceptions of effective health care. *British Medical Journal*, 318(7197), 1532–1535.

Tsang, H.W., Tam, P.K., Chan, F. et al (2003) Sources of burdens on families of individuals with mental illness. *International Journal of Rehabilitation Research*, 26, 123–130.

Turner, B.A. (1981) Some practical aspects of qualitative data analysis: one way of organizing the cognitive processes associated with the generation of grounded theory. *Quality and Quantity*, 15, 225–247.

Turner, B.A. (1987) Connoisseurship in the study of organizational cultures. In A. Bryman (ed.), *Doing Research in Organizations* (pp. 108–121). London: Routledge.

Turner, B.A., Pidgeon, N.F. (1997) *Man Made Disasters* (2nd edn). Oxford: Butterworth-Heinemann.

Turner, M., Beresford, P. (2005) *User Controlled Research: Its Meanings and Potential*. Eastleigh: Involve.

Turpin, G., Barley, V., Beail, N. et al (1997) Standards for research projects and theses involving qualitative methods: suggested guidelines for trainees and courses. *Clinical Psychology Forum*, 108, 3–7.

Tylee, A. (2003) The Primary Care Programme of the National Institute for Mental Health in England (NIMHE). *Primary Care Mental Health*, 1, 1–3.

Tyrer, P. (1998) Cost-effective or profligate community psychiatry? *British Journal of Psychiatry*, 172, 1–3.

Upton, M.W., Evans, M., Goldberg, D.P. et al (1999) Evaluation of ICD-10 PHC mental health guidelines in detecting and managing depression within primary care. *British Journal of Psychiatry*, 175, 476–482.

User Focused Monitoring (2004) *Crisis . . . What Crisis?: The experience of Being in Crisis in Bristol*. Bristol: Bristol Mind.

US Department of Health and Human Services (1999) *Mental Health: A Report of the Surgeon General – Executive Summary*. Rockville, MD: National Institutes for Health.

van der Feltz-Cornelis, C.M., Lyons, J.S., Huyse, F.J. et al (1997) Health services research on mental health in primary care. *International Journal of Psychiatry in Medicine*, 27, 1–21.

van Weel, C., Knottnerus, J.A. (1999) Evidence-based interventions and comprehensive treatment. *Lancet*, 353(9156), 916–918.

Vasquez-Barquero, J.L., Munoz, P.E., Madoz Jauregui, V. (1982) The influence of the process of urbanization on the prevalence of neurosis: a community survey. *Acta Psychiatrica Scandinavica*, 65, 161–170.

Vehviläinen, S. (1999) *Structures of Counselling Interaction: A Conversation Analytic*

Study of Counselling Encounters in Career Guidance Training. Helsinki: Helsinki University Press.

Verdoux, H., Tignol, J. (2003) Focus on psychiatry in France. *British Journal of Psychiatry*, 183, 466–471.

Vieten, B., Ingenleuf, H.-J., Wilm, B. et al (1996) Alte und neue Grenzen – Langzeitpatienten in der Psychiatrie machen sich auf den Weg [Old and new borders: psychiatric long-term patients start moving]. *Sozialpsychiatrische Informationen*, 26, 2–8.

von Cranach, M., Finzen, A. (1972) *Sozialpsychiatrische Text [Readings in Social Psychiatry]*. Berlin: Springer.

Von Korff, M., Goldberg, D. (2001) Improving outcomes in depression. *British Medical Journal*, 323, 948–949.

Wahl, O. (1995) *Media Madness: Public Images of Mental Illness.* New Brunswick, NJ: Rutgers University Press.

Wakefield, A.J., Murch, S.H., Anthony, A. et al (1998) Ileal-lymphoid-nodular hyperplasia, non-specific colitis, and pervasive developmental disorder in children. *Lancet*, 351, 637–641.

Waldmann, K.D. (1998) Die Realisierung der Rodewischer Thesen zu DDR-Zeiten – Versuch einer Analyse aus heutiger Sicht [An attempt to analyse the realisation of the Rodewisch theses in the GDR from today's perspective]. *Psychiatrische Praxis*, 25, 200.

Walker, I., Read, J. (2002) The differential effectiveness of psychosocial and biogenetic causal explanations in reducing negative attitudes toward 'mental illness'. *Psychiatry: Interpersonal and Biological Processes*, 65, 313–325.

Wallcraft, J., Read, J., Sweeney, A. (2003) *On Our Own Terms: Users and Survivors of Mental Health Services Working Together for Support and Change.* London: Sainsbury Centre for Mental Health.

Walsh, E., Buchanan, A., Fahy, T. (2001) Violence and schizophrenia: examining the evidence. *British Journal of Psychiatry*, 180, 490–495.

Walsh, E., Fahy, T. (2002) Violence in society. Contribution of mental illness is low. *British Medical Journal*, 325, 507–508.

Warner, R. (1999) Schizophrenia and the environment: speculative interventions. *Epidemiologia e Psichiatria Sociale*, 8, 19–34.

Warner, R. (2000) Combating the stigma of schizophrenia. *Epidemiologia e Psichiatria Sociale*, 10, 12–17.

Warner, R. (2001) Combating the stigma of schizophrenia. *Epidemiologia e Psichiatria Sociale*, 10(1), 12–17.

Wasow, M. (1983) Parental perspectives on chronic schizophrenia. *Journal of Chronic Diseases*, 36, 337–343.

Weisbrod, B.A., Test, M.A., Stein, L.I. (1980) Alternative to mental hospital treatment. II. Economic benefit-cost analysis. *Archives of General Psychiatry*, 37, 400–405.

Welschehold, M., Berger, W. (2002) Ambulante Basisdokumentation (AmBADO) – Die psychiatrischen Institutsambulanzen der bayerischen Bezirkskrankenhaeuser fuehren ein gemeinsames Dokumentationssystem ein [AmBADO – a new documentation system for outpatient psychiatric departments]. *Krankenhauspsychiatrie*, 13, 164–167.

Wessely, S. (2001) Randomised controlled trials: the gold standard? In C. Mace, S. Moorey, B. Roberts (eds), *Evidence in the Balance* (pp. 46–60). Hove: Routledge.

Wessely, S., Bisson, J., Rose, S. (2000) A systematic review of brief psychological interventions ('debriefing') for the treatment of immediate trauma related symptoms and the prevention of post traumatic stress disorder. In M. Oakley-Browne, R. Churchill, D. Gill et al (eds), *Depression, Anxiety and Neurosis Module of the Cochrane Database of Systematic Reviews*. Oxford: Update Software.

Wetherell, M. (1994) The knots of power and negotiation, blank and complex subjectivities: commentary for the special issue. *Journal of Community and Applied Social Psychology*, 4, 305–308.

Wetherell, M. (1998) Positioning and interpretative repertoires: conversation analysis and post-structuralism in dialogue. *Discourse and Society*, 9, 387–413.

Wetherell, M., Potter, J. (1988) Discourse analysis and the identification of interpretative repertoires. In C. Antaki (ed.), *Analysing Everyday Explanation: A Casebook of Methods*. London: Sage.

Wetherell, M., Taylor, S., Yates, S.J. (2001a) *Discourse Theory and Practice: A Reader*. London: Sage.

Wetherell, M., Taylor, S., Yates, S.J. (2001b) *Discourse as Data: A Guide for Analysis*. London: Sage.

White, S., Evans, P., Mihill, C. et al (1993) *Hitting the Headlines*. Leicester: BPS Books.

Willig, C. (1999a) Introduction: making a difference. In C. Willig (ed.), *Applied Discourse Analysis: Social and Psychological Interventions*. Buckingham: Open University Press.

Willig, C. (ed.). (1999b) *Applied Discourse Analysis: Social and Psychological Interventions*. Buckingham: Open University Press.

Willig, C. (2001) *Introducing Qualitative Research in Psychology: Adventures in Theory and Method*. Buckingham: Open University Press.

Wilson, B.A. (1987) Single-case experimental designs in neuropsychological rehabilitation. *Journal of Clinical and Experimental Neuropsychology*, 9, 527–544.

Wilson, B.A. (1999) *Case Studies in Neuropsychological Rehabilitation*. New York: Oxford University Press.

Wilson, B.A., Baddeley, A.D., Evans, J.J. et al (1994) Errorless learning in the rehabilitation of memory-impaired people. *Neuropsychological Rehabilitation*, 4, 307–326.

Wilson, B.A., Emslie, H., Quirk, K. et al (1999) George: learning to live independently with NeuroPage®. *Rehabilitation Psychology*, 44, 284–296.

Wilson, B.A., Emslie, H.C., Quirk, K. et al (2001) Reducing everyday memory and planning problems by means of a paging system: a randomised control crossover study. *Journal of Neurology, Neurosurgery and Psychiatry*, 70, 477–482.

Wilson, B.A., Evans, J.J., Emslie, H. et al (1997) Evaluation of NeuroPage: a new memory aid. *Journal of Neurology, Neurosurgery and Psychiatry*, 63, 113–115.

Wilson, C., Nairn, R., Coverdale, J. et al (2000) How mental illness is portrayed in children's television. *British Journal of Psychiatry*, 176, 440–443.

Wing, J. (1978) *Reasoning About Madness*. Oxford: Oxford University Press.

Wing, J.K., Babor, T., Brugha, T. et al (1990) SCAN Schedules of Clinical Assessment in Neuropsychiatry. *Archives of General Psychiatry*, 47, 589–593.

Wing, J.K., Brown, G.W. (1970) *Institutionalism and Schizophrenia: A Comparative Study of Three Mental Hospitals*. London: Cambridge University Press.

Wittchen, H.U., Höfler, M., Meister, W. (2000) *Depressionen in der Allgemeinarzt-praxis: Die bundesweite Depressionsstudie [Depressions in Primary Care: The Country-Wide Depression Study]*. Stuttgart: Schattauer.

Wolff, G. Attitudes of the media and the public. (1997) In J. Leff (ed.), *Community Care: Illusion or Reality?* London: Routledge.

Wolpert, L. (2001) *Malignant Sadness: The Anatomy of Depression*. London: Faber & Faber.

Wong, S.E., Liberman, R.P. (1981) Mixed single-subject designs in clinical research: variations of the multiple baseline. *Behavioural Assessment*, 3, 297–306.

Wood, L.A., Kroger, R.O. (2000) *Doing Discourse Analysis: Methods for Studying Action in Talk and Text*. London: Sage.

Workforce Action Team (2001) *Mental Health National Service Framework: Workforce Planning, Education and Training. Special Report*. London: Department of Health.

World Health Organisation (1992) *International Classification of Diseases and related Health Problems* (ICD-10). Geneva: WHO.

World Health Organisation (1996) *Diagnostic and Management Guidelines for Mental Disorders in Primary Care* (ICD-10). Ch. V. Primary Care version. Göttingen: WHO/Hogrefe & Huber.

World Health Organisation Collaborating Centre for Research and Training for Mental Health (1996) *WHO Guide to Mental Health in Primary Care – Adapted for the UK for Diagnostic and Management Guidelines for Mental Disorders in Primary Care (ICD-10)*. Ch. 5. Primary care version. Göttingen: WHO/Hogrefe & Huber.

World Health Organisation (2001) *The World Health Report 2001: Mental health: New Understanding, New Hope*. Geneva: World Health Organisation.

World Psychiatric Association (2000) *The WPA Program to Reduce Stigma and Discrimination Because of Schizophrenia* (vols 1–5). Geneva: WPA.

Wright, A. (1994) Should general practitioners be testing for depression? *British Journal of General Practice*, 44, 132–135.

Yamagami, T. (1998) Psychotherapy, today and tomorrow: status quo of behavior and cognitive therapy and its efficacy. *Psychiatry and Clinical Neurosciences*, 52 Suppl:S236–237.

Yardley, L. (2000) Dilemmas in qualitative health research. *Psychology and Health*, 15, 215–228.

Yardley, L., Murray, M. (2004) Qualitative analysis of talk and text: discourse and narrative analysis. In D. Marks, L. Yardley (eds), *Research Methods for Clinical and Health Psychology*. London: Sage.

Ziguras, S.J., Stuart, G.W. (2000) A meta-analysis of the effectiveness of mental health case management over 20 years. *Psychiatric Services*, 51, 1410–1421.

Index

47